MW01700854

SECOND

PARLIAMENT PARTIES & PEOPLE

AUSTRALIAN POLITICS TODAY

DEAN JAENSCH

LONGMAN

9A
$2

Pearson Education Australia Pty Limited
95 Coventry Street
South Melbourne 3205 Australia

Offices in Sydney, Brisbane and Perth, and associated companies throughout the world.

Copyright © Pearson Education Australia Pty Limited 1994
First published 1994
Reprinted 1995, 1996, 1997, 2000, 2001, 2002

All rights reserved. Except under the conditions described in the Copyright Act 1968 of Australia and subsequent amendments, no part of this publication may be reproduced, stored in a retrieval system or transmitted in any form or by any means, electronic, mechanical, photocopying, recording or otherwise, without the prior permission of the copyright owner.

Edited by Robin Bower
Designed by Judith Summerfeldt
Set in 10.5/12pt New Baskerville
Produced by Pearson Education Australia Pty Limited
Printed in Malaysia, PA

National Library of Australia
Cataloguing-in-Publication data

Jaensch, Dean, 1936– .
Parliament, parties and people.

2nd ed.
Bibliography.
Includes index.
ISBN 0 582 80250 4.

1. Australia. Parliament. 2. Australia – Politics and government. I. Title.

320.494

The publisher's policy is to use **paper manufactured from sustainable forests**

CONTENTS

LIST OF FIGURES

Chapter one

THE CONTEXTS OF AUSTRALIAN POLITICS

DEFINING POLITICS

The title of a famous book called *Politics: Who Gets What, When, How?* (Lasswell 1936) encapsulates all the components of 'politics': it is a human activity and a competitive activity; one which seeks to allocate the material and non-material components of the society among its members; an activity involving conflict over both the components and the means of this allocation and, hence, one which involves the use (and possible abuse) of power.

For most people in Australia, though, politics is something that happens 'somewhere else'. Only a small proportion of Australians are involved in political activity. For most, politics is a matter of media headlines about the latest decision of government, the most recent clash in parliament, the personality of the day, and of occasionally

Lifestyle—a possible factor in apathy?

turning out to vote in elections. Sometimes politics—in times of material scarcity—does impinge deeply on the minds of the average Australian: tax increases, high interest rates, high housing loan rates have an impact. The 'hip pocket/purse nerve' is still the most tender.

For most of the time, however, politics is a matter for politicians; it happens in parliaments and it doesn't really impinge on the daily lives of most of the Australian people. Yet decisions made through the political processes are crucial to the life of every person. Further, the Australian political system offers every opportunity for the citizen to be involved. Why so many do not become involved—why apathy seems to be so rife in Australia—is one question which will be analysed in this book.

Perhaps one reason for the relatively low participation is that politics is a complex and complicated matter. Politics intervenes in the daily lives of Australian citizens more, and more often, than most people realise. Almost every minute of our lives we come under the cover of some law, rule, regulation or by law. Our actions are not only directed by the results of political decisions, but almost every area of our activity is somehow related to, connected with, or comes into contact with an aspect of government and a part of political processes.

Further, political processes encompass a range of institutions, actions, and ideas. They involve voters, pressure groups, political parties, parliaments, governments, the courts, the public service and the media. They involve decisions about aims and ideals, about what is a 'good society' and how to get there. They involve clashes of interests, of beliefs, of attitudes, of cultures and of policies and programmes.

Politics, then, is essentially about conflict. This does not suggest that everything is a matter of conflict. Much of the life of any political society is based on co-operation, consensus, compromise, agreement. But the focus of a study of politics is inexorably a study of the nature of conflict and of the nature and use of power in the society.

SOCIAL CONTEXT

Australia is a nation of a small population occupying a massive land area. At the 1991 census, a total of 16.9 million people lived on 7.7 million square kilometres, a population density well at the bottom of the list of the countries of the world. Of course, over three-quarters of the area of Australia are the deserts and semi-deserts, hardly able to support a settled population. As a result, the Australian population is highly concentrated in a few urban centres along the coast. The concentration has increased over time as cities have grown. In 1921, only 62 per cent of the population lived in the urban areas; in 1991, 87 per cent were urban. Further, in 1991, 68 per cent of the population lived in the eight capital cities.

Until the Second World War, Australia was a white, predominantly British nation geographically situated in the South-East Asian region. After 1945, Australia's society underwent rapid change as waves of immigrants, first from Britain, from north and eastern Europe, and later from southern Europe and, in the 1980s, from Asia, became part of social and political life. Ethnicity became a political issue, as the policies of governments moved from assimilation to integration and finally to multiculturalism.

In economic terms, Australia underwent a transformation from 'living on the sheep's back' to facing the reality of competing with a rapidly changing world economic and trading environment. The traditional world economy of rich nations exploiting the poor nations of the Third World also came under question, especially from the left. At the other extreme, the rise of the New Right and its constellation of ideologies during the 1980s has one common thread—the concept of small government and the free enterprise market place. This has had a strong influence on both sides of politics. As well, both major parties—Liberal with more unity than Labor—began toying with the thought of the privatisation of public enterprises. The ideal of the welfare State also came under pressure, with taxation policies, welfare services, Medicare, and deregulation of business and finance emerging as divisive political issues.

The role of Aborigines in the Australian society and political system is an issue which has come to the forefront only recently. To a large degree, the effectiveness of the voice of the Aboriginal people depends, as with any other sector of society which is seeking political recognition, on its unity and numbers. The former is slowly being achieved, through education and involvement of Aborigines, and by the efforts of Aboriginal and white leaders. Numbers are difficult to establish accurately, for census figures and population estimates have been little more than informed guesswork. The current estimate of the Aboriginal population in 1788 is 750 000. In 1921, the Aboriginal population was estimated at no more than 60 000. The 1966 census estimated an Aboriginal population of 80 207 and in 1991, the census identified 265 387 Aborigines, of whom almost two-thirds lived in Queensland, Western Australia and the Northern Territory.

For much of Australia's history, the Aborigines were a forgotten people. When they were considered, it was more in terms of 'how to solve the Aboriginal problem'. Until recently, the official policy was that until Aborigines showed themselves fit and able to be assimilated into the white community to think, live and act like whites they should be under restrictive laws and remain essentially wards of the state.

In the early 1960s, the welfare, status and rights of Aborigines became a political issue. Under pressure from a rising interest in the more informed white communities, the old paternalistic and restrictive laws and attitudes of governments began to change, except in Queensland where the attitudes and practices of the National Party seemed better suited to an earlier age. Progress was slow. It was not

Aboriginal demonstration, 1988.

until a referendum was carried in 1967 that Aborigines were counted as Australians in the census, and they were finally granted full citizenship. It was not until 1968 that the national government formally recognised its responsibilities with the creation of the first portfolio for Aboriginal affairs.

At the same time, Aboriginal groups themselves began to seek better status and equal rights. In 1966, following a strike by Aborigines on some Northern Territory cattle stations, the first land rights action took place. The Gurindji people left Wave Hill and staked a claim on land they considered to be at the heart of their tribal culture. Such land claims were the beginning of the involvement of the national government in Aboriginal affairs and since the 1967 referendum, successive federal governments have had concurrent powers with the states to legislate for land rights. Recent events in Queensland and Western Australia have brought demands for national intervention to override the state governments, but no such action has yet been taken. The Hawke Labor government prepared a draft Bill for a national uniform Land Rights policy. But the Burke Labor government in Western Australia opposed this concept vehemently, and the Hawke government scheduled the proposal.

In the 1970s, many Aborigines and supportive groups began to bring further pressure on government and the white community. There was considerable response from the Whitlam government, including the formation of Land Councils and an Aboriginal Legal Aid service, a much increased (and much needed) expenditure on Aboriginal affairs, and the formation of the National Aboriginal Consultative Committee (NACC), established to advise the national government. In 1976, the Fraser Liberal government restructured the NACC into the National Aboriginal Conference, which became a forum rather than a representative body. In 1990, the Hawke Labor government transformed the whole arena of Aboriginal affairs with the creation of the Aboriginal and Torres Strait Islanders Commission (ATSIC).

One of the most controversial issues which has emerged is that of land rights. The Woodward Commission in 1974 recommended that land be vested in Aboriginal trusts, and this was finally carried into legislation in 1977. The national government has transferred more than 200 000 square kilometres of the Northern Territory to Aboriginal ownership, and the South Australian government has enacted similar, but slightly more restricted land rights for the traditional Pitjantjantjara and Maralinga lands in the north-west of the state. Other states have been moving slowly on this issue, except in Western Australia, where all political parties are resisting land rights.

However, the ruling of the High Court on the Mabo case has forced all of Australia to re-think the whole issue of Aboriginal affairs. The High Court declared that the former legal situation of *terra nullius* was incorrect; that Australia was inhabited before 1788, and that native title should be recognised by law. This has led to a new impetus in the debate, and has introduced incredible complexity into the legal, social and political questions involved in the area of Aboriginal affairs. The state and federal governments will face pressures from all sides, and there is no doubt that the implications of Mabo will not be easy to resolve.

POLITICAL CLEAVAGES

Many Western nations show evidence of deep divisions in their societies—cleavages which have serious social and political implications. Canada is divided between a French culture in Quebec and an English culture in the remainder of the nation. Scottish nationalism became an important force in British politics in the 1970s. The USA is a nation of great diversity and of many social cleavages based on religion, language, colour, ethnicity and region. Many European nations also show evidence of diverse and deep divisions of religion, class, language and culture.

Australia, on the other hand, is still often described in terms of homogeneity rather than diversity. But Australian society does contain social and economic differences and social cleavages. Like every industrialised nation, sectors of Australian society have different needs, different desires, and demand different things from government. There are cleavages in Australian society between rural and urban populations, between ethnic groups, between unions and business, between black and white (especially in some areas), between states, and between the states and Canberra, between cities (the constant 'war' between Sydney and Melbourne is part of our national history) and between different regions.

But what evidence is there that such differences and divisions have become politically important? The most obvious evidence of a major *political* cleavage is the formation of a political party on the basis of that cleavage. The Italian Communist Party is an example of a class cleavage; the Parti Quebecois in Quebec of a cultural and regional cleavage; Black Power in America of a race cleavage. If we use the existence of a political party as evidence, then class has been politicised in the Labor and Liberal parties (although as Chapter 4 will show, this class basis of the major party politics is far from strong), and the existence of the National Party is evidence of a rural–urban cleavage.

There are many other *social* cleavages in Australia, but they have not been politicised to this extent. Australia is one of the most multicultural nations on earth, but ethnicity is only marginally politicised. Religion has played a role in Australia's political history in the past; for example, during the debate over conscription in 1916 and in the formation of the Democratic Labor Party in the mid 1950s, but it is currently not a source of major political conflict. Overall, while Australia may contain a kaleidoscope of social differences, it is not a nation of deep social and political cleavages.

A CHANGING SOCIETY

At the start of the Second World War in 1939, Australia had a small population, and was politically unimportant on the world scene. Its economy was based almost entirely on rural industries; it depended on Great Britain for many of its exports and imports, as well as for defence and 'cultural heritage'. It was a socially homogeneous, relatively insignificant nation which was slowly and unsteadily emerging from the Great Depression.

By 1970, there had been dramatic changes. The population had almost doubled and become multicultural through large-scale immigration. There had been an 'explosion' of industrial and mining development, making Australia an important trading nation, and the traditional rural industries had become more productive and more efficient. For a quarter of a century after 1945, Australia was an affluent nation with apparently few real social and political problems, a nation which had developed its own foreign policy (increasingly aligned to that of the USA rather than Britain) and was beginning to play a role in international politics.

In the 1990s, as inflation, unemployment, balance of payment problems, and difficulties of economic and industrial restructuring seem intractable, many economic, political and social issues emerge for governments, parties and people. The changing distribution of population, the continuing growth of cities, and the steadily aging population put increasing demands on services. Education, health and social services emerged as major political issues. New demands by ethnic groups, women, the aged, and those in poverty posed difficulties for governments. The result was a rapidly changing environment for politics and for the processes of representative government.

POLITICAL IDEOLOGIES

Politics involves conflict—over the allocation of scarce resources, over who should rule, over which party should be in government, over the level of taxation. Politics also embodies conflict over ways of approaching such specific questions—a conflict between different sets of attitudes and beliefs. That is, it is a conflict between *ideologies*.

For most Australians, the words 'left' and 'right' are sufficient to describe the ideological choices in political life. To Labor partisans, the Liberal Party is 'right wing'; to Liberals, the ALP is a 'left wing' party and that label is enough. But it is far more complex than that. In fact, politics is not a matter of a clearcut conflict between discrete and clearcut ideologies. Rather, there is a spectrum of ideology, a continuum, which has vague internal boundaries. In real political life, some components of some ideologies flow into other ideologies to their left and right. It is valuable, however, to clarify the outlines of the various ideologies which play a part in Australian politics before analysing how they are involved, and the extent to which they are crucial to the political processes.

The diffusion of ideologies in practical political life occurs at least four ways. First, the tightly defined models of the various ideologies often flow into each other in Australian politics. Second, not always do the individuals and groups which either purport to have an ideology, or are so labelled by others, clarify exactly what that ideology is. Third, it has been assumed for much of Australia's political history that there has been little evidence of ideological debate. Fourth, the major players in the political process—the political parties—have not only been vague about their ideologies, but they also contain their own spectrum of ideologies.

In essence, an ideology is a set of attitudes and beliefs about the nature of humanity, society and the State; about what constitutes a 'good society' and prescriptions for getting there; and about the role of government and politics. In its ideal form, the set of attitudes and beliefs would be elaborate, wide-ranging, consistent and internally coherent, explicit, and would serve as the guide for the actions of its adherents. The 'labels' in the practice of Australian politics fall well short of this ideal form. But they do have elements which can be teased out. The following paragraphs provide a brief summary of the 'ideal types' or models of ideologies. After them we will briefly analyse the ideological continuum that addresses Australian politics.

CONSERVATISM

In the narrowest sense, it is those who wish to preserve the status quo who are conservatives. Political conservatives certainly are reluctant to initiate any change, let alone a radical change. But this reluctance flows from a relatively clear set of attitudes and beliefs. Conservatives believe that people are imperfect, and will always be so. Hence the basic requirement of the human polity is to secure 'good order' in a

One interpretation of conservatism.

collectivity of people who are essentially weak and selfish. To build a community, then, conservatives take a 'realist' path as against liberals and socialists who believe that people are essentially 'good', and emphasise law and order, tradition, stability, morality, the commitment to a 'common good'. The society will contain groups and classes who are not, and importantly, *never can be* equal. Hence there is an important, and positive role for the State in conservative ideology.

To conservatives, the State is an indispensable construct, necessary to ensure order; it is accepted as an active and beneficial component of society and politics. Conflict, to conservatives, is an inevitable component of any human society, and the State exists to control and resolve conflict. There is also some flexibility in the perception of the State. While conservatives are keen supporters of capitalism, they also see a positive role for the State provided that it is acting in defence of, or in the promotion of, private property and the free enterprise system. The conservative position also sees a positive role for the State in social welfare. Private property and private enterprise are the bulwarks of a civilised society, but that society, as an organic community, also has a responsibility to care for those of its citizens who cannot succeed. Welfare is a necessary and moral function of the conservative State.

LIBERALISM

This philosophy developed in the eighteenth century, by stressing the rights of the individual *against* the State. The doctrine of humans' natural rights to life, liberty and property set the foundations for the ideology of liberalism. Civil and political rights, as well as an absolute commitment to free enterprise and free trade became the pillars of classical liberalism. Its core belief was the autonomy of the individual; liberals look on the State with great suspicion. Liberals seek to limit the State—small government, free enterprise, rights and freedoms, private property—are the keystones of liberal rhetoric. To a liberal, the welfare system, in offering a 'security blanket', stultifies individual initiative and imposes a 'lowest common denominator' which is based on a concept irrational to liberals of equality.

But classic liberalism split over the issue of *laissez-faire* capitalism. Faced with the plight of the industrial poor in nineteenth-century Britain, many liberals were persuaded that the State should intervene to protect the social and economic rights of the underprivileged. These interventionist liberals assisted in the formation of a theory of a welfare State, and some found a haven in conservatism. These social liberals simply could not agree with the classical liberals. The latter were out of favour for much of this century, but have returned to prominence in the form of the New Right, the neo-liberals, the economic rationalists. This collection of ideologies has a core which is essentially that of the classical liberal—an emphasis on individual rights and initiatives, the rationality of the free market and, above all, the necessity for the size and influence of the State and government to be limited as much as possible.

SOCIALISM

All ideologies have different interpreters and interpretations. Socialism has the most of all. At base, socialists have a common core belief—the advocacy of a socio-economic system which embodies the communal ownership of the means of production, industry, distribution and exchange. But there are important differences among socialists. To some, such public ownership relates only to the key components of the economy, while to others, the aim is the elimination of all private economic ownership and activity. To some, the State is the community; to others, the systems in Stalin's Russia and some modern eastern European communist societies are 'State Capitalist'—they call for 'peoples' ownership'. Socialists are also divided on the means of achieving the desired end. Communists regard revolution as necessary and inevitable. Democratic socialists reject revolution. They advocate

Socialism: then and now?

gradual change, achieved through parliamentary and democratic processes, depending on convincing the people, first, that socialism is the way to go. There are therefore dogmatic socialists, democratic socialists and social democrats. The social democrats may use socialist rhetoric, but their aims are closer to the social liberals than socialists. Social democrats are willing to support and protect a wide-ranging welfare State, and wide intervention in the economy by the State. But they are not interested in bringing about a socialist society.

All streams of socialists see some positive value in the concept of equality—even something as loose as equality of opportunity—and a positive role for the State. Socialists assume people are naturally social, co-operative, and caring, but that through a capitalist system, social and economic justice is not available to all. The State therefore has a major role. The debate, within socialism, is on both the ends and the means of achieving them.

LABOURISM

Labourists borrow from socialism, but they have different aims and different means of bringing those aims about. Labourists seek a better life for the working class. A labourist ideology, then, is based on the trade union movement as the means by which the workers can achieve better conditions and better protection. Labourists do not seek to take

R.J.L. Hawke—first President of the ACTU then Labor Prime Minister.

over or replace the State. They seek a redirection of the functions and activities of the State in favour of the working class. They are not overly interested in ideologies, but are interested in practical gains for the workers.

Labourism was a strong theme in the developing labour movement and Labor Party in colonial Australia. The socialist observer, Metin (cited in McKinley 1977:23) identified the Australian Labor Party in 1907 as

> ... Socialism without doctrines. Its object is to secure instruments by which workers may control industry. It seeks tools rather than proclaims theories, and does not try to harmonise practical attainments with a pre-conceived ideal of Society.

The trade union movement remains labourist; the Labor Party has changed radically.

POPULISM

The essence of a populist ideology is that 'goodness' rests in the 'common person'; they believe that the 'popular will' is subverted by classes, by entrenched interests, by the institutions of capitalism. They believe in 'power to the people', and seek to control the institutions of representative democracy by means of 'people power', through such means as a citizens' initiated referendum. Only then will the groups and interests in society who have power be brought under control. Populists tend to be xenophobic.

Populists also see the world in relatively simple ways, as divided between good and bad, with few grey areas. Wisdom, morality and legitimacy rest with the good people—but it is on the definition of 'good people' that left and right populism diverge. Left populism, embedded in labourism, is based on the belief that goodness rests on the working class, and hence that class should be important in, and protected by, the political processes. Right populism—agrarian populism—is based on the belief that people with a close link to the land—farmers and country town dwellers—are the well-spring of goodness. Hence they should have an important role in politics, and they and their culture should be protected by politics. Populism is a powerful component of the National Party.

THE AUSTRALIAN 'MIX'

The political actors and debates in Australia, like those in all democratic societies, reveal a rich and varied constellation of ideologies. But some strands have been more important than others. Equally, the development of the Australian economy and the State pre-empted some ideologies.

Conservatism, in the British sense of the word, was not translated to Australia. The early squatters may have intended to transplant a British social and economic system, but failed to do so. Equally, the classic liberals were frustrated from the beginning by the early and rapid development of the interventionist Australian State—both in the economy and the society. From this emerged the combination of utilitarianism and populism which dominated the early development of the Australian polity. Utilitarianism, in its emphasis on maximising 'pleasures' and minimising 'pain', led to an essential pragmatism in public affairs and public policies. Populism, based on the belief that goodness rests in the ordinary person, emerged first in the rural areas but also developed in the cities—hence the right-wing populism embedded in the National Party, and the left-wing populism in the early labour movement.

At the formation of the Australian nation, politics contained socialists, social democrats, classical liberals, social liberals, labourists, pragmatists, populists of both left and right, and conservatives. The resultant mix provided considerable complexity and confusion, until the emerging party system moderated the cacophony of voices and brought some order to the ideological debates. The various streams of 'socialists' gravitated to the Labor Party, and the constant attempts by each, embedded within Labor's factions, to control the party and direct its agenda, actually write the history of the party. The conservatives, classical liberals and social liberals found a home in the Liberal Party, as did the early rural populists, but the last decided to form their own separate party in the 1920s.

The modern 'mix' is dominated by the public debates between the left-centre-right in the Labor Party, the wets-damps-dries in the Liberal Party, the 'centrist' Australian Democrats, and the unique 'liberal–socialists' in the National Party. Such positions and debates will be unpacked in detail in later chapters. But we need to note at this stage that the 'mix', in fact, ranges across the possible spectrum. The small, often extremist groups—left, and right—may not receive much media and public attention, but they certainly exist, and occasionally intervene in public politics through minor parties and single-issue groups.

DEMOCRATIC CONTEXT

Australia is one of the minority of countries in the world which can claim to be a democracy. Some nations claim the title; those whose names include 'Democratic People's ...' are certainly not worthy of the name. But democracy is a value-laden word—it conjures up images of freedom, rights, liberty, harmony. It is no surprise that non-democratic countries have sought to benefit from its image.

DEMOCRACY

This term has its origin in the Greek words *demos* (people) and *kratein* (rule), and thus means the rule by the people, rather than by an élite (*aristocracy*), a few (*oligarchy*), or one person (*monarchy, dictatorship*). It is the opposite to authoritarian and totalitarian systems.

Modern democracy differs in one crucial way from the ancient Greek. The Greek practice was 'pure' democracy, in which all citizens met, discussed, and voted to decide what the law and the policy should be. Modern democracy is *representative* democracy, which will be explained further later in this chapter. Of course, even the Greek direct democracy contained some elements of inequality: only some could speak, only some would be active and some individuals were more influential than others. But all citizens had a direct and equal vote on all issues.

Democracy relies upon basic principles in order to operate effectively. These include the right of equality of participation, the principle of 'majority rule', the concepts of 'minority rights', representation, responsibility, and the rule of law. These must be incorporated in every democratic state.

SOCIETY, 'STATE', AND 'NATION'

Australian society is the sum of the interrelationships of the millions of people who live within the borders of the country. This is a complex realm of human relations. Almost all Australians belong to voluntary associations within the country. They may be as small as the family; as varied as sports clubs, stamp collecting clubs, historical societies, and church groups; as worthy as the environmental movement or women's movement; as organised and restricted as the Melbourne Club. Society itself is the least organised and largest of these associations. The important fact is that all of these, including society itself, are *voluntary* associations. But there is one component of 'being an Australian' which is not voluntary. All residents in Australia at any given time are members of the Australian State.

The State has been defined in many ways, and the term is used in a number of senses. Emphasis on legal aspects, on functions, on the people, on the structure of the political system, can produce different interpretations. Australia contains six states—each with a constitutional existence and political processes, each with a distinguishing history—but Australia itself is a State. When we use this term we may be referring to a defined and recognised territory, to a population governed by political authority, to an entity that has sole legitimate control of means of coercion over the citizens, or to an internationally recognised sovereign unit.

The State, in fact, combines all of these elements. It includes territory, people, government and sovereignty. The State is therefore a political system. But a qualification must be noted. Not every political system is a State; the political systems of local government are subordinate to that of the Australian states, and the international political system is composed of States, but is not a State. The Australian State does include all these components. There is a territory, a people, a government, and sovereignty. The last exists in two senses: internal, in that it is the supreme legal authority; and external, in that no external authority can impose its will on Australia. This latter point is confused by some who describe such decisions as placing the Franklin River area in Tasmania on the World Heritage List as 'giving up our sovereignty'. In fact, Australia *agrees* to the protection; it cannot be forced to do so.

A State is a political system. The Australian State involves every aspect of political institutions, functions and processes. The State incorporates such institutions as a constitution, government, executive, parliament, judiciary, public service, and Governor-

General. The processes of politics within the State include the formal actions of these institutions, the relationships between them, and the political parties, pressure groups and other voluntary associations which are involved. In terms of function, any discussion of the Australian State will include such concepts as power, consent, representation, responsibility, authority and the public interest. Even the formal structure of Australia's governments is a complex situation indeed.

The State is more than government. The government provides the means whereby the State functions. While a government can be defeated, the State remains. For this reason, we need to distinguish between Head of State and Head of Government. The Head of State symbolises the sovereignty of the State, ranks first in ceremonial order, and has specific functions in both national and international affairs. The title can be monarch or emperor or president, and the position can be hereditary (the British monarch), appointive (the Australian Governor-General) or elective (the French president). The Head of Government, on the other hand, is wholly a political office. The prime minister (or premier or chancellor), is the leading person in the political and party political processes within the State. Occasionally, in a specific constitutional context, a Head of State may have reserve powers which can override a majority elected Head of State. The constitutional crisis of 1975 was one notorious case.

The various States of the world vary in their structures and natures. Some are federal (Australia, Canada, USA), some are unitary (Britain, New Zealand). Some are democratic; most are not. Some have a constitution which may prescribe a federal structure, when the reality is a totalitarian unitary state (the former Soviet Union). Some are parliamentary; some presidential. The variety is broad. But all are sovereign political entities.

States have existed for millenia. Nations are recent phenomena which developed with the concept of a nation state in the 1500s. From this has developed the powerful force known as nationalism, which can broadly be defined as that state of mind in which individuals feel a supreme loyalty to the nation–state. Americans and Israelis are intensely nationalistic: Australians seem much less so.

The term 'nation' is often used as a synonym for 'State', but 'nation' involves an emphasis on people rather than on institutions, authorities and government. A nation exists because a group of people believe that they possess sufficient common social, historical and cultural attributes and traditions to maintain a common political organisation. A nation can be a State. It can also be part of a State, and can also exist beyond the State if the belief in the existence of common traditions and interest is strong enough. For example: a black nation *within* the American State; a French nation *within* the Canadian State; an Aboriginal nation *within* the Australian State; a Jewish nation *beyond* Israel.

A State, then, is a combination of a state of mind, a nation, a legal entity, a sovereign body, a means and focus of coercion, a society and a political system. Each State is a political system with its distinct political community (divided into fluid or set sub-communities), its distinct régime (the complex of constitutional rules, institutions, conventions, procedures), its separate authorities (state organisations and officials at various levels), and its own political culture. The study of the government and politics of the Australian State, then, includes all these aspects as well as the relationship between them.

What is common to all States, democratic or totalitarian, is that political authorities make decisions, rulings and laws which affect the actions of human beings in their individual, group and social circumstances. Hence our analysis should begin with the principle which is assumed to guide such authorities in the Australian State: a *democratic* principle would seek to balance authority and coercion with representation, responsibility and rights, to balance law and justice, to balance liberty, freedom and coercion. The manner and nature of the balance will suggest some conclusions about the Australian State.

Australian government, *in theory*, rests on the will of the Australian public, and *in theory*, is responsive to the opinions of the public and responsible to the public. The government, *in theory*, should contain such structures, and be formed in such a way that these primary purposes are emphasised and fulfilled. A democratic government will, *in theory*, emphasise the 'three Rs'—representation, responsibility and rule of law.

REPRESENTATIVE GOVERNMENT

In modern States, it is rare for the citizens to be given a direct role in public affairs, as in ancient Athens where citizens assembled in the market place and carried out public business by a direct vote. Procedures used in some local areas of Switzerland and recent direct votes in some American states in citizen-initiative referendums are examples of the Athenian direct democracy modified to fit modern societies.

In large and complex Western societies, the usual method of deciding public issues is for the citizens to elect bodies of representatives to which they delegate authority. Australia has a system of representative government in which representatives are elected to speak and act for groups of citizens in geographically defined electorates or for the citizens as a whole. In Australia there are three levels of such representative government—national, state or territory, and local government—and various types of electorates. Each elected legislature—the national House of Representatives and the Senate, the Legislative Assembly and Legislative Council in the states, and the various forms of local government across Australia—is composed of

The 'new and permanent' Parliament House, Canberra.

representatives, elected by the citizens to act in their name and on their behalf.

Australia was not the first State to incorporate representative government—the Australian colonies modelled their legislative system on the British parliament and the 'Westminster system', and the Australian national government borrowed the model of federalism from the USA and the referendum from Switzerland. But Australia did lead the way with many representative reforms like male adult suffrage in the 1850s, and votes for women and full adult suffrage (inaugurated in South Australia) in the 1890s. Some reforms were slower, and there are still important elements of representative government, notably in the electoral geography in Western Australia, which need to be reformed and 'democratised'.

Having a system of representative government does not automatically produce a democratic State. We need to ask further questions about the nature and *processes* of such representation and establish the extent to which representation is democratic. Later sections will examine such questions in detail.

RESPONSIBLE GOVERNMENT

We need also to establish the extent to which our representatives, and the institutions, are responsible for their actions, and to whom they are responsible. In the Athenian democracy, the citizens at the market place accepted direct responsibility for their actions. In a democratic system of representative government, important means and processes are incorporated to establish responsibility.

Australian responsible government is based on the English model, the distinguishing feature of which is that the executive—in modern times, the cabinet—is formed from the parliament and occupies a place within the parliament. Hence there are close relations between the executive (government) and the legislature (parliament). The smaller body of people which initiates policy and oversees the application and enforcement of laws—the cabinet—works as part of the larger body of parliament whose members represent the citizens, enact the laws and exercise general functions of deliberation, criticism, and supervision. In this system, responsibility is, in theory, both direct and indirect. The cabinet is directly responsible for its policies, executive actions and supervision to the members of the parliament. If the cabinet cannot retain the confidence and support of the parliament—in Australia, the House of Representatives (although the constitutional crisis of 1975 showed the importance of the Senate in this area)—it must resign or seek a dissolution of the parliament and resolve the conflict though an election. Such a procedure would be another example of direct responsibility where the citizens are given the opportunity to make a judgement on the government and, at the same time, make a judgement on one or more of the members of the parliament. In this limited sense, the members of the legislature are, in theory, directly responsible to the public, while the government's responsibility to the citizens is indirect, through the parliament. The USA is the best-known example of an alternative system of 'responsible' government—a republican or presidential system. In this system, the executive (President) and legislature (Congress) function separately from each other. The President and his cabinet are not part of the Congress; the President and the Congress are elected by different methods, from different constituencies, and hold their positions for different terms. Each is directly representative of the citizens, and each is directly responsible to the citizens. Neither can force an election through a lack of majority support (lack of confidence) and neither is directly responsible to the other. Hence, unlike a parliamentary system, there is a formal system of checks and balances between the executive and the legislature.

CONSTITUTIONAL GOVERNMENT

A fundamental characteristic of the Australian State is that a written 'highest law' exists in the form of the Australian constitution. Australia's founding fathers borrowed the concept from the USA of a supreme document which sets out the division of powers in a federal system, along with some basic rules of the system of government. Unlike the USA, the Australian constitution does not incorporate a Bill of Rights, a statement of fundamental rights and liberties which are guaranteed to all citizens by being entrenched in the constitution. There is constant debate on whether it should do so.

Britain does not have a written constitution. But British government, as much as the USA, Australia, and all democratic States, is based on constitutionalism. This is a key value judgement within a democracy, the judgement that the citizens must be protected from arbitrary government, by a constitution—written or unwritten—and that the citizens must have certain rights, especially rights to political activities. Constitutionalism relies upon a specific and protected sector of the State; the judiciary must be independent of government, and it must adjudicate disputes objectively, free of political obligations.

FEDERAL GOVERNMENT

While the Australian colonies incorporated the British parliamentary system, the formation of the national, Australian system of government also included a federal system. The parliamentary system in Australia does not incorporate a separation of powers as in the US presidential system, but it does incorporate the concept of a division of powers, first practised in the USA, between national and the state (and local) governments.

In some nations, the overall authority is held by one single government. Under this unitary system, such as in Britain and New Zealand, the national government is supreme, and the various county, regional and local government authorities derive their powers from, and are subordinate to, the national government.

A federal system is based on a division of the broad powers of government between a national government and a number of state or regional governments, each exercising its authority in its own areas of responsibility. Thus in Australia, and in other federal States such as the USA and Canada, the national legislature has the authority to make laws on certain general and national topics including defence, foreign affairs, the post office and the coining of money, while the state legislatures have formal responsibility for such areas as education, hospitals, highways, state railways and local government.

A federal system is obviously more complex than a unitary system. It is based on a written constitution and a series of formal and informal relations between the levels of government. The Australian federation came into being in 1901, and since then the basic, constitutional *structure* of Australian federalism has remained almost unchanged; no new states have been admitted, and the constitution itself is still virtually as it was when written in the late 1890s. But the *process* of federalism has undergone significant change—relations of governments have been modified, and the balance of power between the national and state governments has swung firmly to the former. We will explore this in Chapter 10.

RULE OF LAW

This principle is an essential component of constitutionalism. The rule of law is based on the concept of a legitimate and responsible authority. For a political system to be democratic, laws must be made by a legislature which is both representative and responsible, by processes of law-making which are recognised as legitimate, and which are upheld by properly constituted courts.

The basic tenet of the rule of law is that government should not be arbitrary, should not be based on mere opinion, should not be at the discretion of any person or group. In a positive sense, it means that government should be conducted through properly authorised procedures, brought about through legislation passed in a proper form; that all people, whether ordinary citizens or law-makers in government, are controlled by laws and must operate according to the terms of such laws; that the rights and obligations of all citizens should be laid down in law; that all citizens, regardless of position or power, are equal before the law and that all laws should be laid down in writing and be available to the public.

As society has become more complex, and as the people tend to expect more and more from their governments, the simple concept of the rule of law has become modified. Hence laws are more often than not passed in general terms, setting a framework of application of certain principles, and details are filled in at a later stage. As one example, consider the laws which are passed in regard to public health, an area which has enlarged tremendously in recent years. The government and the parliament concerned will pass a law setting out in broad terms the aims and purposes of the institutions involved in public health, the services they should provide, and the means by which they will be funded. But this law usually does not cover all the details and explicit applications of rules which will be necessary to regulate public health under the Act of Parliament. Such details are entrusted to public officials, whether in the public service or in a semi-autonomous statutory authority, who use their own judgement to make regulations. This power, usually referred to as 'delegated' legislation, is still within the concept of rule of law as such regulations are, in theory, examined in parliament and can be amended by parliament. In more recent times, many governments have established an ombudsman to ensure that such delegated legislation is applied under the principles of the rule of law.

The application of the rule of law is the province of a third branch of government, the judiciary. The executive and legislative branches of government are separated in a presidential system such as that of the USA. They function together in a parliamentary system such as Australia's. But both systems incorporate a separation essential to democratic government—the separation of the judiciary from both executive and legislative branches.

POLITICAL CULTURE

Almost since the start of recorded history people have attempted to define the main attributes of a particular society, to describe what it is that distinguishes one society from another, to identify the main threads of a particular culture. Since the 1950s students of politics have had available to them the results of survey research, and consequently thousands of comments from people across all sections of society about how they see their society, their political system and their own positions in that system.

A political culture can be described as the environment of attitudes, emotions and judgements within which the political system operates. The political culture of a nation will be the product of the history of the political system, of the leaders and the mass publics, of the attitudes and experiences of individuals and groups and of the political values held privately, and expressed publicly, by the people in the society.

An ideal democratic political culture would be characterised by the majority of the population being aware of politics and political decisions, interested in politics, involved in political activity, and motivated towards continuing involvement. Scandinavian nations are often used as examples.

Such an ideal person would be fully informed about and aware of the political institutions and processes of the nation; with a clear knowledge of events, personalities, issues, and current debates on such issues; aware of rights and responsibilities in the political system; aware of the programmes, policies and platforms of the political parties, especially at election times; motivated by current political events, and interested in discussing politics with others. He or she would approach political questions with an open mind and be willing to consider alternative views and, above all, be aware that the concept of democracy includes a responsibility to be involved in the political process and not to be merely a recipient. This 'ideal political citizen' can be found in all democratic countries, but in a distinct minority.

A study of the Australian political culture seeks the answers to such questions as:

- How much do people know about the political system and the political process?
- To what extent do people participate in the political process?
- What are people's attitudes to the political system—to institutions (parliament, cabinets, elections), to the various components of government and politics (police, public service, courts, pressure groups, political parties)?
- What do people expect from the political system?
- What goals, virtues and aims should government follow or seek to attain?
- What attitudes do people have about their own roles in the system?

In considering these questions, it is obvious that many different answers will be received. Not all Australians believe the same things. Not all seek the same goals. There will be variations in participation, knowledge, judgements, emotions and attitudes. Hence the political culture will be complex and multi-faceted, containing a considerable diversity of ideas, attitudes, feelings and judgements. An examination of the responses to the public debate on any one issue will reveal a range of attitudes and values. For example, any proposition concerning the unions, environment, uranium, or human relations produces a range of positions—those totally opposed, those totally in favour, and (perhaps a majority) those whose opinions and attitudes fall somewhere between the extremes.

In any society, there will be differences between the attitudes and values of individuals and groups and in any nation there will be a wide range of ideas, judgements, goals and aspirations, to the extent that any assumption that a single, uniform political culture exists is questionable. Just as we need to be cautious in referring to an homogeneous Australian society, we need to have doubts about a single, uniform Australian political culture. When the attitudes of a particular part of a population vary considerably in either intensity or content, that part can be said to have its own distinctive political subculture. The description of an 'Australian political culture', then, may be based on heterogeneity, rather than on wide agreement. For example, are there generally held attitudes derived from such questions as the following?

Public Issues: Do the majority of the Australian population identify with a 'mixed economy'? Do they believe Australia should identify more with the Asian region in which their nation is geographically situated? Do they agree on means to solve the energy crisis, on the conflict between exploitation and environment, on the role of trade unions?

Political System: Do Australians consider the 'Westminster system' is the best political system? Do they believe they should be informed and active in political affairs? Do they have trust in political officials? Do they have faith in the political system, and in their political leaders?
Nation: Do most people identify with the nation, or primarily with some regional, ethnic, religious or other sub-group or sub-culture? How do they judge the national (and regional) political system?

Even on this brief list of questions, it is clear that Australia, like other open societies, contains a range of political sub-cultures.

POLITICAL SOCIALISATION

Few Australians would fit the profile of the 'ideal citizen' described above. To explain why, we need to keep in mind that an individual's political attitudes, beliefs and bases for judgements do not just appear. They are not innate. They are taught, absorbed, learned. Political

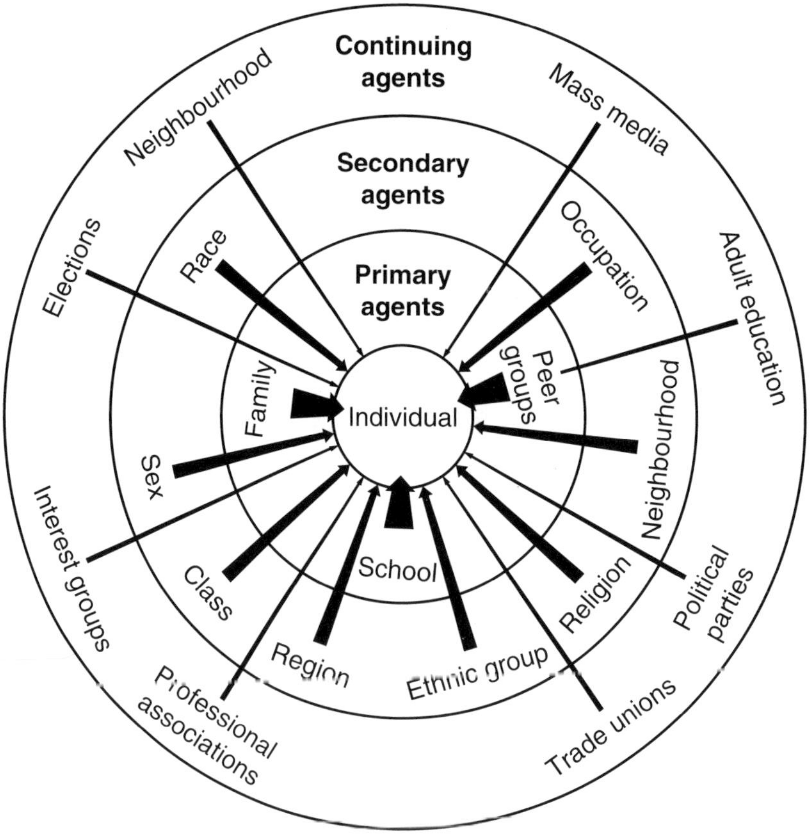

Figure 1.1 Agents of political socialisation

socialisation is the process by which an individual acquires a whole complex collection of information, feelings, beliefs and attitudes which become the framework for him or her to understand, judge and relate to the political system.

Obviously this process of political socialisation varies across society and among individuals. Some people become active participants in politics while many others play no part at all. Some people trust and respect political institutions, leaders and processes. Some others are indifferent or even distrustful. Some people develop commitments to certain ideologies or party programmes; they are confident enough of their own beliefs to be able to say 'I am a conservative/liberal/socialist/marxist', or 'I am committed to the ALP/the Liberal Party/the women's movement.' Others remain uncommitted and uninvolved.

Political socialisation is also a means by which the political system itself transfers sets of values about the system to a new generation. The social customs, values, ideals, systems of belief which are dominant in the political society are not all written into law. Individuals, by a process of political socialisation, become aware not only of the formal laws which govern their actions, but also the more vague but equally strong norms of social and political behaviour that society—or at least a section of society—will expect of them.

How do people *learn* a political culture? Life can be compared to a 'production-line', where number of factors, such as the family, the school, and the mass media pass on information and attitudes about politics which are absorbed as people grow up. This analogy emphasises that the process of political socialisation continues throughout life. The process of political socialisation begins through the family in early childhood. In relations with parents, with the wider family group and with playmates, the child learns something about social and political roles in society. Basic political values, and often party preferences, are developed, perhaps unconsciously, in the home, and these are often retained throughout life. All types of directions, attitudes, emotions and judgements are passed from parents to children, sometimes through deliberate efforts at political education by the parents. The school is also a primary agent. Schools are centrally concerned with attempting to instil at least some patterns of behaviour, although there is a wide variation in the extent to which different nations include deliberate attempts at political education and/or political socialisation in schools.

This process of absorbing a political culture does not end with the school; it continues through much of life. The individual will build up contacts with wider aspects of society, through occupation and work-mates, with the people in the neighbourhood, with church, social and sporting groups, not to mention the police force, bureaucrats, politicians, political parties, judges and so on. Each new influence will have some effect on the attitudes of the individual,

Do Australians protest only when their own personal interests are threatened?

either to reinforce the impact of the early socialisation or to call into question these early influences.

Obviously individuals go through different socialisation processes, formal and informal, primary and secondary, and not all persons react to the same influences in the same way. People grow and learn in different groups and communities—in different social classes, religions, ethnic groups, races, occupations—and each may provide a different orientation to political life and lead to different political attitudes.

Immigrants obviously face a 'rebirth' of their political and social attitudes, and go through a form of political socialisation which is far from simple. In many cases, they will face the task of modifying their own national, political and group identification and loyalty in the face of fundamentally different types of social and political processes. Among many migrants, the process of socialisation is reversed; the adults absorb the new Australian political culture at home from their children who have learnt new ways in their schools and neighbourhoods. It is not surprising that this mix or even clash of social and political cultures has caused tensions within families and groups.

Another important agent of political socialisation is membership of interest groups. In fact, some people consider that their membership of such collectivities as women, blacks, trade unions, Catholics, the Festival of Light, the Communist Party, and so on, is the most important thing in their lives. Others may belong to such groups but be less strong in their identification with the aims and ideologies of the groups.

THE CONTEXT OF REPRESENTATION

Representation involves a transfer of authority. We, the voters, grant our representatives authority to act on our behalf for a specific period of time. After that period of time, we judge our representatives' performance and decide whether or not to continue to grant them our delegated authority. We grant them 'power' to act on our behalf, and we expect them to be 'accountable' to us. But what do we really mean by these terms?

POWER

There is a wide variety of definitions of 'power', but central to all is that power involves a relationship, one which involves

> the ability of a person or group to affect the behaviour of other individuals or groups in specific ways, by the threat or imposition of some form of sanctions (Roberts 1971:171).

From this, we can distinguish political power, social power, industrial power, and economic power on the basis of the component of the society in which the relationship operates, and on the nature of the sanctions which can be applied. A trade union, a person who controls huge economic resources, a leader of the Establishment, a priest—all exercise power to some degree, with 'threats' of sanctions which vary in their scope, nature and potential effects.

All of these relationships can be defined as 'political power' if we define 'politics' as encompassing all human interactions. However, few people would consider religion, the social scene, even economic pressure as part of the political process. By 'political power' we usually mean those relationships within governmental institutions, the various sub-structures such as political parties and pressure groups, and between these and the citizens. In this sense, power is the core component of politics, if politics is defined as essentially a matter of 'who gets what, when and how'. From this flows a range of issues, including the distribution of power, the powers of institutions, the means whereby power is exercised, the nature of constraints, the settlement of political disputes, and the concept of sovereignty.

AUTHORITY

The word 'sovereignty' raises the distinction between power and authority. Both terms, like 'influence', are often used as synonyms, but 'authority' has a specific context. In brief, authority is legitimate power. But that begs the question of the meaning of 'legitimate'. Power, as defined above, is the ability of a person or group to achieve compliance from other persons or groups. Legitimate power—authority—implies that the person or group wielding such power does so with the acceptance of those over whom the power applies. Legitimacy implies that all members of the political system have accepted that those who are in a position of power are rightfully there, are entitled to be there and that the decisions they make have been taken through proper procedures.

That is, we have returned to the concept of representation. The people elect representatives who not only thereby accept authority—legitimate power—but whose responsibility it is to ensure that all other components of the political process act in a legitimate manner. This is especially important in relation to the power and authority of the State, as the State has the right to use coercion to obtain compliance. Such coercion has to be based on legitimate power—on authority. The democratic State obtains this authority from the process of representation, from being responsive to public demands, and from being responsible, ultimately, to the citizens.

Authority implies that the citizens have given their consent to the processes of politics, and to the persons and groups who occupy the positions of authority. But obviously, in a democratic society, not every citizen will agree with every action of the political process. Such people, in a democratic society, have a right to dissent. They can voice their objections, use the political processes to attempt to change the decisions, but to what degree can dissent be carried? A citizen can argue that the right of dissent implies a right to disobey, but that any such disobedience must carry the duty to face the sanctions applied.

DOCUMENTS

1.1 CANADIAN CHARTER OF RIGHTS AND FREEDOMS

Selected Clauses

1 The Canadian Charter of Rights and Freedoms guarantees the rights and freedoms set out in it subject only to such reasonable limits prescribed by law as can be demonstrably justified in a free and democratic society.

2 Everyone has the following fundamental freedoms:

a freedom of conscience and religion

b freedom of thought, belief, opinion and expression, including freedom of the press and other media of communication

c freedom of peaceful assembly
d freedom of association.

3 Every citizen of Canada has the right to vote in an election of members of the House of Commons or of a legislative assembly and to be qualified for membership therein.
4 Everyone has the right to life, liberty and security of the person and the right not to be deprived thereof except in accordance with the principles of fundamental justice.
5 Everyone has the right to be secure against unreasonable search or seizure.
6 Everyone has the right not to be arbitrarily detained or imprisoned.
7 Everyone has the right on arrest or detention
   a to be informed promptly of the reasons therefore
   b to retain and instruct counsel without delay and to be informed of that right
   c to have the validity of the detention determined by way of *habeas corpus* and to be released if the detention is not lawful.
8 Any person charged with an offence has the right
   a to be informed without unreasonable delay of the specific offence
   b to be tried within a reasonable time
   c not to be compelled to be a witness in proceedings against that person in respect of the offence
   d to be presumed innocent until proven guilty according to law in a fair and public hearing by an independent and impartial tribune
   e not to be denied reasonable bail without just cause
   f except in the case of an offence under military law tried before a military tribunal, to the benefit of trial by jury where the maximum punishment for the offence is imprisonment for five years or a more severe punishment
   g not to be found guilty on account of any act or omission unless, at the time of the act or omission, it constituted an offence under Canadian international law or was criminal according to the general principles of law recognised by the community of nations
   h if finally acquitted of the offence, not to be tried for it again and, if finally found guilty and punished for the offence, not to be tried or punished for it again
   i if found guilty of the offence and if the punishment for the offence has been varied between the time of commission and the time of sentencing, to the benefit of the lesser punishment.
9 Everyone has the right not to be subjected to any cruel and unusual treatment or punishment.
10 A witness who testifies in any proceedings has the right not to have any incriminating evidence so given used to incriminate that

witness in any other proceedings, except in a prosecution for perjury or for the giving of contradictory evidence.

11 A party or witness in proceedings who does not understand or speak the language in which the proceedings are conducted or who is deaf has the right to the assistance of an interpreter.

12 a Every individual is equal before and under the law and has the right to the equal benefit of the law without discrimination; in particular, without discrimination based on race, national or ethnic origin, colour, religion, sex, age or mental or physical disability.

b Subsection 1 does not preclude any law, program or activity that has as its object the amelioration of conditions of disadvantaged individuals or groups including those that are disadvantaged because of race, national or ethnic origin, colour, religion, sex, age or mental or physical disability.

1.2 TWO MODELS OF THE AUSTRALIAN POLITICAL SOCIETY

Source: Aitkin, D. 1982, *Stability and Change in Australian Politics*, 2nd edn, Australian National University Press, Canberra, pp. 17–18.

There exist two fanciful portraits of the Australian electorate, which may be labelled the Happy and the Gloomy. The Happy corresponds to the vision of participatory democracy usually attributed to Rousseau and J. S. Mill: all citizens are responsible, rational and concerned; they are alive to problems and issues, and play their part in debating and formulating policies. In turn, governments are quickly responsive to the popular will, and give effect to its decisions. Politics is thus an ongoing dialogue in which every citizen has a say and which the point is the shaping of a better Australian society. No one suggests that the Australian electorate is in every respect like this, but it is assumed to be a state of affairs worth aiming for; certainly the nation ought not to settle for less. In consequence, political leaders and other opinion-makers tend to address the polity at large, citizens accept readily that they ought to vote, newspaper proprietors and other media controllers provide large quantities of political news and information to their publics, and election campaigns continue to be portrayed as occasions on which 'the nation takes stock', on which each of seven million electors reviews the events of the past parliament and the relative performances of government, opposition and other parties, considers the likely problems of the near future, and decides for whom he will vote.

The Gloomy portrait is an antipodean example of what one writer has described as 'the contemporary theory of democracy'. Australia's politics is characterised by apathy; its citizens for the most part take no interest in political issues, and leave the business of policy-making to the political machines, which carry out this function to suit themselves and the vested interests they represent. In consequence, Australians are poorly governed by mediocre men, who are in turn derided by the electorate; and politics ceases to be an activity that can engage the interest or the participation of those best fitted for it. The causes of this malaise are variously located: the absence of deep cleavages in the society, its protective isolation from the rest of the world, a continuing preoccupation with 'growth' and 'development', the lack of a traditional élite that sees in politics an opportunity for disinterested public service, and even the frequency of elections. Indications of a pervasive lack of interest in politics are easy to find, and the phenomenon itself is frequently criticised by those who see external threats menacing Australia, by preachers from the pulpits, and by politicians themselves, especially on having been defeated.

1.3 THE FUTURE OF AUSTRALIAN SOCIETY?

Source: Boyden, S. 1974, 'Australia and the environmental crisis', in Rob Dempsey (ed.), *The Politics of Finding Out,* Longman Cheshire, pp. 15–16.

1 There must be a renewed interest in the quality of life, and a lessening of concern for quantity *per se.* It must involve a total rejection of the gospel of perpetual growth and technological advance at all costs, and also a complete re-appraisal of the current concept of 'progress'. It must lead to a new kind of economy that provides prosperity and opportunity for self-fulfilment and enjoyment of life, in the absence of continued expansion of industry and population.
2 We must turn our minds to the question of what kind of world (and, more locally, what kind of Australia) we really want for the future. In other words, the new thinking must involve our total rejection of the so-called 'inevitability' attitude and of our passive acceptance of our role as victims of the techno-demographic, economic and military spirals. In Australia as a whole, for example, we must ask among other things: Is continual growth of population and of industry and of cities really, taking the long view, the wisest national policy?
3 Society must embrace again the ancient form of human wisdom that still persists among some so-called 'primitive' peoples of the world, namely, a profound respect for the processes of nature on which life depends—and a sound appreciation of the fact that human welfare, on the level of the individual and of society, requires that we live in harmony with nature. In other words, we must cease posing as self-styled 'conquerors' of nature—

conquerors, that is, of that set of processes which not only gave us life in the first place, but on which our civilisation always has, and always will depend for its existence.

4 Perhaps most important of all, this new thinking must involve a genuine and heartfelt concern both for the survival of that unique product of the long evolutionary process, *homo sapiens*, and also for the quality of the lives of our potential descendants.

1.4 POLITICAL SOCIALISATION AND THE FAMILY

Source: Aitkin, D. 1973, 'Electoral behaviour', in Henry Mayer (ed.), *Australia's Political Pattern*, Longman Cheshire, Melbourne, p. 28.

Of the demographic and sociological divisions which underlie Australian party politics, class, however measured, is the strongest. But it is not the best predictor of party identification. That honour is reserved for parents' party identification: three respondents in four remembered their parents as having had a party preference, 83 per cent of them adopted this party for themselves when they first voted; and the majority have retained the same loyalty in later life. The processes by which children acquire their stock of political values and information have been extensively studied. For the most part, it seems clear that children acquire the more or less explicit loyalties of the parents (or dominant parent) by imitation arising from a diffuse loyalty to the family. Where parental loyalties are not explicit, children are likely to adopt the political stance of their parents' social class, if that is obvious. The regularity of the transmission of parental allegiance is the principal cause of the long-term stability of the Australian party system. To say this does not, of course, bring us to the end of the explanation, for we now need to investigate how parents acquired their party identification—an incomparably more difficult job.

We do know that the transmission of parental loyalties is affected to some degree by the circumstances of the times. During the 1930s, about two out of three young voters in their first election supported Labor, at a time when the majority of older voters (including many of their parents) supported the United Australia and Country Parties. More recently, young voters have been voting non-Labor in much the same proportion: in the post-war period, Labor parents have been much less successful than non-Labor parents in reproducing themselves. These changes have long-term implications for the party system because a person's first vote is likely, as we have seen, to represent a continuing disposition.

1.5 IMPACT OF IMMIGRANTS ON POLITICS

a)
Source: Aitkin, D. 1982, *Stability and Change in Australian Politics,* 2nd edn, Australian National University Press, Canberra, pp. 28–9.

On the face of it, the immigration to Australia since the end of the Second World War of more than two million people, mostly unskilled and semi-skilled workers and their dependants, might have led to the growth of migrant parties. Alternatively, it should have been greatly to Labor's electoral advantage. Neither result has occurred, however. Two broad trends can be observed. Firstly, immigration since the Second World War has proceeded during a period of almost continuous and growing prosperity. By and large, immigrants have not needed political structures to help them gain employment, housing or social services—these functions are carried out efficiently by the governmental bureaucracy and private enterprise. No political party has taken much notice of immigrant voters, probably because of the lack of outcry or of demand for political services from immigrants themselves. The Labor Party, which has had most to gain from doing so, lacks the skills to set about welcoming immigrants into its ranks, and suffers from trade union suspicions and hostility besides. For all these reasons, immigrant political behaviour has been barely noticeable. Only a period of major economic and social distress seems likely to change this.

Secondly, immigrants have tended to identify with the non-Labor parties ... Not even the British immigrants, who have had direct experience with a similarly organised and class-based Labour Party, have adopted the ALP in the proportions that might be expected from their class. British immigrants as a group are very similar to Australians in their party choice, while non-British immigrants are even less attracted to the Labor Party.

b)
Source: Jupp, J. 1966, *Arrivals and Departures,* Cheshire-Lansdowne, Melbourne, pp. 84–5.

At the other end of the political scale are thousands of people who have no vote, do not speak English, cannot read the national press or understand the radio or television news, cannot run for office, cannot influence politicians. They have been brought out as labourers in jobs which Australians do not like ... It is often assumed that the absence of political rights, the limited access to power, the political voicelessness of unnaturalised migrants, is unimportant. They can always become naturalised and enjoy the full benefits of citizenship. Yet this is only part of the problem. Living in Australia, owning property, paying taxes and obeying the laws, the European migrant is, nonetheless, largely outside the political framework. His civil rights are not those of British or Australian-born adults ...

Apart from these disadvantages, Europeans find it more difficult to get into positions of influence than do the British or Australians. In trade unions with a preponderance of migrant members they are unlikely to become top-level officials. In local councils where a large part of the ratepayers are migrants, they are not likely to be elected as councillors. If they are not enfranchised they have no pull over local politicians ... The political parties, even where they have special committees for migrants, are almost devoid of European members and officials. This means that migrants are less well equipped than others to get redress against government actions, less well represented in their many dealings with government agencies. It may mean that they will stick by political groups oriented towards Europe rather than Australia, groups which may consciously work against naturalisation, or may exacerbate old rivalries between national minorities.

1.6 MEDIA FOR MIGRANTS?

Source: 'Our multi-racial society', editorial in the *Australian*, 18 April 1980.

The logic behind the proposed establishment of an ethnic television service is hard to follow. The superficial argument is that it will provide programs based on foreign cultures for the many Australians who have come from other countries to make their homes and lives here, thus lessening the traumas of transplantation. But will the Independent and Multi-Cultural Broadcasting Corporation—its name, alone, is dauntingly pretentious—be able to provide a proper service ... even at the estimated establishment cost of $140 million? It seems doubtful.

Estimation of the numbers of diverse cultures and languages native to today's Australians is virtually impossible. We are the world's most multi-racial society so, taking sub-cultures and dialects into account, the number must be large. It would not seem excessive to think 100 different programs would still not cover everybody. Thus, the corporation, broadcasting 12 hours a day, would be able to give each group 45 minutes of programming in a week. Would such a meagre ration help anybody?

The argument that the corporation would be able to cover a large proportion of the migrant population by concentrating on the large groups—such as the Italians and the Greeks—is self-defeating. If anything, members of the large ethnic groups, who can generate their own entertainment and have each other to talk to, suffer less from loneliness and cultural deprivation than do those in the smaller groups, who are often bitterly and depressingly isolated. Indeed, it can be argued the smallest groups are the most in need of the services which the corporation will provide—yet they are most unlikely to be given the lion's share of program time. If they are, it will represent the outlay of an enormous amount of capital and expertise to reach a miniscule audience.

The scheme—a 1977 election promise—gives every indication of being a vastly expensive white elephant, more likely to spread disaffection among migrant groups arguing between themselves about programming rights and program content than to promote national harmony. It must also tend to prolong racial differences rather than settle them, by promoting supra-nationalism instead of nationalism. We are not being racist, simply realistic, when we say we would be much better off bending our efforts toward becoming a mono-lingual society (in English) so that we may all enjoy together the benefits of the wonderful mixture of cultures which our nation encompasses.

1.7 ARE AUSTRALIANS EVERYWHERE THE SAME?

Source: Davis, S.R. (ed.) 1960, *The Government of the Australian States*, Longman Cheshire, Melbourne, pp. 560–1.

... the Australians are a people of an unusual degree of cultural homogeneity. While for some purposes State boundaries define separate units of political action, yet in all the things which determine the content of political behaviour—in their class relations, in their family structure, in the manner in which they gain their wealth, pursue pleasure, instruct their children, worship their gods, in their shibboleths and aspirations, in their dress, speech, diet and interests, there is, despite the great differences in area, vegetation and climate, little to distinguish the mode of life in Camooweal and Fitzroy Crossing, in Cairns and Carnarvon, Collie and Collinsville, or Wagga Wagga and Wagin; and little to mark the passage from the 'Banana' State to the West except for a casual cyclone gate, a modest wooden bridge, or an elusive stone in the Nullarbor Desert. What prospect is there for the collector of political curios in such a society?

1.8 DIFFERING INTERPRETATIONS OF A 'RIGHT'

a 1988 Referendum Question
A Proposed Law: To alter the constitution to extend the right to trial by jury, *to extend freedom of religion*, and to ensure fair terms for persons whose property is acquired by government. Do you approve of the proposed amendment? [emphasis added].

b Extract from Liberal Party leaflet forwarded to private (religious-based) schools during the referendum campaign.

Senator Bishop said the removal of the words 'make any law for' will make the clause similar to one in the American Constitution which has been used to prevent public funding of Church schools in the USA.

c The US Constitution, Bill of Rights, Article 1, extract: 'Congress shall make no law respecting an establishment of religion, or prohibiting the free exercise thereof ...'

d The Australian Constitution, s. 116:
'The Commonwealth shall not make any law for establishing any religion, or for imposing any religious observance, or for prohibiting the free exercise of any religion ...'

ISSUES FOR DISCUSSION

1 Why are governments in Australia involved in more fields and wider activities than they were at the turn of the century?
2 Should citizens in a democracy be free to criticise the laws which they obey? What limits do you consider should be placed on dissent?
3 Identify any group in your community which needs special services or special consideration. Should the government have the responsibility to provide these?
4 Mention several different kinds of authority the government has over you as a citizen. In each case ask whether it is necessary for government to have this authority.
5 Contrast the terms 'equality' and 'liberty'. Can a person in our society have both?
6 Show how each of the following contribute to the success of a democracy: education, economic security, distribution of power, ability to exchange ideas, respect and good will.
7 Should Australia have a Bill of Rights along the lines of the Canadian Bill (Document 1.1)? What would you include in an Australian Bill of Rights? Why are so many people opposed?
8 How should a government balance 'majority rule' and 'minority rights'?
9 'Democracy is more than a political system—it is a way of life.' How would you explain this to a person who has lived all of his or her life under a dictatorship form of government?
10 Should an individual have complete freedom of speech? Of assembly? Of religion? Of thought?
11 What do you think are the major influences that have shaped the Australian political society of today? (See Document 1.2.)

12 Do you think that Australia is becoming too Americanised?
13 In what ways have the migrants who have come to Australia since the Second World War changed Australia's political society? (See Document 1.5.)
14 Do you think the ordinary person has enough say in the political process?
15 Australians are often described as racist. How true is this?
16 Discuss the issues raised in Document 1.3.
17 Discuss the issues raised in Document 1.6.
18 Are Australians 'all the same'? (See Document 1.7.)
19 Analyse the conflicting interpretations in Document 1.8. Why did the Liberal Party argue the wrong interpretation?
20 Should Australia become a republic? If so, what form of republic?

Chapter two ELECTORAL SYSTEMS

Modern democracy is representative democracy. We, the people, are represented in the various legislative forums, by representatives who are assumed to be acting on our behalf. Any comparison of the democratic nations of the world provides a varied collection of electoral laws, practices, and systems. In Australia, with three separate arenas of representation—federal, state, local—there is an even more varied collection.

PRINCIPLES OF ELECTORAL REPRESENTATION

Australia's political institutions are based on a system of representative government. But such a statement immediately begs a whole series of questions:

- How are the representatives chosen?
- Are the elections fair?
- In what sense do our representatives represent?
- What roles do political parties play in choosing the representatives, and in the representation?
- Who has the right to participate in selecting the representatives?
- How important is the election process?
- Are Australian elections 'free, fair and frequent'?

There is no doubt about the frequency of elections in Australia. Citizens have been called on to give their decisions in elections and referendums at a rate above that of most Western nations. And they have been faced not only with frequency, but also with complexity and diversity. The Australian voter, in any three-year period, may be required at least to vote for the Senate with one electoral system, for the House of Representatives with a different system, for two state houses with the possibility of further different election systems in each, and for local government with yet another system. In the same period, the voter may also face referendum questions, state and federal, with yet another different system of voting. The elector may be required on one occasion to mark the ballot paper with numbers in sequence, missing none and filling all boxes (or all but one), on other occasions to put a cross in only one square, and in referendums to write 'yes' or 'no'.

Take the electors of Victoria as an example. In the twenty-four years since 1970 they have been involved in voting in over thirty elections—for the House of Representatives and Senate in the federal arena, and for the Legislative Assembly and Legislative Council in Victoria. As well, they have faced local government elections, and sixteen constitutional referendums. There has been no shortage of opportunity to be involved in representative democracy.

The Australian electoral scene has been complex ever since the nation was formed in 1901. Federalism, which established three separate arenas of representative government, contains the potential for complexity and experimentation. The Australian colonies pioneered major electoral reforms, many well before other democratic nations and before the 'mother country', Britain; reforms such as the secret ballot, male suffrage, and later adult suffrage, and one person one vote. But they went their own ways in terms of the favoured method of translating votes to seats. Tasmania has been the most stable state in terms of electoral systems; proportional representation was introduced in 1909 for the House of Assembly and has been used ever since.

Both voters and political parties have been forced to accommodate themselves to the complexity of the various systems. The majority of voters depend on party how-to-vote cards to guide them; political parties hope that the voters will follow the cards, cast a valid first preference vote and mark their preferences as the party desires. Some voters, estimated at about three per cent of those who cast formal votes, whether through confusion arising out of the complex system or by deliberate choice, cast what is termed a 'donkey vote'. That is, they number the boxes on their ballot papers from top to bottom (or, more rarely from bottom to top) regardless of favoured party or candidate. Hence, in an election with a large number of candidates or the possibility of a close result, the position of the candidates' names on the ballot paper can be quite important.

There is no universally accepted answer to the question of what constitutes a 'fair' election. This is because there is no single body of opinion even on the purposes of elections, on what is a fair and just election system, or even on the nature of electoral representation and the relationships between election systems, elections, political parties and representative government. There are fundamental differences of opinion between political parties on these issues, and any legislation concerning electoral systems is always very controversial. A major reason for these differences is that while political parties may clothe their policies in regard to election systems with 'principles' of representation, they are also very concerned with the actual effects of various election systems on their own chances of success.

Any discussion of the nature of electoral representation in Australia should include a series of questions about the mechanics of the electoral systems themselves. It should also include the broader aspects of pre-selection of candidates by political parties, the effects of election systems on parties (and the impact of party on the choice of electoral system), and the types of representation followed by the representatives once elected.

The study of electoral systems raises at least three separate issues relating to the principles of representation. Each has produced markedly different answers on the practices of electoral systems in Australia. It is necessary, then, to analyse the mechanics of the various electoral systems and ask what principles can be found at their base. Political parties, especially, have shown a tendency to modify democratic principles to produce self-interest even, as in the case of the Queensland National Party, elevating self-interest to a principle.

A FAIR ELECTORAL SYSTEM?

The three issues suggest a host of subordinate questions.

1 Who can (should) vote? Who has the right to vote; who may not vote; what are the procedures for enrolment; who can be a

candidate; under what conditions can candidates nominate; how is the polling conducted; is there a free and secret vote; is there a right to vote, or is there compulsion to vote?
2 Do votes count equally? This is perhaps the most controversial of the questions. It concerns the fairness, representativeness and justice of electoral geography, and electoral practices such as gerrymanders and malapportionment.
3 What is the relation of votes and seats? How are the votes counted; which system is used to translate votes into seats; which is the fairest system?

THE RIGHT TO VOTE

South Australia was the first colony to grant full adult suffrage, in 1894. By 1909 all lower houses in the states, and both the House of Representatives and the Senate federally, were elected by adult suffrage. After political arguments and battles which lasted for over a century, the last two Legislative Councils—which were still not fully elected by adult suffrage—finally accepted this essential aspect of democratic elections in 1973 (South Australia) and 1978 (New South Wales). Today, all adults who have complied with the various Electoral Acts have a right to vote for state and national parliaments. For national elections, any person who is eighteen years of age or older, is an

South Australia introduced full adult suffrage in 1894. Its first Parliament House still stands in North Terrace, Adelaide.

Australian citizen (either natural-born or naturalised), and who has lived in Australia at any time for six months continuously is entitled to be enrolled as a voter. Some people, however, are specifically excluded—people of unsound mind, those who are 'attainted of treason', or those who have been convicted and are under sentence for an offence punishable by imprisonment for five years or longer.

Australian electoral laws go beyond granting the mere right to vote. They include two aspects of compulsion, backed by a legal sanction—compulsory enrolment and compulsory attendance at the polls. Taken together, these are usually referred to as compulsory voting. In fact, the Electoral Acts do not, and cannot, enforce compulsory *voting*. What Australia has is a system of *compulsory attendance* at a polling place. Once a person has been checked for attendance on the electoral roll and has received a blank ballot paper, then there is no legal provision for further scrutiny and any suggestion of such would destroy the secrecy of the vote. For simplicity, however, the term 'compulsory voting' is used.

Compulsory voting obviously aids pollsters and psephologists in their quest to predict and analyse voting patterns. It has also eased the burden on political parties in their quest for power. They have been relieved of the task of getting voters to turn out and have been able to concentrate on their second problem of getting the voters to support them.

Australia remains one of a very small number of countries, and is the only Anglo-Saxon country, to incorporate and enforce compulsory voting. It was introduced in 1924 for national elections following a decline in voter turnout, and justified generally on the grounds that if voters are forced to the polls they will be forced to consider political and electoral issues and hence become more informed and better voters. But there is little evidence to suggest that this has occurred—the level of political apathy in the Australian community has shown no signs of improvement as a result of compulsory voting.

The Australian laws on compulsory voting remove the rights of individuals to decide for themselves; the laws remove the right to vote (the right not to vote). Why, then, has compulsory voting been retained? One reason, applicable to both Labor and non-Labor parties, is that compulsory voting tends to maintain a situation where most electorates are safe for one party or the other. The return to voluntary voting would bring the possibility that changes in turnout may bring some safe seats into the doubtful category. A second reason, which lies at the base of the firm commitment of the Labor Party, is the suspicion in the party that more traditional Labor voters would stay away than would Liberal supporters if voluntary voting were permitted. Hence, as in so many aspects of Australian politics, a policy is maintained more because of perceived benefits to political parties than for its intrinsic democratic value.

Compulsory attendance does not mean that all who do attend cast a valid vote. Whether by mistakes or deliberate action, some voters produce an informal vote. Some do not mark their ballot papers at all, others do not complete their papers correctly. There is evidence that some voters cast deliberate informal votes.

Compulsory preferential voting is almost universal in Australia. Whether on the basis of giving preferences to all candidates in a single-member electorate (as in mainland lower-house elections), or giving preferences to all candidates in a multi-member proportional representation system (as in the Senate or the lower house in Tasmania), the voter is usually compelled to do so or cast an informal ballot. Only in New South Wales is optional preferential voting available, with limited optional preferences in the Legislative Council of New South Wales.

THE RIGHT TO STAND

In a formal sense, the right to stand for election is as wide as the right to vote. Any person can nominate as a candidate if he or she:

- is not less than eighteen years of age
- is an Australian citizen (either natural-born or naturalised)
- is an elector or is qualified to become an elector
- has lived within the Commonwealth for at least three years at the time of the election.

Some people are specifically refused the right to be members of parliament, including those who are not Australian citizens, those who are undischarged bankrupts, and any person who holds an office of profit under the Crown. Any Australian or state public servant must resign before nominating.

But, unlike voting, standing is far from a 'free' right. A deposit is required with each nomination—$500 for the Senate and $250 for the House of Representatives. This deposit is returned if the candidate receives a certain proportion of the vote; in House elections if the candidate's first-preference vote is greater than four per cent of the first-preference votes cast in the electorate; in the Senate if the candidate, or the group of which he or she is a member, received more than four per cent of the first-preference votes.

This establishes a considerable disincentive, especially for prospective independent candidates and minor parties, and is especially a barrier in the Senate. A candidate for the House of Representatives in Victoria in 1993 needed to win around 3000 votes to have the deposit returned. In the Senate, the candidate needed more than 113 000 votes to receive the $500 back. The system aims to discourage frivolous candidates, but who decides what is frivolous?

A second aspect of nomination is that most candidates are pre-selected and endorsed by political parties. We will return in a later chapter to the nature and importance of pre-selection processes. At this point, it is sufficient to ask whether such pre-selection is in accord with the principles of representation outlined in Chapter 1. Who, for example, is a party candidate responsible to—the people in general, his or her electorate, or his or her party?

DO VOTES COUNT EQUALLY?

Of all the various principles of electoral representation, two seem most important in defining a democratic system; 'one person, one vote' and 'one vote, one value'. All national and state electoral laws apply the principle of one person, one vote. All adults have the right to vote and to cast only one vote. But this does not imply that in all electoral systems the vote cast by one person is counted as equal to that cast by another.

A recent decision by the Supreme Court in the USA declared that any electoral system based on some electorates having more electors than others was against the constitution. Shorn of its legal terminology, such a ruling stated that not only should there be one person, one vote—that all eligible adults should have one vote and only one vote—but that all voters should be considered equally. In recent times, some political parties in some states have sought to incorporate both principles into legislation. Some governments have incorporated one vote, one value into electoral systems, and some (South Australia, first, in 1975) have entrenched the principle into the constitution. In 1988, the Hawke Labor government attempted to carry a referendum to entrench the principle into the Australian Constitution to be binding on all electoral arenas. The Liberal Party (except in Queensland) and the National Party opposed the referendum and it was defeated. Hence, some governments can still manipulate electoral boundaries to their advantage.

For over seventy years since Federation, governments consistently and deliberately legislated for inequalities in electoral systems, for *malapportionment* which was designed to favour the party in government by favouring voters in one geographical area over those in another. Such systems of malapportionment, with only one exception, were designed by Liberal–National governments to favour non-metropolitan areas and hence themselves. The only case of a Labor party malapportioning in its own favour was in Queensland in 1947–1956.

In the history of Australian election systems, there has been no shortage of malapportionment. This is often, but incorrectly, termed a gerrymander. There is little evidence that a gerrymander—in strict terms, a deliberate electoral inequality based on odd-shaped electoral boundaries drawn to provide advantage to a political party—has existed except in very minor forms in any Australian system. But deliberate malapportionment has been widely used in Australian electoral systems.

The most obvious examples of deliberate malapportionment in recent times have occurred in Queensland, Western Australia and South Australia, in each case based on a system of electoral zones which allow inequalities and sometimes massive differences. In South Australia in 1968, for example, a rural vote on average was 'worth' more than three times a metropolitan vote, and the largest metropolitan seat contained an enrolment equivalent to the total enrolment in the seven smallest rural seats. In Western Australia in the 1977 election, the metropolitan area, with 66 per cent of the total enrolment of the state, contained only 27 of the 55 seats in the state—less than half the seats. In Queensland, malapportionment after 1958 was based on a system of four zones, with average enrolments at the 1989 election of South-East (metropolitan Brisbane and urban development) 23 171; Provincial City 21 121; West/Far North 10 136; Country 14 569. The intention of this system is shown by the traditional contests: South-East (Labor v. Liberal); Provincial City (Labor v. National); West/Far North and Country (Labor v. National). The system was clearly designed to obtain benefits for the National Party, and to disadvantage *both* Labor and Liberal parties.

In the mid-1970s, two Labor governments moved successfully to reform electoral systems. In 1974, the Whitlam Labor government passed an Act limiting the deviation of the enrolled population in any national electorate to a maximum of 10 per cent from the average. This was strongly opposed by the National Party but was carried in the historic joint sitting of both houses in 1974. This base, approaching one vote, one value to perhaps the maximum practical extent in a system based on single-member districts, was retained by the Fraser Liberal-National Party government, despite strong opposition from the minority coalition party.

In 1975, the South Australian Dunstan Labor government incorporated similar principles, but entrenched the guarantee that votes should be equal in value to the constitution of the state, so that it cannot be modified without a referendum. Tasmania, with a system of multi-member electorates, has had votes of equal value since 1906. The electoral systems for the Legislative Councils in South Australia (since 1974) and New South Wales (1978) automatically produce votes of equal value as they consist of one single statewide electorate, hence overcoming any possibility of 'weighting' one set of votes more heavily than another.

By the 1980s, all but two electoral systems had been reformed, and the comparison with the 1960s is telling (Table 2.1). The inequities in the 1960s are obvious, with only Tasmania's lower house having a fair electoral system. Two decades later, the malapportionment has

Table 2.1: *Measures of malapportionment*

	Gini 1960s	Gini 1980s	David Eisenberg 1960s	David Eisenberg 1980s	Dauer-Kelsey 1960s	Dauer-Kelsey 1980s
Aust	3.1	1.4	42.5	48.3	0.13	0.04
NSW	2.7	1.4	43.1	47.2	0.12	0.05
Vic	4.1	1.8	40.7	45.4	0.18	0.09
Qld	2.6	3.9	41.4	40.3	0.15	0.17
SA	7.7	1.6	24.5	46.1	0.39	0.09
WA	7.2	5.8	33.1	36.1	0.25	0.19
Tas	1.2	1.1	49.0	50.9	0.06	0.04

Range: David Eisenberg—1.0 is perfect one vote one value; the larger, the more malapportioned.
Dauer Kelsey—50.0 is perfect; the smaller, the more malapportioned.
Gini—0.00 is perfect; the larger, the more malapportioned.

Source: Hughes 1977, Hughes 1988. For a description of the indices, see Hughes 1977.

been removed (on every occasion by a Labor government) in all areas except Western Australia and Queensland. In Western Australia, where the Liberal Party controls the (malapportioned) Legislative Council, the Labor government succeeded, after years of conflict with the opposition, in winning agreement to a reform reducing the malapportionment in favour of the non-Labor parties to 2:1. This was a reform, but it retained a strong bias to the Liberal and National parties.

In 1992, following the Fitzgerald Royal Commission, the Queensland electoral system was reformed by an independent commission, and the 'Bjelke-mander' was abolished. Although an allowance was made for two very remote electorates, the Queensland system now incorporates close to one vote, one value for the first time.

The party effects of malapportionment are self-evident. As deliberate malapportionment has the intention of producing an advantage for one party over the others, it would be surprising if the product was not obvious. The 1986 election in Queensland is a prime example (see Table 2.2).

It is no surprise that the National Party is the strongest opponent of one vote, one value!

Is there any justification for malapportionment? Its proponents use two main arguments: that the rural areas are the 'producers' of the nation, those with a 'stake in the country' who merit 'extra' representation; and that the dispersed populations in rural areas can only receive electoral representation, equivalent to that in cities, if the electorates are smaller in population. The former—the 'sheep's back'

Table 2.2: *Effects of malapportionment, Queensland, 1986*

Zone	Seats	Enrolment per seat	ALP% Votes	ALP% Seats	LIB % Votes	LIB % Seats	NAT % Votes	NAT % Seats
South-East	51	20 399	41	37	22	18	34	45
Provincial City	13	17 115	48	62	7	–	42	38
Country	17	13 312	35	12	6	–	57	88
West/Far North	8	9 270	41	13	5	13	54	75
State	89	17 565	41	34	17	11	40	55

principle—is simply not as relevant, if it ever was, in the 1990s. The latter principle is a real one, but it can be resolved by means other than malapportionment. It can be resolved simply by granting larger expense allowances to rural parliamentarians, and by utilising modern communication and transport technologies to the full. The fundamental principle is clear: democracy assumes that every person's vote will be equal in 'political power' to every other person's and any electoral system which departs from this is undemocratic.

Following the report of the Constitutional Commission, the Hawke government decided to put four referendum questions to the people. One was a simple issue: 'To alter the Constitution to provide for fair and democratic parliamentary elections through Australia'. This referendum, if carried, would have required all state parliaments—Assemblies and Councils—to be elected under a system of one vote, one value. It would have ended the power of any party-in-government to incorporate partisan malapportionment to its own advantage. It would not have affected each State's equal representation in the Senate, nor affected the minimum representation guaranteed to Tasmania.

The Liberal Party could have been expected to support this referendum. After all, it has supported one vote, one value in three States and in the national electoral reform Acts. And the Liberal Party in Queensland, which did campaign for a 'yes' vote, had been damaged by the 'Bjelke-mander' for over two decades. But the National Party, with its power base in Queensland depending on severe malapportionment, and with a policy which supports rural-biased election systems, was totally opposed to the referendum. The Liberal Party's ultimate opposition can only be explained by its bowing to National Party pressure.

The official 'no' case, prepared by the Liberal Party, rested on the statements that 'it deprives State Parliaments of the right to tailor their electoral laws to their own needs; it overrides the powers of State Parliaments'. The referendum would have done precisely that but in the process, it would have guaranteed a democratic election system. The majority of the Australian public voted in favour of the Liberal position—that is, to allow malapportionment to continue.

THE POLITICS OF REDISTRIBUTION

Changes in electoral geography—redistributions—have occurred at irregular intervals in the national and state systems. Until the 1970s, the redistribution of electoral boundaries had been a party-political decision. It had been a decision of a party-in-government to decide to inaugurate a redistribution, either because of population movements, or because of a change in the number of members of parliament or, in the partisan sense, to produce or strengthen a bias in its favour. Until the 1970s, and still the case in Western Australia, the party-in-government sets the terms of reference for the redistributing authority and, through its control of the parliamentary members, can decide whether the resultant electoral geography satisfies its desires.

South Australia's Labor government initiated a major reform in 1975 which has now been accepted elsewhere. The principle of one vote, one value is now the overriding term of reference for an independent Electoral Commission, and South Australia has entrenched this into the constitution, requiring a referendum for any modification of the principle. Under the terms of a redistribution, the commission decides when, receives public recommendations, redistributes, and any objections are heard by the Supreme Court. Neither the government nor the parliament can modify or override a redistribution report. The entire process is conducted in the public arena, and South Australia has entrenched the most independent machinery, and most democratic principle, of electoral reform. The reverse—the most secret, party-dominated, and biased procedure—was in Queensland under the National Party.

In the national arena, following the 1983 Electoral Act, a redistribution is carried out for each of the states by an Electoral Commission for each of the states, including a member of the Judiciary, the Chief Electoral Officer and the Surveyor General. The first step is to determine a quota for each state by dividing the total number of people enrolled by the number of members of the House of Representatives to be elected. The number of representatives is determined from the census data, and hence redistributions may be necessary in two or more states following each census. Following the census of 1986 and 1991, a reallocation occurred. The state 'allocation' of seats in 1990 was New South Wales 51, Victoria 39, Queensland 24, South Australia 13, Western Australia 13, Tasmania 5 (a constitutional minimum), Australian Capital Territory 2, Northern Territory 1, total 148; in 1993, New South Wales, Victoria, and South Australia lost one seat, and Western Australia and Queensland gained a seat.

Under the Australian Electoral Act, the Commission is required to arrange the boundaries so that three and a half years *after* the redistribution each electorate will be estimated to contain a number of electors within a 10 per cent variation from the quota. The Commission then takes into account certain guidelines such as community of interest, means of communication and travel, the trend of population changes, physical features and existing electoral boundaries. In South Australia, the Boundaries Commission is required to examine the electoral geography after each election and determine whether a redistribution is necessary.

THE RELATION OF VOTES AND SEATS

The mechanics of an electoral system can have an important effect in deciding the extent of representation of the various parties. There are a number of variations used in Australia in relating votes to seats.

'First-past-the-post'—the 'plurality' system—is used in most Anglo-Saxon countries, and is used for some local government elections in Australia. Under this the simplest system, the voter places a cross in the box next to the name of only one candidate. The candidate who obtains the highest number of votes wins the seat.

Under a system of preferential voting, the system used most widely in Australia, voters are required to rank candidates in order of preference. To be elected, a candidate must have achieved an absolute majority—at least 50 per cent plus one vote—of all formal votes cast. If no candidate achieves an absolute majority on first-preference votes, preferences are allocated, starting with those of the least-supported candidate, until the requisite absolute majority is obtained.

The result in the electorate of MacMillan in Victoria in the 1972 national election shows how different election systems can produce different results. The first preference votes were cast as shown in Table 2.3. If the first-past-the-post system had applied, Mountford would have been elected as he had won the largest number of the formal first preference votes. But he had not achieved the absolute majority demanded by a system of preferential voting. Preferential voting involves two stages: voters decide between the candidates, and record their ranking of candidates by marking the ballot paper with sequential numbers; the second stage is the complex process of counting and distributing the preferences—if they are required. Some electoral systems, such as the House of Representatives and most States, demand compulsory preferences—voters must provide a preference for all candidates. Some systems allow optional preferences—voters can record a preference for only one candidate, or two, or three ... as they choose.

The counting process is complex, especially when an election is close, and when there is a high number of candidates. The following example shows such a case (Tables 2.3 and 2.4). Once the first-preference votes are counted, the candidate with the least number of votes—Buchanan in the example—was eliminated, and his ballot papers were reallocated on the basis of the second-preferences shown on each ballot paper. As an absolute majority was not achieved, the next lowest supported candidate was eliminated. The second-preferences of Houlihan, and the third-preferences of ballot papers which had been transferred from Buchanan, decided the next place for the papers. Finally, to obtain the absolute majority, the second-preferences of Armitage voters, the third-preferences of Houlihan voters who had voted '2' for Armitage, and the fourth-preferences of

Table 2.3: *First-preference votes in federal election, seat of MacMillan, Victoria, 1972*

Candidate	First-preference votes N	%
Armitage (Liberal)	12 025	24.2
Buchanan (Independent)	3 113	6.3
Hewson (Country)	8 282	16.6
Houlihan (DLP)	3 583	7.2
Mountford (ALP)	22 802	45.8

Table 2.4: *Allocation of preferences, seat of MacMillan, Victoria, 1972*

	First-preference votes	Buchanan eliminated	Houlihan eliminated	Armitage eliminated	%
Armitage	12 025	12 835	13 226	–	
Buchanan	3 113	–	–	–	
Hewson	8 282	10 262	13 406	26 096	52.4
Houlihan	3 583	3 721	–	–	
Mountford	22 802	22 987	23 173	23 709	47.6

those voters who had voted '1' Buchanan, '2' Houlihan and '3' Armitage were distributed.

Hence, the candidate who won less than one-sixth of the first-preference vote finally defeated the candidate who won almost half of the first-preference votes.

A third method used in Australia in the Senate, the South Australian, New South Wales and Western Australian Legislative Councils, and in the Tasmanian House of Assembly is the system of proportional representation. Supporters of this system point to it as a means to overcome the biases, inherent or deliberate, in single-member systems. They see proportional representation, based on multi-member electorates, as a solution to the 'evils' of existing systems, in offering representation to a wider group of parties, reducing the problem of the 'wastage' of votes, and reducing the possibility of malapportionment.

Both first-past-the-post and the preferential vote (PV) systems, based on single-member electorates, are designed less to reflect the party choices of the electorate in the parliament and more to produce a majority for one party (or a coalition). In the MacMillan result, if first-past-the-post had been used, the representative would have been elected with 22 802 votes, while 27 003 votes were cast against him. Proponents of a system of proportional representation consider that these 27 003 voters have not had their choices—nor even their interest—represented. One answer is that a representative, once elected, should represent all people in the electorate. The preferential voting system partly overcomes this criticism by ensuring that the successful candidate has absolute majority support through distribution of preferences. However, as the MacMillan result shows, even after the distribution of preferences, there were still 23 709 voters who were not represented by a party of their choice.

A further criticism levelled by proponents of proportional representation is that there is too much 'wastage' of votes in other electoral systems. They point to results such as those in the electorate of Bradfield (New South Wales) in 1977, shown in Table 2.5.

They argue that not only were voters for parties other than the

Table 2.5: *Votes cast in federal election, by parties, Bradfield, New South Wales, 1977 (N and %)*

	Votes	
	N	%
Liberal	49 052	72.6
Labor	9 578	14.2
Democrat	7 378	10.9
Progress	1 518	2.3

Liberal Party 'not represented', but that a proportion of votes was 'wasted'. The Liberal candidate required 33 764 votes to have the necessary absolute majority to be elected; hence, according to supporters of proportional representation, 15 288 Liberal votes were 'wasted'.

Proportional representation (PR) does provide a means of resolving these problems of representation. Proportional representation is based on multi-member districts either as the whole state (as in the Senate, and Legislative Councils in South Australia and New South Wales) or as sub-state electorates (as in Western Australia and Tasmania). The electors are represented by seven members per electorate in Tasmania, twenty-two members for the whole state in South Australia, and twelve members per state in the Senate (increased from ten per state in 1983).

The Senate election result in Victoria in 1990 is shown in Table 2.6. If this pattern of party support had occurred in a single-member electorate then, under a plurality system, the Liberal Party would win the seat. Under preferential voting, the Liberal Party would also have won.

Under the system of proportional representation, the actual results were Liberal–National—three seats, Labor—two seats, and Australian Democrats—one seat. Under PR, the party division in the electorate was more accurately represented in the parliament, and less votes were 'wasted'.

Four types of proportional representation have been used in Australia. The variation used in elections to the Australian Senate is usually referred to as the 'single transferable vote' (STV) type of PR. This allows electors to vote for individual candidates in whatever order they wish. The Tasmanian system, the Hare–Clark system, is the

Table 2.6: *Senate election result, Victoria, 1990*

Party	First-preference votes N	First-preference votes %	Quotes	Seats won
LIB/NAT	1 149 170	44.6	3.12	3
ALP	938 245	36.4	2.55	2
AD	365 376	14.2	0.99	1
CTA	29 608	1.2	0.08	–
VGA	23 420	0.9	0.06	–
AFI	19 439	0.8	0.05	–
EI	16 655	0.7	0.05	–
PPA	15 447	0.6	0.04	–
DLP	14 744	0.6	0.04	–
Other	7 416	0.3	0.02	–

second variant. The variation used in elections to the South Australian Legislative Council for a short time was the List system of PR, a modification which limits the electors' choices to predetermined party lists and does not allow votes for individual candidates. Candidates under a List system are elected in proportion to the votes received by their party list, and in the order they appeared on the list, and thus a List system restricts the choices available to the voters much more than any other electoral system in Australia (see Document 2.1).

In 1989, a fourth variant of proportional representation was introduced for the first election of a parliament for the Australian Capital Territory. This combined a List system of PR with the d'Hondt method of allocation of quotas, arguably the most complex of systems. In fact, negotiations between the Labor and Liberal parties produced a modified d'Hondt system which was clearly *aimed* to eliminate as many minor parties and independent candidates as possible (confirming the self-interest component of party attitudes), but which had the reverse effect in practice. A summary of the system and the results are provided in Document 2.1.

Proportional representation is complex for voters, parties and electoral officers (see Document 2.1). In the 'normal' half-Senate election in 1993, for six Senators from each state, the quota for election was 14.3 per cent of the formal (valid, correctly filled in) votes. In a double dissolution, electing twelve Senators from each state, the quota would be 7.7 per cent. A proportional representation system, therefore, provides a greater possibility for minor parties and independents to win seats.

Supporters of proportional representation point to the fact that the result of the system reflects the (party) opinions of the electorate much more closely than first-past-the-post and preferential voting, and that it overcomes the problem of malapportionment. Opponents of PR claim that the system leads to a proliferation of parties in the legislature, with government dependent on alliances, backroom agreements and small-party coalitions, and point to the experience of some Western European countries—Italy in particular—as the inevitable result. But such extreme proliferation of parties has not occurred under any of the Australian systems of PR (except, perhaps, in the ACT). Because of entrenched parties and party identification prior to its introduction, and the continuation of single-member electorates for the other house, the fragmentation of representation between a number of smaller parties has not occurred. At the same time, with PR, how-to-vote cards become more important as voters face longer and more complex ballot papers, and Senate elections often produced more informal and donkey votes than the elections for the House of Representatives. Since 1983, this has been reduced by the use of 'above and below the line' choices of Senate voting. The former provides a simple method of voting for a party 'ticket' (see Document 2.1).

PARTY EFFECTS AND ATTITUDES

The combination of compulsory voting and compulsory preferences in most Australian electoral systems has an important influence in terms of parties and the party system. In most Anglo-Saxon nations, voluntary voting and first-past-the-post in single-member electorates encourages a two-party system, and offers little encouragement to small groups and parties. In the UK elections of 1974, for example, the Liberal Party achieved 19 per cent of the overall votes, but won only 2 per cent of the seats. For a small party to win consistent representation under such a plurality system it needs a concentration of supporters in a relatively small region—that is, over a few seats.

Those who support the plurality system (with or without voluntary voting), in spite of its shortcomings, do so on the grounds that the prime aim is the formation of strong and stable governments; one major party, under normal circumstances, is usually able to win a majority of the seats. Opponents of a plurality system point mainly to the probability that many members will be elected with the greatest number of votes, but with less than a majority of the voters. Hence, a candidate elected with, say, 42 per cent of the formal votes was elected because *only* 58 per cent of the electors voted against her.

This is overcome by the preferential voting system generally used in Australia. PV ensures that no candidate is elected until he or she secures an absolute majority of the formal votes and also that, except in the closest of results, the member elected also represents a majority of the enrolled adults in his or her district. However, the problems of over-representation and under-representation remain, there are many 'wasted' votes, and malapportionment can be practised. Moreover, even with compulsory preferential voting, there is no guarantee that an absolute majority of votes will produce a majority of seats in a parliament, and there is no guarantee that party representation in parliament will be even approximately proportional to party support in the electorate. For example, in the 1993 election, the national results were as shown in Table 2.7.

The inequalities are obvious. The Labor Party with only 45 per cent of the votes won 54 per cent of the seats, while the Liberal Party's share of the seats showed under-representation. The National Party, with only 7 per cent of the votes, won 11 per cent of the seats, while the Australian Democrats, with almost 4 per cent of the votes, won no seats. Such over- and under-representation can be due to a malapportioned election system, but it can also result from strong regional support and is the inevitable effect of any system based on single-member districts.

It is not surprising, then, that the attitudes of the various political parties to electoral systems show wide variations. The Labor Party favoured compulsory preferential voting until the effects of DLP

Table 2.7: *Votes cast and seats won in federal election, by parties, 1993 (N and %), House of Representatives*

Party	Formal votes %	Seats won N	%
ALP	44.9	80	54
Liberal	37.1	49	33
NP	7.2	16	11
AD	3.8	–	–
Other	7.1	2	1

preferences prompted it to change its policy to optional preferential voting. Labor governments inaugurated the PR systems in South Australia and New South Wales. The Liberal Party is strongly in favour of compulsory preferential voting, partly because the party has benefited from DLP and NP preferences in the past. Minor parties, including the Australian Democrats, generally seek proportional representation. The National Party supports preferential voting in single-member electorates, and is the only party which rejects relatively equal apportionment. The NP seeks a return to a stronger weighting in favour of extra-metropolitan areas; that is, a weighting in favour of the rural electorates where its supporters are concentrated. This policy has been at the heart of all the disputes over electoral systems, especially in Queensland, where the 'Bjelke-mander' had the effect of over-representing the National Party's electoral support and under-representing the electoral support of *both* Liberal and Labor parties.

Overall, a party tends to favour the election system which it believes will be of most benefit to it. All three entrenched parties favour a system based on single-member electorates. The graphs in Figure 2.1 explain why the Liberal and National and, more recently, Labor parties have been so determined. It is a characteristic of any single-member system that a major party often wins a higher proportion of seats than its proportion of the votes would predict. The Liberal Party has clearly benefited from this, while Labor has been relatively disadvantaged until the 1980s, partly because of its tendency to build up massive majorities (and wasted votes) in its safe, urban electorates. The graph also shows the benefits to a party with strong support in a small set of electorates—the National Party has consistently been over-represented.

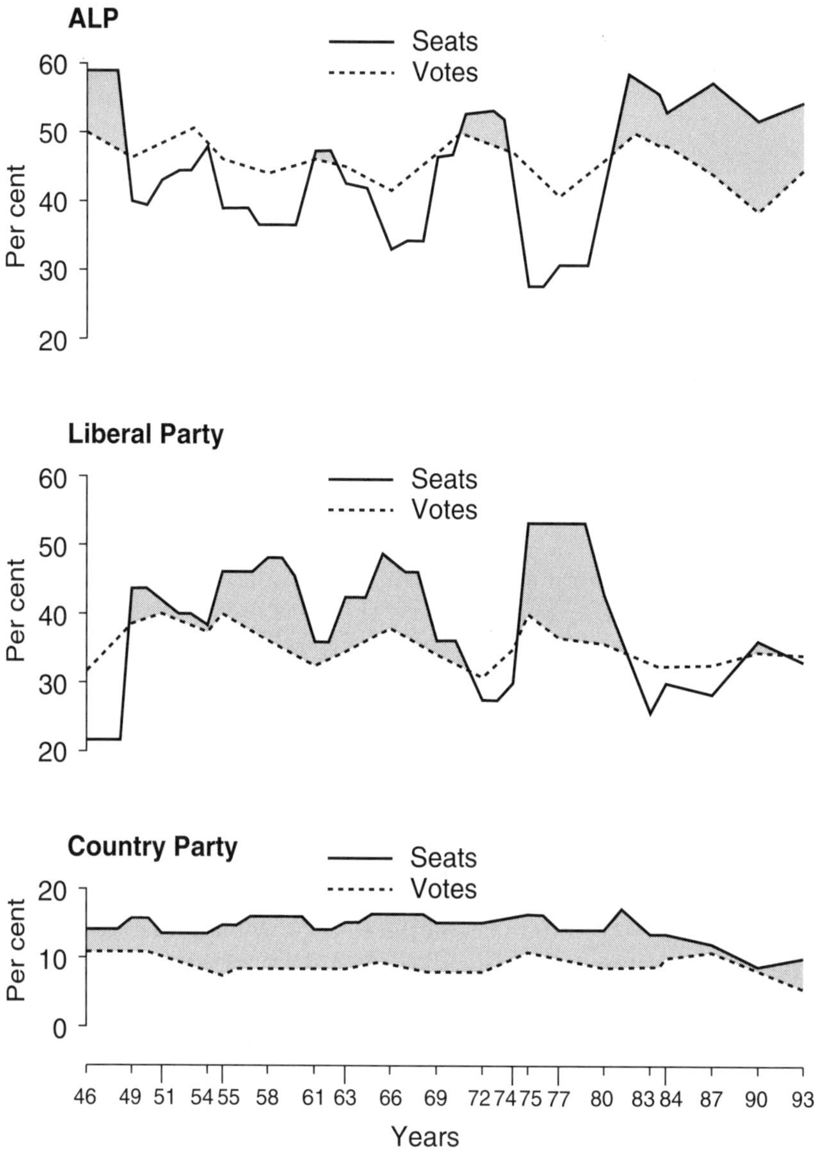

***Figure 2.1** Over-representation—votes and seats, House of Representatives, 1946–1993*

PUBLIC FUNDING

Until 1981, the expenses associated with electoral contests were completely the affair of the parties, groups and candidates contesting the election. Parties and candidates were free to raise any funds they wished (or were able to obtain) from any source. The only constraint was in terms of reporting the expenditure of funds in the campaign. Parties and candidates were required to lodge an official return setting out the extent and nature of expenditure on the campaign—a requirement which was not always fully complied with nor enforced.

In 1981, the New South Wales Labor government introduced public funding—the provision of subsidies to parties and candidates from public funds. For the 1981 elections, the New South Wales state fund was established on the basis of 22 cents per voter, and it was disbursed in two ways: two-thirds of the fund was divided among registered parties in proportion to their statewide support (above 3 per cent) for the Legislative Council; one-third divided among registered candidates for the Legislative Assembly who retained their deposits. The Liberal Party in New South Wales opposed the proposal in principle, and at all stages of the passage of the bill. But it readily accepted the reimbursement following the election.

In the 1983 Australian Electoral Act, public funding was introduced for national elections. All candidates at the 1984 election, or a registered party/group, could claim reimbursement from the fund if they achieved at least four per cent of the total formal first-preference votes in the relevant electorate. The original rates were established at 60 cents for each House of Representatives vote, and 30 cents for each Senate vote. These amounts are indexed to the CPI, and in 1990 had risen to 91.2 to 45.6 cents respectively. The total amount of money involved is considerable; in the 1990 election, it reached almost $13 million. As such, the system is of major benefit to all parties and candidates, but especially to the minor parties whose access to funds from members and donors is very limited.

The main line of opposition to the principle of public funding, an opposition which was most vehement from Liberal and National parties, concerned the other side of public funding—the requirement for public disclosure. Until 1983, parties could raise funds from whatever source, and at whatever level they could obtain. The fear of some parties, especially Liberal and National, which have traditionally been able to secure the largest donations, was that public disclosure would deter some of the sources or, at least, prompt them to seek a balance, and offer donations to all contesting parties.

All parties and candidates are required by the Commonwealth Electoral Act (ss.303–14) to furnish a public return showing the amount and details of all donations and gifts (of $1000 or more to political parties and of $200 or more to a candidate), including the names and addresses of donors. Further, all electoral expenditure during the election campaign must be disclosed, and broadcasters and publishers are also required to furnish details of electoral advertising. There is, therefore, the widest opportunity for interested people to establish who gave what to whom, and who spent what.

VOTER ASSISTANCE

The incorporation of 'compulsory voting' into the electoral laws demanded that special provisions be made available for voters who had difficulty in complying. More recently, provisions have been made for wider types of difficulties. These methods of assistance are of five main types.

ABSENT VOTING

Any elector who cannot attend a polling place in the election district for which he or she is enrolled can vote at any polling place within the state or territory. Such ballot papers are then transferred to the correct district for incorporation into the count.

POSTAL VOTING

This facility is available for voters who are outside their state or territory on polling day, are travelling, are more than 80 km from a polling place, are in prison, are ill or infirm, and for other reasons. Such people vote before polling day, and the postmark must show a date on or before the polling day.

MOBILE POLLING

This concept of taking the polling place to the voters was inaugurated for remote communities in the Northern Territory, and has now been incorporated into national and state election laws. Polling teams, travelling by vehicle, aircraft and helicopter, make pre-arranged visits to isolated communities and hence provide a service equivalent to that available to the more settled areas. Mobile polling teams also visit hospitals and similar institutions.

ELECTORAL ASSISTANCE

There has always been the opportunity for any elector who has needed some form of assistance to request that from the chief presiding officer in any polling booth. This has been extended in recent years, especially in the outback areas where Aboriginal people have only fairly recently been permitted to take part fully in electoral processes. In 1962, all

Aborigines became entitled to vote in national elections and, in parallel with similar developments in the states, especially in South Australia and the Northern Territory, provision was made for official electoral assistants at polling places, specially appointed to offer help to any voter, but especially to Aboriginal and non-literate voters. The appointment of Aborigines as electoral assistants has developed the value of the programme further.

ELECTORAL EDUCATION

For much of the electoral history of Australia, it was a case of political *caveat emptor.* It was up to the voters to politically educate themselves, to sort out and sift through the propaganda of political parties and campaign rhetoric, and to cast an informed and aware vote. In the 1980s, the Australian Electoral Commission not only led the way in public education programmes for the general public in terms of the electoral processes, but it inaugurated a broad programme of Aboriginal electoral education.

In fact, programmes were instituted by the Northern Territory administration and the Western Australian government concurrent with the granting of a full suffrage to Aborigines in 1962. Some efforts, especially through Welfare Branches, were made to inform Aborigines about electoral rights and obligations. This *ad hoc* programme became formal and broad with the formation of the Aboriginal Electoral Education Programme in 1974, and its modification into the Aboriginal Electoral Information Service in 1986.

ELECTION TIMING

From the inauguration of full responsible government in the Australian colonies, through the formation of a national parliament and to the present day, all Australian lower houses have had a maximum term. For most of this time, the maximum term has been three years from the first sitting of the current parliament.

The important point is that it is a maximum term. A leader of a government can, at any time, seek an early election from the Head of State. These have not always been granted, and the history of colonial parliaments is littered with conflicts between Premiers and Governors concerning early elections. Such requests have generally been agreed to in the national and state arenas, and early elections have not been uncommon. All political parties-in-government have at some time requested and been granted an election before the maximum term. In 1975, the parliament elected in 1974 was summarily dissolved by the Governor-General against the advice of the elected majority government.

It should be noted that such requests for early elections are usually, if not always, based on an expected advantage for the party-in-government. They are requested for a range of reasons, but the underlying reason is that one party believes that it has a greater potential to be returned to office at an early election than if it served out its full term.

The upper houses of Australia, the national Senate and the State Legislative Councils, can be forced to early elections only under specific provisions. All have constitutional protection and fixed terms. The Australian Senate can be dissolved early only if the Senate has rejected legislation which has twice (the second after a three months delay) been passed in the House of Representatives. Even then, the Governor-General has to be convinced before such a double dissolution is granted. Hence, the occasions have been relatively few, although they have occurred more often in the past two decades. Double dissolutions were carried out nationally in 1914, 1951, 1974, 1975, 1983 and 1987.

One result of early elections in the national scene is that the House of Representatives and Senate elections can move out of synchronisation. Early dissolutions mean that the fixed term Senate elections may have to be held separately, costing millions of extra dollars. As a result of this trend, three attempts have been made to incorporate simultaneous elections for both houses. The referendum campaigns for these attempts exemplify the nature of party confrontation in Australia.

The first referendum, in 1974, was proposed by the Whitlam Labor government. It was vehemently opposed by the Liberal and National parties. In 1977, following a recommendation of the then Constitutional Convention, the Fraser Liberal government proposed the referendum and strongly supported a 'yes' vote. In 1983, the Hawke Labor government proposed the question for a third time, but the Liberal Party completed its political somersault and had returned to absolute opposition. All three attempts failed to achieve the necessary double majority.

In 1988, the Constitutional Commission recommended what already existed in South Australia; that the maximum term of the House of Representatives should be four years, but that the House should not be dissolved for the first three years unless a motion of no-confidence had been carried and no alternative government could be formed. It also proposed that Senators should hold their seats for two terms of the House, and that there should be simultaneous elections. The Hawke government selected only the four-year maximum term for a referendum in 1988, and this was soundly defeated.

CASUAL VACANCIES

In the case of an electoral system based on single-member electorates, casual vacancies are filled through by-elections. In the case of an election system based on proportional representation and multi-member electorates, by-elections would require the whole electoral apparatus, perhaps the whole state, to be activated. Hence, other means have been devised for such instances.

In the Tasmanian Hare–Clark variation, a casual vacancy is filled by continuing the count of ballots from the original election within the party list of the vacancy. In the Senate, the question of casual vacancies arose soon after the inauguration of PR in 1949. The first casual vacancy raised the question of interpretation of the clause in the Constitution which provided that 'the Houses of Parliament of the state...shall choose a person...'. A convention was established that the person chosen should be a member of the same party as the departing Senator, and this convention was maintained until 1974. During the constitutional crisis of 1974–1975, the National Party government in Queensland, and the Liberal government in New South Wales, broke the convention. In 1977, a referendum was carried to entrench the convention into the constitution.

CONSUMER PROTECTION

Following the 1980 election, the Australian Democrats took a case to the High Court alleging misleading advertising under the Electoral Act. The major parties, in their efforts to destroy the electoral potential of the new minor party were alleged to have acted to break s. 161 (c) which established as 'illegal practices':

> printing, publishing, or distributing any electoral advertisement, notice, handbill, pamphlet, or card containing any untrue or incorrect statement intended or likely to mislead or improperly interfere with any elector in or in relation to the casting of his vote.

The challenge was lost. The High Court interpreted the wording as having a very narrow application, 'limited to the mechanics of marking the ballot paper, and did not extend to the elector's state of mind in deciding which candidate to support' (Stevens 1984:96). This prompted a reconsideration of this section of the Act. In 1983, the entire Act was rewritten, incorporating major reforms. Consumer protection was strengthened, and the new Act contained the clause:

> A person shall not, during the relevant period in relation to an election under this Act, print, publish or distribute, or cause, permit or authorise to be printed, published or distributed, any electoral advertisement containing a statement
> a) that is untrue; and
> b) that is, or is likely to be, misleading or deceptive.

In 1984, the Liberal, Labor and National parties combined to delete this clause from the Act. Only the Australian Democrats voted to retain it. The result, then, is that in practical electoral politics there is little if any constraint on what candidates, groups and parties can say. While there are powerful constraints on the business, financial and retail world for ordinary citizens through consumer protection and trade practices legislation, the political arena remains a matter of *caveat emptor*—let the buyer beware.

THE QUALITY OF ELECTORAL REPRESENTATION

Are elections in Australia free and fair? Do all citizens have an equal opportunity to take part in the electoral processes? Do the various electoral systems provide for an accurate representation of societal views in the parliaments? Are electors offered sufficient choice? This chapter offers some comments on these and related issues of electoral systems.

Certainly, there are unique factors within the systems of electoral representation in Australia. Compulsory voting, preferential voting, and the variety of the systems available are just three such factors. The question to ask is whether Australia has a better quality of electoral representation than other nations.

Electoral representation contains many themes other than the mechanics and geography of election systems; themes which, however, are centrally linked to the systems. The pre-selection process, *within* political parties, clearly affects the quality of representation. Electoral representation, then, is more than the mechanics of the election systems. It incorporates issues such as how well representatives represent, and the roles of political parties in the election and representative processes. Later chapters will focus on these and related themes.

DOCUMENTS

2.1 PROPORTIONAL REPRESENTATION

1 SINGLE TRANSFERABLE VOTE (SENATE-TYPE)

Mechanics

In 1983, a new, 'two-tier' system of voting was introduced for the Senate. Voters could indicate a vote for party lists 'above the line', and the preferences would be allocated as determined by the party of choice. Voters could, however, opt to vote 'below the line', showing preferences for individual candidates.

The mechanics of the 'single transferable vote' (STV) system of proportional representation used in the Senate are set out in an Act passed in 1948, amended in 1983. The steps which have to be followed are:

1 Total the first-preference votes.
2 Calculate the quota: divide the total formal first-preference votes by one more than the number of vacant seats, and add one vote. In the example below:

$$\text{quota} = \frac{2\,579\,520}{6+1} + 1 = 368\,503$$

3 Declare elected those candidates who have first-preference votes equal to or greater than the quota: Alston (Lib.), Ray (ALP). (*Note:* the 'ticket' votes indicate preferences in the order shown on the ballot paper.)
4 Transfer any surplus votes; that is, votes over and above the quota, for those who have been declared elected. This is carried out as follows:
   a Calculate a transfer value for all candidates with surplus votes by dividing the number of surplus votes by the total number of first-preference votes.
   b The total first-preference votes for each candidate who has surplus votes are separated out according to the next preference indicated.
   c The number of votes to be transferred from each batch is calculated by the number of votes in each batch multiplied by the transfer value. For example, using the LIB results below:

Alston	1 141 040
Less quota	368 503
Surplus votes	772 537
Transfer value	0.6771

   d The remaining first-preference ballot papers for candidates declared elected—the number of the quota—are put aside as finally dealt with.

5 After the transfer of surplus votes, any new candidate who has achieved a quota is declared elected: Patterson (Lib.), Cooney (ALP).
6 Any further surplus votes are again transferred as in step 4, and the process continues until all surplus votes have been transferred.
7 If fewer than the number of candidates required to be elected have received a quota following the transfer of all surplus votes, then the candidate who has the fewest votes is excluded and all of his or her votes are transferred in accordance with the next available preference. Transfer of preferences continues until the required number of quotas has been achieved: Kemp (Lib.), Spindler (AD).

Senate election, Victoria, 1990

First-preference votes

Ticket AD	298 180	Ticket L&NP	1 057 250
Spindler	61 481	Alston	83 790
O'Brien	3 659	Patterson	1 238
Paas	430	Kemp	993
Craik	1 626	McGauran (NP)	5 083
		Coatman	238
Ticket ALP	872 519	Clarke	578
Ray	62 609		
Cooney	858	Ticket PPA	13 657
Carr	912	McKay	1 707
Marple	778	Grant	83
Lowrey	569		
		Ticket EI	3 323
Ticket AFI	15 162	McQuilton	2 913
McCormick	4 010	Mcleod	419
Spencer	267		
		Ticket DLP	12 686
Ticket CTA	22 087	Sennel	1 920
Watson	7 254	Taylor	138
Khoury	267		
		Ungrouped	
Ticket	3 576	Fraser	89
Robinson	259	Toscano	215
Giltinan	77	Meggs	82
		Goudappel	119
		Bernard	30
		Guy	2 023
		Cardinal	227

Elected on first preferences: Alston (Lib.), Ray (ALP)
Elected on surplus votes: Patterson (Lib.), Cooney (ALP)
Elected on preferences: Kemp (Lib.), Spindler (AD)
These Senators' terms expire on 30 June 1996

2 LIST SYSTEM, SOUTH AUSTRALIA, 1975

a Mechanics

Voting by placing optional preferences for party lists. Electors were not permitted to vote for individual candidates. Any party which received less than half a quota was excluded and its preferences were distributed. Quotas were then calculated, and sent allocated in the order of the party lists.

b Results

Voted	719 753
Informal	32 690
Formal	687 063
Quota	57 256

First-preference votes

Party	N	%	After exclusion	Quotas/seats achieved	
ALP	324 744	47.3	332 616	5.83	6
Lib	191 341	27.9	211 447	3.71	3
LM	129 110	18.8	140 631	2.46	2
CP	14 640	2.1	–		
AFM	9 966	1.5	–		
FEG	8 141	1.2	–		
SPA	4 273	0.6	–		
AP	3 822	0.6	–		
Ind	1 026	0.2	–		
Total	687 063		684 694	11.00	11

Note:

AFM—Australian Family Movement

FEG—Free Enterprise Group

SPA—Social Party of Australia

3 D'HONDT SYSTEM, ACT, 1989

a Mechanics

Voters were faced with a 'two-tier' ballot paper as for the Senate, but could vote by mixing above- and below-the-line votes, with optional preferences. All parties and candidates who failed to reach a full quota were excluded from the count, and their preferences were distributed. With 17 members to be elected, the quota was 5.6 per cent. The count was very complex, involving eight separate stages, and took nearly 10 weeks to complete. After the count of first-preference votes, the exclusion of parties and independent candidates who failed to achieve a quota, and the transfer of preferences (some of which had to be further transferred if the second preference was to an excluded party or candidate) seats were provisionally allocated. This process of allocation is too complex to be described here.

b Results

Twenty-two parties and nine independents contested the election. Following the exclusion stage, only five parties remained in the count.

First-preference after seats

	First-preference votes	After preferences	Seats won
ALP	32 370	40 643	5
Liberal	21 088	29 853	4
No Self-Government	16 274	20 917	3
Residents Rally	13 647	25 433	4
Abolish Self-Government	10 641	12 407	1
17 Other parties	38 497	–	1
9 Independents	9 344	–	–
Total	141 861	129 253	17

2.2 PARTY STATEMENTS ON ELECTORAL SYSTEMS

LIBERAL PARTY

The preferential/compulsory system of voting has been an essential means of democratic expression and should be continued. An electoral system should be maintained which guarantees substantial equality of voting powers, with regular redistributions based on numbers of electors.

LABOR PARTY

To guarantee the right to vote and ensure the principle of one-vote, one-value in all Australian and State elections. In single-member electorates, adoption of a system of optional preferential voting.

NATIONAL PARTY

The Party is committed to the principle that all Australians should have equal access to Parliamentary representation, ensuring their fundamental right to put before Parliament their special problems. Maintenance of a not less than 20 per cent tolerance in assessing electoral quotas to enable the equating of the value of the vote between densely populated electorates and those affected by sparseness of population, large area and disabilities of transport and communication.

Maintenance of a secret preferential voting system for the House of Representatives and of proportional representation for the Senate.

AUSTRALIAN DEMOCRATS

Several reforms of the electoral system are required to give all voters an equal influence and to provide a more accurate representation of community viewpoints in Parliament. Various Constitution amendments will be put to the public in a Referendum to equalise as far as possible the size of electorates and to prevent gerrymanders. Multimember constituencies with proportional representation will be introduced at all levels of government.

2.3 'PAYING THE PENALTY OF VAST DISTANCE'

Source: Mr Leon Punch, Leader of the New South Wales Country Party, in the *Australian,* 14 April 1980.

With the report of the NSW Electoral Commissioners, something tragic, in my view, happened to country people.

The number of rural seats in the NSW Legislative Assembly was cut from 33 to 27. This means that since 1950, 13 NSW rural seats have been abolished—about 50 per cent of the proposed rural representation in the next NSW Parliament.

This diminution of country representation has been caused by amendments to the electoral laws and by the relative faster population growth of metropolitan areas, particularly Sydney. These two events pose considerable problems for the future, but the central issue is political representation of country areas. Crammed into less than 10 per cent of the State will be the great majority (72 seats) of the elected representatives for the State (99 seats).

Unequal representation? Statistically, no. Fair representation? In my view, no. I say this because one has to contrast the duties of a country member of Parliament with those of a metropolitan member. The country member's duties are the same and more. First there is the problem of distance and the size of country electorates which dwarf city electorates. Within these electorates there is a multitude of extra problems which do not concern a city member. They range from road building to silo construction, from railway line closures to locust plagues. The diversity is often bewildering and complicated. As well, there is the human role of the country MP. In country electorates, the elector rings his MP when he has a problem. A city voter, on the other hand, can easily seek the information with a ten cent telephone call to a departmental office.

The country MP is also the person often called on to make representations on issues which normally do not come into the role of a metropolitan MP. And then there is the incessant travel across the electorate to see constituents, to review progress, speak at schools and talk to government officials. The expenses are higher in terms of cash and time. For the cash, country MPs receive a little compensation which is absorbed in costs. For the time, the compensation is satisfaction but satisfaction achieved at an exhausting pace.

With yet fewer electorates in rural areas, the workload will increase to the point of being ridiculous. The time involved in the country MP's electoral work and the number of representations will significantly rise because of the increase in electorate sizes. It can be argued that State rural electorates are smaller than federal rural electorates. That is true, but a federal country MP's workload cannot be compared with that of a State MP. A State MP deals with the domestic issues involving citizens in every village or on the land. A federal MP, in dealing with the national issues, is not expected to come into such close personal contact.

How do we get around these problems? My answer, more rural seats, is fairly predictable. But it is the readers who have to decide mainly from the comfort of their metropolitan homes what their country cousins should receive in terms of a better deal in State Parliament. And after making their decisions they have to tell their MPs that although the State distribution has been made geographically uneven, country people cannot be neglected as they must be if there is an inadequate representation of country members in our various Houses of Parliament.

2.4 THE EFFECT OF COMPULSORY VOTING

Source: Rydon, J. 1965, 'The electorate', in John Wilkes (ed.), *Forces in Australian Politics,* Angus and Robertson, Sydney, pp. 177–84.

What of compulsory voting? It has obviously affected campaigning. There is no need to persuade people either to register or to vote, no need to provide cars to take them to the polls. For the voter it clearly narrows the choice: he cannot choose to stay at home. Even if he is completely uninterested in the elections and dislikes all the candidates he must in theory express his preference among them. A supporter of a minor party which is not contesting his electorate must choose between the candidates offering. Shortly after the introduction of compulsory voting E.E. Judd claimed that, as a member of the Socialist Labor Party, he was prohibited from voting for any of the candidates, all of whom were supporters of capitalism. The High Court ruled that this was not a valid and sufficient reason for failing to vote. The limited meaning of 'choice' in Australian electoral law was nicely illustrated by the Chief Justice with an example from the Oxford Dictionary: 'I have given thee thy choice of the manner in which thou wilt die.'

Compulsory voting makes it difficult for a committed supporter of one party to express disapproval of the candidate it has selected or of its current policies. Parties can probably be more sure of the support of their committed followers. Though the parties are in some ways strengthened, this may not be so if there is a local split in a major party or a row over pre-selection in a safe seat. If the other major party does not contest the seat its supporters may decide the issue between two Labor or two non-Labor candidates ... Does compulsory voting affect the size of the 'swinging vote'? This depends partly on the use of the term. In Britain and America it is often taken to include all those who make a different choice in two successive elections, including those who change from voting to non-voting and vice versa. If this usage is adopted one would expect the 'swinging vote' to be lower with compulsory voting. If, however, the term is restricted to those who change from one party to another the position is not clear. Compulsion does, of course, raise the turnout at elections. In America it is often less than 50 per cent (one survey showed that 17 per cent had never voted); in Britain it is normally about 70 per cent to 85 per cent; in Australia usually 95 per cent. Studies of non-voters overseas show that they are largely those uninterested, but in Australia all the uninterested and apathetic are required to vote and it is clear that they must often determine the outcome of elections ... In Australia where the apathetic and ill-informed are forced to the polls by law it is even more likely that the 'scum and dregs' of political life will decide who is to govern the country.

2.5 ONE VIEW OF ELECTORAL SYSTEMS

Source: Davis, S.R. (ed.) 1960, *The Government of the Australian States*, Longman Cheshire, Melbourne, p. 565.

It appears that the electoral experience of the Australian States is a mixture of three things—adventure, heterodoxy and knavery. Between them, the States have fathered a crop of electoral devices, confounded their textbook behaviour, and at times and in places used them with a skill which even a funfair poker machine proprietor could admire.

ISSUES FOR DISCUSSION

1 Why do political parties disagree on the 'best' election system? (See Document 2.2.)
2 Discuss the how-to-vote cards on pages 70–74. Try to identify to which parties the preferences were allocated. Discuss these preferences.

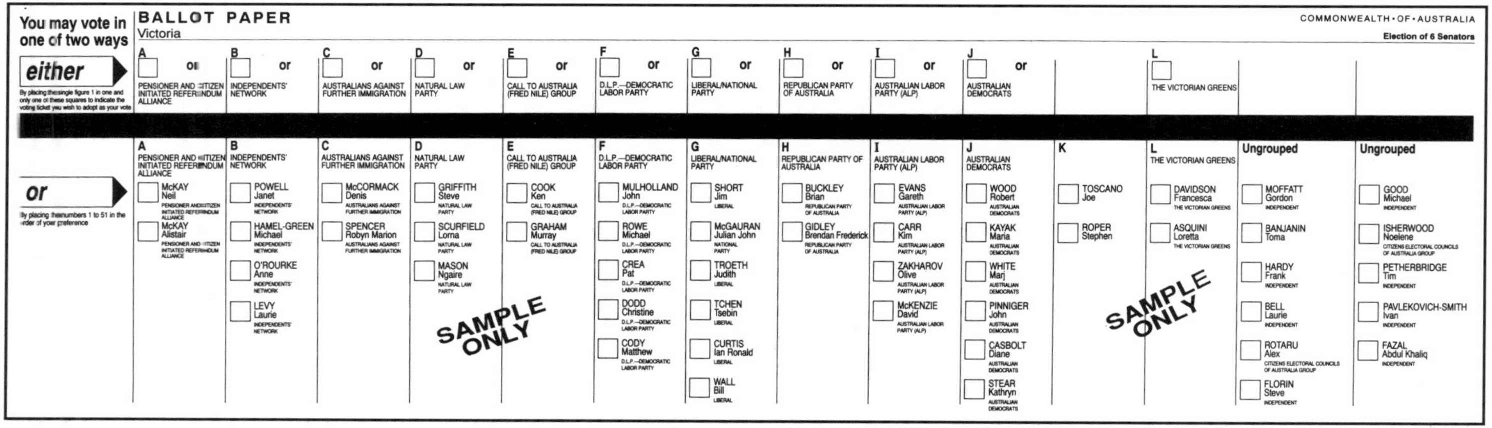

You may vote in one of two ways

BALLOT PAPER
Victoria

COMMONWEALTH·OF·AUSTRALIA
Election of 6 Senators

either

By placing the single figure 1 in one and only one of these squares to indicate the voting ticket you wish to adopt as your vote

A	B	C	D	E	F	G	H	I	J		L		
or	or	or	or	or	or	or	or	or	or				
PENSIONER AND CITIZEN INITIATED REFERENDUM ALLIANCE	INDEPENDENTS' NETWORK	AUSTRALIANS AGAINST FURTHER IMMIGRATION	NATURAL LAW PARTY	CALL TO AUSTRALIA (FRED NILE) GROUP	D.L.P.—DEMOCRATIC LABOR PARTY	LIBERAL/NATIONAL PARTY	REPUBLICAN PARTY OF AUSTRALIA	AUSTRALIAN LABOR PARTY (ALP)	AUSTRALIAN DEMOCRATS		THE VICTORIAN GREENS		

or

By placing the numbers 1 to 51 in the order of your preference

A	B	C	D	E	F	G	H	I	J	K	L	Ungrouped	Ungrouped
PENSIONER AND CITIZEN INITIATED REFERENDUM ALLIANCE	INDEPENDENTS' NETWORK	AUSTRALIANS AGAINST FURTHER IMMIGRATION	NATURAL LAW PARTY	CALL TO AUSTRALIA (FRED NILE) GROUP	D.L.P.—DEMOCRATIC LABOR PARTY	LIBERAL/NATIONAL PARTY	REPUBLICAN PARTY OF AUSTRALIA	AUSTRALIAN LABOR PARTY (ALP)	AUSTRALIAN DEMOCRATS		THE VICTORIAN GREENS		
McKAY Neil PENSIONER AND CITIZEN INITIATED REFERENDUM ALLIANCE	POWELL Janet INDEPENDENTS' NETWORK	McCORMACK Denis AUSTRALIANS AGAINST FURTHER IMMIGRATION	GRIFFITH Steve NATURAL LAW PARTY	COOK Ken CALL TO AUSTRALIA (FRED NILE) GROUP	MULHOLLAND John D.L.P.—DEMOCRATIC LABOR PARTY	SHORT Jim LIBERAL	BUCKLEY Brian REPUBLICAN PARTY OF AUSTRALIA	EVANS Gareth AUSTRALIAN LABOR PARTY (ALP)	WOOD Robert AUSTRALIAN DEMOCRATS	TOSCANO Joe	DAVIDSON Francesca THE VICTORIAN GREENS	MOFFATT Gordon INDEPENDENT	GOOD Michael INDEPENDENT
McKAY Alistair PENSIONER AND CITIZEN INITIATED REFERENDUM ALLIANCE	HAMEL-GREEN Michael INDEPENDENTS' NETWORK	SPENCER Robyn Marion AUSTRALIANS AGAINST FURTHER IMMIGRATION	SCURFIELD Lorna NATURAL LAW PARTY	GRAHAM Murray CALL TO AUSTRALIA (FRED NILE) GROUP	ROWE Michael D.L.P.—DEMOCRATIC LABOR PARTY	McGAURAN Julian John NATIONAL PARTY	GIDLEY Brendan Frederick REPUBLICAN PARTY OF AUSTRALIA	CARR Kim AUSTRALIAN LABOR PARTY (ALP)	KAYAK Maria AUSTRALIAN DEMOCRATS	ROPER Stephen	ASQUINI Loretta THE VICTORIAN GREENS	BANJANIN Toma	ISHERWOOD Noelene CITIZENS ELECTORAL COUNCILS OF AUSTRALIA GROUP
	O'ROURKE Anne INDEPENDENTS' NETWORK		MASON Ngaire NATURAL LAW PARTY		CREA Pat D.L.P.—DEMOCRATIC LABOR PARTY	TROETH Judith LIBERAL		ZAKHAROV Olive AUSTRALIAN LABOR PARTY (ALP)	WHITE Marj AUSTRALIAN DEMOCRATS			HARDY Frank INDEPENDENT	PETHERBRIDGE Tim INDEPENDENT
	LEVY Laurie INDEPENDENTS' NETWORK				DODD Christine D.L.P.—DEMOCRATIC LABOR PARTY	TCHEN Tsebin LIBERAL		McKENZIE David AUSTRALIAN LABOR PARTY (ALP)	PINNIGER John AUSTRALIAN DEMOCRATS			BELL Laurie INDEPENDENT	PAVLEKOVICH-SMITH Ivan INDEPENDENT
					CODY Matthew D.L.P.—DEMOCRATIC LABOR PARTY	CURTIS Ian Ronald LIBERAL			CASBOLT Diane AUSTRALIAN DEMOCRATS			ROTARU Alex CITIZENS ELECTORAL COUNCILS OF AUSTRALIA GROUP	FAZAL Abdul Khaliq INDEPENDENT
						WALL Bill LIBERAL			STEAR Kathryn AUSTRALIAN DEMOCRATS			FLORIN Steve INDEPENDENT	

SAMPLE ONLY

SAMPLE ONLY

Australian Labor

HOW TO VOTE

Victoria

House of Representatives

ASTON
5 CHAPMAN, C
1 CRAVEN, Susan
4 PARRY, A
3 NUGENT, P
2 WISE, D

BALLARAT
6 CAVEN, V
5 RICKARD, J
4 de CAEN, R
3 RONALDSON, M
2 HARDY, G
1 DEVEREUX, Peter

BATMAN
6 THRUPP, M
2 CARR, G
1 HOWE, Brian
3 SIMATKOVICH, G
4 D'SOUZA, N
5 DICKINS, J

BENDIGO
1 HELPER, Joe
2 SEMMENS, D
3 HILL, S
4 TAYLOR, P
5 REID, B
6 HARRISON, D
7 OBERIN, J

BRUCE
2 CHANDRA, L
1 WILLIAMS, Beverley
4 BEALE, J
3 DI TEMPORA, N

BURKE
5 BURROWES, I
1 O'KEEFE, Neil
2 DICKINS, M
3 RALPH, I
4 MITCHELL, S

CALWELL
4 LIVETT, D
5 RODENBURG, V
6 SPENCER, R
1 THEOPHANOUS, Andrew
2 PRICE, S
3 MACKAY, D

CASEY
2 GINSBERG, S
3 KENDI, R
4 HALVERSON, B
1 WARREN, Julie

CHISHOLM
3 JOHNSTON, D
1 McCASKIE, Gordon
2 ALDOUS, R
4 WOOLDRIDGE, M

CORANGAMITE
2 WARNOCK, J
1 EADES, Bernie
7 McARTHUR, S
6 PEARCE, G
5 WINTER, T
4 GOLDEN, I
3 POWELL, N

CORINELLA
3 NELSON, G
4 HOLST, T
5 BROADBENT, R
6 PJANIC, P
1 GRIFFIN, Alan
2 OLDIS, T

CORIO
2 MARTORANA, M
6 TOL, J
1 O'CONNOR, Gavan
5 WINTER, I
4 SMITH, C
3 BELL, A

DEAKIN
3 BACKHOUSE, W
4 NIEUWENHUIS, R
1 ADKINS, Greg
5 ALDRED, K
6 BARRON, A
2 MAGART, P

DUNKLEY
3 NELSON, B
4 FORD, F
2 ROWLAND-HORBLOW, B
1 CHYNOWETH, Bob

FLINDERS
2 CHARLWOOD, J
1 HASSETT, Denise
3 BROWN, M
4 REITH, P

GELLIBRAND
2 BENSON, N
1 WILLIS, Ralph
3 SANKO, P
4 STAROPOLI, L
5 PARKER, A
6 MacGREGOR, C

GIPPSLAND
1 STONE, Judith
2 VAN BAER, P
3 PHILLIPS, B
4 BUCKLEY, B
6 McGAURAN, P
5 STOREY, D

GOLDSTEIN
2 GALE, B
3 HERBERT, G
1 PAKULA, Martin
4 RITCHIE, J
5 KEMP, D

HIGGINS
2 MENDELSON, L
1 CERRITELLI, Joe
4 COSTELLO, P
3 JACKSON, C

HOLT
5 LEWIS, B
4 BLACKBURN, P
3 NEDELJKOVIC, S
2 BURNS, M
1 DUFFY, Michael

HOTHAM
6 HICKS, R
5 PHILLIPS, S
4 PJESIVAC, P
3 DE WAN, G
1 CREAN, Simon
2 SQUILLACCIOTTI, G

INDI
1 LUCK, Jenny
2 MARTIN, J
3 LIEBERMAN, L
4 PULLAR, P

ISAACS
3 HORIN, J
2 RAYNOR, K
1 McSWINEY, John
4 ATKINSON, R

JAGAJAGA
5 VASSIS, C
6 FITZHERBERT, R
1 STAPLES, Peter
7 O'KANE, D
8 WALKER, A
9 KIRKWOOD, E
10 URQUHART, A
2 WEST, B
3 FOLEY, G
4 GRIFFITH, S

KOOYONG
5 PEACOCK, A
4 GREAGG, D
3 ZEMDEGS, D
1 CLARKE, Wayne
2 HARRIS, C

LALOR
4 CANTERBURY, A
3 EVANS, F
1 JONES, Barry
5 GOLDING, A
2 STACEY, C

LA TROBE
7 CHARLES, B
6 HERBERT, P
5 VOIGT, W
4 WIGNEY, R
3 KENDI, J
2 JUNGWIRTH, R
1 PAIN, Geoff

McEWEN
2 MOSLEY, G
1 CLEELAND, Peter
3 GREY, H
4 NIHILL, J
5 BAILEY, F

McMILLAN
2 WHITE, D
1 CUNNINGHAM, Barry
3 MANN, G
4 HOPPNER, H
5 BOSCHIN, C
6 RIGGALL, J

MALLEE
1 ZIGOURAS, John
4 KIDD, A
2 STEAR, C
5 FORREST, J
3 LAWSON KERR, A

MARIBYRNONG
5 HOPPER, M
4 MARINKOVIC, G
3 BELL, J
1 GRIFFITHS, Alan
2 McKAY, F

MELBOURNE
1 TANNER, Lindsay
2 QUIN, D
3 FERRARI, J
4 CLARKE, L
5 SIEVERS, E
6 IVANOV, S
7 COOPER, D
8 KOZANOGLU, R

MELBOURNE PORTS
2 COLBERT, A
1 HOLDING, Clyde
3 CRAIK, C
4 HOCKLEY, C
6 FRIEDMANN, H
5 BROADBENT, B

MENZIES
4 ANDREWS, K
1 DeANGELIS, Peter
2 DOBINSON, J
3 QUINLAN, D

MURRAY
1 SHEEN, John
4 HYLAND, S
2 THOMSON, A
3 LACEY, D
5 LLOYD, B

SCULLIN
3 VEITCH, D
2 GRUJOVSKI, J
1 JENKINS, Harry
7 SMITH, B
6 GEOGIEVSKI, J
5 SIDDONS, J
4 PHILLIPS, N

WANNON
1 MORROW, Richard
2 PHILPOT, J
3 HEMINGWAY, L
4 HORSHAM, Y
5 ANDERSON, D
7 HAWKER, D
6 WILSON, D

WILLS
2 STONE, R
3 SAVAGE, K
4 MURGATROYD, C
5 MANTELL, K
1 KARDAMITSIS, Bill
6 PRICE, J
7 CLEARY, P
8 MINAS, J

Senate

You only have to put 1 in BOX I

I
[1] AUSTRALIAN LABOR PARTY

I
☐ EVANS
☐ CARR
☐ ZAKHAROV
☐ McKENZIE

Authorised by R Hogg, 40 Brisbane Ave, Barton 2600
Printed by Websdale Printing Group, 61 Euston Road, Alexandria NSW 2015

HOW TO VOTE

BRAND
2 EVANS, A
3 CANT, P
4 FAWCETT, A
5 ROBINSON, J
6 TILBURY, R
7 DICKS, N
1 FATIN, Wendy

CANNING
6 JOHNSTON, R
7 TILBURY, R
1 GEAR, George
2 BESSELL, D
3 GOIRAN, G
4 de la HUNTY, S
5 ROBERTS, P

COWAN
2 DIK, O
1 JAKOBSEN, Carol
5 EVANS, R
4 MILES, S
3 GODDEN, S

HOW TO VOTE

Queen

House of R

BOWMAN
2 BICKLE, F
1 SCIACCA, Con
9 WARDLE, D
8 HENMAN, M
7 MARSH, N
6 MAY, R
5 McLAREN, M
4 HENDSTOCK, K
3 WHEELER, B

BRISBANE
4 KELLETT, K
5 ENNIS, N
6 CHOJNACKI, M
7 PRICE, S
8 THURLOW, V
9 VEIVERS, T
10 GUGENBERGER, L
11 DURING, R
1 BEVIS, Arch
2 CHOVEAUX, J
3 GIBSON, M

CAPRICORNIA
6 GOODY, M
7 SMYTH, C
8 WRIGHT, K
9 ALROE, C
10 RUNDLE, J
11 MUIR, B
1 HENZELL, Marjorie
2 TULL, B
3 LAWRENCE, F
4 BRIDGEMAN, D
5 HINTON, M

DAWSON
8 BRAITHWAITE, R
7 FOX, I
6 McCULLOCH, B
5 MAC NEVIN, M
1 GILBERT, Frank
4 MANSELL, J
3 QUADRIO, S
2 HEINIGER, N

DICKSON
8 BEARD, M
1 LAVARCH, Michael
7 St. BAKER, T
6 PEGLER, W
5 MATTHEWS, L
4 FLEGG, B
3 MAHONEY, D
2 SPICER, G

FADDEN
6 DARVILLE, H
7 ABRAHAMSON, I
8 ROSS, J
1 ELDON, Peter
2 KUHNE, O
3 SANDERS, L
4 JULL, D
5 MATHESON, S

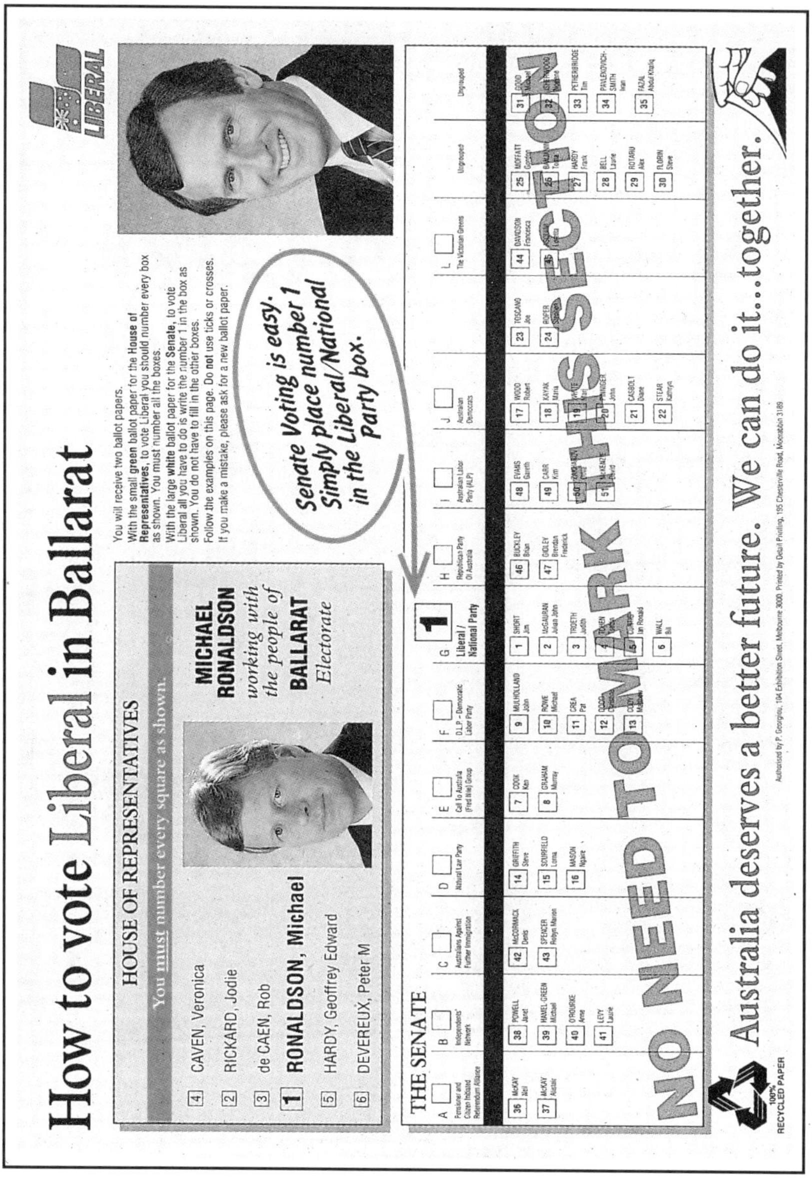
How to vote Liberal in Ballarat
LIBERAL
HOUSE OF REPRESENTATIVES
You must number every square as shown.
4 CAVEN, Veronica
2 RICKARD, Jodie
3 de CAEN, Rob
1 RONALDSON, Michael
5 HARDY, Geoffrey Edward
6 DEVEREUX, Peter M
MICHAEL RONALDSON
working with the people of BALLARAT Electorate
You will receive two ballot papers.
With the small green ballot paper for the House of Representatives, to vote Liberal you should number every box as shown. You must number all the boxes.
With the large white ballot paper for the Senate, to vote Liberal all you have to do is write the number 1 in the box as shown. You do not have to fill in the other boxes.
Follow the examples on this page. Do not use ticks or crosses.
If you make a mistake, please ask for a new ballot paper.
Senate Voting is easy. Simply place number 1 in the Liberal/National Party box.
THE SENATE
NO NEED TO MARK THIS SECTION
Australia deserves a better future. We can do it...together.
100% RECYCLED PAPER

NATIONALS

NATIONALS

How to vote absentee.

You will receive two ballot papers. For the House of Representatives, number every square as shown. For the Senate, follow the example on the back of this sheet exactly. All electorates are listed below in alphabetical order.

BANKS

3	Kirkman, D	Ind
2	Davaris, P	CTA
6	Melham, D	ALP
4	Farleigh, P	Dem
1	TAYLOR, C	LIB
5	Hay, J	Ind

BARTON

1	WHITE, P	LIB
8	Punch, G	ALP
6	McGarry, N	Ind
4	Anderson, T	Dem
3	Mudie, C	CTA
2	Balding, P	Ind
7	Green, R	Ind
5	O'Neill, D	NLP

BENNELONG

1	HOWARD, J	LIB
2	Dalgliesh, G	
3	Dawson, J	Ind
4	Roylance, M	NLP
5	Reddy, S	Dem
6	Rotik, M	ALP

BEROWRA

2	Gallagher, M	Ind
1	RUDDOCK, P	LIB
3	Carr, T	NLP
4	Deane, S	ALP

BLAXLAND

10	Keating, P	ALP
9	Tenenbaum, L	
6	Hennessy, P	Dem
2	Carrick, T	CTA
3	Hillman, J	Ind
5	Kelvin, W	Ind
1	OSMOND, L	LIB
4	Reid, B	Ind
8	Aussie-Stone, M	Ind
7	O'Neill, P	NLP

BRADFIELD

4	Jeans, S	ALP
3	Courtney-Holland, M	NLP
2	Springett, B	Dem
1	CONNOLLY, D	LIB

CALARE

3	Davis, B	Ind
1	**PENNY, R**	**NAT**
2	Staal, J	Lib
5	Simmons, D	ALP
4	Cianfrano, R	Ind

CHARLTON

8	Brown, B	ALP
7	Baldwin, J	Ind
1	BREWSTER, L	LIB
3	Wilson, R	Ind
6	Kviz, Z	NLP
2	Sandford, M	CTA
5	Sievers, C	Ind
4	Godfrey, L	Dem

CHIFLEY

5	Ivor, F	Ind
1	MACKENZIE, J	LIB
6	Price, R	ALP
4	Kumar, T	Ind
2	Bryant, J	EFF
3	Bilyana, Y	

COOK

7	Elphinston, A	Ind
6	Solomon, N	ALP
5	Atkinson, J	NLP
4	Thompson, T	CAP
3	Richardson, T	Dem
1	DOBIE, D	LIB
2	Kinny, W	CTA

COWPER

5	Cranny, J	Greens
4	Wallbridge, D	CAP
3	Forrester, R	NLP
2	Gleeson, N	CEC
1	**NEHL, G**	**NAT**
7	Sekfy, P	ALP
6	Pike, T	Dem

CUNNINGHAM

4	Reverberi, D	Dem
1	LYNCH, R	LIB
8	Martin, S	ALP
7	West, M	Ind
5	Medcalf, C	Greens
3	Sampson, M	Ind
2	O'Neill, R	CTA
6	Misdom, F	NLP

DOBELL

1	BALDWIN, B	LIB
2	Hudson, B	Ind
3	Day, B	Dem
4	Lee, M	ALP

EDEN-MONARO

1	**BARRY, T**	**NAT**
6	Snow, J	ALP
5	Sanders, N	Ind
3	Doyle, G	Ind
2	De Fegely, R	Lib
4	Fraser, P	NLP

FARRER

1	**FISCHER, T**	**NAT**
3	Higgins, B	ALP
2	McKenzie, I	Dem

FOWLER

2	Stevens, M	Ind
3	Josling, G	
4	Hyde, N	NLP
1	ARORA, G	LIB
5	Grace, T	ALP

GILMORE

2	Eddy, B	Lib
4	Leatch, M	Greens
5	Stanborough, J	Ind
6	Butler, G	Dem
3	Devenney, R	Ind
7	Keighley, R	NLP
1	**ATKINS, M**	**NAT**
8	Knott, P	ALP

GRAYNDLER

1	ROBINSON, K	LIB
7	Johnston, P	NLP
5	Fitzgerald, P	Greens
2	Wilson, C	CTA
6	Pepper, L	Ind
3	Shanahan, J	Ind
4	Markham, P	Dem
8	McHugh, J	ALP
9	Kennedy, M	

GREENWAY

1	MORRIS, R	LIB
2	Jerrow, J	CTA
3	Clancy, B	Dem
5	Gorman, R	ALP
4	Alsop, R	NLP

GWYDIR

1	**ANDERSON, J**	**NAT**
3	Stubbins, T	ALP
2	Perrett, J	CAP

HUGHES

4	Young, J	Dem
1	SHORT, N	LIB
5	Buckley, J	Ind
7	Tickner, R	ALP
6	Maher, C	NLP
2	Scott, C	CTA
3	Gunning, S	Ind

HUME

3	Cox, D	Ind
4	Buchanan, I	Dem
5	Archer, P	ALP
2	Ward, S	Lib
1	**SHARP, J**	**NAT**

HUNTER

3	Walker, R	NLP
2	Barnes, C	Lib
4	Fitzgibbon, E	ALP
1	**CROSSING, B**	**NAT**

KINGSFORD-SMITH

1	MARSLAND, P	LIB
6	Brereton, L	ALP
4	Dove, W	
2	Larcos, A	Dem
3	Matson, M	Greens
5	Pearson, P	NLP

LINDSAY

2	Grigg, B	CTA
1	BELLANTONIO, C	LIB
3	Free, R	ALP

LOWE

8	Panzarino, A	Ind
7	Woods, P	Ind
2	Peterson, P	CTA
6	Lowry, E	
5	Eager, R	NLP
4	Jones, E	AAFI
11	Easson, M	ALP
3	Meikle, J	Dem
9	Cummings, K	Ind
1	WOODS, B	LIB
10	Threlfo, B	Greens

PLEASE TURN OVER

100% RECYCLED PAPER. MADE IN AUSTRALIA

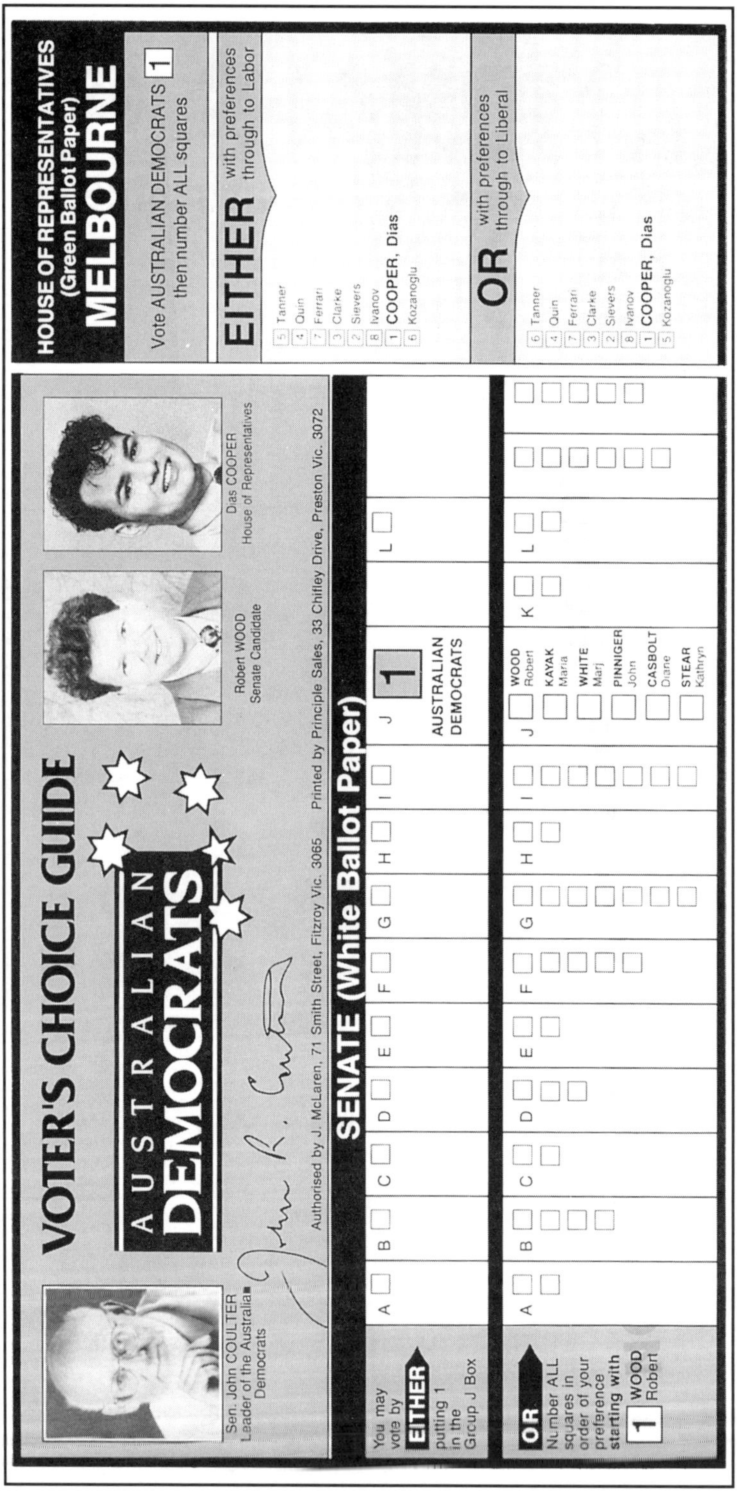
VOTER'S CHOICE GUIDE
AUSTRALIAN DEMOCRATS
Sen. John COULTER Leader of the Australian Democrats
Robert WOOD Senate Candidate
Dias COOPER House of Representatives
Authorised by J. McLaren, 71 Smith Street, Fitzroy Vic. 3065 Printed by Principle Sales, 33 Chifley Drive, Preston Vic. 3072
SENATE (White Ballot Paper)
You may vote by EITHER putting 1 in the Group J Box
A B C D E F G H I J L
1 AUSTRALIAN DEMOCRATS
OR Number ALL squares in order of your preference starting with 1 WOOD Robert
A B C D E F G H I J K L
WOOD Robert
KAYAK Maria
WHITE Marj
PINNIGER John
CASBOLT Diane
STEAR Kathryn
HOUSE OF REPRESENTATIVES (Green Ballot Paper)
MELBOURNE
Vote AUSTRALIAN DEMOCRATS 1 then number ALL squares
EITHER with preferences through to Labor
5 Tanner
4 Quin
7 Ferrari
3 Clarke
2 Sievers
8 Ivanov
1 COOPER, Dias
6 Kozanoglu
OR with preferences through to Liberal
6 Tanner
4 Quin
7 Ferrari
3 Clarke
2 Sievers
8 Ivanov
1 COOPER, Dias
5 Kozanoglu

3 Can the Country Party justify its call for a weighting in favour of rural voters (and against urban voters)? (See Document 2.3.)
4 Australia pioneered a) one man, one vote and one person, one vote, b) votes for women, c) payment for members of parliament, d) the widest possible entry to parliament—all in the nineteenth century. Is it still in the forefront of democracy?
5 Are you in favour of 'compulsory voting'? Why or why not? (See Document 2.4.)
6 Do you agree with this statement: 'All groups must have a voice in government, and no one's voice should be louder than another's.'?
7 Discuss the pros and cons of the proposal: 'The voting age should be lowered to 16 years.'
8 Discuss the statement: 'One person, one vote, one value is an essential part of democratic government.'
9 Some local government elections are based on voluntary voting. Why is the turnout so low?
10 Besides electing a government, what does voting actually do for you? Mention specific personal interests which as a voting citizen you will be able to protect by careful use of the vote.
11 Do you favour the idea of proportional representation? Give reasons for your answer.
12 In the 1993 elections for the Senate, it took only 43 876 votes to elect a senator from Tasmania, but it took 391 540 votes to elect a senator from Victoria. Is this difference justified? Why does it occur?
13 Are how-to-vote cards necessary? Design one for your preferred party, and show preferences.
14 Examine the existing electoral system in your state. To what extent does it support Document 2.5?

Chapter three

ELECTIONS, REPRESENTATION AND THE ELECTORAL PARTY SYSTEM

Elections are the means whereby the citizens of a democratic State select those who will represent them in parliament or congress. Almost from the inauguration of adult suffrage, elections and political parties have been inseparable. Elections in Australia are overwhelmingly contests between parties and between candidates nominated and endorsed by parties. Independent candidates do intervene, but only rarely do they succeed. It follows, then, that political parties and representation in the Australian context are equally inseparable. How do parties contest elections (and referendums)? Who do the representatives represent? What effects are there of the election systems, procedures, and laws outlined in the previous chapter? Is there uniformity in patterns of results of elections in Australia? What, in fact, do elections produce? These are just some of the questions to be asked about the electoral party system.

Australian parties are involved in many more activities than simply contesting elections. Especially in comparison with parties in Canada and the USA, which are essentially electoral organisations brought to active life during campaigns and returned to relative hibernation between elections, Australian parties are permanent organisations, ubiquitous in their involvement in the political process, and key components of day-to-day politics. But elections are the key focus of Australian parties to a degree no less than in the USA or Canada, and the parties' permanence and ubiquity in Australia provides this electoral focus with a greater importance. All policies, programmes and rhetoric of intra-party and inter-party actions either have an electoral implication, or are given such by the mass media.

PATTERNS OF PARTY SUPPORT: AN OVERVIEW

The basic data for a study of the electoral party system are the results of elections and the patterns of party support. Even a cursory glance at the history of elections in Australia suggests that if government and opposition are seen as 'swings of the political pendulum', then the pendulum became stuck for long periods. Rather than swinging fairly evenly between Labor and non-Labor, the Australian national political pendulum has spent much more time on the non-Labor side. From 1910, the history of party government at the national level is a history of short-term Labor governments succeeded by long-term non-Labor governments. Of the 83 years to 1993, Labor held national office for only 28 years, just over one-third of the total. The electoral histories of the states suggest that the pendulum has stuck even more in some sub-national contests but, at this stage, we will focus on the national electoral arena.

When we turn from who won how many seats in the parliament to which parties shared the electorate, then two themes emerge. The first is the remarkable stability of patterns of party choice in the eighty years since the formation of the modern party system. There are peaks and troughs in the graphs of party support, especially the Liberal trough in the 1940s, but the overall picture is one of relative stability. Especially in comparison with other liberal democracies such as the USA, Canada and the UK, the Australian patterns are remarkably stable. This is remarkable simply because the stability has remained over a ten-fold increase in the electorate population, and over three generations. We will examine some reasons for this in the following chapter.

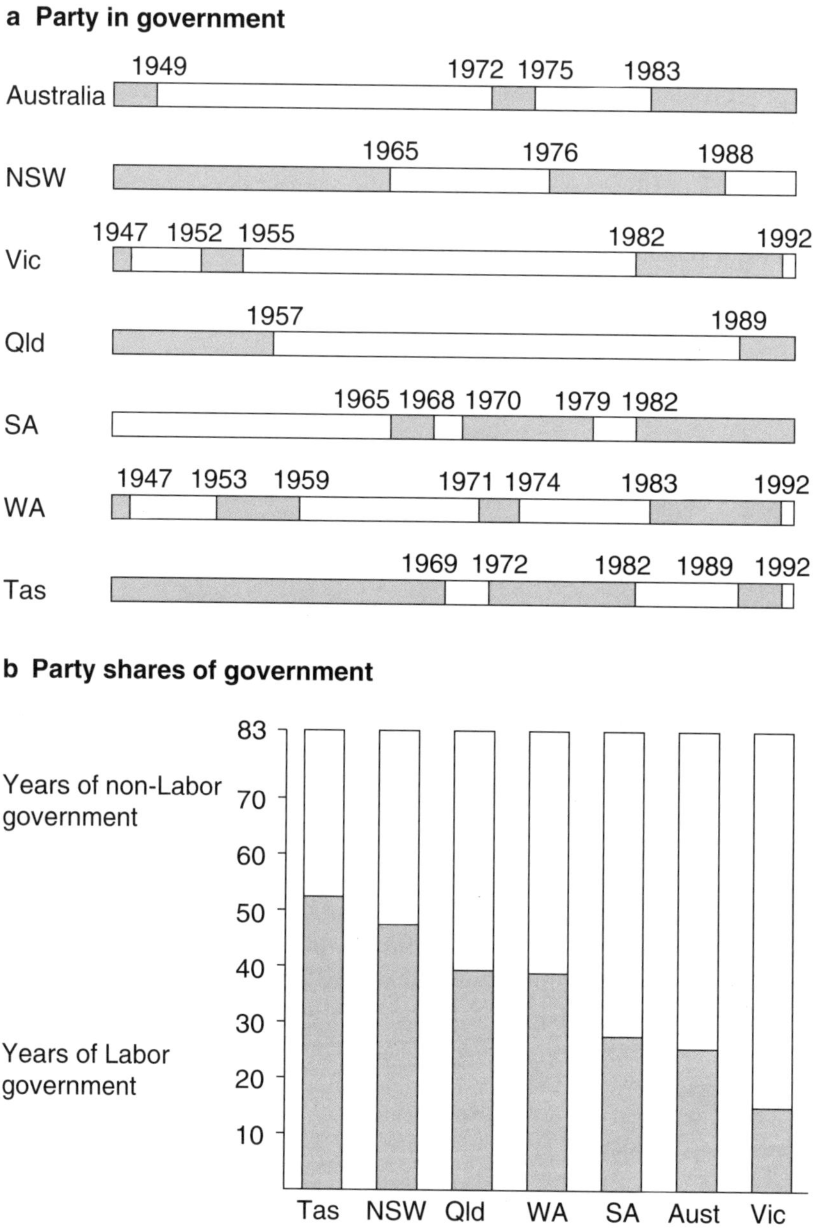

Figure 3.1 *Party composition of Australian governments, 1910–1993*

The second theme is the domination of national elections, over the period of over eighty years, by two parties, Labor and Liberal, and since the 1920s, by the National Party as a minor, but the most stable, participant. The three-party graph on the following page shows this clearly. Other parties have had considerable difficulty in attempting to break into this established pattern.

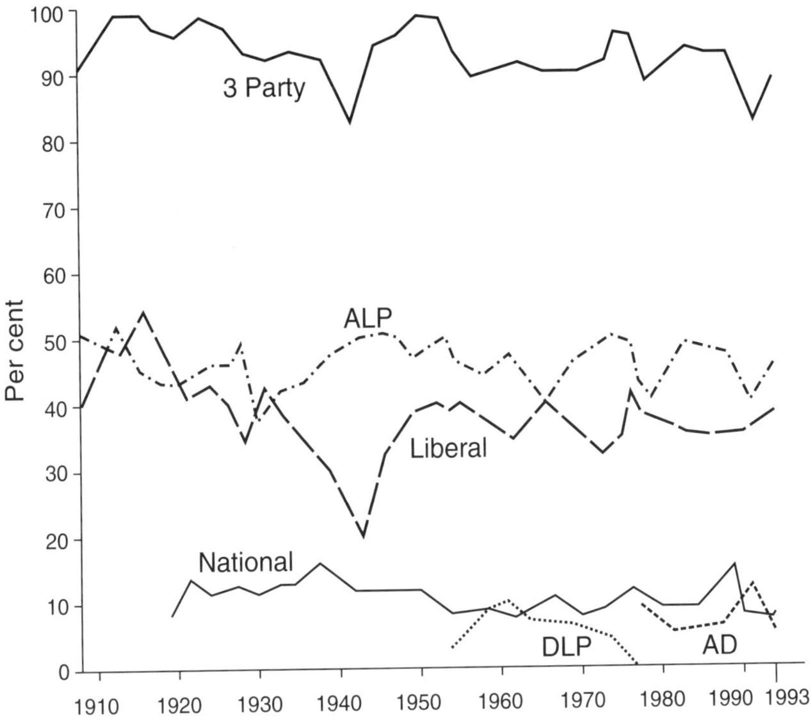

***Figure 3.2** Patterns of party support, 1910–1993 (Percentage of first-preference votes)*

It is apparent, as Aitkin (1977:5) noted, that the 'ebb and flow of party support in federal elections have been most subdued'. At every one of the 35 elections from 1910–1993, the Labor and Liberal parties (Labor and Liberal–NP coalition from 1922) won over 80 per cent of the vote, and at 24 elections won over 90 per cent. As well, there has been a remarkable stability of support for the three established parties. Labor's share of the overall vote has varied between 38 per cent in 1931 to 51 per cent in 1914, with a mean of 45 per cent, and with the largest shift from 49 per cent in 1929 to 38 per cent in 1931. The Liberal Party has a similar history of relative stability of support. If the nadir of 1943, the period of fragmentation of the United Australia party, is excluded, the range is from 30 per cent in 1940 to 54 per cent in 1917, with a mean of 38 per cent. If the remarkably stable pattern of support for the National Party, a mean of 11 per cent, is added to produce a figure for 'coalition' support, then the range is from (again excluding 1943) 41 per cent in 1972 to 53 per cent in 1975.

UNIFORMITY AND HETEROGENEITY

To analyse election results and patterns of party support needs a methodology to deal with a range of factors, some applicable to comparative election studies, some specific to Australia. Encompassed in these issues are the questions of what data can be used, and in what form. If we are seeking to analyse the *national* electoral party system, then we need a methodology which will provide a means of comparing national data over time, which takes into account sub-national variations, provides a means of measuring change, and which does not simplify to the extent of masking significant variations.

At least three questions have a bearing on the direction and focus of the inquiry and on the conclusions which can be drawn:

- To what extent has there been a 'nationalisation' of party voting in post-war Australia?
- To what extent has there been a uniform swing?
- Does the apparent domination by Labor and Liberal justify the concept of a 'two-party vote'?

A 'NATIONAL' VOTE?

Even in an ideal situation—an homogeneous society in which an election is a contest between only two parties, it would be unusual if there were a uniformity of party support across all electorates. Regional and local issues, personalities and events would have some effects on the voters, and result in different patterns in different areas. An aggregate national result in such a hypothetical situation—say, Party A 54 per cent of the national vote and Party B 46 per cent—may well not represent the actual result in any regional or local area. There will always be some evidence of regional diversity. The important question is the *degree* of regional divergence.

The genesis of a party system in Australia occurred with the formation of a federal structure. The centre-periphery cleavage apparent in the 1890–1910 period of party development was reflected in different aspects of parties, pressure groups and processes of politics in the colonies and states. However, as the Labor versus Liberal contest crystallised, then the cleavage theory of party development predicts that core-periphery cleavages would give way to functional cleavages with a trend towards similar patterns of party support across regions and, when shifts to electoral opinion occur, similar shifts across the nation. That is, 'nationalisation' of the vote implies not only similar pattens of support, but evidence of a uniform national swing. We will return to this.

Data from the 1993 federal election and the most recent state elections leave an equivocal conclusion. The 1993 federal election showed inconsistency of patterns of party support across the states. Labor's support ranged from 39 per cent in Western Australia and South Australia to over 50 per cent in the Territories. Liberal patterns were almost as inconsistent. On the other hand, if the latter comparison is based on support for 'the coalition', then relative consistency is apparent. But that is an artificial construct: there is no coalition in Queensland, and the number of three-party contests is increasing.

When comparisons are made between federal and state patterns, in their own context, then there is evidence of more inconsistency. There is sufficient evidence to justify a conclusion that Australia's electoral contests are not characterised by a monotonous homogeneity. State personalities, issues, and political environment do matter.

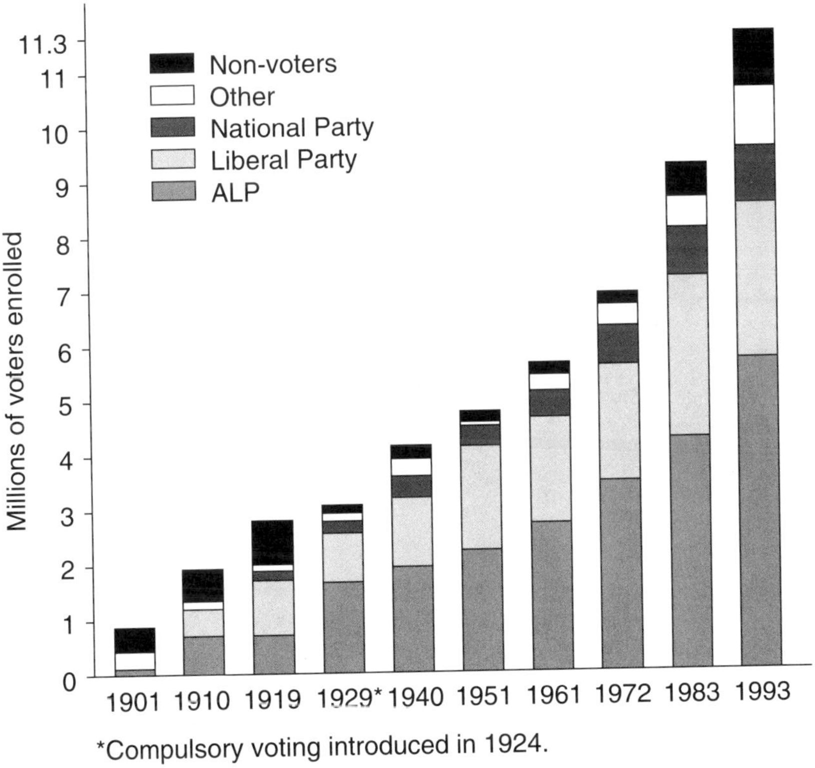

Figure 3.3 *Enrolment, turnout (N) and party support (%), 1901–1993*

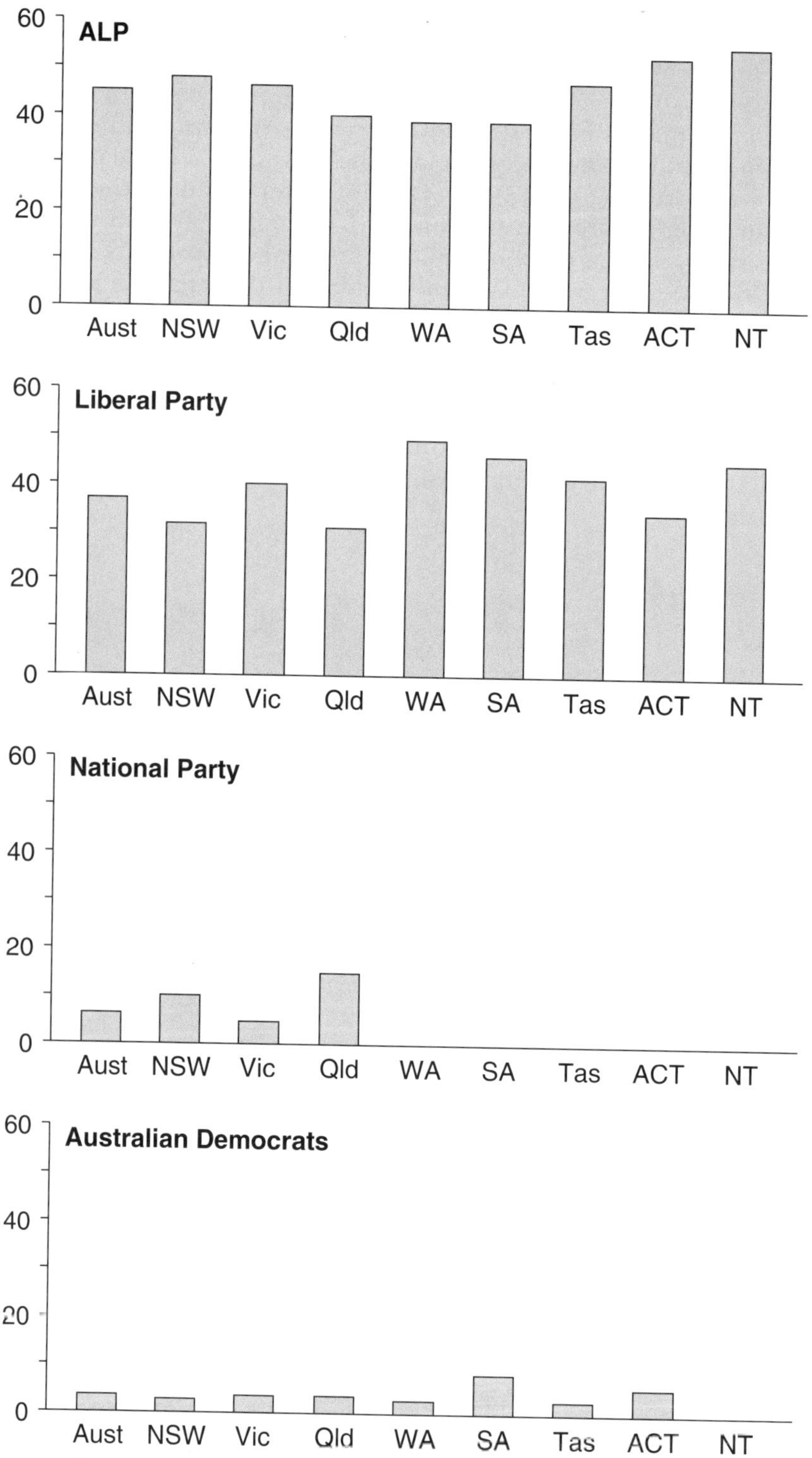

Figure 3.4 *Party support by states, House of Representatives election, 1993 (percentage of formal votes)*

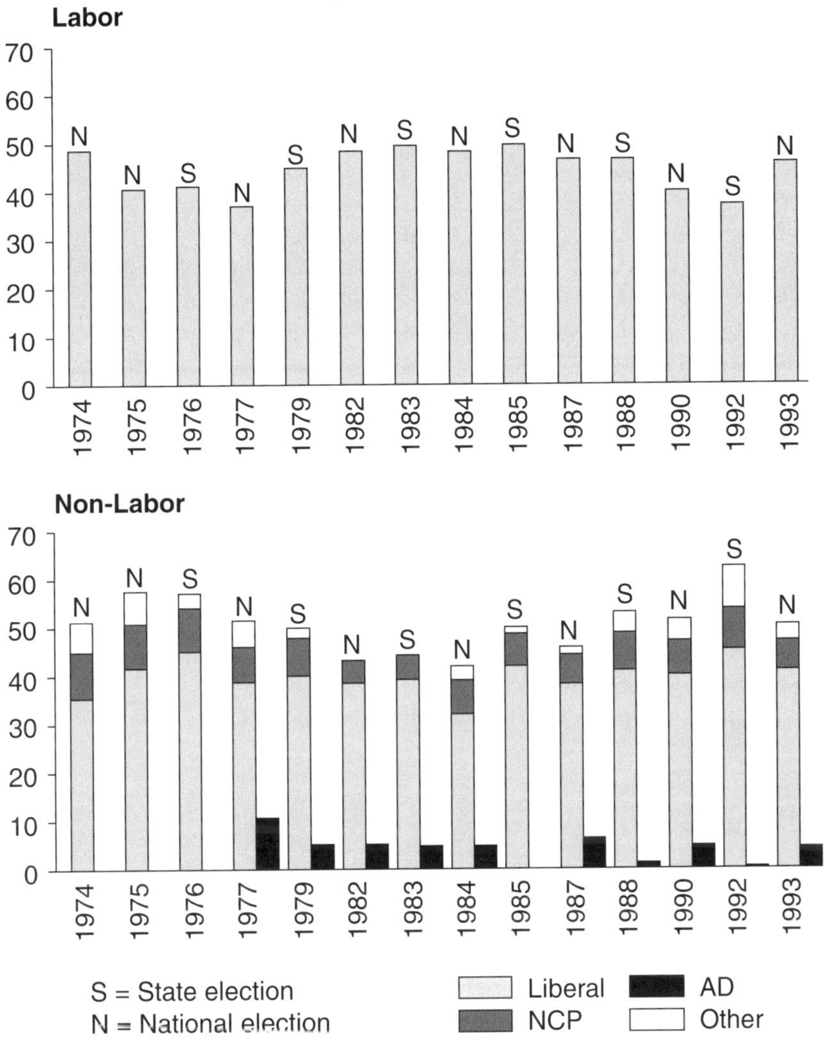

Figure 3.5 *Comparison of national and state voting for relevant parties in Victoria, 1974–1993*

In terms of the electoral party systems of the nation and the states, there appear to be clear distinctions on the basis of patterns of party support over time. The ultimate line of conflict in every state is Labor versus non-Labor, but patterns of voting suggest important variations. The National Party does not exist in Tasmania, it is insignificant in South Australia, and only in Queensland has it even approached a major party status. Labor has consistently outpolled the other parties in Queensland and New South Wales, while the 'pendulum' thesis is most obvious in the Labor/Liberal competition in Victoria.

Table 3.1: *Comparing Australia's party systems*

	1945-1955	1955-1974	1974-1981	1982-1993
Tas	A,L	A,L	A,L,(ad)	A,L,(g)
SA	A,L	A,L	A,L,(ad)	A,L,(ad)
WA	A,L,(n)	A,L,(n)	A,L,(n)	A,L,(n),(g)
NSW	A,L,N	A,L,(n),(d)	A,L,(n)	A,L,(n),(ad)
Vic	A,L,N	A,L,d,(n)	A,L,(n),(d)	A,L,(n),(ad)
Qld	A,L,N	A,L,N,d	A,L,N	A,N,l
Aust	A,L,N	A,L,(n),(d)	A,L,n,(ad)	A,L,n,(ad),(g)

Note: A= ALP; L, l = Liberal; N, (n) = National Party; d (d) = DLP; (ad) = Australian Democrat; (g) = Green

Key: A,L,N—mean support above 20%
d,n,l—mean support in the range 10–19%
(d)(n)(ad)(g)—mean support in the range 5–9%

The conclusion can be drawn that there are regional differences within Australia's party system. On the basis of election results in the last decade, the various systems can be classified as shown in Table 3.1. The differences between the states are significant, as is a trend to the erosion of two-party domination in all states.

UNIFORM SWING?

If a 'national vote' existed, if the Australian voting population everywhere showed general similar patterns of party choice, then we would also expect to find evidence of a uniform swing across the nation. We would expect to find that people, wherever they live, react in similar ways to campaigns, issues, parties and people.

The concept of 'swing' is itself a problem. In the most simple example of a contest between the same two parties in successive elections, the swing is the change in support for each party. In the first example in Table 3.2, the swing is 5.5 per cent against Labor, and 5.5 per cent to the Liberals. But when the successive contests are complicated by the intervention of other parties and by different parties at each election, then calculating the swing becomes difficult. One problem is identifying who shifted where, even in the simple example. The result in example a) could be the result of 5.5 per cent of the voters shifting from Labor to Liberal. It could also have been the result of 2.2 per cent shifting from Liberal to Labor and 7.7 per cent from Labor to Liberal. In the second example, the permutations of possible shifts are very complex. And these comparisons do not take into account new and departed voters.

Table 3.2: *Hypothetical election results*

	Election 1	Election 2	Shift
a Simple two-party			
ALP	52.3	46.8	–5.5
Lib	47.7	53.2	+5.5
b Complicated			
ALP	43.2	33.0	–10.2
Lib	31.6	41.6	+10.0
Nat	8.3	–	–8.3
AD	7.6	8.9	+1.3
CTA	5.3	–	–5.3
Ind	4.0	11.6	+7.6
Grey	–	4.9	+4.9

Some analysts attempted to resolve the problems with the concept of a 'two-party vote'. That is, they assumed that regardless of the complexity of the ballot paper, the final contest would, through preferences, resolve itself into a two-party battle between Labor and a Liberal–National coalition. The counting of votes, in federal and some state elections, assists this calculation as all contests are 'counted out' to a two-candidate contest. One problem, and an increasing one, is that not all two-candidate results are Labor-Liberal. The successes of independents and minor parties, especially in New South Wales, South Australia and Tasmania, questions the idea of a Labor-Liberal two-party contest. As well, the fact that the National Party has forced a coalition in only a minority of electoral arenas asks the question whether such a two-candidate concept matches the reality.

Whether the basis of comparison is first-preference, or two-party preferred votes, there is evidence that a uniform swing does not correctly describe the pattern of elections in Australia. In the 1993 federal election, for example, there was a swing to Labor in New South Wales, Victoria and Tasmania, but a swing against Labor in Queensland, South Australia and Western Australia. Such diversity of swing is apparent in every election, and is the product of different electoral environments, different issues, different personalities and different parties. On the other hand, the differences between swings are not great. It may be, then, that the most accurate description of Australia's electoral party system is 'Unity in Diversity' (Davis 1960).

EXPLAINING ELECTION RESULTS

Elections are not simple contests. They involve a bewildering range of factors to which voters may react. Some of these factors relate to the individual voters—to their backgrounds, attitudes, party identifications, and the impact of family. We will analyse these in the following chapter.

But there remains a whole constellation of possible effects on the electoral choices of the voters. Table 3.6 sets out some of these factors. A government which has had the benefit of a sound and stable

***Table 3.6**: Factors affecting party success*

		Long term		Short term
		Economic environment		
Socio-economic factors	Social cleavages	Class Religion Ethnicity Sex Region Race etc.		
Structural			Electoral system	
Political socialisation	Individual		Mass media	
Political parties			Cohesion Ideology Images Leadership Solidarity	
Party in election				Issues Campaign issues Leaders
Immediate factors				Political events

economy, under which most people, for most of the time, have enjoyed a comfortable way of life, will enjoy a positive benefit in the run-up to an election. Conversely, an economic down-turn, whether due to government policy (one example is the credit squeeze brought on by the Menzies government in 1961), or as a result of the international economic environment, may cause electoral troubles for a government and offer opposition parties some hope.

As discussed in the preceding chapter, electoral systems can play a major part in who wins elections. As an example, for thirty years in Queensland the National Party went into elections with a clear advantage. Electoral laws can influence the potential of parties and individual candidates. These laws may disadvantage some parties and advantage others. The means of allocation of 'free time' by the ABC—based on support won at the *previous* election—is an obvious disadvantage for new parties.

The 'state of the parties' is a very potent factor in elections. One of the accepted wisdoms of Australian electoral politics is that voters do not support divided parties. Labor, on many occasions in its history, the coalition in 1987 and the Liberal Party in South Australia in the 1970s are just some examples suggesting the truth of this assertion. A party which has an ideology or image which accords with that prevailing in the society may start the campaign 'in front'. And, especially after television became the medium used most by most Australians, the image of the leaders of the parties became more important.

Every election campaign is permeated by a range of factors. The voters are bombarded by party propaganda, the media are saturated with advertisements, analyses, reports, and polls. Issues emerge and disappear as leaders and candidates attempt to capture the imaginations of the people. Every event is seen by the parties, the media, the candidates, and pressure groups, as a potential means to win support or to weaken the opposing parties and candidates. For a brief period, usually four or five weeks, the voters live in a maelstrom of electoral politics. How they react to this is one focus of the following chapter. But one point can be noted here: given the nature of the factors present in any election, it is perhaps surprising that Australian aggregate voting patterns show so much stability.

ELECTIONS AND MANDATES

An election decides who will represent whom. Elections produce members of parliaments, and indirectly produce governments and oppositions. But what relationship is there, or should there be, between the opinions expressed by the voters, and the decisions of the representatives who are elected? Do voters provide their representative with a 'mandate'?

The political theory of a mandate is drawn from the linked theories of the sovereignty of the people, of the general will of the people, and of the concept that a government, to be legitimate, must enjoy the consent of the people over whom it governs. In its simplest sense, then, sovereignty and legitimacy in a democracy are derived from, and remain with, the people. Governments are the agents or trustees for the governed, who retain the right to decide who should govern whom, and under what conditions. One immediate problem in Australia is that the Constitution does not recognise, let alone assert, the sovereignty of the people. Where the US Constitution is built on its opening words 'We, the People...', the Australian Constitution is built on a combination of Monarch and parliament.

But the major debate over the term 'mandate' occurs in regard to the phrase, 'agents or trustees'. This debate raises the most crucial controversy within the concept of political representation. One source for the following discussion of 'mandate' is the recognised authority on the subject, H. F. Pitkin's *The Concept of Representation.* In modern democracies, the question of a mandate involves consideration of a range of issues; regular elections, universal franchise, secret ballot, freedom of speech, press and assembly, the right to form political parties and groups, the right of citizens to nominate and so on. But consideration of these leads to the modern usage of mandate, the usage which involves the concept of representative and responsible political parties. This modified concept is based on the assumption that voters not only choose between sets of candidates, but they also choose between sets of programmes and policies. The implicit understanding is that, if elected, the party will turn its programmes and policies into law. It follows, then, that if the elected government refuses to implement its promised policies, or neglects to do so, it can be accused of breaking or dishonouring its promises or of breaking its mandate. Alternatively, if a government initiates policies which it has earlier said it would not countenance, or which it had given no notice that it might carry out, it is accused of exceeding its mandate.

That is, under this 'party' conception of mandate, governments are elected to do certain things, but not others. Their legitimacy is conditional, not unconditional. The only defence against accusations of breaking or exceeding a mandate under this theory is that unforeseen, even unforeseeable, circumstances made it impossible for the government to carry out its election promises, or that new challenges outside the scope of pre-election discussions emerged, and required immediate decisions. But, above the 'party' conception is a debate which is central:

> The question at issue may be summarised as: should (must) a representative do what his constituents want, and be bound by mandate or instructions from them; or should (must) he be free to act as seems best to him in pursuit of their welfare? (Pitkin 1967:145).

This suggests a simple choice between one model or the other, a choice between acting as a delegate or as a trustee. The reality of political life is more complex. The debate about delegate/trustee is embedded in other theoretical questions such as the comparative priority which should be given to local or national interest and practical questions such as the nature of the party political processes through which the debate is resolved in the real world.

Further, the simple dichotomy can mask a number of possible 'positions' between the two poles. The poles establish the representative either as a delegate, mandated to a point where no action is allowed without explicit instructions, or as a trustee, who will act on his or her own perception of what is best, regardless of the opinions of the public. In both cases, an argument can be made that political representation is *not* occurring, that neither a 'pure' delegate nor a 'pure' trustee is a proper representative.

When we extend the potential styles of representative behaviour to include the impact of political parties, then there are three possible models. The *Trustee* model of representation derives from Edmund Burke, a member of the British Parliament in the late eighteenth century. This demands that the representatives act in parliament primarily in terms of their own consciences. They will listen to the arguments of parties, pressure groups and their own constituents but,

Edmund Burke

in the final analysis, they will carry out their parliamentary functions in terms of what they think is in the best interests of the public and of the nation. At the end of their terms, they will face their electors for judgement of their actions. This model is a non-party, even anti-party, concept. It could apply to the very few independent members of Australian parliaments, but the only occasions on which party members of parliament can act as trustees are when party whips are removed, and conscience votes are allowed.

The *Delegate* model of representation demands that the members will also listen to arguments from pressure groups and from their party, and they will obviously have their own consciences to consider. But what decides their vote is what their constituents want. They will seek to establish the views of those who elected them, by whatever means are available, and they will vote in the parliament in accordance with the majority opinion. They can best be described as the conduit through which the electorate's opinions are expressed.

While Australian members of parliament give lip service to their role as delegates, a *Partisan* model best describes all but a handful. Australian politicians acknowledge the need to listen to arguments from pressure groups and constituents, and they all have to take their own consciences into account. But the party line is the bottom line. Australia epitomises the partisan model of representation. Labor members have no choice—their Pledge demands that they follow the party line. They make known their own views and those of their constituents in the secrecy of the party room, but in the public arena of the parliament, the party rules and their lips are sealed. Members of the Liberal and National parties are not pledged but, except for a small number of 'rebels', they are equally partisan.

In the USA, representatives in the Congress are forced to balance all three models. As the US parties are weak, and do not attempt to apply a party line, the US representatives must continually balance their own consciences, the pressures from various groups, the majority opinions in their electorates, and their party. In Australian parliaments, there are also these pressures on members from electorates, pressure groups, and conscience. But politicians do not have to balance the pressures. The party line must be followed by Labor members, and generally is followed by Liberal and National members. This enforced cohesion, almost total in its effect, has obvious implications for parliament and its functions.

In the theory of representation, however, the models need further consideration. Each, like the polar models of mandate/independent, has an internal logic, and can be argued coherently and sensibly. The dilemma for representatives is that they must make decisions based on a range of competing pressures, each of which may demand a different decision. The representative, after all, is elected to represent a collectivity of people among whom there will be a range of views, opinions and interests, and a range of levels of information at the base of these opinions. The representative will also (usually) be a member of a party, and will be under some pressure to support the party policy or party line. The representative is also deciding within an environment of pressure groups. The representative will also have his/her own opinions concerning the question at hand. Finally, the representative will consider the impact of any decision he/she makes on his/her chances for re-election. The final action of a representative on any specific question requires these various, and probably competing influences, to be balanced, judged, assessed, and a final decision made. Which one should the representative consider to be decisive?

This raises the issue of 'interest' within the representative's equation. Any decision by a representative raises at least the following questions:

- In whose interest has the decision been made?
- In which interest—local or national, pressure group or whole society—has the decision been made?
- Can a representative make a decision which is *not* in accord with the expressed wishes of the majority of his/her constituents and still properly represent them?

The answers depend on the model of representation which the representative has decided to follow. A trustee, for example, will focus on the national interest, and obviously answer 'yes' to the third question. A delegate will follow the local interest and answer 'no' to that question.

Any representative must be *responsible* to the wishes of his/her constituents. But the models differ in relation to whether the

MPs must be seen to be representing their constituencies, and constituents.

representative should automatically follow those wishes. It can be argued, within a democratic theory of representation, that there are two bases for a representative *rejecting* the majority opinion of his/her constituency. The majority interest of the local constituency may conflict with the national interest. The national interest can be applied within a theory of representation, *and of the mandate.* The second basis is that the information and awareness levels of the constituents may not have been sufficient for objective and rational opinions. In such cases, the representative may well decide to reject local interest. That is, the representative may decide on the basis of what the people *ought to want* if they were fully informed, fully aware of the consequences, and fully rational.

Two examples suggest that this type of representation can logically be applied. One example is the well-known case of Proposition 13 in California. A majority of electors, in a citizens' initiated referendum, mandated the Congress to lower property taxes. It was in the immediate, short-term, and local interest of the people to do so. But the decision, and its effects of cutting services, was against the 'national' interest. It was reversed. A second, hypothetical, example would be the general question of taxation. Most people would have a personal interest in lower taxes, but it may not be in the 'national' interest to do so. A decision to lower taxes would accord with a delegate/mandate theory of representation; a decision not to lower them also accords with a democratic theory of representation. That is, as Pitkin (1967:164) puts it,

> Acting contrary to their wishes is not necessarily wrong, not necessarily bad representation or a violation of a representative's duty. It may, indeed, be required of him in certain situations.

On what grounds? Very simply, because the representative has twin duties—to 'represent' the national interest, and the interest of the people as a whole. In cases of conflict, the representative has to decide from where the mandate is drawn.

Further, it can be argued that if the Australian voters were fully informed, aware, active, openminded and discussive, there would be no conflict between the 'personal' and 'national' interest. But the majority of Australian voters are not so. Most are not the open-minded, interested, aware, discussive and rational voters that the ideal is built upon. Most are apathetic. Hence, there may be a case for a representative to act against the opinions of the local electors on the grounds that, if informed and aware, they would have different opinions.

In summary, any decision taken by a representative will be the result of a constellation of factors: party, constituent opinions, local interest, national interest, individual conscience, and the effect on re-election prospects. Each representative must decide what weight to apply to each factor.

In Australia, the practical application of the concept of mandate is through political parties. Except for the rare independents, and arguably the Australian Democrats, political representation is a matter of cohesive and disciplined parties, and the party line sets limits of a mandate. Whether this constitutes democracy is a matter for debate.

A NEW VOLATILITY?

In the first section of this chapter, the focus was on stability of patterns of party support. That focus is justified on the basis of the results in eighty years of elections in Australia. But the late 1980s, and the 1990 and 1993 federal elections, provided some evidence to suggest that the stability of the two-party domination was being tested. Three state elections in 1988 and 1989 also suggested that something different was happening in the electorates.

In the 1988 New South Wales election, independent candidates managed to win 8.1 per cent of the votes and seven of the 109 seats in the Legislative Assembly, the most since 1944. In South Australia in 1989, the Australian Democrats received 10.3 per cent of the votes, and two independent Labor members were elected, forcing a 'hung' parliament and a minority Labor government. The third example, the 1989 election in Tasmania, is the most important but, at the same time, the most idiosyncratic. Green Independent candidates won 17.1 per cent of the votes and five of the thirty-five seats, producing a 'hung' parliament and a minority Labor government.

These are examples of something new in Australian electoral patterns, an apparent willingness of a significant proportion of voters to abandon, at least in terms of party of first-preference choice, the traditional Labor, Liberal and National parties. And this trend was very noticeable in the run-up to, and in the results of, the 1990 federal election. Throughout the five-week campaign, the surveys indicated three related trends. First, a very high proportion of voters, in some surveys up to 30 per cent, had not made up their minds. Given the strength of party identification in Australia's electoral history, this suggested that short-term factors in 1990 had become very important indeed. Second, the surveys, and the spokespeople for the parties, commented on a new level of cynicism in the electorate. Third, there was evidence in the surveys, and in the election, of a significant shift away from the entrenched parties.

The 1993 election showed different trends again. Public opinion polls showed considerable volatility; the Democrats' support collapsed, but other minor parties and independents increased support; there were disparate shifts across Australia; and the Australian electorate proved to be even more unpredictable. Overall, there is a new volatility in the Australian electorate. The level of voter uncertainty and vote shifting would be unremarkable in, say, the USA, Canada or the UK. But, given the strength and stability of major party support until the 1980s, it does raise important questions about the electorate, and about Australian voters.

DOCUMENTS

3.1 NATIONAL ELECTION RESULTS, 1974–1993

House of Representatives (% of first-preference votes)					
	ALP	Lib	Nat	AD	Other
1974	49	35	11	–	5
1975	43	42	11	–	4
1977	40	38	10	9	3
1980	45	37	9	7	2
1983	50	34	9	5	2
1984	48	34	11	5	2
1987	46	35	11	6	2
1990	39	35	8	11	9
1993	45	37	7	4	7
Seats won					
1974	66	40	21	–	–
1975	36	68	22	–	–
1977	38	67	10	–	–
1980	51	54	10	–	–
1983	75	33	17	–	–
1984	82	45	21	–	
1987	86	43	19	–	–
1990	78	55	14	–	1
1993	80	49	16	–	2

3.2 VICTORIAN ELECTION RESULTS, 1979–1993

• *National: House of Representatives*
• *State: Legislative Assembly*
(% of first-preference votes)

	ALP	Lib	Nat	AD	Other
1979 (Vic)	45	41	6	5	2
1980 (Fed)	46	39	5	8	2
1982 (Vic)	50	38	5	5	1
1983 (Fed)	51	37	5	6	2
1984 (Fed)	49	37	6	5	2
1985 (Vic)	50	42	7	–	1
1987 (Fed)	47	38	6	7	2
1988 (Vic)	47	41	8	1	4
1990 (Fed)	37	40	6	12	5
1992 (Vic)	38	44	8	–	10
1993 (Fed)	46	40	5	4	5

ISSUES FOR DISCUSSION

1 Compare the votes and seats for federal elections (Document 3.1). What conclusion can be drawn?
2 Why was there such a big shift in the 1990 federal election?
3 Can the Labor Party really claim to have won government in 1990?
4 Compare and contrast the elections held in Victoria in the last decade (Document 3.2). What significant patterns emerge?
5 Is there any evidence in Document 3.2 that voters do not sufficiently distinguish federal and state issues and elections?
6 Is the concept of a 'two-candidate' ('two-party') vote valid?
7 Why did Labor win the 1993 election?
8 Did the 1993 election produce a mandate for the Keating government?

Chapter four

VOTERS AND VOTING BEHAVIOUR

The Constitution of the USA starts with the words 'We, the people...', emphasising that the polity and all of its institutions are responsible to the citizens. While the Australian Constitution does not state the sovereignty of the people, the whole construct of representative and responsible government nevertheless rests on that assumption. It follows then that voters and their votes are key components of the Australian political system. The electors produce the representatives who act for them, who form governments and oppositions on the basis of the support given in elections to the various candidates and political parties. It is therefore important to ask 'What makes voters tick'?

STUDYING VOTERS

The study of aggregate electoral patterns and of the voting patterns of groups and individuals is an important means of analysing the linkages in the processes of representation. The Australian electoral systems offer close to the maximum possible degree of citizen participation in political life in general, and in electoral politics in particular. Do the citizens avail themselves of such opportunities? Do they play a full role in elections and in the representation process? What roles do political parties play in the process of electoral choice? What are the major influences on voters?

Elections are critical events in liberal democracies. Governments change as a result of elections, and social and economic policies can be significantly altered. The policies of the government, the programmes which were inaugurated or abandoned, were different after the 1972 (Whitlam–Labor), 1975 (Fraser–Liberal) and 1983 (Hawke–Labor) elections. And State elections can be equally important. The Tasmanian election of 1989 which resulted in the unique Labor–Green Independent alliance government produced a new set of policies for that State. Important sections and groups in society attach great importance to elections marked by the effort and money they put into the campaigns. On the other hand, a 'crude' Marxist would have a different view, along the lines that the people, the oppressed class, are permitted now and again to decide which members of the oppressing ruling class should be in parliament to oppress them. Few of the represented and representatives would agree.

The most readily accessible database for a study of voters is the results of elections. These tell us what happened, who won and who lost. But they tell us nothing about why it happened. They show the patterns of aggregate party choice which were discussed in the previous chapter. But we need different sources of information to establish the 'why' of voting behaviour. The main basis for modern studies of voting behaviour is the sample survey. People, selected at random, form a sample of the population which is then used to attempt to understand individual and group political behaviour. Interviews with these respondents seek a range of information predictions, tracking of voter opinion over time, political attitudes and preferences, and explanations for political behaviour. Such studies have become increasingly sophisticated, and are a major aspect of the campaigns and strategies of candidates and political parties, and the prime source of data for psephologists.

Such data are the bases for the generalisations in this chapter. But a *caveat* is necessary. In the first place, the study of voting behaviour is often based on what people tell interviewers. Hence, any conclusions drawn assume that the respondents have been open and honest about their opinions. Second, much of the data available are from a sample of the population, and we must be cautious about extrapolations to the population as a whole, and even more cautious about making any firm statements about the political behaviour of individuals. Finally, we must remember that most people's memories are relatively short, and that the electoral population is constantly changing;

conclusions about patterns of voting behaviour may be affected by new events, new personalities and by changes in the social and economic environment.

Before we turn to the Australian voter, it is worthwhile outlining some of the theories of voting which have emerged from various studies over time and across nations.

1 The *adjudicating* voter model suggested that electors considered the campaigns as consumer marketing exercises. Voters examined the products in the political supermarket and chose the one they wanted. The problem with this model was that many, if not most, people went into a campaign with a strong brand loyalty—their party identification. They had decided how they were going to vote.
2 The *social group* voter model emerged when it became obvious that the way people voted was strongly related to the various types of social and economic groups to which they belonged. There were obvious correlations between voting behaviour and such aspects as class, income, ethnicity, education, religion, urban or rural residence and other social cleavages. The problem was that not all members of a socio-economic group voted the same way, and patterns of electoral choice within a group varied over time.
3 The *ideological* voter model proposed that peoples' attitudes were the most important aspects. This emphasises three major influences: the strength of the individual's commitment to and identification with an ideology and a political party; the effect of the issues in the election; attitudes to the candidates and party leaders.

The problem is that none of the models of voting behaviour offers a means of explaining, beyond doubt, why people voted in a certain way. None provides a certain method of predicting the results of a future election. Psephology will always remain an inexact science.

THE 'IDEAL' VOTER

The classical democratic theorists based their support for representative democracy on the belief that, if given the opportunity to be involved, the citizens would react in a positive manner. What, then, was the expectation of the 'Ideal' voter? Has that expectation changed? What does psephology say about voters in practice?

The expectation remains the same today as it was in the time of the classical theorists. Democracy expects that voters will play a full role in the electoral process. It demands that voters should be informed about politics, and especially about the issues and events of the

Ideal voter of the 1990s?

elections. Voters should be aware of the political scene, and motivated to keep in touch with events. They should be open-minded, willing and able to consider all views, opinions and programmes, and able to come to a rational decision. Finally, the voter should be discussive, involved in constant discussions of political matters with others, seeking to come to an aware, informed decision after considering all the options.

Few voters match this ideal picture. For most voters, politics, even at election time, is not a matter of primary concern. For most people participation in politics is not attractive; only about 4 per cent of Australian adults belong to political parties. Many Australians have low levels of political information and knowledge, little interest in politics, are not motivated to be involved, and are far from open-minded. The questions for this chapter, then, are: why are many, if not most, Australians apathetic? Is there reason for concern about this? What effect does it have on the electoral and political processes, especially for representation and responsibility? If apathy is rife, how do people decide for whom to vote?

PATTERNS OF ELECTORAL SUPPORT

As the previous chapter showed, the most obvious feature of the history of Australian elections has been the remarkable stability of support for the entrenched political parties. These data, alone, pose questions about Australians as 'ideal' voters; if the voters were open-mindedly adjudicating, then it is surprising that the overwhelming majority, over three generations, have come down with such consistent and stable choices.

One explanation for the stability of aggregate electoral patterns is that party identification is strong in Australia. As one observer put it (Aitkin 1982:1)

> the shape of Australian politics has been largely unchanged since 1910 ... the causes of this stability are to be found in the adoption, by millions of Australians then and since, of relatively unchanging feelings of loyalty to one or other of the Australian parties.

Party identification, for most voters, provides the major means by which they interpret and make sense of political events, issues, leaders and of the accusations and counter-accusations which constantly flow between them, especially via the media.

The relative stability of patterns of party identification is emphasised by the findings of three national surveys (Graetz and McAllister 1988:268). Over three surveys, over 15 years, more than 70 per cent of the respondents claimed 'fairly' or 'very' strong partisanship. These data provide a major part of the explanation for the stability of the party system and of aggregate election results. Strong partisans are unlikely to change their votes; those with weaker or no party identification are more likely to cross the party lines. And these potentially swinging voters are the focus of all political parties. Find them and convince them and success is probable.

Table 4.1: *Strength of partisanship, 1967–1990 (%)*

	1967	1979	1987	1990	1967–1990
L–NP					
Very strong	27	29	19	19	–8
Fairly, Not very	73	71	81	81	+8
ALP					
Very strong	37	33	21	17	–20
Fairly, Not very	63	67	79	83	+20

Source: Adapted from Stewart and Ward 1992:126

On the other hand, elections in the 1980s and 1990s have shown increasing evidence of volatility and instability. The 1988 election in New South Wales and the 1989 election in Tasmania showed, in comparison with past patterns, significant swings, as did the 1990 federal election. Table 4.1 suggests that part of the explanation may be a decrease in the proportion of strong partisans. If this trend continues, then political parties will face a new and much more challenging electoral environment.

There has been an erosion of the 'very strong' identifiers between 1967 and 1990, most apparent among Labor identifiers. But this is still 'at the margins'; it is clear that a majority of voters retain an identification with political parties, and the overwhelming majority of these cast their votes in accord with that party identification. Australia is still a long way from the 'collapse of party' which has occurred in the USA.

FACTORS AFFECTING VOTING BEHAVIOUR

The factors which, at any election, may have a bearing on electoral behaviour, can be loosely divided into two main types. Long-term factors are those which are related to the individual's party identification, the effects of political socialisation and the groups to which he or she belongs—class, occupation, religion, race and place of residence (urban or rural) may all be important. At the same time, short-term factors which concern only one specific election may be important, and the student would need to take into account the events, issues, personalities and emphases of the election campaign and attempt to establish the effects these had on the individual. Such factors as the issues brought forward by the parties, the nature and style of the campaigns, the images of the parties produced by the media, the role and impact of the party leaders and events in and outside of Australia all could have some effect on the voter's final decision.

Every election includes short-term influences on the voter, which have the potential to reinforce or to change the party choice, if not the party identification of the individual. Examples abound in recent history: the intrusion of the Petrov Affair in 1954; the issue of the McMahon leadership in 1972; the Vietnam War in 1966; the change of leader from Hayden to Hawke in 1983; the 'Joh for PM' campaign in 1987.

Given the multiplicity of long-term and short-term factors which can influence voting behaviour, the analyst needs a means of organising the multitude of issues, events, trends, social cleavages and

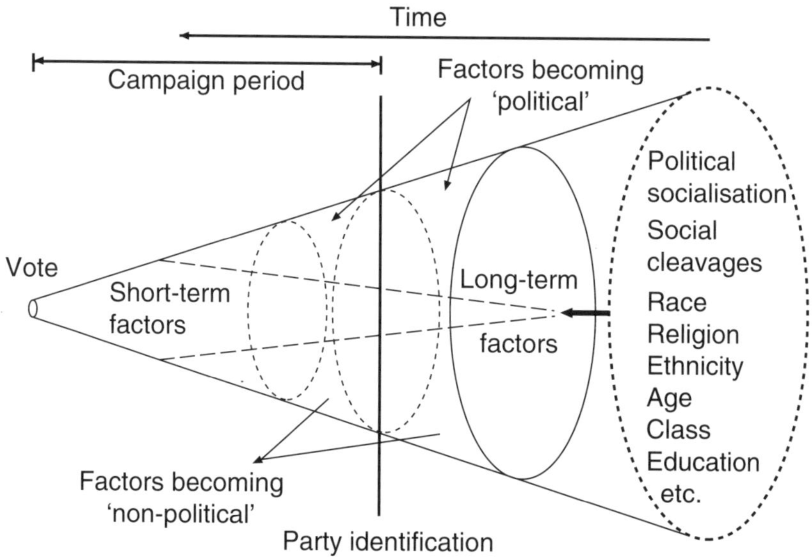

Figure 4.1 *The funnel of causality*

Source: Modified from A. Campbell et al., *The American Voter*, Wiley, Michigan, 1964.

patterns of party identification which are present in and around an election. The diagram above suggests one such means. It was proposed originally for the analysis of American elections, but has been adapted to Australia. This model of analysing an election is in the shape of a funnel, with the tip of the funnel representing the election. Back in the funnel are the long-term influences on voting behaviour, starting with the formation of attitudes to political parties in early life. Such long-term factors as party identification and social group characteristics, which are usually taken as affecting both party identification and voting intentions, are at the mouth of the funnel. Closer to the election are the short-term factors of the campaign which may affect the voting decision. As the campaign starts, the individual voter will already carry a predisposition to one party or another. Once the campaign gets under way, a host of other, short-term, factors will influence the voter. Some political events, personalities and factors will become issues, by means of the policy speeches and subsequent decisions by the parties themselves or by simple intrusion into the campaign via media or word of mouth. Other events, personalities and factors which one or more parties may have planned to make into issues working either for them or against the opposition, will become non-issues and unimportant in the campaign.

THE SOCIAL BASES OF ELECTORAL BEHAVIOUR

In some countries, notably in Western Europe, it appears that every possible social and economic cleavage in society has produced a political party. Most European nations are multi-party in elections and in parliaments. In comparison, Australia appears to have a relatively stable party system, dominated by a 'two-partism' of Labor versus non-Labor and relatively stable patterns of party support.

One explanation could be that some European societies are deeply divided by religion, language, class, region, ethnicity, and so on, and that the fragmentation of parties reflects this. To what extent does Australia show evidence of social cleavages, and to what extent are these reflected in the party system and in electoral behaviour? On the evidence of the history of the party system, there appear to be three obvious cases of clear social bases of electoral behaviour. Since 1910, there have been two major parties, Labor and Liberal, and this could suggest that the most important political cleavage in Australian society is socio-economic or class-based. The emergence of the Country/National Party and its stability over time could suggest a cleavage based on urban versus rural. Finally, it could be suggested that the existence of the Democratic Labor Party for twenty years from the mid-1950s was evidence of a religious cleavage.

CLASS

If we depend only on the rhetoric of the two major parties, at least until the 1970s, then electoral politics has been dominated by 'class'. But what do we mean by 'class'? For the purpose of this chapter, the term is used in two restricted senses:

1 objective class—a classification based on the occupations of people
2 subjective class—the class to which people see themselves as belonging.

To a Marxist, not only are these two senses really the same, but to ask whether class is the basis and focus of the whole political system is to state a self-evident truth; class is the natural, in fact the *only* real, basis of politics, conflict and division in a capitalist society. To a non-Marxist though, the explanation is less deterministic; if class is the dominant social and political cleavage, then it is so because other socio-economic and socio-cultural cleavages have not developed with sufficient salience to crosscut class. This was clearly the case until the

Second World War, and arguably until the 1970s. As one observer (Epstein 1980:6) put it,

> little stood in the way of Australian class identification. Neither regional or ethnic cleavages, nor a large population of small farm owners, worked significantly against the solidarity of manual workers, or against the response of middle and upper classes. Perhaps this is to say that the sense of economic class became strong primarily because of the absence of other salient cleavages in Australia.

But how strong was class in terms of partisanship? The findings of a survey in the 1960s (Aitkin 1977:130) suggests that the link was far from complete. And when the three variables—objective class, subjective class and party identification—are brought together, the connections require further questions.

Two preliminary conclusions can be derived. First, class is apparently an important basis of party preference. Nearly three-quarters of those in non-manual occupations who also saw themselves as members of the middle class identified with the Liberal–Country coalition. Of those in manual occupations who saw themselves as working class, 70 per cent identified with the Labor Party. Here, then, is some explanation for the stability of voting patterns, and of the stability of the party system itself.

But a second important factor was evident. The link of class, party preference and vote was well short of an exact relationship. For

Table 4.3: *Party identification, by subjective class (percentage of respondents)*

Party identification	Middle class	Working class
Liberal–CP	70	34
ALP	27	62
DLP	3	4

Table 4.4: *Party identification by occupational and subjective class (%)*

Occupational and subjective class	Total	L–CP	ALP	DLP
Non-manual workers				
See self as middle class	34	73	24	3
See self as working class	12	52	44	4
Manual workers				
See self as middle class	21	56	42	2
See self as working class	33	26	70	4

Source: Aitkin and Kahan 1974:455

example, a quarter of those whom the Labor Party could expect to be its strongest supporters—those manual workers who saw themselves as working class—voted for the Liberal–Country coalition and a quarter of those whom the Liberal Party would expect to be its strongest supporters—the non-manual people who saw themselves as middle class—voted for the Labor Party.

In the 1980s, the linkage weakened still further, and to analyse this we need to refine the concept a little more. If we refer to class and electoral politics, we can be talking of any one, or all, of three relatively distinct meanings. We may be referring to an *appeal* for the votes of a class; we may refer to electoral *support* based on class; we may be referring to the representatives actually *representing* class interests. The generalisation that Australian politics are class politics combines all three.

Since 1967, when Gough Whitlam began the process of reforming the Labor Party, and with its greatest impetus under the Hawke leadership, allied with Labor leaders in the states, the ALP has changed its *appeal* to, and increased its support from, the middle classes. Further, it can hardly be said to be *representing* only working-class interests in the 1980s and 1990s. The effects of this change on the party system will be explored further in later chapters, but the impact in electoral politics and voting behaviour has been significant. The Australian electorate in the 1990s is more volatile than ever before, and the salience of party identification, while still there, seems weaker.

RELIGION

Religious denomination was connected with party politics in Australia from their earliest beginnings. In the late nineteenth and early twentieth centuries, Catholics in Australian society were a minority in a political and social system dominated by English and Scottish Protestants. They were generally Irish, poor, and in manual occupations. It is not surprising, then, that the early Labor party was strongly Catholic in its membership, both in the organisation and in parliament, and that Catholic electoral support for the ALP was strong.

The Democratic Labor Party, which emerged from the ALP split in the mid-1950s, had the potential to change this link. The DLP was led by Catholics, its membership was overwhelmingly Catholic and the majority of its supporters were Catholic. But while the DLP was a party of Catholics, it was not a Catholic party. It did not succeed in attracting the majority of Catholic voters. Three factors are obvious from Table 4.5. First, that religious denomination does seem to have some influence on party choice; second, that the DLP identifiers were overwhelmingly drawn from Catholics; third, that the majority of

Table 4.5: *Religion and party identification (percentage of respondents)*

	Catholic	Anglican	Methodist	Other Protestant	Presby-terian
ALP	51	42	40	35	29
Liberal–NP	38	58	60	64	70
DLP	11	*	*	1	1
Other	*	*	*	*	*

* = less than 0.5%

Source: Adapted from Aitkin 1977:166.

Catholics in the sample still identified with the ALP. In fact, the DLP all but disappeared from Australian politics in 1974, suggesting even more strongly that it was not able to effectively politicise a religious cleavage.

Yet religion has remained a factor in electoral politics. The Call to Australia Party contests elections and has won seats in New South Wales. Issues such as divorce law reform, homosexuality and abortion law reform have all mobilised religious-based groups. Even so, the failure of the DLP to form a Catholic party suggests that the religious cleavage is not a powerful one.

AN URBAN–RURAL DIVISION?

Tension between urban dwellers, especially those in the capital cities, and people in the rural areas, has been an important part of Australia's political history. The formation of a Country Party by rural people because of a strong feeling that neither Labor nor Liberal (then Nationalist) parties were adequately representing rural interests was evidence of such tension. Patterns of party support in the last twenty

Table 4.6: *Party identification, rural–urban (percentage of respondents)*

	Farmers	Urban business	Farm workers	Urban unskilled
Liberal	44	70	20	37
National	37	0	25	1
(Lib–Nat)	(81)	(70)	(45)	(38)
ALP	14	29	50	59
Other	5	1	5	3

Source: Aitkin and Kahan 1974:421

Some issues reveal animosity between country and city dwellers.

years and recent pressure group activity by rural interests, suggest that the urban–rural division remains a continuing feature of Australian politics.

The Australian electoral system has also been a focus of an urban–rural cleavage. Australia is one of the most urbanised and centralised nations on earth, with almost 90 per cent of the population living in urban areas. Further, almost 70 per cent of Australia's population live in seven major cities—the six state capitals and the federal capital of Canberra. Recent elections have supported and emphasised the historical evidence of an urban–rural cleavage reflected in electoral patterns. The ALP depends on urban areas for the bulk of its support while the Liberal–National Party coalition virtually owns the extra-metropolitan areas. One of the reasons for this is the apparent tendency for many rural manual workers and working-class residents to identify with non-Labor parties and to have a weaker class orientation to politics (see Table 4.6).

ETHNICITY

The overwhelming British-born nature of Australian immigration for nearly two centuries has been transformed by successive waves of immigration since 1945. In the 1947 census, 90 per cent of the Australian population was Australian born. By 1961, this figure had been reduced to 83 per cent, and by the 1980s to 76 per cent. However, at the 1986 census, almost 40 per cent of the population who were born

Table 4.7: *Party identification by birthplace*

Party identification	Australia	Britain	Southern Europe	Eastern Europe	Northern Europe
Lib–NCP	45	34	29	50	55
ALP	44	52	57	37	33
Other	3	3	4	2	7
None/DK	8	11	10	11	5
Total	100	100	100	100	100
(N)	(15960)	(200)	(49)	(46)	(42)

Source: Aitkin 1982:335

overseas still came from the UK. As such, their political experiences would have been drawn from a party system not unlike that of Australia and dominated by Labor and Conservative parties. In fact they are stronger Labor voters than the Australian born.

Approximately one million migrants of non-British origin, mainly from Europe and especially from Italy, Germany and Greece, have had a marked impact on Australian society and its patterns of social behaviour. But their impact on politics in general, and on patterns of voting, has not been as great. To some degree, this relative similarity of voting patterns is derived from the occupational background of migrants—there was a dominance of semi-skilled and unskilled occupations, especially in the early post-war wave of immigrants. But despite the working-class bias among the migrants, the overall patterns of electoral behaviour of non-British migrants suggest a tendency for slightly lower support for the Labor Party than among Australian-born voters except among Southern Europeans. Part of the explanation for this seems to be the communist issue, based on the nature of the political environment in some of the source countries and the apparent success of some anti-Labor electoral propaganda in painting the Labor Party as quasi-communist.

GENDER

For most of Australia's electoral history, there has been a crucial gender gap in patterns of party support, a differential of around 10 per cent between men and women. Labor suffered consistently from the long-term tendency for women to be more inclined than men to vote for the conservative parties. The ALP recognised this, noting in its 1978 internal self-assessment (ALP 1979:31), with an understatement, that 'the appeal the Party has for women may not be all it could be', and that the differential was 'a formidable handicap'.

Table 4.8: *Party identification and gender, 1967–1990 (percentage of respondents)*

	1967		1979		1984		1990	
	L-N	ALP	L-N	ALP	L-N	ALP	L-N	ALP
Male	53	44	47	50	40	57	45	43
Female	63	35	54	43	43	53	44	41

Source: Graetz and McAllister 1988:282; McAllister 1992

The evidence of the difference, and for a significant change in the 1970s and 1980s, is in data from national surveys. The author of two of the surveys, Don Aitkin, left no doubt about the importance of the shifts shown in Table 4.8:

> Of all the changes that have taken place in the Australian electorate in the past 20 years, the most profound has been in the political outlook of women (*Bulletin,* 22 May 1984).

By the 1984 survey, the differential had all but disappeared, especially through a particularly strong Labor identification among younger women. We can suggest a number of causes of this change; the changing status of women in the society, the growing importance of issues concerning women, the increased participation of women in the labour force and the commitment by the Whitlam, Hayden and Hawke Labor parties to 'women's issues'.

A GENERATION GAP?

While the realignment of the women's vote is a very significant factor, an even stronger realignment in the former patterns of party allegiance across the age groups may be of more long-term importance. Aitkin and Kahan (1974:458) point out that on the basis of the 1960s data:

> In the 1930s and 1940s, Labor pulled disproportionately from the pool of new voters. Since the early 1950s, on the other hand, the balance has swung away.

In the 1970s, 1980s and 1990s, the balance swung back, and further than before. Labor support among the 18 to 24-year-old voters has changed from 39 per cent in 1967 to 49 per cent in 1979, to a massive 62 per cent in 1984 (Graetz and McAllister 1988:279). These data suggest that Labor may be on the threshold of capturing a solid majority of a generation of voters despite the economic situation and especially high unemployment among the young.

A KALEIDOSCOPE OF PREFERENCES

One possible explanation for the leakages from a class-based political system is that while class is the most important political cleavage in Australia, it is a relatively weak cleavage and is affected to some degree (either strengthened or weakened) by such socio-economic variables as religion, age, sex, ethnicity and geographical region. In the late 1970s, even this qualified generalisation about the class basis of Australian electoral politics began to come under question. There have been election results in the 1980s and 1990s which have suggested that the stability of the party system, and of patterns of electoral support, is weakening.

Analysts have pointed to an apparent new volatility in the electorate, an apparent willingness of more people to cross the lines of party identification. Some recent election results support this argument. The swing against Labor in 1975 was one of the largest in recent history; over 12 per cent of the Australian electorate, almost three-quarters of a million voters, abandoned the traditional parties for the fledgling Australian Democrats in 1977; the 1979 election in South Australia showed swings of up to 24 per cent; there were unprecedented swings against Labor in its safe seats in the 1988 New South Wales election and there was the shift to Green Independents in Tasmania in 1989. All these support the contention that the electorate is less stable and more volatile and that traditional patterns of party support are breaking down. A typical, and valid, interpretation of the history of Australian electoral politics, at least until the late 1960s, was that in Australia, as in Britain and New Zealand, 'the primacy of occupational class as the rock on which the party system rests and as the major influence upon electoral behaviour, is firmly established' (Aitkin and Kahan 1974:477). Such a view has become increasingly under challenge. Increasingly, as the Australian electorate becomes more educated, more affluent, more mobile, more middle class in economic terms and ambitions, the previous stable bases of party support are being eroded.

THE APATHY OF AUSTRALIAN VOTERS

What is apathy? To one theorist (Mannheim 1975:112–13): 'Apathy refers most simply to an absence of concern with the outcomes of political affairs'. Even in the USA, where political participation is taken as a public good, and political education in schools is emphasised, the accepted description of the average citizen is one whose political knowledge is generally low, one who, even during election campaigns, is unlikely to be aware of specific issues and who seldom engages in much political discussion; when he/she does it is likely to be with people who agree with him/her.

What of Australia? All studies conclude that Australia's political culture is passive. For most people, government is there to do things for and to people; it is not seen as something that people should be interested and involved in, unless the products are not satisfactory. Very few people, less than 4 per cent of the adult population, join political parties and even fewer actively work for a party. As a rough calculation, the population can be divided into three main groups:

1 about a quarter are aware of (and fewer are active in) politics
2 about 40 per cent are a passive audience of politics
3 about a third are indifferent and uninterested.

There is a low level of knowledge about politics in the Australian community. One survey found that, for two-thirds of the people interviewed, 'politics is simply a vacancy, an unused space'; they represent, in the evangelical phrase, 'the Great Unreached'. Another concluded that 'most electors have a very limited knowledge ... in some respects they are almost incredibly ignorant'. A summary of survey findings suggests that most Australian voters are not informed, and show a low level of knowledge of personalities, institutions and issues. Few people know the names of their own local members, of the candidates at elections, or even to which party they belong. Many do not distinguish between state and national politics and many who vote for a particular party have no idea of the policies of their party or of the issues at an election. The great majority of people are firmly committed to a particular political party and tend to gravitate to their party and its propaganda whenever any political decision is required of them. Most people tend to use their chosen party as a fallback position for any political question or issue; 'my party, right or wrong'. Overall, a picture emerges which differs markedly from the ideal democratic citizen. Of course there are people in the Australian society who do match the ideal. But they are in a tiny minority.

What factors are responsible for this situation? Some general influences can be suggested. Australia's history has been relatively quiet, with a relatively affluent society insulated from many of the serious problems of the world starvation, famine, constant warfare and tension. With a minimal amount of internal conflict, Australia has offered to its citizens a lifestyle which has not encouraged (or forced) large numbers of people to dissent from the system to seek new or radically different solutions. Hence, most people have been satisfied with the political and economic system and have been satisfied with what they have been able to obtain from the system.

Only recently have some education systems allowed, let alone encouraged, the teaching of politics in schools. In Victoria, South

Australia and Western Australia, a course in politics is fully established. But there is little opportunity for all trainee electors to study their own Australian political system, let alone be acquainted with wider aspects of politics. It does seem illogical for society to expect a person who turns eighteen to suddenly become an informed, rational voter without any prior education. A further reason may derive from the effectiveness of one aspect of political socialisation—the dependence on, and commitment to a political party by the majority of Australians. Many people leave politics to their party, the policies and practices of which they will support, come what may. The development of the suburban society has also been suggested as a reason, if not for apathy in the broadest sense, at least for the evident lack of participation. According to Elcock (1976:69–70), there are four characteristics which a good citizen in a liberal democracy should possess:

1. He/she must know a certain amount about politics and recognise that this knowledge is of some importance.
2. He/she must believe that he/she can have some influence upon the course of political events.
3. He/she must believe that he/she will normally get fair and reasonable treatment from the government, both in policy making and in his individual contacts with its servants.
4. He/she should hold political institutions and actors in a certain regard.

Too many Australians seem to lack one or even all of these characteristics. That is a problem for our system of representative and responsible democracy.

This broad picture of apathy, depressing to those who seek a more participatory public, may be undergoing change. The results of national and state elections in the last decade suggest a new volatility in what was, in the past, an electorate with remarkably stable allegiances to parties. Whether this is due to greater awareness and the development of the thinking voter, or whether it is due to vacillations caused by the hip pocket nerve is a matter for conjecture. But as Australians become more aware of events, tensions and rapid social changes in other parts of the world, and especially in our own region, it may be that the effects of this communication from outside may engender change in the patterns of voting behaviour and electoral interest and involvement. Especially if the formerly stable socio-economic bases of party support are in the process of being eroded, then all political parties will have to react to, and perhaps modify themselves to suit, the new electoral environment.

At a broader level, if it is the case that the majority of Australian citizens do not accord with the 'ideal voter', do not accord with the demands of the theory of representation in a liberal democracy, then what should be done? There are three types of prescriptions suggested by various thinkers on the subject. To some, the classical democratic theory is outmoded. What is obvious is that voters are not, and can never be, the model of the 'ideal voter'. Hence, the theory of voters should be rewritten to match the real world. A second position is that the voters are not at fault; they have the innate ability to become 'ideal voters', but the system of politics in which they live does not encourage them to do so. Hence, the system needs changing to more open government, less party discipline, political education for all, a better media, and so on. A third position holds that the classical democratic voter is an ideal, a set of goals to which every democratic society should aim. The fact that Australia has not yet achieved that is no reason to abandon the aim and the ideal. The problem is how the system, the practices, and the processes in Australian representative democracy be reformed so as to move in the direction of the goals and values.

DOCUMENTS

4.1 AUSTRALIA: A SUBJECT POLITICAL CULTURE?

Source: Emy, H.V. 1974, *The Politics of Australian Democracy*, Macmillan, Melbourne, p. 355.

Australia comes nearest to the pattern of orientations which Almond and Verba classified as a subject-participant political culture. In such a cultural mix, most people are still oriented primarily towards the output aspects of the system (that is, towards the results and benefits they expect and demand from the government), and relatively few people have developed a strong orientation towards the input aspects (that is, they don't see the system in terms of their reciprocal duties and obligations as active, participatory citizens) but still adopt the passive role associated with a subject culture. Indeed, a distinct emphasis remains upon the subject culture, for although most people are aware of specialised governmental authority (that is, of 'structural differentiation'), can be effectively oriented towards it, and can evaluate its legitimacy, they still show only a limited political competence. They have little sense of their own political significance (their ability to influence policy-making procedures), they do not seek information, and government (and press) do not dispense much information. Overall, the Australian system still shows periodically strong paternalistic tendencies which may seriously restrict the experience and self-confidence of the small minority of active participants.

4.2 PARTICIPATION AND NON-PARTICIPATION

Source: Dahl, R.A. 1976, *Modern Political Analysis*, Prentice-Hall, pp. 103–7.

1 You are less likely to get involved in politics if you place a low value on the rewards expected from political involvement relative to the rewards you expect from other kinds of activity.
2 You are less likely to get involved in politics if you think there is no significant difference in the alternatives before you and, consequently, that what you do won't matter.
3 You are less likely to become involved in politics if you think that what you do won't matter because you can't significantly change the outcome anyway.
4 You are less likely to become involved in politics if you believe that the outcome will be relatively satisfactory to you without your involvement.
5 You are less likely to get involved in politics if you feel that your knowledge is too limited for you to be effective.
6 Finally, the greater the obstacles placed in your way, the less likely you are to become involved in politics.

4.3 WHY APATHY?

Source: Mannheim, J.B. 1976, *The Politics Within*, Prentice-Hall, New York, pp. 112–13.

Apathy refers most simply to an absence of concern with the outcomes of political affairs. The apathetic individual is in effect the end case of the low-involvement political actor of whom we have spoken earlier. He makes no political judgements, he establishes no political preferences, and he maintains no stake in the flow of political events. He remains, in other words, politically inert. If he is cynical by nature, he may evolve to a state of alienation; if he is lazy by nature, to a less purposeful state of aloofness. In either event, he will disparage political activity as an undertaking of dubious utility ...

No single explanation can account for the adoption by an individual of minimal levels of political involvement. Indeed, political inactivity may derive from any of a large number of highly individualised experiences, some, all, or none of which might be expressly political in nature. Nevertheless, we are able to identify at least three underlying factors pertaining to choice and circumstances which may help us better to understand particular non-active patterns of behaviour. These factors include the ability, the opportunity, and the preference for participation in politics.

Many individuals, for example, may lack the time or the skills requisite for political activity in their particular society. They may, in a very real sense, be unable to engage in politics. A person who holds down two jobs to support a family, for instance, might be less able to become politically active than a well-paid professional worker, not because of any purposeful avoidance of or disinterest in political affairs, but simply because he has less available leisure time to distribute among his non-work interests. Similarly, a person who is functionally illiterate or physically handicapped or an individual who has not had the opportunity to develop certain group activity skills may be reduced to a role of inactivity not because of a negative inclination toward politics, but because of a fundamental inability either to comprehend or to fully respond to political stimuli.

4.4 'EVERYONE VOTES AND NOTHING HAPPENS'

Source: Sun, Sydney, 10 October 1969. Quoted in Mayer, H. and Nelson, H. (eds) 1973, *Australian Politics: A Third Reader,* Longman Cheshire, Melbourne, p. 336.

Today's question: Are you interested in the coming Federal elections?

Linda Davies, 17, receptionist: 'No, they are dull. Politics just seem to go on and on. Nothing changes. Everyone votes and nothing happens. Politicians don't seem to try to interest people. You're not going to be much better off no matter who you vote in.'

Vicki Gray, 20, receptionist: 'Just a little. But the government never seems to change and nothing happens. I would like to see Labor win, so that we could see what they could do. Any change in Australian politics would be a change for the better. I don't listen to every policy speech but I do make an effort to know what both parties are saying.'

Dierdre Gray, 16, typist-clerk: 'Not really. Nothing exciting ever happens. No one seems to care about politics in Australia. We never talk about politics. The only things I know about elections come from school and even then we didn't talk about them often.'

Anne Armitage, 19, hairdresser: 'No, I'm just not interested. Whoever is in power is going to be blamed for what's going wrong. That's all there is to politics. Having rallies or parades like the Americans would just be ridiculous. Who cares about politics? I don't think I'll ever bother about voting.'

Louise McNeilly, 18, secretary: 'No. There is nothing exciting about Australian politics. In America they have rallies which make it interesting to young people, but I can't see that happening here. The same party has been in power too long. When I am old enough to vote I will make an effort to find out a bit about political policies.'

4.5 EXTRACTS FROM AUSTRALIAN ELECTORAL OFFICE RESEARCH REPORT, 1983

The purpose of the research covered by this report was to acquire detailed information on the beliefs and attitudes about enrolment in order to provide necessary guidelines for the development of an integrated information campaign.

Twelve discussion groups were held with 17 1/2 to 21-year-olds and six more with those between 21 and 30 years of age.

The single most important reason why young people fail to register to vote is because they do not see any direct link between the Government or Government institutions and their own lives. They become apathetic and will not take the steps necessary to become enrolled.

The same apathy is responsible for their failure to acquire any real political knowledge leading many young people to feel incapable of recording a meaningful vote. They feel that if they can't vote wisely there is little point in bothering to enrol.

Central to an understanding of enrolment failure in young Australians is the realisation that the majority of this group reach 18 years without any feelings toward or knowledge of our political system and what it means to live in a democracy.

Politics is a thing apart yet another of the institutions of our society that controls us while we can have no effect on it. As the young people see it there is a wide gap between these institutions and 'me' and they have no feeling of participation or belonging associated with the electoral system nor any belief that anything that they can do would have any effect. In short the vote has no personal relevance.

More than any other single factor, the lack of any perceived direct relevance of the political system (and, equally, their concomitantly perceived inability to influence the course of political events) forms the basis of electoral inactivity amongst the young.

The group as a whole can be further subdivided into five main types. These are:

- Apathetic—politically aware
- Apathetic—politically unaware
- Seekers for enlightenment
- Afraid of retribution
- Hostiles.

ISSUES FOR DISCUSSION

1 Do you think voters today are more aware of national or local candidates and issues at elections? Give reasons for your answer.
2 Which factor do you think has most influenced your political party preference—your family, your school, your friends, your independent thinking? What advantages do you see in 'independent' voting? What advantages lie in choosing and working with a particular party?
3 What were the main reasons Labor won the 1993 election?
4 The Labor Party originally set out to be the party to represent the working class. Has the change in Australian society—the growth of the middle class and the contraction of the working class—caused problems for the Labor Party?
5 Do recent voting patterns suggest that traditional party loyalties are breaking down?
6 Why was the DLP most effective in Victoria?
7 Is apathy 'the cancer of democracy'? (See Document 4.3.)
8 Would voluntary voting increase the interest and involvement of the average Australian voter?
9 Why are most Australians apathetic? (See Documents 4.2, 4.3.)
10 Is your class a collection of ideal democratic citizens?
11 Are the attitudes in Document 4.4 common?
12 Analyse and explain Document 4.5.
13 Analyse the recent election results in your local seat. Is it safe for one or other of the parties? Is it a marginal seat? What effect do you think this would have on the type of election campaign in this area?
14 Using the list of factors affecting party success, explain the last election in your state.

Chapter five

AUSTRALIA'S POLITICAL PARTIES: THE 'ENGINES' OF REPRESENTATIVE DEMOCRACY?

Most people, when they think of politics in Australia, think first in terms of political parties. The mass media, more often than not, report on the positions taken by political parties on various issues in more depth than they report on the issues themselves. Most Australians view politics almost exclusively in terms of 'their' party. The most obvious and visible actors in the Australian political system are the political parties.

This tendency is not unique to Australia. Any study of the political system of any modern nation must stress the role of political parties. In all Western democracies, political parties have become part of a way of life and it is difficult to imagine elections, parliaments and the organisation of political matters in the USA, Britain, Canada and other nations without parties. But the evidence suggests that parties are more ubiquitous, more salient, more internally cohesive, and more dominant in the political processes in Australia than in other democratic nations. If so, we need to closely examine the natures of the major players in the party arena and the roles they should play, and do play, in the processes of representation and democracy.

The existence of parties as such is not a new phenomenon; defined as a more or less cohesive group of people involved in attempting to control some type of body of authority, parties have been in existence at least since Roman times. But the *political* party is a *recent* invention, with origins in eighteenth-century Britain. The nature of political parties and party systems provides a diverse and complex picture, one which can be studied in many ways and from many approaches: ideologies and policies, the social composition of party members and their supporters, the internal structure of the organisational wings of the parties, and the ways in which the parties interact and relate within the system.

This chapter examines a number of aspects of political parties in Australia: emergence and development; the financial and group supports of parties; structure and organisation including the all-important issues of selection and control of candidates; the relationship between ideology, policy and practices of the parties; campaign styles and some general comments about the Australian party system. The emphasis is on the two major parties, Labor and Liberal, on the grounds that these two parties, since 1910, have been the only two serious contestants for the control of national government. Two other parties are examined in less detail: the National Party, due to its continuing influence within the non-Labor coalition; and the Australian Democrats who merit examination on the grounds of their electoral support in recent elections and the unusual features of their organisation and ideology. Mention will be made of other minor parties.

EMERGENCE AND DEVELOPMENT

Australian politics underwent a remarkable transformation in the twenty-odd years prior to 1910. Before the 1880s, despite more than thirty years experience of self-government, the colonies had not produced a system of party politics in the modern sense of the term. Political leaders worked within the system of responsive government by means of factions—complex, variable and often hidden from the public view, but essentially personal and individualistic. By 1910, a clear transformation had taken place. In all seven parliaments, formal political parties had developed and the old faction systems had disappeared. What is more, although there have been subsequent changes in the number and names of these parties, the broader social

Charles Cameron Kingston. Colonial politics were dominated by individuals and personality factions rather than parties.

and ideological divisions they reflected and the character of the party life they established at the turn of the century remained important in setting the essential patterns of politics in Australia until today. By 1910, Australia had a two-party system in function, Labor versus Liberal Party, and despite the formation of the Country Party, the Democratic Labor Party and the Australian Democrats together with a constellation of ephemeral minor parties, the functioning Australian party system is similar in the 1990s.

The Labor Party and the Country Party both began as the political wing of an organised, sectional group *outside* parliament. The Labor Party was the creation of the various trade-union organisations in the colonies while the Country Party was formed by elements of rural industry. The Liberal Party, on the other hand, was created by a group of members *inside* parliament. The DLP and the Australian Democrats emerged following the fission of existing parties, although the latter also attracted many who were not currently members of political parties.

By federation, the Labor Party was established as a cohesive, unified and increasingly national party. At the same time, non-Labor (and anti-Labor) parties had also formed, but these were far from united in opposition to Labor. In the first federal parliament, for example, Labor members from all states shared the legislature with Free Trade, Protection and independent members. In the various states, and in

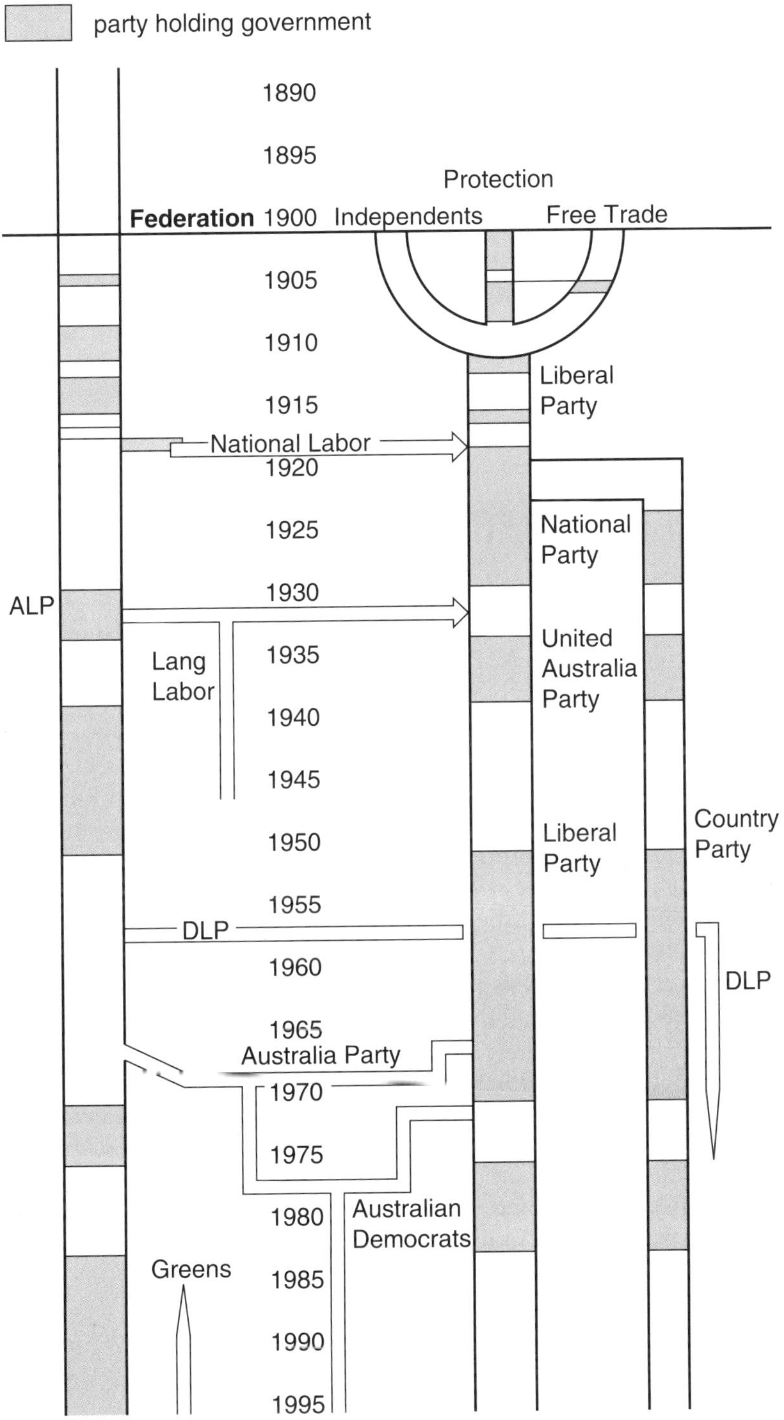

Figure 5.1 Evolution of Australian political parties

the national parliament, the following eighty years were kaleidoscopic. Alliances formed and reformed, factions and parties fought for dominance, and a varied collection of political combinations were produced. In South Australia in 1906, for example, the Labor Party was in alliance with a rural-based Liberal and Democratic Union and in opposition to an alliance of the urban Australian National League and the Farmers' and Producers' Political Association. As this first decade proceeded, however, the non-Labor factions and parties nationally gradually moved towards an alignment against Labor, a process given impetus by the election of a Labor government in 1908. This resulted in a fusion of the Protection and Free Trade parties in 1909, and by 1910, the two-party system had emerged. The major developments in the history of the party system since 1910 are shown in Figure 5.1.

AUSTRALIAN LABOR PARTY

The history of the Australian Labor Party, despite being the oldest continuously active political party in Australia, is a history of internal division and schisms. The ALP split openly and with long-term effects on three occasions: in 1916, in the early 1930s and in the mid-1950s. Each of these damaged the party electorally, aided the non-Labor side of politics, and brought long-lasting strains.

In 1916, the party split over the moves by the Labor prime minister, W. M. Hughes, to introduce conscription. The majority of the federal Labor caucus refused to support the proposal, and Hughes led many of the senior members of the federal party, and many of the state Labor politicians and members, over to the Liberal Party, which was happy to change its name to the National Party to accommodate them. Hughes continued as prime minister—a rare Australian case of national leader achieving the position under the labels of opposing parties.

The 1921 federal conference adopted as the Labor Party's objective 'the socialisation of industry, production, distribution and exchange' but immediately qualified this with the 'Blackburn declaration' in an attempt to reassure the voters: 'the party does not seek to abolish private ownership even of the instruments of production where such instrument is utilised by its owner in a socially useful manner and without exploitation.'

A second major schism occurred in 1931. The election of a Labor government in 1929 came as the depression deepened, and the party divided over the economic crisis. Scullin, who was prime minister, and five state premiers proposed cuts in salaries, pensions and government expenditure as a means of countering the depression. J. T. Lang, premier of New South Wales, rejected the Premiers' Plan,

Labor leaders. Above: Billy Hughes, John Curtin. Below: Ben Chifley, H.V. Evatt

as it was called, and was expelled from the party. On this occasion, the Labor Party split into three; one group joined the Nationalist Party to form the United Australia Party (UAP), Lang formed a separate Lang Labor Party, the remaining federal and state Labor parties were reduced virtually to impotence.

The third major split had it genesis in two of the major ideological components of the party. A strong Catholic component had played an important role in the party from its formation and Catholics became concerned as trade unions in the 1940s came under communist influence. The formation of the Catholic-based 'Movement' and 'Industrial Groups' in the unions led to tensions in unions and party. These came to a head in 1954, when Labor leader Evatt publicly attacked the Catholic-based faction, accusing them of disloyalty and subversion. In 1955, the strains culminated in the formation of the Anti-Communist Labor Party by Movement and Industrial Group members who had been expelled from the ALP. From this grew the Democratic Labor Party which played a major role in keeping Labor's electoral hopes dim, especially in Victoria and Queensland.

Except for one election in 1961, when the Menzies government had instituted a credit squeeze and Labor came within one seat of winning office, the national Labor Party was in relative limbo for twenty years following defeat in 1949. In 1969, the nadir of Labor's fortunes, no Labor government held office anywhere in Australia. In the 1960s, however, the Labor Party set out with determination to win back power. Some factors and events leading to the Labor victory in 1972 include the election of Whitlam as federal leader in 1967; the federal intervention in the Victorian branch which began to win the party more support in that important state; changes in the policy, image and structure of the party which were spearheaded by a reformed federal conference and executive; and the growing uncertainty and disunity in the Liberal Party after the resignation of Menzies.

The Whitlam Labor government was in office from 1972 to 1975 and survived a double dissolution impelled by the opposition majority in the Senate in 1974. After its defeat in the 1975 and 1977 elections, a national committee of inquiry within the party carried out a major internal reappraisal, the effects of which assisted Labor to victory in 1983.

LIBERAL PARTY OF AUSTRALIA

The modern Liberal Party of Australia was founded by R. G. Menzies in 1944, and since then it has been the major non-Labor party nationally, and in all states except Queensland. But the ancestry of the party goes back to the various quasi-parties formed in the Australian colonies in the 1890s as a reaction against the new Labor Party. From 1909 until the present day, this party has had a continuous history as the major non Labor party, although it underwent three changes of name; Liberal to 1917, Nationalist to 1931 and United Australia to 1944. The UAP was far from united, and by 1944 had become little more than a loose collection of factions with a general anti-Labor orientation. In 1944, Menzies rebuilt a political party from these fragments, and on 28 August 1945 the modern Liberal Party was formally inaugurated.

Liberal leaders. Above: S.M. Bruce, Sir Robert Menzies.
Below: William McMahon, Malcolm Fraser.

For over twenty years, the structure, organisation, style and policies of the Liberal Party were what Menzies had designed them to be. The party was an organisation designed by Menzies, as a support for Menzies and with a structure and process planned by Menzies. The party was founded on three basic tenets: that it should be federal in structure with considerable autonomy for the state organisations; that it should have a mass base and a large and broad membership; and that there should be a definite division between the mass organisation and the parliamentary wing.

Until 1972, these tenets were hardly ever questioned. In the first place, in a formal sense there was hardly a Liberal Party of *Australia* in existence; the national party was founded on, and functioned through, its state organisations. A second aspect has been a feature of the Liberal Party: its membership was the largest of all parties, and these members served the function planned by Menzies—to give a stable and steady income, and to provide a willing work force at elections. The third aspect—the autonomy of the parliamentary wing—has always been a tenet of the party and its ancestors. Formed inside the legislature, and as a reaction to the organisation-controlled Labor Party, Liberal parliamentarians have always resisted any attempt by the organisational wing to apply any form of control, let alone discipline, over them.

The long Menzies era was characterised by a relative stability of electoral support for the Liberal Party. It was also characterised by the consummate political skill of Menzies himself. Aided by the Labor split in 1954–1955 and the existence (and preferences) of the DLP, Menzies skilfully exploited political issues, especially the 'communist threat'. When Menzies retired in 1966, latent strains within the party came to the surface and various proto-factions emerged. Menzies had not made any real effort to arrange a transfer of power to a successor and in the leadership vacuum which existed, factions began to act openly. After twenty-two years of stable leadership, the Liberal Party had nine national leaders in 24 years: Holt (1966–1967), Gorton (1968–1971), McMahon (1971–1972), Snedden (1972–1975), Fraser (1975–1983), Peacock (1983–1985), Howard (1985–1989), Peacock, again (1989–1990), and Hewson (1990–).

The basic tenets of the Menzies model came under question following the Liberals' defeat in the 1972 election. The organisation began to demand more say in the affairs of the parliamentary wing and the party established an efficient national organisation for the first time. Faction fighting also became common in the state branches. Winning government back in 1975 brought only a superficial appearance of unity. Differences within the party's own ideology, policy and programmes, especially differences between progressive (small 'l' liberal) and conservative components, and the growing tension between the 'wets' and 'dries', became open battles after the election defeat of 1983.

In essence, the labels 'wet' and 'dry' are shorthand terms for ideologies which have existed within the Liberal Party since its formation in 1909. The 'wet' faction includes those who believe in a positive role for government in the economy and in the lives of citizens. This role includes assisting, protecting, or 'pump priming' business and industry, a commitment to a strong social welfare system, and a mixed economy. The 'dry' faction believes that government should, as far as possible, keep out of the economy and out of the lives of citizens. The 'dries' are opposed to government 'ownership' and seek to privatise. They believe that 'market forces' provide the best economic environment, and they generally take a harder line on the availability of social welfare. The Fraser government, (1975–1983), was 'dry' in rhetoric, but it did not put it into practice. After the 1990 election, the Hewson front bench is dominated by 'dries', but whether that will be translated into action remains to be seen, if the Hewson Liberal Party can win office.

NATIONAL PARTY

The Country parties in Australia emerged in the colonial period as rural, especially pastoral, pressure groups. When the party system began to form in the 1890s, these rural interests found a home in the non-Labor parties, especially in Free Trade.

During the first decade of national government a number of rural political parties emerged in the states, often including the names 'Farmers and Settlers' or 'Farmers and Producers'. The impact of the First World War, together with rising tariff levels and other financial actions which benefited the urban areas, brought accusations that the Liberal and—later—Nationalist Party were too urban-oriented and prompted rural interests to form a separate political party. In the 1919 election, there were nineteen candidates from a range of rural electoral organisations, including Farmers and Settlers, Victorian Farmers' Union, Primary Producers' Union and a Farmers' candidate, and eleven seats were won. The reasons for this success included the concentration of support for such candidates in a few electorates (a factor which has always been important) and that the new parties managed to obtain support from residents of country towns. In 1920, the Australian Country Party was formed and the history of a national rural party in Australian electoral politics dates from the 1922 election when it won fourteen seats. Early in 1923, it joined in a composite government with the Nationalists. Since then, the now National Party has achieved remarkably stable electoral support and representation in the national parliament. This stability is especially evident in the last two decades. Constant assertions by its opponents about the imminent disappearance of the National Party have been based on hopes rather than facts. But, at the same time, the party has had to face the realities of Australian demographic movements.

Its ability to achieve what it sought in politics has always rested on two factors: the 'captive vote' in the rural areas which provided it with a relatively stable core of seats in the House of Representatives; and its 'coalition potential' its control of a sufficient number of seats to be essential to the Liberal Party as a coalition partner in government. Only on rare occasions has the Liberal Party had sufficient numbers in the national arena to govern in its own right. The National Party is not only constrained to rural areas but its electoral strength is in

Country/National leaders. Above: A. Fadden, Joh Bjelke-Petersen. Below: Doug Anthony, Ian Sinclair.

mainland Australia (it has never had permanent existence in Tasmania) and especially in the eastern states. As the rural population declined and as many small towns became ghost towns, the party was forced to reconsider its policies and image.

The change of image was attempted first in Queensland when the Country Party became the National Party, and began contesting suburban seats. After some resistance, especially in New South Wales and in Western Australia (where the Country Party had a brief flirtation with the DLP in a National Alliance) the National Party was accepted as the new national name. But the party has not been able to shed its sectional base. To become a 'catch-all' party and contest with the other two broad parties would remove its major strength—its core of support in the rural areas. At the same time, the non-Labor coalition has faced internal tensions. The federal coalition collapsed in the late 1980s during the Joh–push out of Queensland, and since its re-formation in 1990 it has hardly been a happy family. In the states, only New South Wales has a history of a stable coalition. The National Party has only recently forced a coalition in Victoria; the Western Australian non-Labor relations have been far from peaceful, and there is no coalition in South Australia.

The NP is more federal in structure than the two major parties: power resides in the state branches. Beyond that fact, its general structure, from local branches to state council and executive, resembles other parties. Its future must be described as in doubt. The 1975, 1977 and 1980 federal elections provided the Liberal Party with sufficient parliamentary numbers for it to govern without it; the continued coalition was based on tradition, not necessity. Only in Queensland, and only there due to the 'Bjelke-mander', was the party the dominant partner in the parliamentary non-Labor coalition, and in 1983, the NP excluded the Liberal Party from government. In 1988, the National Party went into its most serious crisis, brought by factions, ambitions, personality conflicts and, most important, the findings of alleged corruption by the Fitzgerald Commission. In the 1989 Queensland election, the National Party was soundly defeated, and its crisis continues.

RELEVANT MINOR PARTIES

The emphasis so far in this chapter has been on the three entrenched national political parties—Labor, Liberal and National. But the *form* of the Australian party system is multi-party, and most national elections are contested by thirty or more political parties and groups. Most are limited to contests in one or two seats, and few have any real existence beyond one or two elections. But in its functioning, rather than its form, the Australian party system is best described as two-partism—a competition for government between Labor and the anti-Labor coalition (with the qualifications noted above).

Some minor parties have achieved, if briefly, an important place in the party system. Some have become relevant. On what grounds? A minor party can achieve relevance if it has a coalition potential, if it is able to exert influence over a major party and its policies by its necessity in obtaining the numbers to form a government. This is the basis of the relevance of the minor National Party. A second means exists if a minor party can use its preference power to pressure a major party. The Democratic Labor Party was a past master at this. A third basis for relevance is when a minor party manages to win a balance of power in at least one house of parliament. The Australian Democrats, with that balance of power in the Senate and some Legislative Councils, have achieved relevance in this way. These three parties achieved relevance in the national scene. Others have emerged as important in the State arenas. The Call to Australia Party in the New South Wales Legislative Council, and the unique situation of the Green Independents in Tasmania in 1989 are two such cases.

The DLP was an important minor party in Australian history in terms of electoral success and political power. The genesis of the party lay in the history of the labour movement, both in the increasingly strained coexistence within the union movement of Catholic and communist elements and within the ALP of socialist and Catholic elements. By 1953, the Movement and Industrial Groups had developed to the stage where they dominated the executive of the Victorian branch of the ALP and had a major influence in the New South Wales branch. The ALP federal executive acted against the Movement and the Industrial Groups in late 1954 and early 1955. Seven federal parliamentary members were expelled from the party in April, and the Cain Labor government in Victoria was defeated when ten Labor members with Movement backing crossed the floor and supported a no-confidence motion. Labor had split openly. Not surprisingly, R. G. Menzies took advantage of the split and called an election in 1955, two years before time. The Labor Party was soundly defeated, but the only success for the ALP (Anti-communist)—as the splinter group was then called—was the narrow win by McManus as fifth senator for Victoria. By 1957, the split was complete; in August 1957, the Democratic Labor Party was formed. The Gair Queensland Labor Party joined in 1962.

The DLP organisation was similar to other Australian parties, but its main membership was drawn from Victoria. It was notably weak in South Australia and Western Australia from the beginning, partly because the Catholic hierarchy stood aside from the new party in those states. The organisational strength of the DLP came through three major areas: the Victorian branch, a group of senators, and the National Civic Council. The DLP never achieved sufficient support to win a seat in the House of Representatives (nor, in fact, in any lower house, except for the unique case of the 1974 New South Wales state election—a DLP candidate was elected when the Liberal sitting member for a seat forgot to nominate), but it achieved a small group in the Senate which wielded considerable political power, derived from the fact that it held a numerical balance of power in that chamber. This control of the Senate disappeared at the 1974 double dissolution, when the DLP lost all its Senate seats. It has not had parliamentary representation since then.

Former Liberal minister Don Chipp formed the Australian Democrats in 1977.

The prime aim of the DLP, from its inception, was essentially a negative one—to keep the ALP from government—and there is evidence that the tight preference distribution of DLP votes was a major factor in elections during the 1960s. The policies of the DLP were based on anti-communism in both internal and in foreign policy and it emphasised a hard conservative line on social issues. From the beginning, the DLP was a party overwhelmingly of Catholics in leadership, membership and electoral support, but it did not become a Catholic party. Only in Victoria did it succeed in capturing a majority of Catholic voters. Its brief history provided some evidence of a religious cleavage in Australia, but even more evidence of ideological strains in the Labor Party. It showed the difficulties faced by any political party which is based on a single issue and which is unable to adapt to a changing world.

The Australian Democrats formed in 1977. Its genesis lay in two existing minor parties and the resignation from the Liberal Party of Don Chipp. Both the Australia Party and the Liberal Movement had fallen on hard times in the double dissolution elections of 1974 and 1975 and the latter split in South Australia with the formation of the New Liberal Movement. Discussions had occurred between the Liberal Movement and the Australia Party seeking alliance if not amalgamation, and this came to fruition following Chipp's resignation. Following a barnstorming tour of Australian capitals by Chipp, the 'third force' was formed by June 1977.

Since then, the Australian Democrats have been remarkably successful, relative to the history of minor parties in Australia. By 1993, it had achieved seven seats in the Senate, and representation in two state Legislative Councils, again with a balance of power. This record certainly exceeded that of the DLP. But the Democrats still face an uncertain future, especially after the 1993 federal election when its electoral support collapsed from 11.3 per cent in 1990 to only 3.8 per cent. Further, the relevance of the party rests on its balance of power in the legislatures and this could be eroded by changing opinions in the electorate. The rise of the environmental movement in the late 1980s, which the Democrats spearheaded, could in fact work against the party. If the Tasmanian Green Independent initiative is followed in other electoral areas, then the Democrats could find one of its bases of support eroded.

The Democrats do have components which are unique in the Australian party system. The party applies participatory democracy at all levels. It does not apply discipline nor enforce cohesion on its parliamentary members. The party does not attempt to direct preferences in elections, leaving it to voters to decide. It is the archetype of 'new politics', of issues of a post-industrial society, especially issues defined as 'quality to life'. Its ideology is most accurately termed environmentalism.

One reason for the long-term relevance of the National Party is that it has a stable base of support in a specific sector of the society. The DLP attempted to form such a base, and failed. The Democrats have resisted this mode, attempting to appeal across all sections of the population. The question for the Democrats in the 1990s is whether the party's support has built up some secure base, or whether it is still essentially a 'protest' or 'haven' party for voters dissatisfied with the major players. The Australian Democrats have attempted to become a 'different' political party, especially in terms of ideology. Where most other minor parties have been of the left or the right, and have allied themselves with either the Labor or Liberal parties, the Democrats have tried to be a 'third alternative', even to the point of not allocating preferences. Their only rigid 'ideological plank' is total opposition to uranium mining. Whether the party is more than a temporary haven for dissatisfied voters is a long-term problem for the Democrats.

In the last decade, there has been a proliferation of minor parties and single-issue parties in Australian elections. The constellation of green parties burgeoned in 1990; from only two parties in 1987, to 14 in 1990, and to 16 in 1993. The 'environment' became a major issue in 1990, to the point where Labor was forced to appeal for second-preferences.

The 'moral' collection of minor parties included such parties as

Call to Australia, Christian Democrats, Independent Christian Party, and the United Christian Party. On the far left were a range of parties, including four communist/socialist parties, but these have faded from the scene in recent years. Parties on the extreme right include the National Front, the White Australia Progressive Party and the National Socialist Party, and most have an ideology based on social issues.

THE PARTY SYSTEM

The Australian party system can most accurately be described as multi-party in form, but essentially two-partism in function. Certainly, until the formation of the Australian Democrats, competition for government, for control of the legislature, was between the two major parties, Labor and Liberal. The DLP and the National Party aligned themselves to the Liberals and the two-partism become entrenched. The Democrats added a third 'pole' to the system, a centre party, but it remains to be seen whether their influence will grow to the point where the two-partism is threatened.

Labor and Liberal have also dominated the electorate, consistently winning over 80 per cent of the votes cast at almost every election and in almost every election arena in Australia. This dominance has been challenged, notably in Queensland, and in the 1989 election in Tasmania by the Green Independents. The long-term pattern had been two-partism in the electorate. But the dominance has been by two quite different party types—at least until the 1960s. Australia is one of only a handful of nations (including New Zealand and Britain) in which a Labor party is one of the dominant components of the party system. Labor and Liberal were different types of parties at their formation, and the influences of their genesis are still evident today. The distinction between the two types is that between an expressive (Labor) party, and a responsive (Liberal) party. The term 'mass party' can equally be applied to Labor. The models need to be clarified, as they are one key to the transformation in both parties which has occurred recently.

A *responsive* party is one which has only a weak social base, and which does not rely for funds, members, and electoral support on any specific stratum of society. A responsive party will seek to identify and reflect the changes in the majority public moods, remain flexible in policy terms, and will not have a clear and binding ideology. This model describes the Liberal Party for most of its history, as well as the Australian Democrats.

An *expressive* party has the reverse characteristics. It will be based on a distinct sector of society and will aim to, and be expected by the sector to reflect its wishes, demands and needs. That is, it will have a social base, and will be expected to represent or express that base. It will therefore have a set of aims, an ideology that flows from the interests of that base and an organisational structure which enables the base to ensure that the party continues to reflect and represent it and to express its demands. Such a party is a mass party and will continually be involved in a mobilisation process involving all levels of the party, as well as continually emphasising the necessity for intra-party cohesion. This model describes the Labor Party for most of its history, as well as the National Party.

INTERNAL PARTY POLITICS

There seems to be a general agreement about the ideal internal organisation of a political party in Australia, for all have sought similar structures. Each party in Australia is trying to achieve a bigger membership, to be a large party, presumably on the assumption that more members mean steadier income, more electoral helpers and more committed supporters. Each party puts great stress on unity and cohesion. Unlike the party systems of the USA where diversity and heterogeneity are the keynote, Australian parties fear diversity and disunity. Each party also attempts to give an impression (if not the actuality) of being a dynamic party. Finally, each party spends considerable time in continuing discussions of its own internal organisation—the extent of internal representation, responsibility and democracy.

STRUCTURE AND ORGANISATION

There are obvious problems implicit in such a model based on these attributes. Increased membership could mean greater potential for factions to emerge and hence for unity to be threatened, and a large party may find that may create inertia, and a moribund rather than a dynamic organisation. There is also the question of whether a large organisation can be run on democratic lines. The Australian Democrats have deliberately incorporated decision making by participation—all party questions, including policies and leadership, are decided by a vote of the total membership. Such a system of participatory democracy obviously becomes more difficult as size increases.

In general terms, the structure of each major political party can be described as an hierarchical pyramid, with individual members at the bottom level and the supreme decision-making body of the party at the top. The ALP, the Liberal Party, the National Party and the Democrats are all federal parties, with roots in the states, and with more or less autonomy and authority in the hands of the state branches. The National Party is the most state-oriented, with a weak national organisation which has little authority to produce cohesive, national action by the party. In the formal sense, the Labor Party is the most national party; its central organisation is strong, and the ultimate decision maker of the party, especially in the area of platform, is the national conference held every two years. In 1994, the structure of the Labor Party still reflects the forces which formed it. The ALP is organised on the basis of six state branches and branches in the ACT and the Northern Territory, all of which have their own organisation and structure, yet are closely linked in a federal organisation. The basic organisations of the ALP are sub-branches of the state parties and affiliated trade unions, and membership is achieved through either or both. At the top, the state branches are governed by a state conference (or congress). Between these levels are the multiplicity of various types of intermediate organisations, including electorate and regional committees, Young Labor groups, a women's organisation, a state council and a state executive.

The modern Liberal Party is also based on a federal model, but with power in the hands of state divisions, a weak national organisation and a general structure which offers the greatest possible support for the parliamentary party without the organisation having the authority to direct or control it. This last point reflects the origins of the Liberal Party inside parliament, and the view held by the party almost since its formation that members of parliament should be safeguarded from direction by the party.

Since 1972, a national Liberal organisation has been developed, with considerable research, planning and co-ordination functions, but this change has not seriously altered the model. The apex of the representation ladder of the national hierarchy is the federal council, whose membership emphasises the party's attempt to provide a federalised structure.

In general terms, then, the structures of the parties are not fundamentally different. The major differences between the parties concern such aspects as discipline and a pledge, the relations between the organisational and the parliamentary wings, the authority given to caucus in the leadership of the parliamentary wing of the ALP and pre-selection.

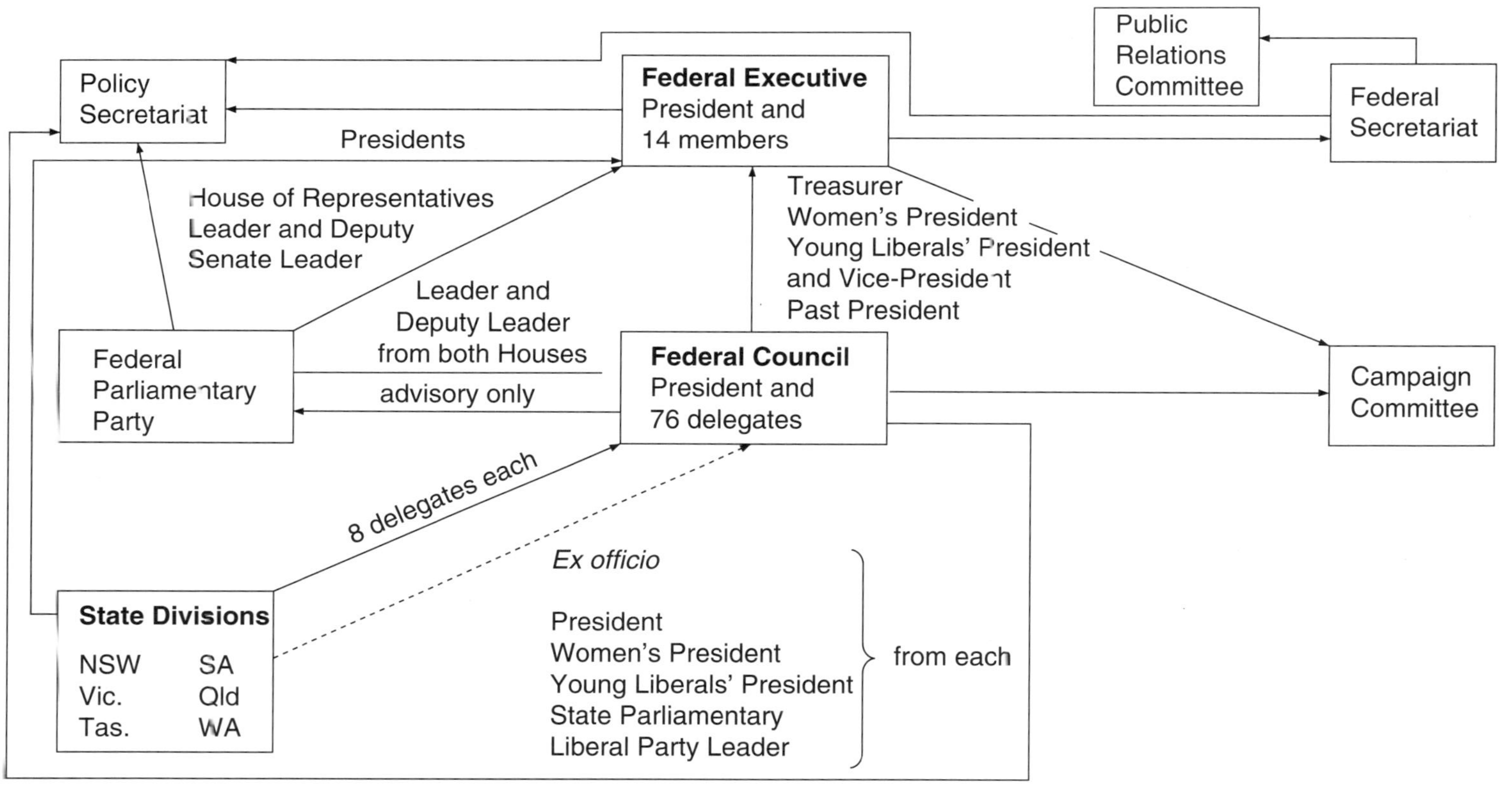

Figure 5.2 *Structure of the Australian Liberal Party*

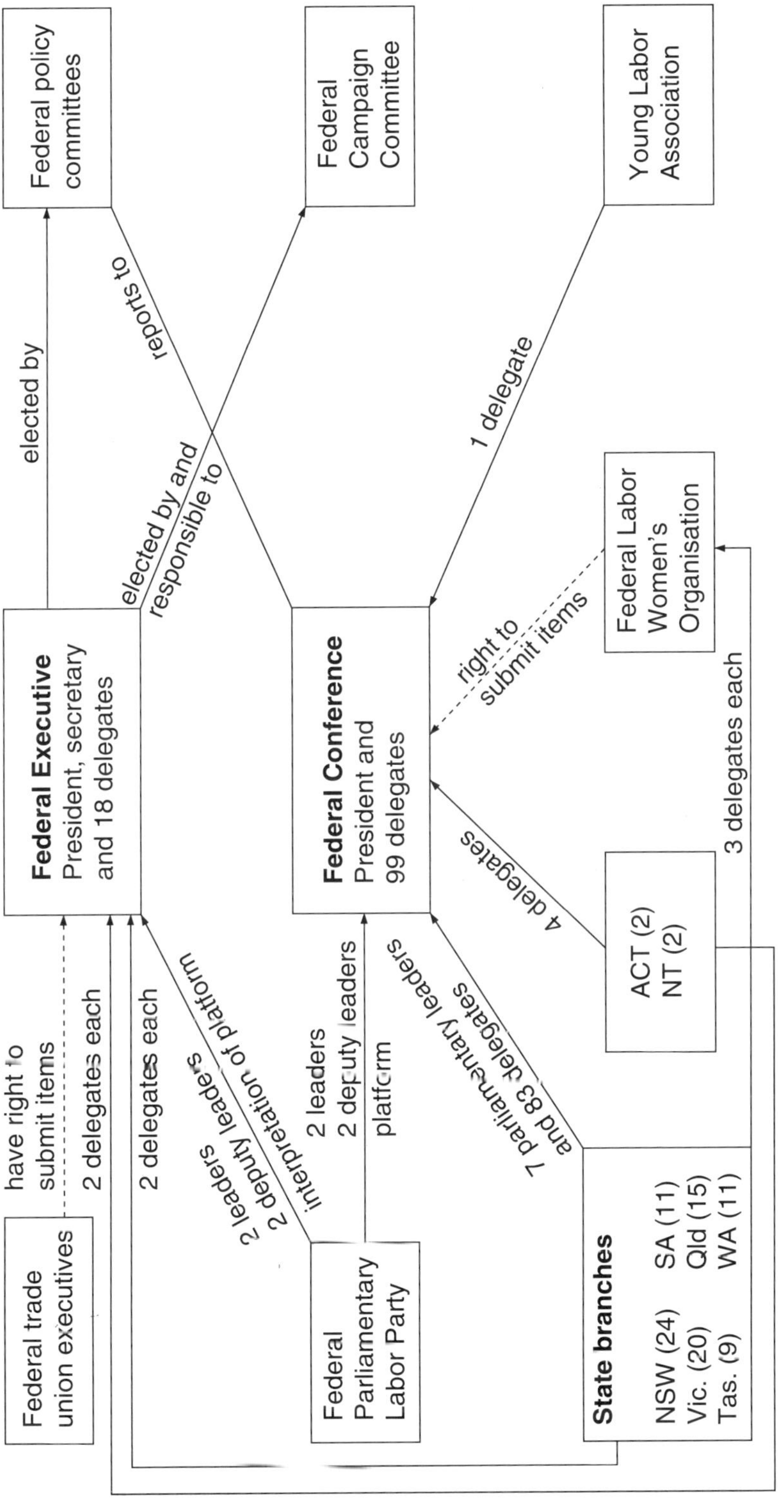

Figure 5.3 *Structure of the Australian Labor Party*

COHESION AND DISCIPLINE

The Australian Labor Party is quite open about its demand that its representatives shall be its delegates, and it enforces discipline over parliamentary members with a formal pledge. Members of the party pledge themselves to be bound by the platform and rules of the party and by the decisions of the executive and conference, not to oppose any endorsed Labor candidate at any election, and to vote according to the majority decision of the caucus of the parliamentary party on all questions in parliament. They face expulsion from the party if they break any aspect of the pledge.

The Liberal Party has always asserted its 'fundamental law' of parliamentary behaviour that members elected to parliament as Liberals would not be pledged in any way which would conflict with the right of a member to act as an independent. Where Labor's pledge contains three essential elements of complete support for the principles of the party, a promise not to oppose an endorsed candidate, and a pledge to abide by majority decisions of caucus, and these elements are strictly enforced, the Liberal Party makes much capital of its refusal, *in theory* to bind its members in any way.

Once a Liberal member of parliament has been elected then he or she is virtually a free agent—*at least in the terms of the party's constitution.* In a formal sense, Liberal members cannot be directed by their local organisation, although members will certainly keep their interests in mind, and will religiously attend their local meetings. Members may take advice from the party organisation, but are under no pledge to follow that advice. At the same time, the parliamentary leader, his or her lieutenants and the backbench ranks do work under constraints. All will be constantly subjected to pressures from parliamentary colleagues, from local organisations, from upper levels of the extra-parliamentary wing and from professional and business pressure groups. Liberal parliamentarians' so-called freedom must take account of suggestions and support from the party organisation, although they have formal discretion and freedom of action.

There is almost no avenue for the party *formally* to discipline recalcitrant members, and the party's ideology would not allow such discipline. But there is one important sanction which the Liberal Party has used—the power of the party to remove pre-selection from a member who has not sufficiently followed the party line. Given the tendency for most voters to support a party rather than a person, this has been an effective sanction.

CAUCUS CONTROL AND LEADERSHIP

The particular circumstances of the formation of the Labor Party, and the peculiar parliamentary environment in its first twenty years until 1910, produced an ethos of political behaviour in the party which is still dominant. The party was created by the labour movement outside parliament. From this flowed two consequences. First, the concept of the movement's sovereignty and hence the pledge which clearly states that parliamentary representatives of the Labor Party are delegates of the wider labour movement and stipulates its role as supreme policy-maker by way of the national conference. Second, the party was created from the trade union movement, hence the formal power of the union movement in the Labor Party was, and remains, central.

A third characteristic derives from the necessity in the early years for cohesion in the embryonic parliamentary group. The parliamentary Labor Party—the caucus—demanded a dominant role in parliamentary politics. Moreover, the party entered parliament as an alternative to the existing faction system which placed loyalty and participation at a relatively low level of priority. The concept of cohesion based on participation soon became entrenched as the concept of caucus dominance. This practice is undoubtedly based on the concept of representation—the parliamentary leadership of the Labor Party is seen as the *delegate* of caucus; it must report to caucus and obtain caucus agreement on actions. Such a system caused problems for the Whitlam government, with several well-publicised instances when caucus overruled a cabinet decision, and the Hawke and Keating governments have also had problems.

The Liberal Party rejects any suggestion of such caucus domination. The first non-Labor parties were forced to become more cohesive than their faction predecessors, simply in response to the new approach to parliamentary politics inaugurated by the Labor Party. In fact, some early state Liberal parties toyed with the idea of a pledge similar to that of Labor. But the Liberal Party had been formed in parliament by members who held a strong commitment that members of parliament should be representatives not delegates, not partisans, and should be independent representatives. Hence there is no formal pledge with formal sanctions in the Liberal Party, and no concept of caucus control. The parliamentary Liberal Party meets as a caucus, and it is not unusual for leaks from the party room to show that the leadership came under strong criticism from backbench members. But strong criticism is a far cry from a formal commitment to caucus control. In practice, of course, the Liberal Party in parliament is as cohesive and internally disciplined as the Labor Party.

The Liberal Party places great importance on leadership; on the need for parliament to lead the nation, on the need for cabinet to lead the parliament, on the need for its own leaders to head the party.

This is not to say that a Liberal leader is unchecked. He (all have been men so far) is elected by the caucus and can be removed by it. He must obviously take into account the views, demands and the proto-factions within his own party. But, providing that the Liberal leader can accomplish one thing, then the caucus will generally follow. Electoral success is fundamental. The recent history of the Liberal Party provides a number of instances where an unsuccessful Liberal leader found his leadership immediately tested by the caucus. A Liberal leader who loses, or who looks as if he may lose, has a very unsteady hold on the leadership.

PRE-SELECTION

In Australia, any person who fulfils certain legal requirements, such as a minimum age and Australian nationality, and who can afford the nomination fee, can stand as a candidate for election. For most individuals who stand as independents or minor party candidates, however, the exercise is doomed to defeat. In all but a handful of over 800 seats in Australian parliaments, success will be achieved by a nominee of a political party, and in all but a handful of seats the elected member will belong to one of three parties. In the majority of seats the contest will be little more than a formality; most are safe for one party.

As a result of this last factor, which depends on relative stability of party voting, the selection of a candidate by a party is, in effect, certainly in safe seats, the election of a member of parliament. In such cases, where the incumbent party is in no danger of defeat, the 'election' process is carried out by the party, not by the public. Hence it is important to establish how parties undertake the selection of their candidates.

The first point to be noted is that pre-selection in Australian party politics is usually a secret, internal party matter. Unlike the primary elections in the USA where members of a party (and sometimes the general public) have an open say in a primary (pre-selection) election, the Australian parties regard candidate choice as a private party matter and not for the scrutiny of the public. Should pre-selection be open to public scrutiny?

Procedures vary from state to state, from election to election, and in terms of which house of parliament and which level—state or national—is being contested. Methods used include: a centralised form in which candidate selection is carried out by the executive of the party; selection by a central body formed by delegates from all levels of the state branch; selection by regional or electorate sub-committees specifically formed for this purpose; or the Australian form of the US primary where a plebiscite of all party members in the relevant electorate decides the issue. In general, the Labor Party uses more centralised methods of pre-selection, and the Liberal and National state parties tend to pre-select by electorate or regional committees. The Australian Democrats use a full plebiscite of members.

Which is the best method? The answer, like so many answers in politics, depends on what end is being sought. The most centralised form of pre-selection by a state conference, used by the South Australian Labor Party, allows the delegates to view, question and decide on which candidates would be the best representatives of the party. But inherent in this method is the potential to overlook specific local interests and pressures. Selection by regional or electorate committees does allow local interests to be recognised. While this decentralised system may produce locally supported members, it may not provide the special expertise that the party requires. Of course, it must be remembered that for the hopeless seats the problem for parties is usually that of finding a candidate at all rather than choosing between a list of hopefuls.

PARTY AND PARLIAMENTARIANS

When Menzies re-established the Liberal Party in 1944, he planned a federal structure with a hierarchy of authority based on a clear division between the parliamentary and organisational wings of the party. The federal structure of the new Liberal Party was set up by Menzies to be a support for himself, not an external pressure or constraint. The structure remained relatively moribund, and throughout the Menzies era, both principle and practice included the autonomy of the state branches, the subordination of the parliamentary members to the cabinet and of the cabinet to the Prime Minister.

In the 1990s, the relations of the parliamentary and organisational wings of the Liberal and Labor parties remain almost as they were at their formation. Relations in the Labor Party are best defined in terms of unity of purpose—the parliamentary wing is drawn from, is part of, and is ultimately responsible to the mass party as a whole, and is a delegate of the mass party. Relations in the Liberal Party are equally clear. The organisation has responsibility for support, for pre-selection and for the platform which the party presents to the public; the parliamentary wing has sole responsibility for policy and for legislative activity, and cannot be bound by decisions or platforms of the extra-parliamentary wing of the party.

The National Party differs from state to state in terms of relations with its parliamentarians. In general, the National Party constitutions contain more potential for direction, control and discipline of the parliamentarians by the organisation than does the Liberal Party—a difference possibly explained by the origin of the Country Party, like the Labor Party, in organisations outside the parliament. The Australian Democrats do not seek to apply any form of enforced cohesion on its members of parliament.

IDEOLOGY, POLICY AND PRACTICE

Australian political parties are often described as ideological and the party system as based on ideological divisions. To analyse this view, we need to first establish what we will describe as an ideology, then establish whether Australian parties can be described. We also need to ask whether these ideologies are transmitted into the policies, platforms and practices of the parties.

'IDEOLOGY'

When we refer to a political party as having an ideology, we are saying that it has a reasonably elaborated and closely connected set of ideas and attitudes. These involve:

- some conception of history and the place of humanity in history
- a set of values and moral views
- a social theory which can be applied to specific situations
- a conception of the best form of the future state of society, and prescriptions about how to achieve it
- a clear idea of the relationship between ends and means
- an explicit conception about the role of government and politics in society.

Two qualifications need to be made in applying these to Australia. First, there will be different degrees of articulation of an ideology. One party may set out its ideology in detail while another may also reflect its ideology in a range of policies and programmes. Second, it is a common assumption that only radical programmes are derived from an ideology. However, a clear commitment to the *status quo* can be just as much part of an ideological framework as a commitment to a utopian society.

When we examine literature about the Australian party system we find little serious analysis of ideology. This derives from one or more of four assumptions about Australian parties.

1 The notion that Australian parties are essentially syndical—that they see their major function as the serving of certain interests.

2 The common view that the party system is centripetal—battling for the 'middle vote', seeking the centre of the political spectrum, and hence deliberately underplaying ideology.
3 The description of Australian politics as pragmatic, 'market-place' politics, in which ideology gets in the way of bargaining and compromise.
4 The fact that Australian political parties show an ideological spread within their membership, and hence make difficult any attempt to label the whole party under an ideology.

To attempt to come to some conclusion concerning the ideologies of the major Australian parties, we need to examine both what the parties *say* their ideology is, and also whether the attitudes, policies and actions of the party reflect such an ideology. It must be stressed, however, that while parties may consider themselves as committed to certain ideals, generalisations about a party or its members may ignore the wide range of viewpoints and attitudes within a party membership, differing commitments to the ideology among the membership, and the possibility that the propaganda of a party (on which judgements concerning ideology are sometimes made) may be for electoral purposes only.

LABOR—THE END OF IDEOLOGY?

The Labor Party has always maintained that it has had a commitment to socialism and is, in some sense, some sort of a socialist party. At the same time, the party, and various factions within it , have never been sure about what was meant by 'socialism', and there have been different, even conflicting ideas on the strategies, the means, and the methods they should use to arrive at 'socialism'.

At its birth, in 1890, there was no doubt about Labor's ideology. The first two points on its 'fighting platform', demanded unequivocal socialism:

1 The nationalisation of all sources of wealth and all means of producing and distributing wealth.
2 The conducting by the State Authority of all production and all exchange.

But this history of the party since then is a history of the erosion of the 'socialist objective'. A major change in 1921, the 'Blackburn Declaration', modified the original hard-line statement to include these important qualifications.

a That the Australian Labor Party proposes collective ownership for the purpose of preventing exploitation, and to whatever extent may be necessary for that purpose

Labor in the 1980s: ideology and popularity?

b That wherever private ownership is a means of exploitation it is opposed by the Party; but
c That the Party does not seek to abolish private ownership even of any of the instruments of production where such instrument is utilised by its owner in a socially useful manner and without exploitation.

By the late 1960s, commitment to 'collective ownership' had disappeared, proposals for nationalisation had been deleted and the party stood for democratic socialisation, which it defined as:

a social justice and economic security
b freedom of speech, education, assembly, organisation and religion
c the right of the development of the human personality protected from arbitrary invasion by the State
d free election under universal, adult and secret franchise, with government by the majority, with recognition for the rights of minorities
e the rule of law to be the right of all.

At a special conference in 1982, the Labor Party finally abandoned any commitment to any form of socialism. The 22 Clauses of the Objective even included a guarantee of 'The right to own private property'.

The Hawke and Keating governments and the modern state Labor leaders and parties have moved Labor even further. The terms *pragmatism* or *electoralism* are now used more often to describe the ALP. In its economic policies, Labor has become a party of deregulation, of private enterprise, of the 'market', and has even incorporated privatisation. Ideology, especially socialist ideology, has been downplayed almost to the point of invisibility.

LIBERAL—IDEOLOGY DISCOVERED?

Parliamentary members of the ALP have few problems in working out what party policy is and whether it has to be followed. Liberal Party members also have few problems about party policy, but for a different reason—a Liberal platform is remarkably devoid of detailed statements, but full of 'beliefs in', 'principles of' and 'fundamental philosophies'. It is a matter not of establishing what the detailed party policy is, but deciding whether or not an action fits within a wide, ambiguous and generalised ideology, what one observer has called a 'party theology' (Turner 1973:368). And when party theology is questioned, the 'Liberal way' remains to emphasise the clear separation of parliamentary and organisational wings.

Unlike the Labor Party, it is only in recent years that the Liberal Party has attempted to clarify what it means by 'liberalism'. Consequently, the party and its predecessors have not had to face the constant pressures for interpretation and re-interpretation of basic philosophy from inside. But in the 1980s, when the party *was* forced to think about itself, a virtual crisis developed.

For its first 70 years, the Liberal Party rarely thought about issues of ideology. Yet it contained from the beginning a potentially divisive ideological difference. It was formed by a fusion of free enterprise ('classical') liberals, and the Deakin protectionists who were best described as social liberals. In the 1980s, these strains re-emerged in the form of conflict between 'dries' and 'wets'. Why did they not emerge before? One reason was that the Liberal Party could expect, at almost every election, to win support from a majority of voters. There was no need to clarify its ideology. Another reason was the division in the structure of the party between the organisational and parliamentary wings. That is, despite what the party members and the platform said, the party leaders could be as pragmatic as the environment demanded.

It was not until the 1970s, when the Liberal Party found itself in opposition, that ideology began to be considered. It was not until 1978 that the first, albeit brief, comment on what the Liberal Party's ideology was emerged from the party. A later document, *Our Aims: What Liberals Stand For*, was apparently a formal and definitive statement as it emphasised that it 'deals with philosophy only, and not with policies.' That document included the following:

> Liberals believe that the government is responsible to the people through a parliamentary system in which elected representatives of the people are free to act upon their own convictions.
>
> The Liberal Society is a free association of individuals who believe that everyone has the right to develop their own personalities and choose their own ways of life.
>
> Liberals aim to create an environment in which individual initiative and private enterprise can flourish. They recognise that the competitive market economy is the key factor in achieving general economic progress.

In the 1980s, the party was forced to clarify some of these vague statements. Following the Fraser government (1975–1983), which expressed a dry rhetoric but pursued a wet practice, the party decided it needed to clarify better what it was and what it sought to achieve. But this brought into the open the latent ideological tensions in the party. These tensions were essentially based on the input of the 'dries' and the New Right group, who placed emphasis on the need for free enterprise, small government, and competition through the market. These social liberals, who saw a need for social benefits and who were not opposed to government intervention and the welfare state, found themselves in a minority in the 1983–1989 Howard Liberal Party and had only limited input in the Peacock Liberal Party. They are in a clear minority in the Hewson Liberal Party. One result of this ideological tension is that the Liberal Party has formed proto-factions.

FACTION POLITICS

A faction is a group of people within a political party, a group which is organised and has a measure of cohesion and which seeks to control the ideology, policies and practices of the party. Major parties are very fertile environments for factions to emerge. They are concerned with a range of activities—winning government, having nominees elected to parliament, formulating platforms and policies, debating ideology, and putting policies into practice. People and groups will have different views about the processes and ends of these activities—hence factions. But, until the late 1980s, there was a major difference between the Labor and Liberal parties.

Factions in the Labor Party have always been formal, structured, permanent and public. 'Factions' in the Liberal Party have tended to be ephemeral, loose, and private; in the past they could have been termed tendencies rather than factions. The National Party has also been remarkably free of factions (until the crisis in Queensland in 1988), partly because it managed to combine an ideology of free enterprise in rhetoric, a pragmatic approach to policy, and a quasi-socialist practice in relation to its rural base. In the late 1980s, however, the Liberal Party developed proto-factions, and the Queensland National Party became a faction.

By the mid-1980s, the Labor Party had coalesced its internal divisions into three national factions: Left, Centre Left, and Right. The Left can be subdivided into the *old* socialist left (essentially based in Victoria, but represented in other State branches), and the new socialist left, which gives more emphasis to issues such as uranium and environment than to 'socialism'. The Right can also be considered as containing the Catholic Right, a non-socialist, conservative group based on the trade union movement, and the more pragmatic Right. The Labor Party nationally, and in most States except Victoria, is dominated by the combined members of the pragmatic Right and Centre Left.

In 1990, the Liberal Party had developed two proto-factions—these were less clear than those in the Labor Party. The 'progressives'—the wets—see merit in the welfare state, in planning and in the role of government in the economy and the society. These comprise the social liberals. On the other hand are the anti-socialists, the 'dries' (compared to the non-socialist 'progressives'), who seek market forces, and minimal government intervention in the economy, are willing to maintain a welfare state only in the cases of severe need yet who support conservative social policies. The Liberal Party under Howard was dominated by the latter; under Peacock by the former; under Hewson the 'dries' are dominant.

A SENSE OF DIFFERENCE?

A casual observer of election *propaganda* in Australia would be excused for assuming that the two major parties were separated by an ideological chasm. But to what extent does party propaganda describe the actuality? In other words, how socialist is the Labor Party and how liberal is the Liberal Party?

In the late 1960s and early 1970s it seemed that the major parties had mellowed, had become closer to the centre and hence closer to each other, a trend which may have been the result of changes in Australian society. The Liberal Party was forced to react to new economic situations, changes in the economic structure of society and demands from the public for more rather than less government intervention. The Labor Party was forced to recognise that an increasing number of people were not employed in manual occupations, were not members of trade unions and were therefore not automatically Labor supporters.

As a result, both major parties have had to rethink their ideologies and policies. The Liberal Party was better situated to redirect itself; its loose ideology allowed for policy change, whereas the Labor Party's more concrete commitment to a 'socialist objective' made radical change of policies a potentially painful process. The period of the Fraser government, 1975–1983, appeared to reverse this. The hard-line Fraser rhetoric of free enterprise was in confrontation with Labor's semi-socialist platform. But the confrontation did not go beyond rhetoric. And since the 1983 election of the Labor government some observers, especially Labor's own socialist left, have accused the Labor government of policies and actions which 'out-Liberal' the Liberals.

Both major parties must take into account the real world of politics. Ideological commitments are valuable propaganda at election times; conflicting policies, programmes and philosophies offer the voting public some choice of teams of people to govern them, and party competition does provide some means for the government to be 'kept on its toes' if only in election campaigns. But there are real constraints on political parties in Australia, in terms of ideology, policy and practice. The economic system is firmly and apparently inextricably, based on a mixed system of private and government enterprise. The social system is apparently stable. The constraints of government—constitutional, bureaucratic, economic—all act as a moderating influence on party policy and practice. These and other factors tend to produce two parties which, in the long run, in ideology, policy and platform, tend to look very much like each other.

SUPPORTS AND INTERESTS

Political parties do not exist in a social vacuum. They are inextricably linked with society in many ways. In financial terms they depend on money raised from their membership and from broader sections of the society, not only for the short-term demands of election campaigns, but for the day-to-day affairs of the party. They are also linked, formally and informally, to certain pressure groups, cleavages and classes in society, and these links can produce problems for the parties.

FINANCE

Political parties are constantly spending money and, at election times, they may go deeply into debt. Unlike the USA and Canada, where party organisations virtually disappear between election campaigns, Australian parties are permanent, ubiquitous and constantly involved in society. Parties therefore need a steady infusion of funds to keep their central offices open, to pay their permanent staffs—organisers, research workers, secretaries, stenographers—to pay for the constant stream of publicity, propaganda, position papers and assorted material which the offices and the leaders produce, and to service the membership with regular material pointing out what the party is doing for them. The parties seek as much cash as possible when elections are announced. They have to pay for nomination fees for candidates, the production of pamphlets and assorted propaganda, the employment of temporary staff and the major expenditure—the production and presentation of the media publicity for the election.

Parties do not like to reveal how much they spend in these various areas, nor where their money comes from. Many observers and some participants have long pleaded for legislation to require that all donations to political parties should be a matter of public record, a proposal strongly resisted by all parties except the Australian Democrats. The purpose of such legislation, according to its proponents, was to ensure that the public was given the means to judge the responsibility of parties and to identify any potential or actual conflict of interest. Opponents of the proposal denied the need for full public disclosure and emphasised that many donations would simply not be made if the transaction were to be made public.

Without detailed information from political parties about their cash flows and balance sheets, it is impossible to come to any definitive, detailed conclusions about party finances. What can be said with reasonable confidence is that political parties could not exist simply on the basis of membership fees alone, and that a considerable amount of their time and energy is spent soliciting donations from any possible area. At the local level, as any branch member will tell, party life is a constant stream of fund-raising activities—fêtes, dinners, raffles—and general money gathering. Branch meetings often consist of members analysing the last fund-raising attempt, congratulating those concerned, and planning for the next.

In 1983, the national Electoral Act included public funding of political parties. This was inaugurated in New South Wales in the late 1970s, and will probably apply in all state elections before long. At the 1984 election, registered candidates and parties could claim 60 cents and 30 cents respectively for each House of Representatives and Senate vote they received. By 1990, the amounts had risen to 91.2 and 45.6 cents respectively. To be eligible, a candidate or party had to receive at least 4 per cent of the formal votes in the respective electorate.

The other side of the expenses equation was also modified. Until 1983, existing legislation covering election expenditure by candidates required that a detailed return of expenses be made by all candidates. This law was constantly broken, either by members (including ministers) refusing to submit returns, or by members reporting expenditure above the limit with no action taken against them. Under the new Act, parties have to report all donations above $200 for a candidate and above $1000 for a party. This information is available for public scrutiny.

INTERESTS AND PARTIES

One of the most persuasive arguments used by proponents of open disclosure of party funding is that a party in government is not likely to act against the interests of an individual, group or company which provides substantial financial assistance. Hence, the argument goes, to ensure that it is the public good rather than any private interest which governs the action of a party in government, all substantial donations should be made public so that the public can judge.

The relation of parties and interest groups goes beyond the question of finance. Australian political parties have formal and informal links with interest groups, especially economic groups, or are able to call on the support of a majority of the members of such groups. A group seeking access to political influence, either to obtain a certain benefit or to seek immunity from a certain constraint, often uses political parties as one of its means to achieve its aims.

The party system shows strong evidence of both formal and informal links between economic groups and political parties. This is partly a result of the origins of the parties; the Labor Party was formed by the trade union movement to represent the interests of the working class, the Liberal Party had its origins among the business sector engaged in manufacturing, finance and commerce and was formed to oppose the Labor Party, and the Country Party was formed by members of the rural industries to represent rural industry. Of the four, only the Australian Democrats has no identifiable sectional base.

The ALP has remained *formally* tied to a specific economic group. The affiliated units of the trade union movement are part of the Labor Party organisation and the party cannot ignore the strength of its industrial wing, nor the wing's demand for action on its behalf. The influence of the trade unions is felt throughout the party, and this influence is expressed by powerful voting blocs in the organisation. At the same time, the Labor Party in the electorate and in the parliament has found it necessary to be more than a trade union or workers' party. It has been forced to broaden its electoral appeal. One crucial fact of Australian electoral politics has made this a necessity: not all working people vote Labor, and even if they did, the party would still be short of a majority. Hence it has to appeal beyond its original sectional base, and even risk alienating it.

The Country Party in the mid-1970s, faced with a declining rural population, made a deliberate decision to attempt to broaden its base and appeal. But their new name—the National Party—achieved only after much dissent, was essentially a cosmetic change. The Country Party claimed to be national in its policies, but in organisation, support and policy emphases, it was in fact sectional and regional. Its membership (and steady income) came essentially from a rural population. Although during the 1970s the National (Country) Party had been seeking closer links with, and financial support from, the mining, minerals and export industries, its support and seats are still almost exclusively rural. These are facts which a mere change of name cannot obliterate. The party's non-parliamentary organisation developed out of various farmers' and graziers' organisations and, for a time, this formal link was retained. Unlike the Labor Party, the National Party severed these connections, but with mixed blessings. The party has autonomy of action, but at the same time has faced criticism and even direct opposition from some rural groups, who complained that the National Party was not sufficiently looking after their sectional interests. The National Farmers' Federation is the most recent manifestation and arguably the most important.

The Liberal Party's own view of itself is that it integrates and serves the interests of all social and economic groups in society, that it is non-sectional in its supports and policies, and that it represents the national interest in contrast with the 'sectional' Labor Party. It argues that the Labor Party's formal association with the trade union movement is a constraining influence and implies that the National Party's sectional supports have a similar effect. But the supports of the Liberal Party also show strong evidence of a functioning, if informal, link with a socio-economic stratum in Australian society.

The Liberal Party has a large membership, a support valuable at elections for canvassing and manning of booths and equally valuable in terms of membership dues. This membership also shows evidence of a distinct social composition in the Liberal Party, beginning at grassroots levels at the branch meetings of the members and at meetings of Young Liberals. The upper-middle-class membership in the city and suburbs meets in an atmosphere of social harmony often in comfortably furnished living rooms—and spend as much time on organising coming social events as on political party activities. The leading activists are overwhelmingly upper-middle-class, Protestant, and have usually been to private schools.

In terms of external supports, there has been a two-way link between business and industrial interests on the one hand and the Liberal Party in government on the other. These interests have generally been treated agreeably by the party in government and they in turn have been generous in adding to the Liberal coffers at election times. It is inaccurate, however, to assume that the Liberal Party is nothing more than the voice and political wing of these business interests or that the party is merely the political wing of the propertied and privileged classes. Business was not pleased with some of the activities of the Gorton and Fraser ministries, especially with what were seen as moves towards central government control, but there was no public disavowal of the Liberal government while it was in office. Where criticism is necessary, the business world often, but not always, tends to make its views known to the party rather than in the public arena, partly because while business, primary industry and the professions have provided much of the funds for the Liberal Party, they have also provided many of the parliamentarians and the

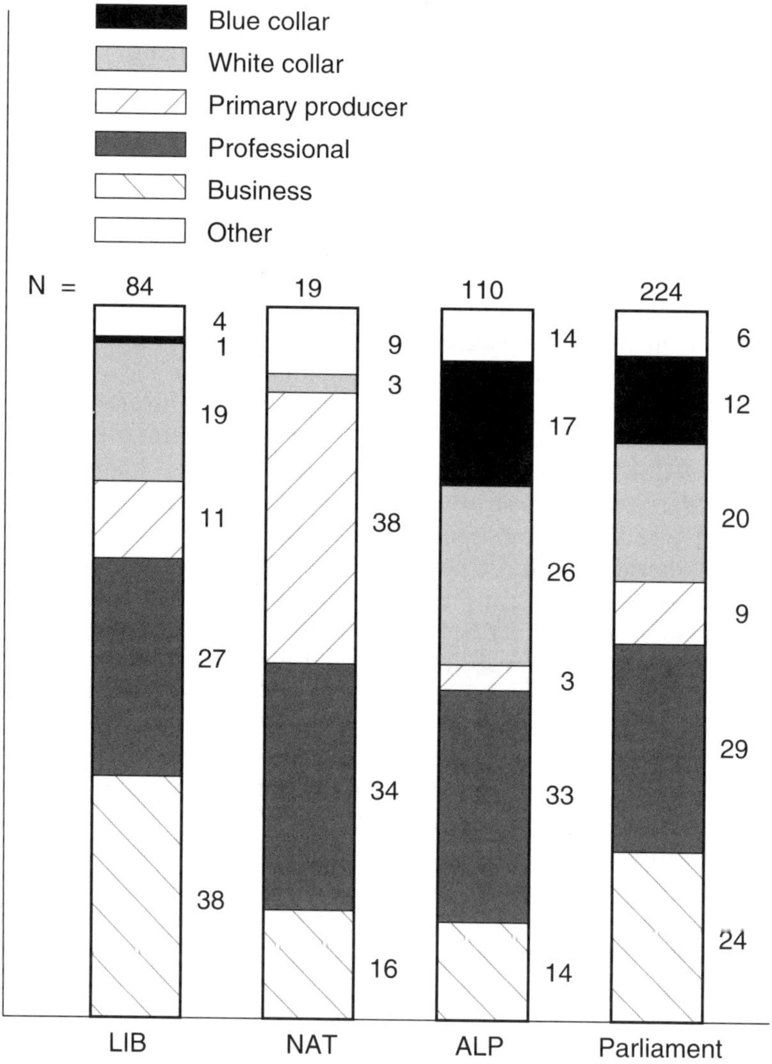

Figure 5.4 *Social basis of Australian parliamentarians, Australian parliament, 1990–93*

wielders of power in the extra-parliamentary wings. It is, to a considerable degree, a matter of like talking to like.

The party with the least dependence on, or link with, the organisational and financial support of identifiable sectional interests is the Australian Democrats. This party did not emerge; it was deliberately formed by an amalgamation of parties and groups with a history of non-sectional politics and it attracted many people who had not before been involved in parties and party politics. This is both a strength and a weakness of the party: on the one hand, the party is not required to reflect the ideals and demands of a sectional group; on the other, it lacks a steady base of electoral support.

One means of identifying the syndicates at the base of political parties is to examine the type of person who has risen to membership of the parliamentary wing. Such success depends to some degree on satisfying the various pressures within the party and the subjective judgements made by those in the party who select candidates as a fit and proper person to represent the party. The data shown in Figure 5.4 on the thirty-sixth parliament of Australia have been extracted from the *Parliamentary Handbook* 1991 and apply to the membership at 31 August 1990. No less than 65 per cent of Liberal members of federal parliament were from business or professional occupations, over one-third of the National Party membership was drawn from primary production, and it was the Labor Party which showed the greatest spread. The membership was also overwhelmingly male, and did not mirror the age structure of the population.

The extent to which parties and interests are related is not only a function of the origins of the parties. As demographic and social conditions change, so a party such as the former Country Party will be forced to re-assess its organisation and supports. Equally, the Labor Party has had to come to terms with the changing nature of the Australian population and with a relative decrease in the number of blue-collar workers.

REPRESENTATION AND POLITICAL PARTIES

The Australian parliamentary system is based on the theory of representative democracy. Political parties are an integral part of the processes of representation. How well do Australian political parties function as representative institutions?

Parties permeate the political process. Their existence is a necessary component of representative democracy. It is difficult to imagine how elections, parliaments and representation could perform efficiently and effectively without the parties. So, what functions *should* parties perform in a representative democracy, and how well do Australian parties carry out their functions?

One analyst suggested the following as functions of political parties (Hagopian 1984:239).

1 Mobilisation of voters
2 Education of the public
3 Political socialisation
4 Policy making
5 Interest aggregation
6 Political recruitment
7 System integration
8 Communication conduit

Some of these functions are clearly observable; parties do recruit candidates and nominate party members for elections, they dominate the electoral process, they have policies on almost all matters which affect the Australian nation and they are continually in the process of revising, rewording and publicising such policies. They are also involved in the actual running of government and opposition. Other functions include aggregating and representing the interests of unions, individuals, groups and classes in society.

In fact, the various specific functions can be reduced to three broad functions relating to three aspects of the process of representative democracy: providing representation in the various parliaments; identifying problems and issues and providing policies and programmes to the public as means of dealing with them; and organising and managing the process of government. In Australia all three functions are seen by the political parties as equally important and as interrelated. Australian political parties contest elections with teams of candidates and with detailed policies and programmes which are put before the public. If the party is elected to government, then it expects its representatives to put such policies and programmes into practice. Once elected to parliament with party endorsement and support, a member of parliament is expected to follow the party line and support the party policy. It is a brave member indeed who does not; on the rare occasions where such rebels do emerge, they usually do not remain members for very much longer.

In addition to providing the political leaders, parties in Australia are the prime movers in matters of policy. The parties, in government or opposition, during elections and at their many meetings, stress the major problems and issues—social, economic and political—which they feel require the attention of members of the society, if only to enhance the electoral hopes of the parties. These problems and issues may arise from the ideologies and policies of the parties themselves—each party has a vision of what the good society should be and do, and how it should function—but they may also arise from a reaction in the parties to a groundswell of public opinion in the electorate. Parties, then, define and refine various attitudes in the society and produce alternative policies and programmes for the members of the society to consider and ultimately to choose between. Australian parties spend a considerable amount of time on this process. Anyone who is or has been a member of a party can attest to the constant meetings, conventions, discussions and debates on general and specific aspects of the party platform.

The third general function of political parties is to organise the various levels and processes of government. After an election the majority party (or coalition of parties) will not be concerned only to put into action the policy on which it was elected; equally important is its responsibility of organising the complex process of government cabinet, parliament, public service, statutory authorities and the like. The minority party (or parties) has an equally important function—to criticise the programmes of the government, to ensure that programmes are carried out in a responsible manner, to offer alternative policies and programmes and to probe constantly the means and methods of the government to ensure that the various levels of government are functioning as they should.

Not all political parties discharge these functions equally well—in fact, some parties, especially some minor parties, do not have the opportunity to carry out some of these functions at all. Nor are political parties the only organisations that are involved with such activities. Interest groups, pressure groups, factions, and other associations in society also participate in the electoral process, providing alternative programmes and suggesting solutions to various social, economic and political problems, attempting to influence the government, the opposition and the people, and criticising the processes in the various levels of government and suggesting changes. But it is the constellation of parties which plays the dominant role in the Australian political process.

A political party has three major components: the party in parliament—the members elected as representatives in the name of the party; the party organisation—members, committees, executives; and the party in the electorate—the (changing) 'population' which identifies with, votes for, or generally supports the party. Given the importance of the party system in Australian politics and the extent to which parties are involved in all aspects of the political process, it is surprising to note that relatively few people in Australia ever join political parties. Most parties are notoriously shy about releasing information about membership, hence any figures are approximations, but it is certain that less than 4 per cent of the adult population of Australia are members of a party.

More important, it is surprising that the citizens seem to offer few constraints to the domination by political parties of the processes of representative democracy. Australia's political parties—the National Party less so, but Labor, Liberal and Democrats unquestionably—

have become catch-all parties, efficient and effective vote-catching organisms. But at the same time, they have become increasingly centralised, organised and disciplined. Parties are natural and inevitable developments in an open society. Party government is inevitable. But it should be the voters' responsibility to continually ensure that the parties themselves are representative and responsible. The 'problem of party' in Australia's representative democracy is not that parties exist, but the mode of behaviour of the parties. Party in Australia has become a matter of conflict, confrontation, and point-scoring. The question to be asked is whether they have sufficient commitment to principles of representation and responsibility. The rapid growth in the constellation of single-issue groups, in the range of success of independents and in the general disaffection of people with the political process, may be signs that political parties need to reconsider the role they play.

DOCUMENTS

5.1 LABOR'S IDEOLOGY: FROM SOCIALISM TO 'ME-TOOISM'?

General Objective: 1890

1 The nationalisation of all sources of wealth and all means of producing and distributing wealth.
2 The conducting by the State Authority of all production and all exchange.
3 The pensioning by the State Authority of all children, aged and invalid citizens.
4 The saving by the State Authority of such proportion of the joint wealth production as may be requisite for instituting, maintaining and increasing national capital.
5 The maintenance by the State Authority from the joint wealth production of all education and sanitary institutions.
6 The just division among all the citizens of the State of all wealth production, less only that part retained for public and common requirements.
7 The reorganisation of society upon the above lines to be commenced at once and pursued uninterruptedly until social justice is fully secured to each and every citizen.

Blackburn Declaration: 1921

That this Conference declares:

a That the Australian Labor Party proposes collective ownership for the purpose of preventing exploitation, and to whatever extent may be necessary for that purpose.

b That wherever private ownership is a means of exploitation it is opposed by the Party; but
c That the Party does not seek to abolish private ownership even of any of the instruments of production where such instrument is utilised by its owner in a socially useful manner and without exploitation.

Interpretation of 'Democratic Socialisation': 1980

The Australian Labor Party believes that:

Democratic socialisation is the utilisation of the economic assets of the State in the interests of citizens, and that man is greater than the machines he uses or the environment in which he lives. Scientific and technological advancement shall serve the interest of all and not be the exclusive right of the few. The economic aims of social control are full employment, higher production, a rising standard of living and social security; and seeks to secure through democratic socialism:

a social justice and economic security
b freedom of speech, education, assembly, organisation and religion
c the right of the development of the human personality protected from arbitrary invasion by the State
d free election under universal, adult and secret franchise, with government by the majority, with recognition for the rights of minorities; and
e the rule of law to be the right of all.

1982 Platform: extracts

Objectives

The Australian Labor Party is a democratic socialist party and has the objective of the democratic socialisation of industry, production, distribution and exchange, to the extent necessary to eliminate exploitation and other anti-social features in these fields.

To achieve the political and social values of equality, democracy, liberty and social co-operation inherent in this objective, the Australian Labor Party stands for:

- Redistribution of political and economic power so that all members of society have the opportunity to participate in the shaping and control of the institutions and relationships which determine their lives.
- Establishment and development of public enterprises, based upon federal, state and other forms of social ownership, in appropriate sectors of the economy.
- Democratic control and strategic social ownership of Australian natural resources for the benefit of all Australians.
- Maintenance of and support for a competitive non-monopolistic private sector, including small business and farming, controlled

and owned by Australians, operating within clear social guidelines and objectives.

- The right to own private property.
- Recognition and encouragement of the right of labour to organise for the protection and advancement of its interests.
- The application of democracy in industry to increase the opportunities for people to work in satisfying, healthy and humane conditions, and to participate in and to increase their control over the decision-making processes affecting them.
- The abolition of poverty, and the achievement of greater equality in the distribution of income, wealth and opportunity.
- Social justice and equality for individuals, the family and all social units, and the elimination of exploitation in the home.
- Equal access and rights to employment, education, information, technology, housing, health and welfare services, cultural and leisure activities and the law.
- Reform of the Australian Constitution and other political institutions to ensure that they reflect the will of the majority of Australian citizens and the existence of Australia as an independent republic.
- Recognition and protection of fundamental political and civil rights, including freedom of expression, the press, assembly, association, conscience and religion; the right to privacy; the protection of the individual from oppression by the state; and democratic reform of the Australian legal system.
- Elimination of discrimination and exploitation on the grounds of class, race, sex, sexuality, religion, political affiliation, national origin, citizenship, age, disability, regional location, or economic or household status.
- Recognition of the prior ownership of Australian land by Aborigines and Islanders; recognition of their special and essential relationship with the land as the basis of their culture; and a commitment to the return of established traditional lands to the ownership of Aboriginal and Islander communities.
- Recognition and encouragement of diversity of cultural expression and lifestyle within the Australian community.

5.2 LIBERAL PARTY

How Liberal is the Liberal Party?

Source: Sir Robert Menzies speaking at the twenty-first birthday of the Liberal Party in 1965.

We have learned that the right answer is to set the individual free, to aim at equality of opportunity, to protect the individual against oppression, to create a society in which rights and duties are recognised and made effective. In this free society, the tyrannical notion of an all-powerful state is rejected, and dogmatic socialism with it. In its place we have put opportunity without any class privileges, social and economic justice, and the civilised democratic conception that governments are not the masters of the people, but their servants.

1982 platform: extracts

The Spirit of Liberalism

Liberalism's central task is to safeguard and advance the freedom of the individual and to subject all constraints on him to ever more stringent scrutiny. In a liberal society governments and other institutions, such as public and private corporations and trade unions, must be made to serve individuals, not master them...

Liberals reject attempts to promote class division, to restrict social mobility, to divide city and country, or to separate those in one occupation from those in another...

Liberalism supports the institution of the family, wishing to strengthen it as the fundamental social group...

Liberals favour independent decision making, preferring individuals, families, associations and businesses to decide as many things as possible for themselves without government intervention and to accept responsibility for their decisions. Within government, Liberals encourage decentralisation; decision making by state and local governments, which are closest to those affected...

Australian liberalism means support for constitutional monarchy and freedom for all under the rule of law. It supports the Constitution...

Liberals believe in private property, private enterprise in a competitive market and economic growth. They believe in reward for effort, minimum but effective government and low taxes.

Australian Democracy

The basic elements of Australia's free, democratic political system are:

- Constitutional monarchy as a symbol of unity and continuity.
- A Constitution capable of being adapted to changing requirements by democratic processes.
- The rule of law and an independent judiciary.
- The Federal System of government in which the powers of the Federal Government are specially conferred by the Constitution of the Commonwealth and the residue of powers resides with the States.
- A Federal Parliament which consists of the Crown, the Senate and the House of Representatives.
- The Ministry, drawn from Parliament and accountable to it.

- An informed and effective Parliamentary Opposition with full freedom of expression.
- Free, fair and regularly held elections.
- A free press.
- The preservation of the rights of individuals and minorities.
- A dedicated, efficient and objective Public Service of integrity.

A Liberal Philosophy?

Source: D. Kemp, in Mayer H. and Nelson H. (eds) 1980, *Australian Politics: A Fifth Reader*, Longman Cheshire, Melbourne, pp. 302–4.

There is a broadly shared consciousness within the Liberal Party that the party 'has' a philosophy: the philosophy of liberalism. There would be an equally wide awareness that there is little conscious consideration of that philosophy, and most members of the party would probably claim only a very limited ability to state its main elements...

Over the party's history a number of documents have been produced which attempt to formulate the basic elements of the philosophy, and to express its implications for policy. These include the platforms of the party, as well as brief documents which are specifically philosophical in intent, such as 'We believe' and the more recently issued 'Our Aims'.

Despite the fact that the party could hardly be called an ideological party, and undoubtedly sees itself as responding to problems in a practical and non-doctrinaire way, ministers and backbenchers may still be heard to argue with (to the outsider) surprising frequency that such-and-such a policy is, or is not, in accord with the party's philosophy. To overlook the frequent references and significant organisational effort devoted to the party's philosophy or to dismiss it as insignificant, is to assert the unimportance of something which many party members, particularly the leaders of the organisational and parliamentary wings, believe to be important. It may be of some interest to the political scientist to find out why.

'Our Aims': (Future Directions 1988)

The time for short-term, instant solutions is over: what Australia needs and what we will provide is consistency, realism and plain thinking, in pursuing the right long-term aims for our country:

- To enhance individual freedom and opportunity.
- To restore the family and family values to their central role in Australian society with policies designed to help people become home owners; raise educational standards; give Australia's youth a new deal; uphold law and order; and encourage self help within families so we can concentrate welfare support on the elderly, the sick and the genuinely needy.

- To create One Australia, a nation in which all Australians are proud of their diverse heritage but united by shared values, common beliefs and an overriding commitment to Australia and the Australian way of life.
- To create the conditions for a more productive, thriving economy in which there is greater incentive to work hard, save and invest; inflation is under control; interest rates are affordable; bureaucratic regulation is minimised; and ownership is expanded so that more Australians have a direct share in their community.
- To create a more flexible labour market (with greater responsibility for good industrial relations placed directly on the participants themselves) as the basis for a more competitive economy and expanded employment opportunities.
- To establish a fair balance of rights and duties for the trade union movement.
- To reduce the scale of government and control expenditure so our country can live within its means.
- To extend genuine freedom of choice and individual responsibility for parents in the education of their children; for patients in access to health care; for consumers in the selection of goods and services they want by a programme of deregulation and privatisation designed to transfer decision making from remote bureaucrats to the individuals affected.
- To restore Parliament to its pre-eminent role in our national life and thus better protect the rights of the individual against the excessive power of the bureaucracy, unions and large corporations.
- To strengthen our defences; to work with out allies to protect our interests; to promote the values of the Western democratic way of life; and to provide consistency in our relations with other countries.

5.3 NATIONAL PARTY

A Dual Objective?

Source: J. McEwen, leader of the Country Party, 1965.

We conceive of our role as a dual one of being at all times the specialist party with a sharp fighting edge, the specialists for rural industries and rural communities. At the same time we are the party which has the total co-ordinated concept of what is necessary for the growth and safety of the whole Australian nation.

1982 Platform: selected

The National Country Party of Australia seeks to protect the rights, foster the aspirations and preserve the freedoms of the individual, and advocates:

- Preservation of democracy, the Westminster Parliamentary system of government and the Commonwealth Constitution.
- Preservation of a bicameral system of government, with the Senate as a house of review in the interests of upholding the rights of the individual and the sovereignty of the states.
- Adherence to the federal system of government with its three-tier structure—federal, state and local.
- Maintenance of the rule of law.
- Assuring Australian security by ensuring strong defence capacity.
- Preservation of freedom of communication, speech, worship, assembly and association.
- Protection of the security of private ownership and the advancement of free enterprise through individual initiative, as against the socialisation of industry, production, distribution and exchange.
- Promotion of an efficient and prosperous primary industry sector to provide appropriately priced food and fibre, with stability of supply, to the people of Australia and of other nations.
- Encouragement of economic and efficient mining, secondary and tertiary industry, recognising the need to assist decentralised development.
- Implementation of measures to achieve a more balanced population distribution throughout Australia. Recognition of the family unit as the basic element of a strong and stable society.

5.4 AUSTRALIAN DEMOCRATS: AN IDEOLOGY?

Statement By National Executive 1977

No Ideology
First though, let it be said that the Australian Democrats will not have a bar of any 'ideology' if it means a rigid adherence to some set of ideas laid down by a writer or a school of thought years ago. As Don Chipp has put it, 'The party will insist on its basic principles of humanitarian concern being adapted to meet new conditions as they arise, and it will respond to new concepts setting ever higher levels of human love and justice.' Indeed, from our viewpoint, it is largely because the two older parties are tied to ideologies which are outdated, increasingly irrelevant to today's problems, and in fact, destructive and divisive in their confrontation, that they have both proved so incompetent in managing the affairs of the nation.

Objectives of the Australian Democrats

Policy Objectives
1 To be beholden to no group or groups in the community but to serve the best interests of all Australians.

2 To accept the challenge of the predicament of mankind on the planet with its exponentially increasing population, disappearing finite resources and accelerating deterioration of the environment.
3 To recognise the interdependence of all people and all nations, to co-operate fully with the United Nations, and to accept our obligation to the developing countries by co-operating with them in their social and economic development.
4 To seek the transition to a sustainable economy, in equilibrium with world resources and ecosystems, with a minimum of dislocation by planning the necessary changes in good time, and by increasing public awareness of the problems ahead.
5 To use our positions as a party in the middle ground, even-handed to capital and labour, to reconcile their real interests by encouraging industrial democracy and all other forms of co-operation.
6 To foster greater mutual understanding, as well as greater equality of income per hour of work, between city and country dwellers.
7 To stimulate the development of a multi-faceted national culture, with full opportunity for all ethnic groups to contribute.
8 To further unite the people of Australia by co-operative, indicative national planning, taking account of social as well as of economic objectives, seeking consensus of all sections of the community, including political parties, so that there may be continuity.
9 To seek improvement in the quality of human relationships in all aspects of society and the economy, through honesty, tolerance, compassion and a sense of mutual obligation.
10 To decentralise power, to oppose its concentration in the hands of sectional groups, and to ensure that the power of large groups or of bureaucracies is not allowed to override the interests of individuals or of smaller groups.
11 To achieve and defend effective participatory democracy and open government by appropriate constitutional, parliamentary and governmental reforms.
12 By supporting existing rural and provincial industries and in other ways, to stem, and finally reverse, the flow of population to the cities, the firm belief that given better facilities, many people would prefer to live in the country.
13 In social and health services to emphasise prevention rather than cure.
14 To foster community activities and the growth of community spirit, bringing government and health services closer to the people.
15 To enable people to pursue lifestyles of their own choosing so long as they do not interfere with the rights of others.

16 To provide education for living, as well as for earning a living, throughout life.
17 To ensure ready access to the media for public communication.
18 To ensure that the basic needs of all people are securely met, and to distribute income, wealth, social services and opportunity more equitably without undermining either incentive or self-respect.
19 To encourage individual initiative and enterprise and to recognise the need for self-fulfilment.
20 To allow neither avidity for material gain nor 'sporting' instinct override our concern and compassion for animals.

5.5 THEY'RE ALL THE SAME?

Source: Turner, K. 1976, 'The Party Contest in the 1970s', in Mayer, H. & Nelson, H. (eds), *Australian Politics: A Fourth Reader,* Longman Cheshire, Melbourne, p. 463.

A common criticism of two-sided systems is that the parties provide rival formulae but no choice, because the formulae are indistinguishable in any significant respect. Such charges arise not only out of simple cynicism as represented in statements like: 'They're all the same' or 'Vote informal: otherwise you get a politician'. They arise also out of worldwide observations about policy convergence.

Parties in a two-sided competition find 'me-tooism' irresistible. At recent Australian elections, observers have highlighted this phenomenon by references to 'Gortlam' or 'Gill Sneddlam' policies or to Snedden's 1974 program as 'Whitlamism at half pace'. Neither party can allow the other an edge. Electoral opportunism induces each party to woo those in the middle who alone have a choice. The loyalty of hardcore supporters can be taken for granted for they have nowhere to go however much they complain of 'ratting' or 'betrayal of principles'...

But the similarity of the parties' programs is not simply due to electoral opportunism. 'Consensus politics' could be partly a product of societies where political temperatures are low and agreement considerable. Besides wide acceptance of the 'broad rules of the game', there may be fundamental agreement about a whole range of 'settled issues'. Perhaps the Welfare State has softened political conflict to a dispute about priorities?

In well-off homogeneous Australia there may be more agreement than in some countries. Still, even disagreements about scope, method, speed, and priorities can be important. Moreover, supposedly settled issues can come unstuck. Indeed 'fundamental agreement' then turns out to be agreement only at a level of rhetoric or ambiguity, or arrived at only by avoiding consideration of divisive issues...

Finally, 'responsible' major parties are likely to find similar answers because they face the same contextual constraints. Both sides know that in office they will face similar problems and demands, and that in meeting them they will have the same resources, and similar limits to their opinions. They will experience the same international constraints. They must manage the same economy, working with the same private power groups and working through a Public Service whose 'departmental line' can be altered only with great effort, despite changes of political master. Despite the rhetoric of party debate, the two sides do not offer a choice between systems but about how a given system might be run.

5.6 EXTRACTS FROM CALL TO AUSTRALIA PARTY FEDERAL PLATFORM 1990

Call To Australia is firmly committed to preserving the independence of Australia as a Sovereign Nation. We deplore the commitment of Labor, Liberal and Democrat parties to 'international' goals through the deliberate misuse of the 'External Affairs' clause in Section 51 of our Constitution.

We therefore propose:

- To withdraw Australia from membership of the pro-Socialist, pro-Communist United Nations Organisation.
- To modify, by referendum, the 'External Affairs' clause in the Constitution in order to prevent politicians signing International Treaties which become law without first consulting the Australian people.
- To resist the transfer of Australian sovereignty to the United Nations or to new Aboriginal States.

We support an urgent review by all States to consider, with the intention of initiating referenda on:

- a proposed re-introduction of capital punishment by humane methods for specific crimes.

Call To Australia has conclusive evidence to confirm the fact that most of the rhetoric concerning the 'greenhouse effect' and the 'depletion of the ozone layer' is blatant propaganda.

The objective of the propagandists is to create sufficient panic among our populations so that central planners may be justified in grabbing more power through environmental issues for Canberra and then transfer this power to international bodies.

Global control of the environment is the ultimate goal and is the real issue at stake. We therefore take the following position:

- We will expose the fallacies of the 'environment' movements by funding and promoting properly organised scientific research.
- We claim that most matters affecting the environment can be dealt with at Local Government level and power should be retained at that level.

- We believe that, as a Christian-based party we are bound to be faithful stewards and protectors of our environment, but that God's promises to Noah and Job establishing His dominion over His creation are still relevant and binding.
- We believe that all foreign aid to totalitarian governments should be abolished and any aid provided to the citizens of such countries be administered by approved charitable groups, supervised according to strict humanitarian guidelines.

5.7 SELECTED LIST OF MINOR PARTIES WHICH CONTESTED ELECTIONS, 1988–1990

Australian Alliance Party
Australian Conservative Party
Australian Democrats
Australian Ethnic Democrats
Australians Against Further Immigration
Australian Family Movement
Australian Green Party
Balonne Independence Movement
Central Coast Greens
Citizens Electoral Councils
Cowper Greens
Combined New Australian Party
Communist Party
Community Independent Party
Call To Australia Party
Defence and Ex-Services Party
Democratic Labor Party
Democratic Socialist Party
Green Alliance
Green Independents
Greens in Lowe
(The) Greens
Grey Power
Senator Brian Harradine Group
Illawarra Greens
Illawarra Workers Party
Independent Christian Democrat Party
Independent Conservative Party
Independent Enterprise
Independent Labor
Macarthur Green Party
Nuclear Disarmament Party
National Party of Australia
One Australia Movement
Pensioner Party
Rex Connor (Sen.) Labor Party
Referendum First Group
Sydney Greens
Socialist Alliance
Socialist Party
South Sydney Greens
Socialist Workers Party
Torres United Party
United Australia Party
United Peoples Party
United Tasmanian Group
Victorian Green Alliance
Vallentine Peace Group
Western Australian Green Party
Western Suburbs Greens

5.8 ARE PARTIES NECESSARY FOR DEMOCRACY?

Source: Sir Mark Oliphant, Speech to First Conference of Australian Democrats, 16 February 1980.

I have a deep conviction that the two-party system in politics is destroying democracy. Politicians, in State and Federal Parliaments, pursue their calling as did the soldiers at Waterloo. They are arrayed in opposing ranks, firing broadsides at one another, and trooping obediently into the division rooms at the commands of their leaders. Their insults are hurled back and forth, like a clash between two 'bikie' gangs of larrikins, neither ever admitting that the proposals of the other could have any merit whatsoever. Since it is every politician's ambition to become a member of a government, he or she must obey without question. *Once elected to parliament, the member no longer represents his constituency.* He becomes an automaton, representing only his party, often in blatant opposition to the wishes of the people who put him there. And the party leaders are, in turn, manipulated by the well-off and powerful, on the one hand, and by the even more powerful trade unions on the other. There are still kingmakers among us.

ISSUES FOR DISCUSSION

1 Compare and contrast the various party documents. Do these official statements suggest differences, or similarities of ideology and policy?
2 Are political parties necessary for democracy in Australia? In other words, could Australia do without parties? (See Document 5.8.)
3 What features of Australian political society have encouraged a functioning two-party system?
4 Would a multi-party system be better for Australia?
5 Given the history of minor parties in Australia, what future has the Australian Democrat Party?
6 How, and why, has the National Party succeeded where other minor parties have failed?
7 To one observer, 'the ALP is organisationally and ideologically fogbound within capitalism' (McQueen 1972:345). How socialist is the Labor Party? (See Document 5.1.)
8 'The Liberal Party is ideologically a coalition ranging from very conservative to liberal with a small "l".' How liberal is the Liberal Party? (See Document 5.2.)

9 Can a Country Party be a National Party as well? (See Document 5.3.)
10 Do political parties put their major supporting groups first? That is, does the National Party serve rural industry, the Labor Party serve trade unions, the Liberal Party serve business?
11 Can Australia be referred to as having a two-party system? (See Document 5.7.)
12 Under normal circumstances, over half and up to three-quarters of all of the electorates in Australia—national and state—are safe for one party or another. In such seats, the pre-selection of the candidate by the party is really the election of a member to parliament. Is this system adequate for democracy? Should Australia incorporate a 'primary' system, as in the USA, where candidates compete openly for selection?
13 What is the ideology of the Call To Australia Party? (See Document 5.6.)
14 Select a political party and discuss the extent to which that party:
  a speaks for the wishes and demands of its members and supporters
  b publicises these wishes and demands
  c attracts electoral support
  d wins seats
  e ensures democracy within its organisation
  f maintains unity
  g is ideological
  h (if it has won office, or shared office) has provided an effective administration, and has put its policies into practice.

Chapter six
PRESSURE GROUPS, PUBLIC OPINIONS AND THE MASS MEDIA

Australian society is a kaleidoscope of interests. People belong to many groups, formal and informal, organised and ad hoc, large and small. The spectrum of such interests is very broad indeed, encompassing sporting groups, trade unions, hobby groups, farmers' associations, service groups, and so on. Normally, members of an interest group, such as a group of butterfly collectors, go happily about their collecting, analysing and sharing a common interest. But if a government decided to impose a tax on butterfly collecting, the interest group would rapidly become a pressure group.

Pressure groups are active everywhere in Australian politics. In modern industrial societies, one individual is not likely to carry much weight in the political process. People have found by experience that they need to join together with others of like opinions, interests and aims if they are going to exert an effective influence in an attempt to attain their common objectives—that is, collective action through pressure groups. Wherever government—whether national, state or local—is involved, there will be many kinds of organised pressure groups.

Three terms are often used as synonyms in the analysis of groups. In fact, they describe different modes of activity. An *interest group* is a formal or informal group of people with common interests, attitudes or aims—for example, a commercial interest, a church interest or a rural interest. A *pressure group* is a formal organisation of people who share one or more interests or objectives or concerns and who try to influence the course of public policy to protect or to promote these objectives. In the USA, a third term is widely used—the *lobby*. This refers to pressure groups acting directly on individual members of the legislature in an attempt to achieve their aims. For simplicity, this analysis will include lobbies under the term pressure group.

We need to distinguish between pressure groups and political parties. Although the functions and activities of pressure groups and parties sometimes overlap, they can be distinguished in three ways. First, political parties are usually far broader in aims, policies and support than single-issue pressure groups. Most political parties in Australia seek to win support across the nation and to seek support from voters from every socio-economic background. As a result, the programmes of the political parties are broad. A pressure group usually has a narrow programme, and its appeal (and membership) is usually limited to a relatively small group of people who are directly interested in such a policy. Second, political parties are distinguishable from pressure groups because the major political parties in Australia, when in government, are in a position to set the rules for the activities of pressure groups. Third, a party nominates candidates for election for political office; a pressure group does not. Overall, a political party contests elections with the aim of achieving a position where it can *make* policy; a pressure group seeks to *influence* policy, policy-makers, and the policy-making process.

Two qualifications are needed for such a clear distinction. First, some pressure groups live in a grey area between group and party, and on occasions, cross the line. The group Defence of Government Schools (DOGS) was a pressure group in the 1960s. In the years 1969–1972, when the debate over state aid to private schools was bitterly fought, DOGS nominated candidates for state and federal elections but without any success. It was, for a short time, a single-issue political party; it then returned to its pressure group activity.

Second, some pressure groups have a very close relationship with political parties. The most obvious example of group-party interaction is that of the trade-union movement and the Labor Party. The affiliated unions constitute the industrial wing of the party—in fact, in terms of numbers of delegates, they control the party. They are therefore engaged in policy-making through the party, and are also constantly engaged in pressure group activities. In a similar style, the close relationship between some rural pressure groups and the (then)

Country Party, at least until the 1970s, led some observers to suggest that the party was little more than a single-issue party, the conduit in parliament for rural pressures. More recently, the (now) National Party has faced considerable dissent from rural areas, and organisations such as the Cattlemen's Association and the National Farmers' Federation are evidence that the rural groups have not been satisfied.

All pressure group activity takes place in the political arena. A group applies pressure on one or more levels of the decision-making processes of government. The pressure is political, and seeks a political decision. Individual pressure groups, asked for their interpretations of their roles, gave markedly differing answers. Some were quite clear about their political role in the interests of their numbers:

- To advocate, promote and procure the passing of such legislation, both federal and state, as may be conducive to any of the objects of the Association (South Australian Association of Permanent Building Societies)
- To co-operate with government departments and representatives to ensure that government policies be to the best advantage of the industry (Housing Industry Association).

Some clearly understood a key distinction:

- The Association shall be and remain non-party political...[objects include] to raise and obtain moneys for expenditure in accomplishing the objects of the Association, provided that no such moneys shall be used for party-political purposes (United Farmers and Graziers of South Australia).

Others, however, did not distinguish the political from the party political:

- I wish to advise that Women's Christian Temperance Union is a non-political organisation.

Pressure groups *are* political. Their reason for existence is to influence politics and policy-making. To do so, they undertake political activities.

A PLETHORA OF PRESSURES

Any interested person has only to examine the classified pages of a telephone directory or one of the daily newspapers to be aware of the number and diversity of pressure groups in Australia. One direct cause of this extent and intensity of activity is the fact that governments have slowly but steadily extended their involvement in, and regulation of, the economy and of society. As this has occurred, new pressure groups have emerged seeking to benefit or to react. As well, government has become increasingly dependent on such groups for information, co-operation and even co-ordination of governmental activities. In particular, as governments have been increasingly involved in social and economic legislation, so new pressure groups have emerged.

Another reason for the proliferation of pressure groups in Australia is the federal system, which has meant that some pressure groups may have to be involved with national, state and local authorities. Some groups are organised and active only in their specific states or areas; others, especially economic groups, are increasingly national organisations. A further reason is the ever-increasing complexity of modern society. The division of labour and increasing specialisation has caused more and more specific interests to emerge, each of which may spawn a group to protect or further its interests. One example is in the field of medicine. Until recently, the medical profession's pressure group was the Australian Medical Association. Partly because of the constantly changing concept and application of Medibank and Medicare, the AMA split, and three other pressure groups formed—the General Practitioners' Society, the Doctors' Reform Society, and the Procedural Surgeons, each with different interests to promote and/or protect.

Finally, the organisation of one interest has a tendency to produce the organisation of a counter-interest. One can argue over which came first, of course, but the formation of trade unions was matched by the emergence of employers' associations. The Abortion Law Reform Association and the Right to Life Association were formed over one issue, and Australia's involvement in the Vietnam War spawned a number of pressure groups, both for and against.

A TYPOLOGY OF PRESSURE GROUPS

The most obvious fact about pressure groups in Australia is their tremendous heterogeneity. There seem to be pressure groups in and around every aspect of human activity. To make sense out of their activities, we need to classify them in some way. One means of classification is based on the group's reason for existence, and distinguishes two major types.

1 Sectional groups, which are concerned with the specific interests of their members, either to achieve something, or to protect the interests of the group from incursions by government or by some other interest. These are essentially self-interested, and usually

economic—often subdivided into agriculture, labour and business pressure groups.

2 Altruistic groups, which are other-interested rather than self-interested. These exist and function on the basis of public-spirited motives, for causes which they believe are in the public interest. They include such groups as the Royal Society for the Prevention of Cruelty to Animals, and the Council for Civil Liberties.

This distinction faces the problem of the many groups which, in some of their activities, can be defined as altruistic, but in others are in the sectional, self-interested category. Churches and church organisations, the Returned and Services League, education groups, all at some time may be arguing for public-spirited purposes—for moral re-armament, for better defence, for better education—and at another time applying pressure to the government for some advantage for their membership. Hence, the boundaries between these classifications may become blurred.

Most pressure groups are naturally concerned with maintaining their own existence, and this results in the formation—especially in the large groups—of an internal organisation and bureaucracy. It can also lead to the group being involved in protecting itself against another group pursuing similar aims and goals. Some rural groups may find themselves opposed by other rural organisations, although one would expect the overall goals of groups in the rural sector to be relatively similar. Membership poaching in the trade union movement is a constant theme, although it could be assumed that the overall goals of most unions in the industrial field are relatively similar.

The most obviously and most openly sectional and self-interested pressure groups are those in the economic area. These range over the whole spectrum of the economy of Australia. They encompass all industries—sugar, wool, wheat, wood-chipping, minerals, coal, chemicals, oil companies and the building industry. As well, there are peak associations—groups of similar pressure groups which come together under one umbrella. For example, there are many specific pressure groups within the business sector, and these have formed peak associations such as the Chamber of Manufactures and the Confederation of Australian Industry. There are hundreds of individual trade unions, many under the umbrella of the Australian Council of Trade Unions. Each will be involved in constant activity to seek to obtain benefits for, or to protect, the interests of its members, whether such benefits and protection are in the form of tariffs, bounties, subsidies, wages, conditions or whatever. Such self-protection is not limited to the areas of business and industry. Professions—medical professionals, lawyers, dentists, teachers, academics—are all protective of their own interests and have established formal, organised pressure groups to further these.

Other analysts have proposed different typologies. Some, for example, distinguish between five types. One is the self-interested and self-protective groups in any industrial society—business, agricultural, manufacturing and so on—which seek specific benefits for their members. A second type are those larger aggregates of people who share a common characteristic, but who rarely become pressure groups, and when they do, rarely achieve the unanimity and cohesion of the first type. One example is the aggregate of aged people in Australia. In the 1980s, when governments faced severe economic pressures and began to limit, even cut back, benefits for the aged, a number of pensioner pressure groups, and even a Grey Power Party, were formed. A third type can be referred to as institutional pressure groups. These are part of the institutional structure of government, but have interests to protect and enhance. The defence forces, the police, statutory authorities, even the parliament itself, can act as pressure groups on government. The fourth type are the selfless, altruistic groups like Friends of the Earth or Save the Children Fund. Finally, public perception is often focussed on the less organised, more ephemeral, but very public pressure groups that emerge over specific issues. These usually form when a specific issue becomes contentious, and disappear when the issue is resolved.

TARGETS, MEANS, ACCESS, SUCCESS

Pressure groups, by definition, seek to bring pressure on the policy-makers. The activities of pressure groups, in the final analysis, can be refined to a single statement; they seek to influence the making of public policy, whether in their favour or from some altruistic motive. To clarify the nature and the differential successes of pressure-group activities, we need to ask four questions:

1 Where do groups apply pressure in order to obtain what they are seeking?
2 By what means and methods do they hope to achieve their aims?
3 Which channels of access do they intend to exploit?
4 What are the characteristics of groups and the political society which make for success for some and failure for others?

In other words, an analysis of the role and effectiveness of pressure groups needs to examine the nature of the institutions of government, the characteristics of pressure groups and the strategic position of pressure groups in the society, the economy, and the governmental structure.

TARGETS AND MEANS

The foci of group pressures and the means used by pressure groups have changed over time. As the range of government activity and involvement has broadened and the area of public administration has widened, so there has been increased opportunity and incentive for pressure groups. As the power of government and cabinet has strengthened and the power of parliament and parliamentarians has correspondingly decreased, so pressure groups have recognised that new forms and targets of pressure need to be considered so that the greatest benefit can be achieved.

In Australia, access and potential influence are more limited than in a presidential system such as in the USA. We can simplify matters by considering five major potential points of access to decision-makers for pressure groups.

PARLIAMENT AND THE LOBBY

Parliament in Australia has changed to the extent where lobbying—direct attempts to influence members of parliament—is almost a waste of time. For most legislation the function of law-making has passed out of the control of parliament to the cabinet—parliament debates and almost inevitably ratifies, but does not often initiate legislation. Individual members of parliament have become subservient to their parties; for most legislation, the party line will be maintained. As a result, for most legislation, pressure groups have found that the lobby is a waste of resources, energy and time.

On the rare occasions when the party whips are removed, when the parties decide that a free vote should be permitted, the lobby is very effective. On such social issues as drinking laws, abortion law reform, prostitution and homosexuality, political parties find themselves faced with internal differences of such intensity that a free vote is granted to members to avoid a public party split. On such occasions, the individual members of the parliament are subjected to the efforts of pressure groups for and against—delegations, lobbies, letters, petitions and phone-ins—to an extent not normally seen in Australian parliaments.

During the last decade, a lobby industry has emerged, especially in Canberra—pressure groups rightly recognise the place of power! This lobby industry consists of a range of lobby companies and individual lobbyists, who are employed by a range of interests in the society to bring pressure on government, either directly, or through ministers, parties and even private members. It is a comment on the nature of federalism that the Northern Territory government employed a lobby to push its interests to the national government. However, parliament and individual members of parliament are usually not an effective means of access for pressure groups. The role of governing, legislating and policy-making has shifted to three other areas, and pressure groups have naturally followed.

THE EXECUTIVE

Pressure groups increasingly direct their activities to cabinet, ministers and the public service. This is based on a realistic assessment of where the powers of decision-making really lie—with cabinet rather than parliament, ministers rather than backbenchers, with the top civil servants, that is, the expert advisers to the ministers, and with those with the power of delegated legislation. The aim of the pressure groups is, after all, to bring pressure to bear where it will produce the most effective results.

Each year before the budget is brought down, major national pressure groups present a brief to cabinet, but these are only the most publicised forms of communication between groups and government. The continuing process of pressure is less formal, less public, but has great potential for pressure groups. If the cabinet can be convinced that a policy sought by a pressure group merits support, then the pressure group has succeeded. The task may remain to seek urgent application of the demand, either through legislation or through the public service, but if cabinet can be convinced, then the battle effectively has been won. At the same time, pressure groups have concentrated increasingly on the bureaucracy. In fact, the most constant (but least open) contact between government and pressure groups occurs at the upper levels of the public service. This is a recognition of the power, influence and ubiquity of the public service in the Australian political process.

The institutionalised relationships of the executive and pressure groups are based on a recognition that while pressure groups have to live with government, so governments have to live in a political process dominated by group activity, and need advice, specialised information and co-operation from pressure groups. Governments, then, have established formal links with some pressure groups to maintain a flow of information needed to frame viable, realistic and, in the final analysis, acceptable policies. Hence a cabinet may consult with the Australian Medical Association about a medical benefits scheme, with manufacturers concerning tariffs and import policies, with trade unions about industrial legislation, with banks about economic policy and with primary industry groups about world markets and export matters.

A further formal relationship has been established in the area of delegated legislation and in the proliferation of statutory corporations of government. These joint efforts by government, bureaucracy and pressure groups encompass such bodies as advisory committees—formed by a combination of these three elements to act as a permanent source of expert advice to government in that area—and administering bodies such as marketing boards, public corporations and statutory authorities in which the pressure group has a specified and important role.

POLITICAL PARTIES

The interest shown by pressure groups in political parties in Australia is based on a recognition that politics has become *party* politics. If a pressure group can win the support of a major political party, to the extent that the aims of the group are ultimately written into party policy, then electoral success for that party ensures virtual policy success for the pressure group.

The extent and degree of group alignment with political parties varies from group to group. Association to the point of absorption occurs only in the case of the unions and the Labor Party. Some groups have an informal alignment. Business and commercial interests have tended to be closer to the Liberal Party, have sought concessions from it and funded it when requested. Others claim a specifically neutral position and support the idea of, say, the Australian Institute of Management which claims in its constitution to be 'non-party, non-partisan and independent'. Others adopt a formal neutrality, but find themselves closer to one or other of the two major parties for a specific period or over a specific issue.

In general, the relationship of a pressure group with a political party will depend on the extent to which the aims of the group and the ideology of the party coincide. Rural pressure groups have generally aligned themselves with the National Party and with the broader Liberal–National Party coalition, but a recent development of interest has been the formation of rural based pressure groups—such as the National Farmers' Federation—which have not been satisfied with National Party representation.

The relationship between pressure group and party will also depend on the likelihood that the party will achieve a position of power or influence. The Liberal and Labor parties have the potential to form a government; the National Party has considerable influence in the coalition. But groups would find little benefit in close relations with a minor party. The relationship can also be affected by the attitudes of the party itself. Some political parties attempt to incorporate as many interests as possible; such parties are under pressure from many groups and are forced to judge and to balance these. Elsewhere, special interests have a strong foothold in a particular party and this provides a strong lever. Sometimes an entire minor political party, such as the Nuclear Disarmament Party, may consist mainly of one interest group.

THE ELECTORATE

This point of access to decision-making is based on an indirect method, an attempt to influence government through public opinion, public pressure and the ballot box. This often involves large-scale and costly publicity campaigns and it is usually a means of last resort for a group. Pressure groups generally turn to the public only when other means of access have been tried and have failed to bring the desired result. In the context of Australian politics, it has been mainly altruistic promotional groups which have taken this action of last resort; only rarely do sectional, business and producer groups seek to influence the electorate and by so doing, to influence the government.

The means of such attempts by pressure groups to influence the public and their votes vary widely, from direct action (marches, demonstrations, sit-ins) to media campaigns. In the last two decades, Australia has seen direct action from two groups which could be considered to be on opposite sides of the ideological fence—from farmers and from groups opposed to Australia's involvement in the Vietnam War. Both claim that their direct action was a significant factor in influencing government decisions of the time, but all groups recognise that this focus on the electorate is the most uncertain in terms of positive results. Most groups, of course, would consider this style of pressure entirely inappropriate and resort to the public only rarely; it is a costly and often fruitless exercise, given the strength and stability of party identification and voting patterns.

CHARACTERISTICS OF PRESSURE GROUPS

The nature of the pressure group can be an important factor in its success or failure. In simple terms, a group which has resources, a large membership, is united internally in the formulation of aims and in regard to methods of action, which has developed organisation skills and has professional expertise and a clear knowledge of the machinery of government has a head-start to success. It follows, then, that a group which is small, poor, disorganised and uninformed about the process of government is under severe constraints.

Unity is important. It is of no value to a pressure group to have a large membership if most members are not actively committed to the cause. Leaders of any group can attest to the constant difficulty of obtaining a commitment from many members, even to the extent of attending meetings. Usually a mass-membership group is similar to a political party or to the electorate as a whole: it consists of a small number of totally committed leaders, devoting much of their time, effort and money to the campaign; a hard-core of willing and active supporters who identify closely with the aims of the group, attend meetings, and work for the group; and the remainder, often a majority, who are little more than nominal members.

A combination of size, wealth, sense of unity, and clear and distinct aims is the basis for a powerful pressure group. Wealth is increasingly important, especially as the complexity of government demands more and more detailed knowledge and professional activity. Pressure groups are depending more on costly public relations, the relations with government authorities may require legal skills and the very diversity of government—national, state, local, and the development of statutory authorities—demands a wide spread of activity by a pressure group.

STRATEGIC POSITION

A pressure group may have size, wealth and unity, but it may find that its aims are frustrated by an opposing group. The explanation may well be that one group occupies a position in relation to government, the economy or even society at large which gives it a certain advantage.

Pressure groups based on key sectors of the economy are indeed powerful. One simple example is the extent to which certain industries have obtained and retained such benefits as tariff protection. Rural industries have equally been able to protect their interests and their benefits for over a century. In contrast, economic groups which do not have a strategic position will find that their arguments fall on less sympathetic ears.

Some groups have a strong bargaining position because they control a scarcity of some sort. Oil producers are a powerful pressure group and will probably become even stronger as supplies dwindle. A monopoly or near-monopoly control of an industry provides inherent strength at the bargaining tables; it is commonly said that if BHP sneezes, the government will supply a handkerchief. A third instance would be the situation of farmers in a marginal National Party seat—in fact, any major pressure group in any marginal seat—who are likely to receive the benefits and services they seek.

At the same time, the political culture of the society regards some pressure groups as more acceptable than others. The activities of such groups as the Returned and Services League and the Australian Medical Association can achieve a mantle of respectability, even of supporting the common good, when in fact these pressure groups have aims little if at all different from other groups seeking benefits for their members. To this extent, then, the RSL, the AMA, the trade union movement, the Cattlemen's Association and the oil industry are all in the same game. The difference is in the level of acceptance and respectability given to each group and the tactics they use to achieve their desired ends.

If a pressure group intends to win what it wants, it may have to be willing to change its methods. It may also be forced to do so. Rural pressure groups, through their informal links with the National Party, expect and commonly receive what they want when a Liberal–National Party coalition is in government. But when the coalition is in opposition, or when relations between the National Party and a Liberal government are strained, such groups find that the access to the policy-making level is not as smooth.

The trade-union movement, like other pressure groups, modifies its tactics to fit circumstances. Given the special relationship of the union movement with the Labor Party, it is not surprising that some unions and some sections of the movement have, on occasions, seen a Labor government as Father Christmas, a direct line to benefits for the union pressure group. Consultation and direct collective bargaining is one type of union pressure-group activity; strikes are another type, both within the range of tactics available to pressure groups.

At the same time, some groups and types of groups have been reluctant to act openly as pressure groups and have rejected any suggestions of militant, direct action. But tactics change with circumstances, and some professional and white-collar groups—doctors, teachers, nurses and others—which, in the past, were never militant, have tended to become so in recent years.

Finally, the success of a pressure group will depend on the extent to which government wishes to heed the demands, the extent to which it is committed by circumstances to do so and the extent to which it is forced to do so. Hence a pressure group which has built up a positive attitude to itself in the political culture, which has a large membership, which has formal and informal relations with government at all levels and which has members of the group in the parliament and in the government, is well placed for success. Some industries have continued to receive special benefits such as tariff protection as the government has been forced to protect employment.

In summary, some powerful pressure groups in Australia have access, status and potential for a veto power. These groups will have means of access to the various levels of government, to decision-makers, either formally or informally and may even be connected in some formal way with decision-makers. They will also have their activities and roles recognised as legitimate by the decision-makers and by the society. Finally, such groups will have some ability to impose further pressure—even a veto—if a decision or policy is not in their favour. In contrast to such groups with strategic positions in the society some groups have little or no direct representation in parliament, cabinet or bureaucracy; they often swim against the tide of public opinion and their activities are often limited by circumstances to public agitation and the seeking of publicity for their causes.

GROUPS AND THE POLITICAL PROCESS

Pressure groups are an integral part of the political process in Australia. There is a constant ferment of activity at all levels of government as various groups battle to obtain the benefits they seek. On the other hand, pressure-group activity in Australia is not as public, as recognised, as legitimatised and as seemingly effective as in the USA and Canada. The reason suggested for this is that the functions of aggregating and articulating the demands of various pressure groups have been pre-empted in Australia by dominant, ubiquitous and permanent political parties. But this question needs to be considered; is it the case that while pressure groups are more public and more publicly active in North America, are they as powerful (if not more powerful) in Australia, but just not as public?

Even given the problem of establishing the real power and influence of pressure groups, there are two opposed theories about the role of pressure groups in the processes of democratic government.

PLURALISM

The pluralist argument sees activity by pressure groups as natural and valuable in a democracy. This argument holds that pressure groups reflect conflicting divisions in society, but they also contribute to the social consensus by providing the informal institutions whereby these inherent conflicts may be peacefully resolved by compromise within the society to the existing political system. As the pressure groups are a part of the existing political system, they therefore have a vested interest in its maintenance. Pressure groups are therefore seen as a valuable two-way channel of communication and pressure between the government and the governed. Through pressure groups, complaints and grievances of members are taken up to the government along with those views and opinions on policies which especially affect particular groups. This channel is continuously open and therefore, along with other channels such as the press and the parliament, covers the gap between elections when the governed actually choose the government. Pressure groups are therefore seen as alternative channels of communication for those who dissent from the discipline of political parties and for those who are unsuccessful in winning acceptance for their policies in the programmes of parties and an alternative means whereby the voices and opinions of the governed can be heard by the government.

This argument describes pressure groups as additional and complementary to the system of geographical representation through local constituencies and a local member of parliament. Thus, in representing diverse functional groups in a complex industrial society, pressure groups complement and enlarge the degree of representation. One MP cannot represent all the different interests in his or her one geographical area. Nor can two or three large political parties completely fulfil this task for the nation.

Many analysts of Australian politics describe the system as a pluralist structure. The major features of this model are that:

1 The political society is essentially composed of groups which are diverse in nature and membership.
2 Individuals have the freedom and the potential to join what groups they wish, within the rules of those groups, and can work within such groups to further their interests, but participation is not an essential requirement for the operation of a pluralist polity.
3 The issues of politics are matters of values, of different ideas about what is best for society as democratic processes do not seek authoritarian solutions to problems and issues, but seek solutions by consensus, accommodation and compromise of many differing views.
4 Power is not centralised or monopolised, but is dispersed among groups, and is organised by them.
5 The groups involved in politics are led by an élite within each group which at the same time, reflects the opinions and demands of the mass membership of the group.
6 Groups genuinely compete for power, and for public support in pursuit of power, and no one group or combination of groups obtains a dominant position, for it will always be matched by an opposing group or set of groups.
7 Governments play a role similar to that of an umpire—a government's task is to adjudicate between the competing claims of such groups and, more often than not by compromise, to arrive at policies and decisions which will be satisfactory for the majority.

Pluralists therefore argue that the participation by a wide range of groups and interests in the decision-making processes, at all levels, produces a balance which, in the broad sense of democracy, produces the best policies and decisions for the greatest number of people.

CRITICS OF PLURALISM

Critics of the pluralist model argue that while the benefits may be there in theory, the model does not work in real life. Further, they argue that it *cannot* work. They point to the facts, acknowledged by pluralists, that some groups have more wealth, better organisation, a good strategic position and better access to the decision-makers.

To some analysts, then, Australia is governed by élites. Their theory is based on the following grounds.

1 The mass of individuals in society do not have power (beyond an electoral decision).
2 Groups exist, but most do not achieve a position where they can in any real way influence policy and policy-making.
3 Those who control the bases of power—the economy, the mass media, the upper levels of the bureaucracy—form élites which, by their control of such key areas, can influence decision-making and even dictate it.
4 The parliament, the parties and the public contain some members of the élite, but have little function other than to ratify decisions already made by the élites.

A second criticism is based on the obvious strength of some economic groups; the term 'neo-capitalism' is used to describe a

Pressure groups—planning for action?

system which is characterised by the pervasiveness of business in the institutions of the State, in planning, co-ordination and control. This argument criticises the pluralist thesis on at least two grounds: that the various groups in society do not compete on even relatively equal terms; that some are so powerful and so formally and informally linked with government that they give opposing groups little opportunity for real influence, and that the important groups are representative of the 'ruling class' in society which excludes ordinary people from decision-making. One such view is put by Connell and Irving (in Mayer and Nelson 1973:33).

> In what sense does a ruling class rule? Firstly, in the sense that its members make economic decisions that shape the lives of the whole people. They direct the production of goods, their distribution, pricing, and so on; and in the modern economy they direct the stimulation of wants and tastes through advertising and fashion. In a more general sense, the class rules jointly by preserving the power structure within which its members individually hold the right to do these things. That is, it is able to preserve the system of private ownership and prevent alternative systems emerging. This preservation involves much more than purely economic power. For one thing, it involves political power. A ruling class exercises that by its members actually managing the affairs of government, by sponsoring politicians who will manage them in a way that does no damage to the system of property, or by destroying political movements that do threaten damage. It is also likely to involve cultural power. A really well-established ruling class dominates the culture of its time.

Still others described Australia as similar to the power structure of American politics described by C. Wright Mills in his book *The Power Elite* (1956).

> Across the bargaining tables of power, the bureaucracies of business and government face one another, and under the tables their myriad feet are interlocked in wonderfully complex ways.

The reality of the process of policy-making and decision-making in Australia is probably somewhere between these models. Sectional pressure groups are concerned with their own interests and will seek to obtain as much influence and power as possible. Some groups have attained a degree of influence which does put them well ahead of their rivals. The Chamber of Manufactures, the oil industry, the mining industry, the private banking system, for example, do not have to appeal to the electorate and do not have to take to the streets to achieve their demands from government. They have established other means of influence and their importance in the Australian economy ensures that they will be listened to by government.

Most of the organised, articulate and powerful pressure groups represent economic interests. These can and do make a stream of specific demands on governments. In fact, they and their interests often represent the decisive factor in the framing of public policy and some have developed for themselves a position where they are, in effect, necessary for the government. With the tremendous advances in industry, communications, science and technology, more and more economic interests have found ways of entering, or have been specifically asked to enter, the actual process of policy-making and government.

At the same time, there are some means of checking the power of pressure groups. For example, those pressure groups which seek to exercise influence through particular political parties (especially trade union and business interests), are restricted in these endeavours by the fact that political parties must compromise between various sectional interests if they are to win an electoral majority. Individual MPs can resist the claims of local pressure groups on their vote by pleading the demands of party discipline. Many pressure groups are counterbalanced by opposing pressure groups: unions versus employers, urban versus rural, Catholic versus Protestant. The government and its departments and the political parties must balance the competing claims of different pressure groups, and government intervention and regulation may check improper pressure-group tactics; for example, laws relating to conspiracy, bribery and illegal strikes and regulations regarding the management of the affairs of companies and trade unions.

PRESSURE GROUPS AND REPRESENTATION

Any representative system has to include the principle that the representatives have been elected to represent. But how should they do so? Chapter 3 analysed the concept of a mandate and pointed out some of the complexities involved with that concept. But pressure groups raise a similar question about the potential conflicting concepts of representation and responsiveness.

The concept of responsiveness is a key element of a democratic system. Governments are expected to listen to the opinions of the citizens, consider them, weigh them up, and to devise laws accordingly. If a government decides to act in opposition to a clearly-stated majority decision, then it has a clear responsibility to explain why. But the key question is to which 'opinion' should a government be responsive? To which pressure group, if any, should governments grant most credence?

There is one view, the *trustee* model of representation, which suggests that pressure groups should not be influential. Prime

Minister Robert Menzies put a clear view about pressure groups (cited in Westerway 1965:120).

> There are plenty of pressure groups in Australia and there are plenty of pressure groups in the world... It is the age of pressure groups. It is a period of time, politically and internationally, in which people seek to promote differences and seek to promote a clash of interests so that in the waters they stir up they may fish to their advantage... Therefore I say: Away with all this pressure group idea.

The suggestion in this view is that there are 'national interests' and that sectional pressure-group interests are, by definition, antithetic to these. But it can equally be argued that the 'interests' of a democratic society are, in fact, the aggregates of the interests expressed by and through the multitude of interest groups. Democratic societies are heterogeneous, containing a multiplicity of interests, and to argue that these are somehow inimical to democratic representative government is to reject the importance of responsiveness within representation.

The problem is to which pressure group(s) should a democratic representative government give credence, and which should they reject? One cliché from the USA was coined by the head of a major car corporation: 'What is good for General Motors is good for America.' Should democratic governments give special consideration to the major industries of the nation, on the grounds that the economic health—including production, income and jobs—depends on such industries receiving favourable government consideration? The growth of the environmental movement established a counter-pressure, one which has growing public support—that is, votes. Governments are forced to consider such competing pressures as development versus environment, and decide who to 'represent'.

A MULTITUDE OF PUBLIC OPINIONS

Pressure groups are organised opinions, collections of people who have similar views, and who need to have decision-makers in governments reflect and apply those views. Any democracy is based on a concept of government by the people. The system of representative democracy is based on a concept of government in accordance with the will of the people. Australian politicians put considerable stress on the latter concept and constantly attempt to justify their actions, policies and programmes by referring to 'the people'. We also constantly hear statements such as 'the people demand it', 'it is in accord with the public interest', 'the public will not stand for it'. How do politicians determine what the view of the public is? Is there just one view? How is this view communicated to government? What is meant by 'public opinion'?

There is no such thing as a single public opinion in Australia, let alone a uniform, or permanent, or consistent public opinion. In any society, there will be a number of different, even contradictory, public opinions because there will be a number of different 'publics'. These publics will react to events, issues and policies in different ways; some will be nearer to an event than others, some will be affected by a policy in a different way from others, different occupational, social or economic publics will react in different ways and different basic attitudes will also predispose different opinions in different publics. There is a tremendous complexity of public opinion. If, for example, a government announces that it intends to legislate for compulsory secret ballots for all major trade-union decisions because 'public opinion' has demanded it, then the proposal would certainly not reflect the opinion of all members of trade unions. An announcement about tariff protection or subsidies or a tax increase will bring different reactions from different interests—from different publics.

Who represents public opinion?

As well as emphasising that a complex society such as Australia will not show only one, uniform, public opinion, there are some further qualifications to keep in mind. There may be differences between the opinions which are held privately by people, and the opinions which they express publicly. There are public opinions which are vocal, which are usually expressed through pressure groups. There are public opinions which can be tapped through such agencies as public opinion polls. There are also public opinions which are latent and contingent, on which politicians gamble at election times. When opinions are expressed in public, they are more often than not the opinions of specific groups and often the opinion of leaders of groups. Not all members of the public have formed opinions on all issues and not all opinions will be based on full information. Finally, Australia's political culture is characterised by widespread apathy, hence the concept of an aware, rational, public opinion is even more doubtful. Thus, when a politician refers to a public opinion as a reason for an action or decision, it may be that he/she is really referring to the opinion of a political party, or to the opinion of a specific interest group which is important, or even to his or her own particular opinion.

As well, opinions can be fluid. While it is apparent that one general type of opinion—party identification—appears to be relatively stable in Australia, people do change their minds about issues, personalities and political issues. What may have been a divisive and controversial issue yesterday may not arouse any interested opinion today. Opinions are also held with different intensity by different people. For example, some may be strongly in favour of government aid to private schools; others may be totally opposed; still others are mildly in favour or mildly against; and others may not have any opinion on the issue one way or the other. Given these factors, the use of the term 'public opinion' by politicians needs to be interpreted as something other than the relatively uniform, mass opinion that is often suggested by the term.

From where do our public opinions come? The primary, and most pervasive, influences are in the political culture in which we live—our family and immediate peer group. Many of our attitudes and opinions are set for us early in life. But there are many other influences on our opinions. Our individual political attitudes, formed through early political socialisation, will affect the type of opinions we form and largely affect the way we react to political issues and events. But we will also come under a kaleidoscope of other influences. People, interests, and groups will constantly be pouring their points of view onto us and seeking to win our support.

Politicians, parties, interest groups, governments and oppositions are all centrally concerned with the opinions of the public. Their plans, policies and, for many, their futures depend on such opinions. Hence, they will be constantly concerned about political communication—attempting to produce change in opinion, or to emphasise certain opinions rather than others.

POLITICAL COMMUNICATION

The process of communication is important in any society, and in any political system, regardless of its nature. The concern of an authoritarian or totalitarian government will be to ensure that there is only one official public opinion—the opinion which the government demands. The concern, then, will be to suppress dissenting opinions and to create and reinforce a unanimous, controlled public opinion in favour of the regime. Even in such situations there will be dissenting opinions but these will be voiced in secret.

The concern of a democratic government should be to encourage the expression rather than the suppression of different opinions, to encourage diversity rather than uniformity, to guarantee freedom of opinion and expression.

The simplest example of political communication is when an individual comes into direct contact with an event. If a prime minister makes a major policy statement at a public meeting, the audience is in a situation of direct communication. At the same time, of course, the impact of such a statement will be affected by the interest, attitudes and involvement of each individual in the audience—by the political culture of the individual.

For most of us for most of the time, direct communication or actual presence at an event is simply not possible. We therefore depend on indirect means of communication. Between the event and the individual, there may be any number of links in the chain of communication, and any number of screens which may modify the message which is being communicated. All of us have at some stage played the game where a message is transferred verbally along a chain of people and we have noted the garbled version which emerges at the end of the chain. A similar process can occur in political communication.

When a prime minister makes a major policy statement, the screens between him and individual members of the public include at least the following: a member of the staff of the government will prepare a summary for the mass media; a journalist will prepare a story; a sub-editor may have to modify the story to fit the space available; one newspaper may give the story front-page treatment, another may put it as a minor story on an inside page; editorial writers may vary in their interpretation. When the story reaches the individual, the way it is received and interpreted may depend on party identification, political attitudes and the individual's interest in politics, economy and community.

Direct communication.

But political communication is not just a one-way process. Governments also need communication from the public. This process is even more indirect. Few people bother (or manage) to seek out their own local members of parliament to communicate opinions and it would be a rare occasion indeed for a private citizen to be able to discuss political issues with the members of cabinet. Hence government and opposition have to depend on such indirect methods as letters from the public, petitions and especially public-opinion polls to give them some idea of the mood, or moods, of the public.

MASS MEDIA

The media play a crucial role in the process of political communication. The democratic model of politics and government requires a continuous and full flow of information between government and public. According to the model, the better informed and aware the public is, the better will be the discussion, the better will be the bases of electoral decisions, and the better and more representative will be the policies of the government. The public, then, has the right to expect to be fully informed and the government has the duty to provide the information. What responsibilities do the media have?

The average Australian will come into contact with the mass media for a considerable proportion of every day. Most people read (more or less fully) at least one newspaper each day. Most will listen to the radio and almost all will watch television for some time. The press and the electronic media are the most obvious means of mass communication. At the same time, there is a whole range of other means of communication—magazines, pamphlets, billboards, books, films—which also play a role in the formation of public opinion. Our analysis of the Australian media will concentrate on the press and the electronic media.

If we are to assess the Australian media we need to have something by which to judge. The first point is that in a democratic society the mass media are not solely, nor even basically, concerned with political communication. In a totalitarian society, the political content and effect of the media will be the overriding concern—political communication would have to be 'of the right type'. In a democratic society, the mass media are large industries and, unless owned by the government and funded by the taxpayer, will be concerned to remain financially successful industries. Newspaper publishers and owners of the electronic media will primarily be concerned with audience ratings, with making a profit and with keeping their shareholders happy. Hence, they may place political communication as a high priority only if it is likely to bring results in the commercial area. When we make judgements about the role played by the mass media in the realm of political communication we need to remember that this is only one of the functions which the media perform and it may be considered by the media as less important than entertainment, sport, fashions and similar themes.

An ideal mass medium, in terms of political communication, would provide at least:

1 A source of political information for the public which gives all the facts.
2 A source of informed political opinions and views which provides access for all shades of opinion.
3 An uncensored communication of political matters.

But this is a utopian ideal, one which simply could not be achieved in the real world. No element of the media could include all the facts and encompass all opinions. No element of the mass media is read by all people. No two people read or hear the same element of the media in the same way and no two people will be affected in the same way by the same story or programme.

There are many ways in which the mass media in any democratic society can fall short of the ideal. Most can be put under the general heading of *bias*. No individual, no group, no element of the media can be totally objective, totally unbiased. The media are owned, controlled, managed, produced, and reported for by people, and people are not totally objective neutrals. Hence, we can expect to find bias in all types of media. Some elements of the media are deliberately biased—a publication by any group for circulation to members of that group, whether Labor or Liberal or rural or Catholic or communist or hippy, would not unnaturally be a sectional, biased production. But the mass media—the wide, public media on which the public depends for its political communication—cannot be simply propaganda sheets. In fact there is a clear economic incentive in the commercial mass media to avoid too much bias; they need to avoid antagonising any sizeable group of readers or listeners. Thus while we would not expect to describe the daily output of any element of the mass media in a democratic society as propaganda, we need to ask how biased the media are.

MASS MEDIA IN AUSTRALIA

As in other democratic countries, the mass media in Australia have a tremendous potential for influence and power. As the main means of political communication for the great majority of the people, the media can be very influential indeed. There are three aspects of the media in Australia which parallel and reflect trends and developments in other Western nations. These are not necessarily undemocratic, but they may raise problems for a free media—concentration, commercialism and conservatism.

The first factor is most clear in the history of the Australian press: a marked decrease in the number of newspapers available for the public and a concentration of ownership to the point of oligopoly. In the 1920s, there were twenty-one separately owned daily metropolitan newspapers in Australia. In 1985 there were only fourteen metropolitan dailies and these were divided between only three commercial companies: Herald and Weekly Times Ltd, News Ltd, and John Fairfax Ltd. Only in three cities did readers have a choice between morning newspapers from different companies; only in Sydney was there such a choice in afternoon papers. In Perth, the same company owned both the morning and afternoon newspaper, and there is still no afternoon newspaper in Hobart. This concentration has continued into the 1990s.

This concentration has two major implications for political communication. The first is the tendency for news and opinions to become similar. The media tend to obtain the bulk of national and international news from the large news-gathering organisations such as Australian Associated Press, Reuter and United Press International.

As a result, it is not unusual to see and hear the same film clip and the same comments in the news times of all radio stations and on all TV channels. A similar trend is noticeable in the printed media; newspapers in the same stable often show little difference in the basic presentation of a specific news item or in editorial comment. The newspaper is under no real pressure to improve its quality of political communication—the public is a relatively captive audience, with little if any choice available. In Adelaide, for example, the daily newspapers, the Sunday newspaper, and the suburban free papers, are all in the Murdoch News Corporation. There is no competition.

Since 1985, there have been kaleidoscopic, complex and often confusing changes in media ownership, changes which are continuing. The government's decisions on allowable 'coverage' for TV stations, the impact of satellite transmission, and the potential of cable TV and 'people meters', resulted in major changes in the structures of the electronic media. But the development of an oligopoly of ownership did not slow and its negative implications for media in a democratic society need to be debated.

The commercialism of the Australian mass media is immediately obvious. The ABC is an important component of the electronic media, but the majority of stations are owned by private interests and the entire printed media network is privately owned. Within the commercial networks, communication is first and foremost a business. Ratings and sales—the figures which determine the level of advertising, and therefore of income—become the dominant, and some critics would suggest, the only consideration. The possibility is there, then, for the commercial broadcasters to give the people what the media thinks the people want—whether it be comics, scandals, sport, features, crime, fiction—at the expense of full and balanced political communication.

The third element, conservatism, is a direct result of the concentration and commercialism. As the mass media become bigger and bigger private enterprises, they are increasingly under the influence of big business and of businessmen. Businessmen tend to take a conservative position on most political questions and we would expect this conservatism to be reflected in the people they choose as editors and hence in the style and approach of their newspapers, radio and television. At the same time, as businesses, the media are forced to give a receptive ear to the major customers, the readers and listeners and viewers, for these produce the all-important ratings, but more fundamentally to the advertisers who provide the bulk of the income. Any fall in ratings or sales would threaten support from advertisers. Hence, the commercial media, especially commercial radio and television, are businesses in which audiences are 'sold' to advertisers.

Two Australian media owners: Packer and Murdoch.

THE AUSTRALIAN BROADCASTING CORPORATION

The ABC was created as a Commission in 1932, an independent statutory authority created by the national parliament. It began with eight metropolitan and four regional radio stations and with a staff of less than 300. Today it is one of the largest electronic media systems in the world, with over 200 radio and television stations throughout the nation. It also includes symphony orchestras, Radio Australia (broadcasting 24 hours a day in ten languages), a concert management structure and a publication business.

In the late 1970s, the ABC became a political issue, especially when the Fraser government decreased its funding. The major problem for the ABC has been that it was financially dependent on the national government on a year-to-year basis. Hence the potential for financial control to become political pressure. As one ABC executive put it, 'the Commission is aware that if you go too far, someone in Canberra's going to turn off the tap.' The granting of 'freedom' to the ABC by the creation of a Corporation in 1983 was, therefore, a major step towards a truly independent national broadcasting authority along the lines of the BBC. However, the Corporation found its funding continually cut, and this has had serious effects on the breadth and quality of the products of the national broadcaster. The major issue in the 1990s remains that of security of funding.

CONTROL OF THE MEDIA

There are no formal or constitutional means (at least in peace time) whereby the national government can exercise direct control over the press. Nor should there be. Australia can still claim to be in the ever-shrinking minority of nations that can boast of a free press. But this is not to say that there are no restrictions on the press, nor that attempts at political persuasion are always unsuccessful.

In the first place, a government can control the amount and nature of information which is made available. The simplest method is the retention of information within the walls of government and government departments, a trend which has not decreased in recent years; this has resulted in the situation where the media have used 'leaks' from various levels of government as means of obtaining news stories. Although the Crimes Act makes it an offence for public servants to divulge any unauthorised information from their employment, this has not prevented major leaks to the media.

A second means of control involves Defence-notices, a system which is, in effect, an agreement by the media to be censored. If the government decides that a certain topic is crucial to Australia's security then the media are requested to refrain from reporting on it by the issue of a D-notice. There are no formal sanctions to back up this voluntary agreement, but the media usually accept the censorship—partly through the implicit threat of withdrawal of access to government if a D-notice is violated. A third means is the simple exercise, or attempted exercise, of political influence. It is rare, indeed, for such instances of attempted political pressure to reach the public arena, but there is no doubt that such attempts occur (see Document 6.5).

The control of the electronic media is more formal and direct. In 1948, the Australian Broadcasting Control Board was established as a statutory authority with functions including the determination of technical details of radio and television stations, standards of equipment, hours of service, the quality and comprehensiveness of the commercial sector of the electronic media and whether the media were serving 'the best interests of the public'. The ABCB held inquiries and advised governments on media policies, especially in regard to commercial licences.

In early 1976, the Fraser government commissioned an inquiry into broadcasting, and the resultant Green Report was released after the government had already announced its decision in regard to the structure and control of the commercial electronic media. One decision was the abolition of the ABCB and the formation of an Australian Broadcasting Tribunal. The ABT is a statutory authority responsible for the broad areas of licensing and supervision of the commercial sector of the electronic media. In 1978 the Tribunal began public hearings in the area of application and renewal of commercial radio and television licences. It has the authority to 'grant', renew, suspend or revoke licences and to determine programme and advertising standards'. The Tribunal has been the centre of political controversy, especially over the extent to which it can, or is willing to, act on its terms of reference, including advertising and programme standards. All licences reviewed to date have been renewed, but there is no doubt that the commercial interests and the many pressure groups in and around the industry will continue to make hearings interesting events.

BIAS

Opinions have been, and probably always will be, divided on the question of whether the mass media, and especially the press in Australia, show a bias. There are a number of reasons for this uncertainty. Perhaps the most important is that bias is often in the mind of the beholder. What is seen as bias may well be an objective treatment of a topic, but the strong political views of the reader perceive this as bias. Hence, it is theoretically possible for a Labor supporter and a Liberal supporter to perceive bias, in opposite directions, in the same story. The party identification of the individual is important. A Labor supporter may read a Labor-oriented story and not see bias because it accords with his or her view of politics, whereas a Liberal reader who does not find the story in accordance with his or her views would call it biased.

A second reason for the uncertainty is a lack of clear definition of what constitutes bias, and how it should be measured. How much of the alleged bias was actually bias? Was the bias in editorials, or was it in placement and style and content of news stories? Did the readers have sufficient knowledge of politics in general, and of the specific issues, to be able to judge?

Attitudes to the media's political line differ markedly. In a retrospective comment ALP leader Arthur Calwell asserted (*Advertiser*, 22 March 1967) that 'for the 80 years of its history the ALP and its leaders have been maligned by the press.' But academic surveys are not always so harsh. There is no doubt that the press, and the media generally, do take sides, at least editorially, at election times. In 1972, the Murdoch-News group swung firmly to advocating 'vote ALP'; in 1974, the same group swung even more firmly back to the Liberal Party.

And in recent national and state elections some components of the media were deliberately and consistently partisan.

Some elements of the press, even editorially, sit uncomfortably on the fence. One of the clearest examples of this occurred in the 1970 South Australian election when *The News* included the following in its editorials:

> Liberal Premier Hall's promises were all reasonable, within practical limits, and were all constructive plans for the future.
>
> Labor Opposition Leader Dunstan looked forward to a busy future, setting his sights high, but made no reckless promises.
>
> Voters should think, consider, evaluate, then determine which party's programme is in the best interests of the state.

In recent years, especially following the polarisation in national politics, such attempts at 'non-influence' have become rare, and in the 1979 South Australian election, *The News* was strongly anti-Labor, to such an extent that the Press Council criticised it.

The final comment on bias comes from the extreme-Right organisation, the Australian League of Rights, and it indicates the extent to which perceptions of bias flow from preconceived political ideologies.

> The mass media are most definitely penetrated to varying extents by subversives ... much of the world's news is, in fact, left-slanted propaganda disguised as news ... e.g. the 'line' now taken on South Africa by the capitalist and the communist press is identical ... the impact of the revolutionary students on our society would be negligible were it not for the adulatory attentions and reportings of the 'capitalist' mass media ... the bias normally shown against letters of a conservative flavour is the well-known experience of many League of Rights supporters. Only small, free, independent organs of fact and opinion, such as our journals, can now project that truth into our society which can still make us all free.

THE INFLUENCE OF THE MEDIA

Newspapers, and the media in general, are not merely sources of political information and comment, nor are they bought merely for that purpose. Indeed, if we bear in mind the general lack of interest in politics of the majority of people, this is probably a very minor reason for their purchase. Apart from political information and comment, newspapers provide all sorts of information, entertainment and diversion: sport, finance, women's pages, children's pages, social notes, gossip columns, law reports, shipping, commercial news, weather forecasts, cultural comment and criticism on the various arts, comic strips, crosswords, film, TV, and radio programmes and advertisements for an enormous range of products. As one analyst (R.W. Connell) put it: 'Nobody reads a paper intelligently or critically. That's not what it's for. It's there for splashing around in.' Any attempt to assess the political influence of the mass media must take this into account. In relation to the electronic media it must also take into account a marked difference between the ABC and the commercial television networks in terms of emphasis.

Do the media affect voting patterns? The shift in the News Ltd section of the media to a pro-Labor position at the 1972 election was welcomed by the ALP, and annoyed the coalition government. The shift back (and further) in 1974 incensed the ALP and pleased the coalition. Yet the net electoral swing at these two elections was 2.5 per cent and 0.4 per cent respectively. Is it, perhaps, reasonable to conclude that the shift of partisan alignment by a major component of the Australian media was of little significance?

AN AGENDA FOR ANALYSIS

If we are attempting to analyse the components of the media rather than simply accuse them of bias (from the position of our own bias) we need to consider the extent to which media are setting the agenda, and especially the political agenda. That is, the important effect of the media is not that they tell us what to think, but that newspapers, radio and television contain a clear guide to what we should think about. That is, the media set the agenda for public debate, especially by excluding some items from the agenda.

The Australian media are criticised by some, praised by others and ignored (except as entertainment) by many. The political communications in the press, radio and television will reinforce the views of some, change the opinions of others, and simply pass the majority by.

The ABC clearly places emphasis on political communication; its charter demands this. Its independence both from explicit government control and from the implicit and explicit pressures of ratings and advertisers allows it to continue this emphasis. Whether the changes occurring within the ABC and in its relations with the government will modify this intention and opportunity remains to be seen.

The commercial media are, above all, businesses. They therefore react, above all else, to popular appeal, ratings, advertising pressures and profits. Given a relatively apathetic audience, a community not over-interested in politics and political communication, can the commercial media be blamed for these emphases? Any discussion of the issues of and around the politics of the Australian mass media should examine the following broad questions.

- *Who?* Who is communicating with us—the readers, listeners, viewers? Does the tendency to oligopoly in the commercial media limit the range of news and views? What role do owners, editors, sub-editors and journalists play?
- *Says what?* Is content of our newspapers emphasising the 'right thing'? Are radio and television informing and educating? Should they?
- *To whom?* Who reads and listens and watches? To what aspects?
- *By what means?* How are newspapers prepared? How are radio and television programmes produced? Does this affect quality?
- *Under what circumstances?* Do deadlines mean that investigative journalism is not possible? How independent are journalists?
- *For what purpose?* Do the media have a responsibility beyond that of entertainment? A responsibility to whom? For what?
- *With what effects?* Do the media influence the way we think? Should they? Is there a problem of bias in the Australian media?

Overall, if the media 'give the public what the public wants', then is reform of the media dependent on the precondition of reform of the Australian political culture? That is, if we feel the media can and should be improved, it is up to us to bring sufficient pressure to demand improvement.

DOCUMENTS

6.1 WHEN IS AN INTEREST GROUP NOT A PRESSURE GROUP?

Source: Correspondence with pressure groups during research for this chapter revealed wide variations among interest groups in their attitudes to political activity. Three groups interpreted 'political' in fundamentally different ways.

'It would be correct to say that we [the Housing Industry Association] are a political body, insofar as we spend considerable time lobbying parliamentarians ... However, we are affiliated with no political party, and are prepared to criticise any or all of them.'

'I wish to advise that the Women's Christian Temperance Union is a non-political organisation.'

'[The object of the United Farmers and Graziers of South Australia is] to promote by legal process or legislation, or in any other manner, all matters considered beneficial to primary producers and when occasion demands, to resist within the law, legislation deemed to be oppressive.'

6.2 PRESSURE GROUPS SPEAK FOR THEMSELVES

Sources: The following quotations have been extracted either from official rules of pressure groups, or from correspondence with the groups.

Association of Employers of Waterside Labor
The Association does not become involved in the political processes as in the case with say the Chamber of Manufactures and the Metal Trades Industry Association in regard to tariffs or the Master Builders in regard to the availability of finance for home building. The principal purpose of the Association is to represent its members in all fields of industrial relations involving waterfront unions.

Automotive Chamber of Commerce: Rules
The objects of the Association [include]: a) to protect and conserve the interests of members; b) to promote support or oppose legislative or other measures affecting the retail motor industry ... and to deal with any restrictions affecting the retail motor industry.

United Farmers and Graziers of South Australia: Constitution
The Association shall be and remain non-party political and non-sectarian throughout its existence. A Member of Parliament may become a member, but shall not be appointed as an Officer or Delegate of the Association. If any Officer or Delegate to the Association is elected as a Member of Parliament, he shall *ipso facto* vacate his office...

[Objects include] to raise and obtain moneys for expenditure in accomplishing the objects of the Association, provided that no such moneys shall be used for party-political purposes.

South Australian Dairyfarmer's Association: Correspondence
... the types of activities that would normally be associated with the activities of such an organisation, that is to say, initiating, supporting, or opposing the passing of legislation which affects the interests of dairy farmers, pressing for increase in the prices of milk and dairy produce, and generally looking after the interests of members as dairy farmers, and as individuals ...

Public Service Association of South Australia: Objects
To represent, act for, provide assistance to, and secure preference for

members in any matters connected with their callings and their employment with loyalty to the Government of South Australia.

South Australia Association of Permanent Building Societies
To advocate, promote and procure the passing of such legislation, both Federal and State, as may be conducive to any of the objects of the Association.

Housing Industry Association: Objects
To co-operate with Government Departments and representatives to ensure that government policies be to the best advantage of the industry.

6.3 PRESSURE GROUPS: GOOD OR BAD?

Source: Westerway, P.B. 1965, 'Pressure groups', in *Forces in Australian Politics*, Angus and Robertson, Sydney, p.120.

In Australia the term 'pressure group' is still regarded as an insult, and the Prime Minister only put the usual view when he recently told a Liberal Party meeting:

> There are plenty of pressure groups in Australia and there are plenty of pressure groups in the world ... It is the age of pressure groups. It is a period of time, politically and intentionally, in which people seek to promote differences and seek to promote a clash of interests so that in the waters they stir up they may fish to their advantage.

Here are implied all the usual charges against pressure groups that they are selfish, that they profit from conflict, and that they have a secret, unexplained capacity to cause trouble. No doubt his audience suffered no surprise when he went on to claim that the Liberal Party is neither backed by nor responsive to pressure groups. This, he said, was the party's peculiar contribution to Australian political history. Peculiar it certainly is. One apparently acknowledges 'great and powerful friends' only in the international sphere. But Mr Menzies was expressing a very popular view. And he was also speaking for a great many people when he added: 'Therefore I say: Away with all this pressure group idea.'

Fortunately in my opinion this is not possible. We live in a complex society which, if it is to remain democratic, must allow the free organisation of interests to influence or 'pressure' governments. Of course, this assumes a certain view of what constitutes democracy. If we take it to be a system which allows the 'real' interests of the community to prevail over what its constituent individuals and groups think to be their interests, then we will probably consider pressure groups undemocratic. Again, if we take democracy to be a set of ideas which must be realised no matter by what methods, we may regard pressure groups as obstructionist and therefore undemocratic. But there is a third view of democracy that it is a system which makes the governors highly responsive to the wishes of the governed. If, as I do, you accept this view, I hope to persuade you that pressure groups are not only consistent with democracy but essential to it.

6.4 IS THERE A RULING CLASS IN AUSTRALIA?

a)

Source: Connell, R.W. & Irving, T.H. 1973, 'Yes Virginia, there is a ruling class', in Mayer, H. & Nelson, H. (eds), *Australian Politics: A Third Reader*, Longman Cheshire, Melbourne, p. 33.

We are now in a position to say what we mean by a 'ruling class'. It is not simply a top group or an 'elite'. It is in a sense an 'elite', but one whose position and power has its roots deep in the culture and basic institutions of the society. In modern history that has chiefly meant the institution of property. A ruling class, then, is the owning class in a society that is divided in the way we have just discussed. It is a class that has successfully replaced earlier power groups (we would not call business a ruling class where it is still competing with a landed aristocracy), and is in a position to fight off current challenges to its position from below. When we speak of an 'Australian' ruling class, it is understood that we are speaking of only one section of an international system which has close relationships with the others, and in many ways is dependent on them.

In what sense does a ruling class rule? Firstly, in the sense that its members make economic decisions that shape the lives of the whole people. They direct the production of goods, their distribution, pricing, and so on; and in the modern economy they direct the stimulation of wants and tastes through advertising and fashion. In a more general sense, the class rules jointly by preserving the power structure within which its members individually hold the right to do these things. That is, it is able to preserve the system of private ownership and prevent alternative systems emerging. This preservation involves much more than purely economic power. For one thing, it involves political power. A ruling class exercises this by its members actually managing the affairs of government, by sponsoring politicians who will manage them in a way that does no damage to the system of property, or destroying political movements that do threaten damage. It is also likely to involve cultural power. A really well-established ruling class dominates the culture of its time.

b)
Source: Connell, R.W. 1977, *Ruling Class, Ruling Culture*, Cambridge University Press, Melbourne, pp. vii, 58.

If there remained any lingering doubt about the class nature of Australian politics, the events of late 1975 must have resolved it. There is hardly a clearer case, in the recent history of the 'western democracies', of the way a threatened ruling class is able to mobilise fragments of state power, business connections, financial resources, and the legitimacy given them by the dominant culture, in a campaign to remove an offending government ...

It may seem odd to argue that the society has a ruling class, and then to suggest that the most powerful officials in it are not members of that class, or at least not members of its leadership (since civil servants may well be small property owners). Yet this is what the argument implies. The difficulty is partly an ambiguity of language: the phrase 'ruling class' does not imply 'rule' in the sense of executive control (no one, and no group, rules a capitalist society in that sense). What is implied is a collective domination, the maintenance of an institutional structure within which the class appropriates benefits, the choking off of alternatives—the only sense in which a class can intelligibly be said to rule.

c)
Source: Dwyer, P. 1978, *How Lucky Are We?*, Longman Cheshire, Melbourne, p. 59.

It would be foolish to underestimate the extent to which those who dominate our economy really do constitute a ruling class. I say this for two reasons.

First, they have effective political power. This does not mean that they are constantly interfering with our democratic processes, but it does mean that dominant business concerns are capable of exerting considerable power during those occasional periods when they consider that their own interests are under threat. The experience of the Chifley government in the late 1940s and the more recent experience of the Whitlam government from mid-1974 (pre-Khemlani) onwards demonstrate this all too clearly ...

Second, precisely because these interests have the dominance they do, they exert a powerful hold over the lives and outlook of others ... the minority of Australians ... have benefited from our past economic developments ... economic constraints of home ownership and competitive education foster a conformity to 'the system' that is further reinforced by the influence of the mass media and the isolation that is part of Australian life ... challenges to the dominance of capitalist values are made to appear 'unacceptable' ...

What all this means is that economic considerations begin almost inevitably to dominate people's lives and their attitudes towards others. The ruling force of capital interests engenders self-interest, as people come to measure themselves and others in terms of competitive economic advantage.

6.5 AN EXAMPLE OF ATTEMPTED POLITICAL PRESSURE ON THE MEDIA

Source: Letter from the President of the Liberal Party to Prime Minister McMahon, 7 March 1972, quoted in Reid, A. 1976, *The Whitlam Venture*, Hill of Content, Melbourne.

May I direct attention to two or three things which at the moment seem to be particularly important?

The first is the attitude of the press. I want to say that, after mature reflection, I do not believe that the individual journalists are going to improve. People like Allan Barnes are coldly determined to destroy us, and I do not think that, however well we perform, they are going to alter their tune very much. The *Age* is having a very destructive effect in Victoria, and is much more bilious than most of the other Australian newspapers which I see.

Unless the Editor of the *Age* can be persuaded to alter the tune, their attitude will be increasingly serious. I am unable to find out how the *Age* really works internally. Are you? Am I correct in assuming that Graham Perkin really calls the tune, and that Ranald Macdonald is little more than the creature of Perkin? What influence has Warwick Fairfax? I wish I could be of some help to you here, but frankly I am a babe in that sort of jungle, and all I am really sure of is that whoever the real enemy is in the *Age*, and I think it is probably Perkin, he must be brought into line or circumvented.

I am much less concerned about the *Herald* and the *Sun*, for the *Herald* is reasonably trustworthy, whilst Oakes of the *Sun* is less damaging than Barnes. I know that Henry Bolte has very strong links with the *Herald*, and I wonder whether you have spoken to Henry about this, or whether I ought to do so myself. In straightening out the press, it is much more important that this should be done thoroughly, than that it should be done in a hurry.

6.6 PREFERENCES ABOUT MEDIA

Source: Mayer, H. & Nelson, H. (eds) 1980, *Australian Politics: A Fourth Reader*, Longman Cheshire, Melbourne, p. 561.

'Which medium would you want most if you could only have one of the four?

	Total %	14–19 years %
TV	45.4	59.5
Newspapers	34.2	22.3
Radio	15.9	14.0
Magazines	2.5	2.9

'Which medium is best for accurate and reliable news and other information?'

	Total %	14–19 years %
TV	47.0	68.1
Newspapers	28.1	16.0
Radio	15.5	8.1
Magazines	2.6	5.6

6.7 HAVE THE MEDIA A BIAS?

Source: Dwyer, P. 1978, *How Lucky Are We?*, Longman Cheshire, Melbourne, p. 22.

Of course, it has become common practice to accuse the media of bias whenever they present a point of view different from one's own. It has become common too for the media to deny bias. However, the point at stake here is not primarily one of bias but of accuracy of information. It is not necessarily subscribing to a 'conspiracy theory' to claim that the media often seem more concerned about maintaining the image of conformity than with the facts of the situation. The influence this can have is not simply a question of the monopoly control of the media, although that is obviously an important factor in restricting the access people have to alternative sources of information. It is not even simply a question of the use of the media by commercial interests, such as advertisers, whose job it is to encourage the general public to conform to the particular images they are sold. It is perhaps much more a question of what the media actually take to be, and present as, the reality of Australian society.

ISSUES FOR DISCUSSION

1 Are all interest groups pressure groups? If an interest group states it is 'non-political' what does it mean? Can an interest group which is seeking to influence public opinion not be a pressure group? Why are some pressure groups more open about their 'pressure' than others? (See Document 6.1.)
2 In the USA, the lobbies of the various pressure groups have to register their activities, and they are controlled by laws. Should pressure groups in Australia be controlled by law?
3 How powerful are pressure groups in Australia? Are some more powerful than others? Why are they?
4 Is the National Party better described as a major rural pressure group in parliament?
5 To what extent are the groups in Document 6.2 pressure groups?
6 Are pressure groups good or bad for democracy in Australia? (See Document 6.3.)
7 Is Australia governed by a ruling class? (See Document 6.4.)
8 Discuss the proposition that 'pressure groups are the means by which the rich and powerful in the society are able to influence the governing of Australia'.
9 Identify three pressure groups in your area which focus on local government, three which are attempting to influence state government, and three which are seeking some action from the national government. Which issues are of concern to them? What methods are the groups using? How successful have they been?
10 Identify a problem within your community. Devise your strategy as a pressure group to obtain some action on this problem from those in authority.
11 It is often said that pressure groups have important functions in a democracy. In your local area, identify groups which have carried out any or all of the following functions. How successful have they been?
   a Promotion of ideas which the group believes are for the good of the society as a whole.
   b The public expression to government of the interests and opinions of a minority group (say an ethnic or Aboriginal group).
   c The clarification of election issues by seeking and publicising information from candidates and parties (for example, the Women's Electoral Lobby).

d An alternative means of contact with a member of parliament to obtaining action on a grievance.
e Encouraging interest in the political process.
f Providing information to government.

12 Political opinion is often labelled as either reactionary, conservative, moderate, liberal, or radical. Analyse the qualities which characterise each of these types of political opinion, perhaps on a specific issue.

13 Which do you think is the most powerful influence on public opinion—newspapers, magazines, radio, or TV? Give reasons for your answer. (See Document 6.6.)

14 'Faced with criticism, many politicians fall back onto blaming the media.' Is this a comment on the media, or on politicians?

15 Is it possible to have an unbiased media? (Documents 6.5 and 6.7.)

16 Given the relative powerlessness of a party in opposition, should the media take over some of the opposition's role—criticising, exposing, analysing governments?

Chapter seven

PARLIAMENTARY DEMOCRACY AND AUSTRALIAN PRACTICE

INTRODUCTION

A visitor to the Stranger's Gallery in the House of Representatives or Senate in the national parliament house is often disillusioned. The visitor has arrived probably expecting an impressive parliamentary panorama, pageantry, sparkling but dignified debate and occasional fiery clashes between leading personalities. If the house is involved in question time, the visitor may be lucky enough to observe some of the expected attractions, but more often than not there will be a dull, inactive, almost somnolent scene. Of the 147 members of the House of Representatives less than a dozen may be present in the chamber; of the 76 senators only a handful. A member will hold the floor, attempting to spark some interest among the other attenders; a minister will be working at the table; some members will be reading newspapers or writing their own speeches for later that day; one or two may even be asleep. Such a view from the Gallery is not a reliable guide to the parliamentary process in Australia. Parliaments go about their work by means of complicated (and often archaic) processes which are not all obvious from an observation of the members in formal sessions.

For most Australians, politics is a matter of occasional elections and of the 'goings-on' in parliament. Members of the parliaments in Australia often complain about the low standing they and their institutions have in the minds of the voters. They have cause to be concerned about such opinions, but perhaps their complaints might be also directed inwards, to themselves, and to the way they manage and manipulate the institution.

Parliament is the keystone of representative and responsible government. Its members are charged with a range of functions which are supposed to nurture and protect representation and responsibility, which are supposed to maintain the model known as parliamentary democracy. This chapter analyses and explains the Australian national parliament, sets out what it should be, and should be doing, and compares that with what actually happens. It concludes with a proposal for reform, a proposal that the Australian parliament should be allowed to become what it is supposed to be—the central authority in the Australian democracy.

CONSTITUTIONAL DEFINITION

In Britain, parliament and parliamentary democracy evolved over a thousand years but nowhere is parliament formally defined. In Australia, parliament is defined in, and constrained by, a written Constitution. At first sight, this difference appears relatively insignificant, but it is crucial in terms of the functions and authority of the Australian parliament. Further, the Australian Constitution established a federal system, in which the national parliament is contained within certain defined functions, by the division of powers.

The Constitution is Australia's supreme law, so it should contain the definitive statement not only of parliament, but of its purpose, roles, and functions within the system of parliamentary democracy. It does not do so, and hence any study of parliament must compare the model within which parliament was established, the formal statements of its powers and functions, and the processes, procedures and conventions which have been necessary for it to function. That is, as with the study of federalism, we need to analyse and compare the structures and processes of parliamentary democracy.

The opening words of the Constitution do not tell us very much. (Section 1)

> The legislative power of the Commonwealth shall be vested in a Federal Parliament, which shall consist of the Queen, a Senate, and a House of Representatives, and which is hereinafter called 'The Parliament', or 'the Parliament of the Commonwealth'.

The presence of the Queen in this formal definition is the first problem. Obviously, the Queen, in any practical sense, is not part of the Australian parliament. Sections 61 and 62 of the Constitution clarify the matter—but only a little:

> The executive power of the Commonwealth is vested in the Queen and is exercisable by the Governor-General as the Queen's representative. There shall be a Federal Executive Council to advise the Governor-General.

According to the formal definition of Parliament in the Constitution, then, the Parliament contains a Governor-General, appointed by the Queen, who then forms an Executive Council by appointing Ministers to advise him, from the Parliament which the people elect. But in that interpretation is the first important message about Australian politics; the Constitution may be the 'supreme law', but it is by no means a full, or even accurate, description of how the political processes actually work. For example, the Queen does appoint the Governor-General to exercise her 'executive power', but the person is chosen by the Australian government and recommended to the Queen for her approval.

According to the Constitution (Section 62), the Executive Council is chosen and summoned by the Governor-General, and it 'shall hold office during his pleasure'. In fact, the ministers are produced from the party (or coalition of parties) which has managed to win a majority of seats in the House of Representatives.

These ministers are selected by the prime minister in the case of a non-Labor ministry, and elected by the caucus in a Labor ministry. Their appointments as ministers, and as members of the Executive Council, are made constitutionally by the Governor-General; in practical politics, they are chosen by the party with the majority. The limitation of the constitutional definition are apparent, especially as key offices—the cabinet and prime minister—do not even rate a mention!

PARLIAMENTS: THE MAP

We need, therefore, to start with some minimal definitions of terms which will recur throughout this chapter. The parliaments of Australia are, at basis, the assembly of elected representatives. The 223 members

Table 7.1: Membership of Australian parliaments

Parliaments	Lower House	Upper House	Total
National	147	76	223
NSW	99	42	141
VIC	88	44	132
QLD	89	–	89
WA	56	34	90
SA	47	22	69
TAS	35	19	54
ACT	17	–	17
NT	25	–	25
Total	603	237	840

of the Australian parliament are divided between the House of Representatives (147) and the Senate (76). The parliament also contains a cabinet, a shadow cabinet, and caucuses. The cabinet is a convention (see below) of parliamentary democracy, not mentioned in the Constitution, the senior parliamentary members of the party (or coalition) which holds a majority of the members of the House of Representatives. The shadow cabinet is the group of senior parliamentary members of the party (or coalition) which is the official opposition. The caucus is the total parliamentary membership of each party with representation in the parliament. Liberal and National parties each have a separate caucus, but they form a coalition and meet in a joint party caucus as well.

To clarify these points it may help to describe the situation in 1994. The Keating Labor Party is in government in Canberra as it holds a majority of seats in the House of Representatives. It does not have a majority in the Senate where seven Australian Democrats, Senator Harradine, and two Green senators hold a numerical balance of power. The Keating Labor government contains the prime minister and twenty-nine ministers, some of whom are members of the Senate. This government is divided into nineteen senior ministers who comprise the cabinet, and the remaining eleven who form the outer ministry. There are ten Parliamentary Secretaries—quasi ministers.

The Australian Democrat senators constitute a caucus, but with one important difference—the Democrats do not apply a party discipline (as does the Labor Party), nor demand a party cohesion (as do the Liberal and National parties), the effects of which will be examined later in this study. For our purposes, when we talk of 'cabinet–caucus' relations, the term 'caucus' will refer to the back bench (non-ministerial) members of the party.

WESTMINSTER SYSTEM: THEORY AND PRACTICE

The model of parliamentary democracy evolved in Britain, and the structures and processes which are at the foundation of the system in Britain are termed the *Westminster* model. Its key concepts are representation and responsibility, the former involving such processes as elections, and the manner in which the elected representatives actually represent, and the latter encompassing a range of levels of institutions and groups, all which should function within an ethos of accountability.

Parliament should be the keystone of the Westminster model. It is the product of representation of the citizens and is responsible to the citizens. It forms the government which is directly responsible to the parliament. It has authority to call the public service to account and has the power to dismiss members of the judiciary. But such a preeminent position of parliament in the theory of the Westminster model is not matched by the practice of Australia politics.

THEORY

Explicating the Westminister model needs to be conducted with care, for we are in a confused and confusing area. As Parker (1978:349) put it:

Parliament House, London.

it is rather important to unravel the tangle of intellectual constructs, emotional responses and pictures of the real world evoked by the phrase 'the Westminster system'.

The emotional responses are a constant component of political rhetoric. For some, the term conjures up a range of images of a British system of constitutional monarch and parliamentary democracy, images which combine to form an idealised picture of how the British system is believed to function. To Anglophiles, the term 'Westminster system' carries the whole history of the development of parliament in Britain, a belief that it was exported unchanged to the colonies, that it still exists in Australia, and a firm belief that it is the best form of government.

The term has also become part of the rhetoric of Australian political parties. But, more often than not, the Westminster system is a term which is *used* for whatever party purposes are required at the time. Hence, we find the opposition—of whatever party label—invokes the term when it has been unable to win a battle of party tactics, either in the parliament or in the public arena; we hear constant assertions that 'the government has not followed the Westminster system'.

A government also tends to invoke the term as a justification for whatever it is planning, or doing, whether it is 'Westminster' or not.

As a consequence, the term has all but lost any meaning except as a convenient weapon with which to beat the other side. As one senior public servant put it: 'The Westminster system is all things to all people—that depends on whom you are asking to define it' (cited by Thompson 1980:32). Or, as Parker put it (1978:350), too many politicians, and particularly officials, hypocritically profess to live by the Westminster system while making decisions in ways that pay no respect to it at all. It is obvious that if we are to assess Australia's political practices in terms of what the Westminster system says they should be, we do have to clarify the concept. To do so, we need to consider three levels within it: the principles that define the system; the practical requirements which flow from these principles; and the various informal processes which have developed outside the formal structures, but which are no less important in influencing the way in which the system functions.

Principles: Parker outlines the first level, the principles, as the 'four axioms' of the 'Westminster syndrome':

1 Responsible ministers in parliament
2 A partnership of elected ministers and appointed officials (the public servants)
3 A relationship between ministers and officials; the minister should be able to have the last word at any level, and officials should be loyal to the current minister

4 Accountability which runs from official to minister to cabinet to parliament to voters.

There is no argument that these principles are present in the Australian system of government—as principles. But there is considerable debate as to whether they are followed in practice. That is, there may be a commitment to the principles, but there may also be a rejection of them in the practices of politics. When James Killen as Minister for Defence in the Fraser government refused to allow senior public servants from his department to be questioned by a Senate committee, he based his decision on 'Westminster principles'. Equally, the committee based its demand on the Westminster principle that parliament has the duty to ensure that the chain of accountability functions effectively.

The problem with any principle is that it may, and probably will, contain terms which are complex and open for interpretation. Consider Parker's 'axioms'. What do the terms 'responsible', 'partnership', 'relationship', and 'accountability' mean in practice? What actions can be described as 'responsible'? What actions fall outside of the principle?

Practical Requirements: If we describe the principles as the skeleton of the Westminster model, then the second level can be thought of as the muscles. The principles establish the fundamental foundation; the second level, the practical requirement, establish the political structures and processes that are necessary for the system to be put into operation. These practical requirements include at least the following:

1 A non-elective and non-party political head (Queen in Britain, Governor-General in Australia)
2 The sovereignty of parliament
3 The lower house as the 'house of government'—the house to which government is responsible
4 The government proposes, the parliament legislates.

Obviously there are many questions to be asked about the extent to which these apply to Australia. As just one example—if the parliament is to be the central component of the whole construct of the Westminster system, then it should be sovereign, it should be the place of the 'last word'. The Australian High Court has the authority to overrule any Act of any Australian parliament!

The events of 1975 which led to the dismissal of the Whitlam Labor government focussed attention on these practices and their application in Australia. The role of the Governor-General, of the House of Representatives as the 'house of government', and of the Senate, emerged as crucial questions during 1975 and raised the issue of whether the parliament is indeed sovereign.

Conventions: The third level—the various informal processes, the conventions, is the most difficult to pin down in exact terms, so much so that some people argue that it does not exist! If we continue the analogy, then this third level—the conventions of the Westminster system—is the blood supply which is necessary for the skeleton and the muscles, in fact for the whole system, to function at all.

These conventions are the unwritten 'rules of the game'. They are in informal understandings between the actors in the political processes which allow the principles, and the political structures and practices, to be put into operation. They are an undeniably important component of the Westminster system in Britain. As there is no written constitution in Britain, the application of the model, developed over more than a century, became dependent on a whole constellation of conventions.

In Australia the formal, written Constitution is silent on many of the principles, let alone the practices and procedures of responsible government. As a result, the Australian parliamentary and governmental processes have also become surrounded by, and dependent on, these agreements, mutual understandings and rules of the game—the conventions.

This third level is the most diffuse of all, and the importance of conventions is a matter of debate. In the field of constitutional law, they simply do not exist. A legalist interpretation of the Australian political system and processes would be based on a combination of the Constitution and the rulings of the High Court interpreting that document. But the Constitution is simply inadequate as a description, let alone a prescription, about how politics work in Australia. For example, the keystone of the process of governmental decision-making is the cabinet. But the cabinet does not exist according to the Constitution. The tacit agreements, the practices based on such agreements and the understandings between the participants—have become fundamentally important components of the political processes of Australia.

WESTMINSTER IN AUSTRALIA

Any analysis of parliamentary democracy in Australia which starts from the premise that we applied a Westminster model is doomed to irrelevance. If we are comparing what happens in the structures, practices and processes of parliament in Australia with the theory, we need to use the correct theory in the comparison.

The Washminster Mutation

As Thompson (Thompson 1980:38) puts it,

> What is being argued is that the concept of responsible government is inadequate and misleading as an analytic tool describing the Australian political system... The objection is not to using either the terms 'Westminster model' or 'responsible government' as departure points in the analysis of the Australian political system. The objection is to their use in ways that imply they are the models of government best suited to describing the Australian system.

The remainder of this chapter will describe 'what is' in the processes and practices of parliamentary democracy in Australia. But where analysis is needed, where practice is compared to theory, the model which will be used is that which was incorporated from the beginning—the Australian model of parliamentary democracy.

THE QUEEN AND HER REPRESENTATIVE

In the system of government in the UK, the monarchy is permanent, constitutionally powerful, and symbolic. Parliaments are formed and

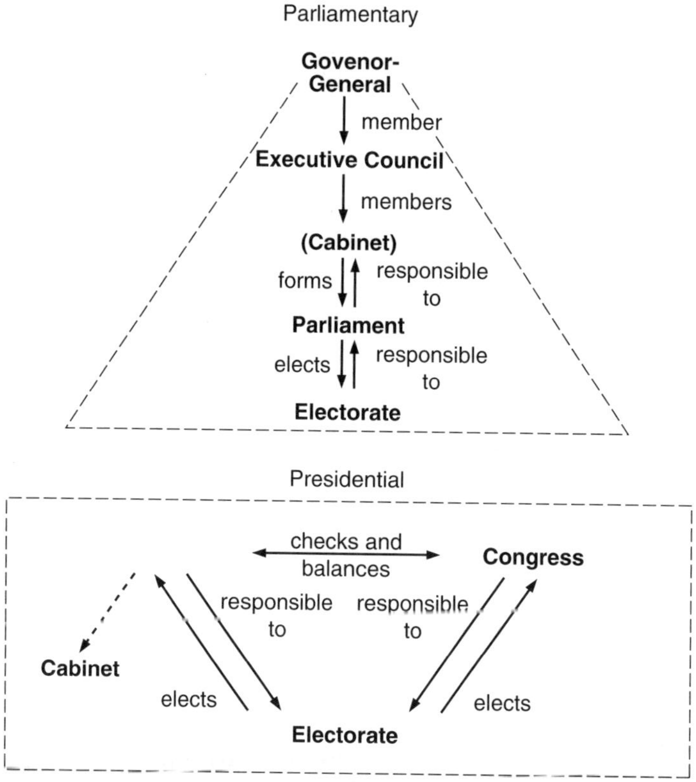

Figure 7.1 Parliamentary and Presidential systems of government

Australia's Governor-General, H.E. Bill Hayden.

dissolved, ministries, ministers and cabinets come and go, elections decide the fate of governments and form others, but the monarch continues to reign separated from party politics, factional and sectional interest, and above political strife. At the same time, the monarch is formal head of government in the UK and the assent of the sovereign is necessary before any law can be passed by parliament or any executive action can be put into effect. In modern British practice, of course, this power has become a formality. Finally, the monarch has an important symbolic role, identifying the British nation.

The British monarch is also monarch of Australia, represented by a Governor-General in the national capital and by a Governor in each state, all of whom are direct representatives of the monarch. They all have the same formal, legal powers in their own constitutionally defined area as the monarch has in Britain.

THE IMPACT OF FEDERALISM

The founding fathers of the Constitution in 1901 incorporated the practices and the conventions of the British parliament but mixed the Westminster model with federalism. The result was the 'Washminster mutation' (Thompson 1980), a marriage of two different structures

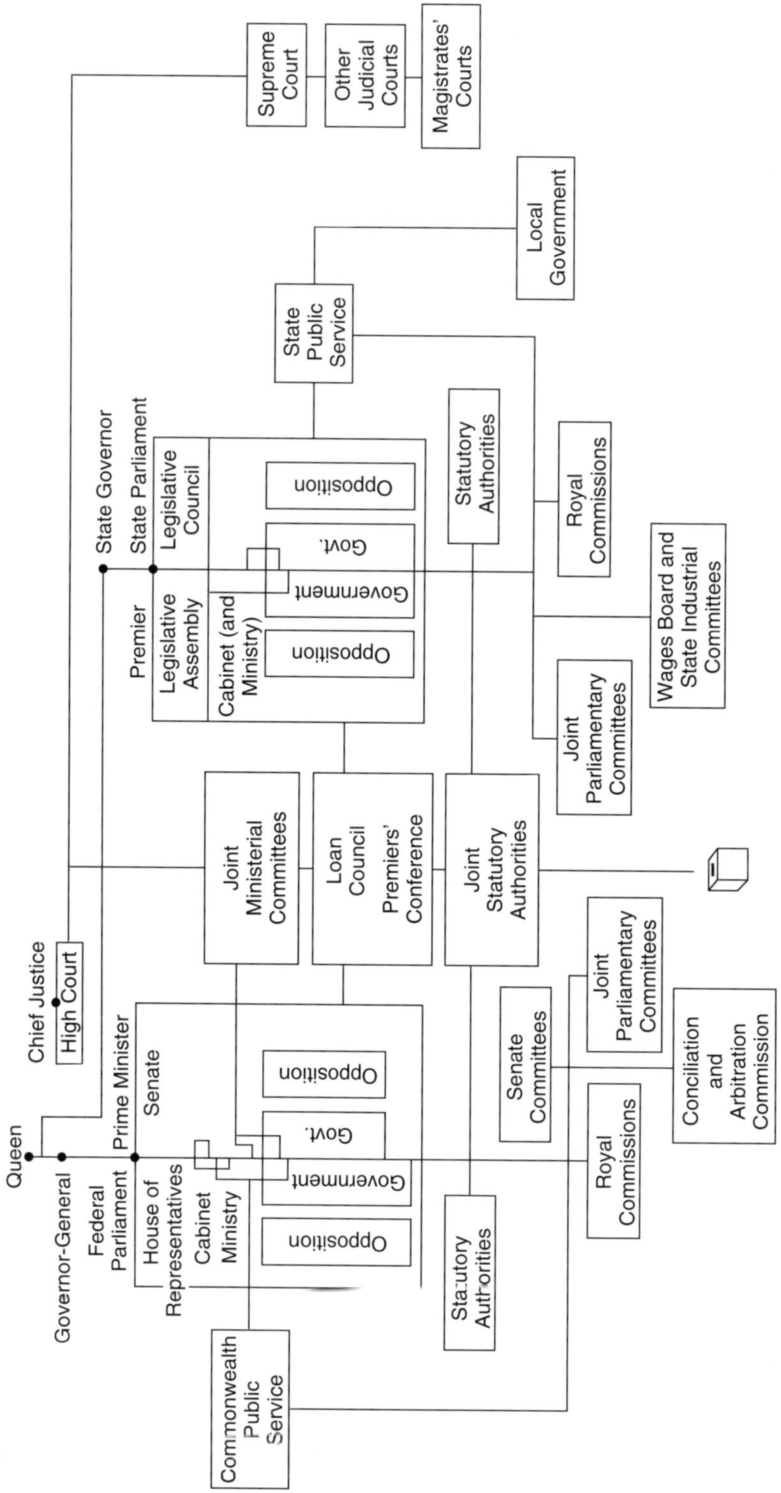

***Figure 7.2** The structure of Australian political institutions*

and principles of government. The structures and principles are mutually incompatible, and were so from the beginning.

Obviously, then, Australia did not incorporate a Westminster system of parliamentary democracy. Yet claims are still heard that we did and that any suggestion or action which may be in conflict with the model should be resisted. For example, a senior Liberal minister, James Killen, one of the most vocal and impassioned defenders of the Westminster system, opposed the development of a committee system in parliament because 'we stand in high danger of commingling the American system with the Westminster system of government'. In fact, the 'commingling' occurred in 1901. The result was that an *Australian model* of federal parliamentary government was inaugurated in 1901. As further structures developed, invented through necessity, the plan became even more complex, and the workings of the peculiar Australian model became more complicated.

Four implications of a federal structure are sufficient to show that the Australian model is very different from the Westminster system. First, the prime function of the High Court of Australia is to arbitrate on cases concerning federalism. The Court is the final interpreter of the Constitution. It has the authority to rule that law passed by the national parliament (or by a state parliament) is unconstitutional and therefore invalid. The High Court was specifically established with this authority as a key structure within federalism, to ensure that the division of powers, which is the kernel of federalism, was not subverted by any government, national or state. But this authority places the Court above parliament. It denies the essential sovereignty of parliament. It establishes a structure of government significantly different from Westminster.

Second, the federal Constitution limits the area of competence of the national parliament. Under Section 51, the national parliament is given authority to legislate on a specific list of topics. All other topics are the sole responsibility of the state parliaments. The national parliament is therefore not only not sovereign, but it is limited in its field of authority. Again, this is a fundamental change from Westminster. The British parliament has no limits on what it can do. No court, nor any other institution, can overrule its acts. It is a sovereign parliament.

Third, a federal structure requires the existence of a house of parliament which is specifically established as a house of the states and for the states—one which will represent the states and will protect their interests. The Australian Senate, modelled on the US Senate, is formed by equal representation from each state, and it has equal powers with the House of Representatives. Hence the 'People's House', the house which is the keystone of the Westminster system, can be checked in Australia by the federal upper house. This is not the case in the British Westminster parliament. The upper house, the House of Lords, has strictly limited powers. It can delay legislation for a limited period of time, but it cannot veto any Act of the House of Commons.

Finally, the British parliament within a Westminster system has total control of all the structures and processes of the political system. Because the British 'constitution' is not written in a single document, but is the aggregate of all Acts of parliament, then the parliament itself is the custodian of the 'constitution'. A simple Act of parliament is all that is required for the 'constitution' to be changed. The parliament has the sole authority to undertake this. In Australia, the fundamental law is the written Constitution. It cannot be changed by the parliament. Any modification of the Constitution requires a referendum of the people, and hence the parliament may propose, but it cannot enact changes to supreme law which governs it.

THE IMPACT OF PARTY

Australian parliaments are essentially party parliaments. So are all other parliaments—in Britain, Canada and New Zealand, for example. Any parliamentary system contains a powerful drive towards the development of party cohesion. Major parties will see themselves as winning government at the next election. The governing party will therefore emphasise internal cohesion to show its capacity to be returned. The opposition party will also have an incentive to be cohesive, both as a response to a cohesive government, and as a sign to the electorate that it is an alternative government.

But Australian parliaments contain *disciplined* political parties, and this has important effects. The Labor Party imposes discipline through its pledge. All Labor members are bound by the rules and platform of the party, all are pledged not to oppose any endorsed Labor candidate, and all are pledged to vote in accordance with the majority decision of caucus. The Liberal Party rejects any such pledge. It has always asserted a formal independence for Liberal members of parliament. But a Liberal caucus, in practice, is bound by a party cohesion which is almost a discipline. Only rarely does a Liberal member speak, let alone vote, against the party, and such instances usually bring down the wrath of the party. The National Party is just as cohesive. Only the Democrats actually put into practice the independence within their rules.

The impact on parliament is obvious. To one observer (Clark 1971:49).

> No member of parliament, or parliamentary candidate, of any party, is allowed to dissent in the slightest degree from the decisions or actions of his party leaders, whatever he believes to be his duties towards his constituents, the needs of the country as he understands them, or the voice of his own conscience. If by any public word or

> action, or even by any implication or inaction, he expresses the slightest disagreement, the whole weight of the party machine is turned against him.

This comment was written before the formation of the Australian Democrats, but it remains accurate as a description of the Labor, Liberal and National parties. The result, to translate a description of the British parliament (Beer 1965:350–1) into the Australian context, is that:

> In the House of Representatives were two bodies of freedom-loving Australians, chosen in 148 constituencies and subject to influences that run back to an electorate that is numbered in millions and divided by the complex interest and aspirations of an advanced modern society. Yet day after day, with a Prussian discipline, they trooped from one side of the House to the other at the signals of their whips, and in the service of the authoritarian decisions of their parliamentary parties.

This authoritarian cohesion has major effects on the functions, practices and procedures of parliaments.

There is one set of issues on which the party discipline is not applied. Conscience votes are allowed when parties allow their members a 'free' vote. These occur on social issues such as abortion law reform, divorce law, homosexual law reform, rape law reform, and so on. The parties announce a free, conscience vote on such matters of grave social concern. But there is another interpretation. These matters are deeply divisive, and most people hold strongly committed views. A conscience vote is therefore a case of parties protecting themselves. For example, any attempt to impose a pro-abortion party line in the Labor Party would split the party. Further, a party line on a social issue would alienate a significant sector of the voting public, and threaten the chances of a party to win a majority. On most issues, however, the party line will be enforced, and this has had major effects on the theoretical functions of parliament.

FUNCTIONS OF PARLIAMENT: THEORY AND PRACTICE

FORMING A GOVERNMENT

In all but a handful of cases in this century, the government has been decided by the election result. Given that the parties are cohesive, then there is no doubt that the party (or coalition) that wins the majority of seats in the lower house of parliament will be the party which produces the prime minister and the government. There are some cases when the parliament has had to decide who should govern. These have been the result of a 'hung' parliament, one in which no party has achieved an absolute majority of the seats in the lower house. Recent examples include Tasmania (1989) when the house divided thus: Liberal 17 seats, Labor 13 and Green Independent 5; and South Australia (1989) with Liberal 22, National 1, Labor 22 and Independent Labor 2 seats. In most cases, however, one party (or the Liberal/National coalition) has won an absolute majority of seats and has formed the government.

LEGISLATING

A parliament, in theory, is a law-making body. But this legislative function of parliament has become little more than a formality. Given that political parties expect the party line to be followed and they do not take kindly to members who abstain, let alone cross the floor, then what the government wishes to be carried in legislation almost inevitably will be carried. Hence, the legislative function in practice has passed from parliament to cabinet, or to the prime minister, or to the party caucus, or to a combination of the three.

The only exception to this pattern, the rare occasions when parliament regains its pre-eminence and power in regard to legislation, is when the party whips are removed and members of parties are given a free or conscience vote. These are the only occasions when parliament is fulfilling its theoretical legislative role, and then only because the political parties are unable or unwilling to produce, or to enforce, a party policy on such questions.

In one sense, then, the parliamentary legislative process has become a formality; cabinet decides what laws shall be made and cabinet controls the voting decision in parliament through the instruments of party loyalty and party discipline, which are tighter in Australia than in any other parliamentary system. Even with this development, the legislative process still contains provisions for extended discussion and debate on government policies and programmes and on broad questions of foreign affairs, economic matters and a wide range of subjects. But governments vary in the degree to which they are willing to offer such rights and opportunities to an opposition, and to backbench members of parliament. The business of the house, in the final analysis, is in the control of the government, the party in power, and there are a number of means which can, and are, used by government to limit debate, to stifle criticism, and to force legislation through the house in a short period of time.

Governments of all parties have used the gag—a means to end debate. Any member of parliament has the right to move 'that the question be now put', but the gag is usually moved by a minister or the whip; oppositions usually seek more, rather than less, debate. The motion must be put to a vote, and if necessary a division, without further debate and if it is carried out the question under the discussion is also voted on without further debate. Governments of both parties in recent years have used the gag with increasing frequency to rush legislation through, to stifle opposition, or to silence an opposition speaker, the last by moving 'that the Member be no longer heard'. Governments also have recourse to the guillotine, a procedure by which discussion on certain subjects is governed by a time limit. The guillotine is generally applied when legislation is being strongly contested by the opposition, or when the government is in the process of attempting to complete a legislative programme within a certain time. Under the terms of a guillotine, a time limit is applied to the various stages of the passage of a bill. Its use sometimes reaches ridiculous proportions at the end of a session when important bills are guillotined through all stages in a matter of minutes. In such situations the idea of a legislative debate becomes farcical.

REPRESENTATIVE FUNCTION

Members of parliament are supposed to represent their constituents, bring to the parliament the ideas, ideals, interest and grievances of their constituents and report to their constituents on their actions. Most MPs at least attempt to carry this out, but party discipline is a constraint.

INFORMATION FUNCTION

Parliament provides information and informed opinions for the public. There is a question as to whether Australia has sufficient 'open government', and, indeed what is 'sufficient'! Further, given the confrontation style of party politics, information often takes second place to point-scoring.

RESPONSIBILITY

This is a complex area, and is usually considered as the keystone of any system of parliamentary democracy. The following chapter examines its theory and practice in detail, but some brief comments are necessary at this stage.

In the model of parliamentary democracy, all components of government—ministers, the public service, the statutory authorities and the ministry as a whole—are ultimately responsible to parliament. It is parliament which is the final arbiter of government proposals, plans and policies. It is parliament which has the authority and power to call the government and individual ministers to account for their actions.

In practice, this responsibility function has passed out of the hands of parliament. Neither individual members nor the opposition have much opportunity to test, question and force the government to justify its policies and actions, and parliament's authority to exercise the ultimate sanction and remove a government is simply not available under the system of party government in Australia. Even in 1975, the dismissal of the Whitlam government during the constitutional crisis was by the Liberal–NCP in the Senate and the Governor-General, not the parliament.

The functions of representation and information are still carried out, on occasions relatively effectively, by parliament. In fact, the primary function of Australian parliaments today is to provide a forum for discussion. There is a constant dialogue between government and opposition (some critics would call it a diatribe), and there is also a two-way process of political communicating between government and opposition and the general public—through the forum of the national parliament and through indirect means of political communication such as the mass media.

This process of contact between people, parliament and government occurs as a continuing process and in a number of ways. Individual members of parliament express to the government the views, opinions and grievances of the people, publicly through the parliamentary debates, or confidentially to ministers and their staffs, or directly to the public service, or in the party room during discussion of policy. The members of parliament inform the public generally, and their own electorate, of the views and policies of the government and opposition.

THE SENATE

Each of the four broad types of functions of parliament outlined above is specifically that of the House of Representatives. In the practice of Australian legislative politics, they apply equally to the Senate. In fact, following the 1975 constitutional crisis, it is clear that no government is truly in power unless it also controls the upper house.

The Australian Senate was a direct result of two basic concepts accepted by constitution planners in the 1890s. The first was drawn from the traditions of the Westminster system and reflected the existing initiations of the colonies—the perceived need for a bicameral or two-chamber system. It was an axiom of Victorian constitutional theory that there should be two houses of parliament; the lower house to provide representation for the people and to be the house of policy, of government, of legislation; and the upper house where the actions of the lower house could be independently examined and judged.

The second concept was that of federalism. The House of Representatives was planned to represent the people of Australia. The Senate was also a representative house, but its prime purpose was to represent the states. The constitutional plan specifically designed the Senate as a house of the states, for the states, representing the states equally regardless of population (originally six senators per state) and a house which would be powerful enough to match the House of Representatives to protect state interests.

Until recently, the Senate was not a highly regarded institution in Australia. Since the 1960s, however, the image of the Senate has undergone a change, partly because of changed party composition and partly because of radical changes in the legislative process within that house.

For two periods, the control of the Senate, and hence control of all legislation, has been in the hands of minor parties. In the 1967–1974 period, the DLP held the balance of power in the Senate. In the main, the DLP supported the Liberal Party, and in 1972–1974 parliament used its numbers on more than one occasion to block the Whitlam government. The Australian Democrats and Greens now hold the balance of power. One major difference from the DLP period is that the Australian Democrat party is allied with neither government nor opposition, and can be said to hold a real balance of power. Whether the control of legislation and of the parliament, through a veto power exercised by just ten out of 223 members of parliament is a democratic situation is a matter of debate.

The second significant change in the Senate has long-term effects. The development of a committee style of legislative procedure in the Senate has been a significant change for the better. Both houses individually, and jointly on occasion, had utilised a series of committees of inquiry into specific matters since federation—these were select committees, appointed on an *ad hoc* basis, for specific purposes. Since 1970, the Senate has a number of permanent committees which carry out important activities in audit areas; that is, detailed investigations and analyses of government financial proposals, including details of supply and budget bills and in general areas of legislative investigation, including committees into public accounts and delegated legislation, as well as *ad hoc* committees of investigation into specific matters.

Despite the new public image of the Senate, there is no doubt that it is no longer what it was planned to be. There is marginally less disciplined party-line voting, but only marginally less. The modern

Senate is not a house of independent review, nor is it a house of and for the states. It is almost a replica of the party-dominated House of Representatives and generally can be described as either an echo or an obstruction. When the political chips are down, party loyalties for most senators are, and always have been, stronger than the concept of independent representation.

SUMMARY

In summary, parliament is no longer pre-eminent. Political parties dominate, and the government controls the parliament by means of party discipline. Parliament has retained some important roles:

- it is a national forum for government policies and the alternative policies of the opposition
- it is a two-way channel of communication between the government and the governed—the electorate
- it is a training ground for future ministers
- it is one avenue for the protection of the rights of individual citizens.

But if these are the functions of parliament which remain relevant, then there are questions which need to be asked about whether the other prime functions are adequately followed. Hence:

- How efficiently does parliament perform its tasks?
- Does parliament have the resources to perform its tasks efficiently?
- Does parliament have adequate sources of information which are independent of the government and its public service? Do MPs have adequate research and secretarial facilities? Are MPs paid enough?
- Are there enough MPs?
- If the parliament is the major national forum of debate, are its proceedings sufficiently publicised?
- Are parliament's procedures effective and efficient for the purpose of fulfilling its functions?

THE PEOPLE OF PARLIAMENT

The people of parliament are of two types—the elected representatives and the officials who serve them. The elected representatives can be further subdivided into the backbenchers, the organisers and the leaders.

MEMBERS' BACKGROUNDS

The members of parliament in Australia do not show much evidence of a 'mirror' representation; they do not provide a cross-section of the society. The parliaments are, in a clear majority, male and middle class. Of course, any proposal to produce a parliament which 'mirrors' society would face insoluble problems. Should women be represented in proportion to the population? Should the young, middle-aged, and old have proportional representation? Should the major religions be 'mirrored'? Ethnic groups, Aborigines, the unemployed, the wealthy, the poor could all claim the right to be representatives. In fact, *who* is represented is essentially a matter of pre-selection processes in the political parties and the effects of these are evident in the membership. In the parliament elected in 1990, 29 per cent of the parliamentary membership were professional, 24 per cent in business, and 15 per cent white collar workers—a total of 68 per cent who could be described as middle class. Further, 71 of the 111 Labor members, 58 of the 84 Liberals, 7 of the 19 Nationals, and all but one of the nine Democrats and Independents have achieved a higher education qualification. This picture is hardly a mirror of the electorate, and certainly a major disjunction exists between the backgrounds of the majority of Labor MPs and their traditional labour base.

THE BACKBENCH

This term is generally used to describe members of parliament who are not members of either the ministry or the shadow ministry. The term 'backbencher' derives from the convention that ministers and opposition shadow ministers occupy the front seat on the right and left sides of the Speaker respectively. As the Parliamentary system developed into a cabinet government, the frontbench members became more dominant; as the party system developed, this tendency was confirmed. In recent years, rumblings from the backbenchers are occasionally heard in regard to lack of power and participation given to them and in regard to what some backbenchers see as a deliberate plot by the frontbench members on both sides of the house to keep them in their place. Some backbenchers feel the term itself is derogatory and claim that 'private member' is a more fitting description.

The backbench is expected to be supportive of the party leaders, to do what it is told by the organisers, to make speeches when requested, and generally not to question the existing order. A Liberal backbencher, Edward St John (1969:22–3), presented a first-hand account of the life and worth of this group (see Document 7.3). Most backbenchers, especially those in marginal seats, faced with the reality of their parliamentary life, turn their efforts and involvements to the electorate and the party organisation. Being returned to parliament at the next election becomes the overriding concern.

THE ORGANISERS

As parliamentary democracy became cabinet government and eventually party government, each party in parliament developed a hierarchy within its own ranks, with a small internal party group given the task of managing the party, the members, the legislative involvement of the party and, if in government, the legislative business of the house. They also became a means of communication between the backbench and the party leadership, especially as these two sections became increasingly separated.

Each party caucus elects one or more party whips for each house of parliament. These became the key managers of the party in parliament with the often difficult task of ensuring that party members attend the house when required, and they attempt to keep the party line intact in important votes. With strict party discipline, the role of the whip in such areas is formal and mechanical. On occasions, a Liberal or National whip may need to pull into line a potential rebel, or admonish an absentee, but the task has become more administration of such matters as lists of speakers (and occasionally making sure there are sufficient speakers on legislation no one is very interested in) and of recording votes or divisions.

As the role of whip for the government party in the Australian parliaments has become less important, so the leader of the house (in the lower house) and the leader of the government (in the Senate) have become more important for the efficiency of parliament and its business. The whip is responsible for administration and occasionally for an element of discipline; the leader of the house is a senior member of the governing party who has the responsibility for the overall planning of the activities of parliament, the order of business which the government intends to follow and, most important, the front-line responsibility for tactics. As parliament has become less a place for discussion and debate and more an arena for confrontation, so tactics have become more important. Manoeuvres in parliament take on as much importance as manoeuvres on a battlefield, with potential embarrassment awaiting the loser in a battle of tactics, if not more serious political implications.

The opposition also elects a senior person to manage the attacks on the government, plan tactics and liaise with the leader of the house or the leader of the government in regard to the order and arrangement of parliamentary business. Both types of organisers have received official recognition and both are granted extra salary for their efforts (which are, in the main, efforts in and on behalf of a party first, and parliament second).

THE LEADERS

As the backbenchers of the parties in parliament have become less important in almost all senses except as numbers necessary at times of voting on divisions, the frontbench members have enlarged their authority and power. On the government side, the leaders on the front bench are the prime minister and his ministers; on the opposition side, the leader of the opposition and his shadow ministers. These frontbench members play the dominant role in parliament; procedures, and ultimately, the party line, are used by the leaders who face not only the leaders on the other side of the house, but pressure from their members on the backbench behind them for more involvement and more say in legislative process.

Obviously the leaders on the government benches are the dominant force. They attempt to control, and generally succeed in controlling, the parliament and what is done within it. The methods used to achieve such control are many and various. There is an incentive for backbenchers to conform—their hopes for promotion will depend partly on faithful service to the party. Sanctions are available within a party—demotion or a threat of no promotion. Procedures allow a government to overwhelm any opposition member, or the opposition itself. By imposing the party line, a government can gag an opposition member who is raising embarrassing questions, and can impose a guillotine, setting time limits for the passage of a bill and hence limit the opportunities for oppositions to oppose.

SPEAKER

One office of leadership in parliament can also be included under the term 'manager'. The office of Speaker in the tradition of British parliamentary government has been considered as one of the most senior, most demanding and most important in parliament and is granted great prestige. British tradition and modern practice require a Speaker to be a presiding officer of stature, independence, impartiality and with full knowledge of the rules of parliament. The Speaker of the House of Commons, when elected to the position, resigns from his or her party and is usually never opposed in an election. Thus, the independence and impartiality of the Speaker are seen to be assured and usually are so assured.

Australian parliaments broke early from this tradition and today there is little comparison with the British Speaker, except in the prestige claimed by the incumbents in Australia. In theory the authority, role and judgement of the Speaker in the House of Representatives and of the President in the Senate are crucial to the

The Speaker

proper functioning of a legislature. But this role in Australia has been modified in practice: by a lack of impartiality of a Speaker or President; by lack of an adequate knowledge and understanding of standing orders; by a lack of recognition by the opposition or even their own party, of the status of their rulings from the chair and by the limited degree of independence from the party that they actually have. Australian Speakers are almost invariably members of the majority party. The extent to which a Speaker removes him or herself from an overt identification with his/her party varies from individual to individual, but the ideal of independence has been more and more departed from in Australia in recent years. A Labor Speaker remains a member of caucus, bound by the party pledge; a Liberal Speaker continues to attend party meetings and it has not been unusual to hear a Speaker at a non-parliamentary function supporting government policy. The Chairman of Committees carries out functions similar to those of a Speaker or President, but only in the area of management of parliamentary business and only when the house is in a committee stage (see below).

THE OFFICIALS

Both houses of parliament have established a team of officials necessary for the running of the business of parliament. The various departments of Parliament House have grown in size as the business of the parliament and the number of its members have expanded.

The Clerk is the chief official in both House of Representatives and

Table 7.2: *Parliamentary staff, 1901–1986* (selected years)*

	1901	1964	1975	1986
Senate	10	19	107	175
Representatives	18	29	138	174
Library	3	15	134	181
Joint House	10	50	131	265
Reporting	12	26	51	78
Totals	43	139	561	873

* Figures at 30 June for the years cited do not include temporary, casual or sessional staff, of which there are many, especially during sessions.

the Senate. The Clerk is a permanent officer in the Commonwealth public service and is the person responsible for the administration for the house and of its proceedings. The Clerk is responsible for a number of functions, including preparation of agendas for meetings, recording of proceedings, publications and general staff administration. The Clerk also provides valuable support for a Speaker or a President, especially in terms of standing orders and questions about proceedings of the house.

In the House of Representatives, a Serjeant-at-Arms is the officer in charge of all ceremonial functions, accommodation of members and their staff, transport, broadcasting, and clerical facilities. The parallel officer in the Senate, Black Rod, has similar functions, but with more history and ceremony attached to the office. The title—Gentleman Usher of the Black Rod—derives from fourteenth-century England and refers to the symbol of office he carries. Black Rod is involved in much of the ceremony of parliament, especially in relation to the opening of parliament, and has the role of a Royal Messenger, as well as policing the Senate chamber.

David Solomon (1986:419) identified an explosion in the staff and the bureaucracy employed to serve the parliament and the parliamentarians.

PROCEDURES OF PARLIAMENT

For most people, knowledge of the formal proceedings of parliament is usually limited to the occasional time when they turn on the broadcast of proceedings and, perhaps, make a brief visit. And more often than not, there is a rather bemused reaction to what appears to be excessive formality of procedure and constant repetition of certain phrases. There are two reasons for what may appear at first sight to be excess formality: first, the fact that procedures of parliament in Australia are based on the historic traditions of the House of Commons and have retained those traditions as part of the heritage of the Westminster system; and second that, in theory, such formal procedures should provide a guarantee that the functions of parliament are undertaken seriously and correctly, especially as the function of law-making will affect all citizens.

Most of the forms and procedures of the parliament are set out in the Standing Orders of each house. These provide comprehensively for the conduct of proceedings, the means and process of the passage of legislation, the rules of debate, the presentation of order and the operation of the various committees.

A normal day in a house of parliament in Australia follows an order of business laid down in the Standing Orders, and usually follows a set routine.

1 **Prayers**
Each sitting opens with a standard prayer read by the Speaker (or President).

2 **Petitions**
Any citizen or group of citizens can organise a petition to parliament calling for some action. Such petitions can only be presented to parliament by a member of parliament, and are accepted only if they conform to a standard form of address. The presentation of petitions has been streamlined to the extent that the Clerk merely records publicly the topic of the petition and which member presented it, and the petitions do not seem to be given serious consideration.

3 **Notices**
A formality, a statement of an intention to move a motion or present a bill at some time.

4 **Questions without Notice**
The period allowed for question time is forty-five minutes in the House of Representatives, but there is no statutory time limit in the Senate. Questions are usually directed to a minister and must be on a matter within the responsibility of that minister. The Speaker usually alternates government and opposition members, and ensures that questions are in order. A minister is not required to answer a question and is entitled to answer a question in a manner he or she thinks fit. In the practice of confrontation politics in Australian parliaments, question time is less a process of seeking and giving information than a chance for scoring partisan points. A growing number of questions are of the 'Dorothy Dix' type (from the government backbench) and attempts to win political points (from both sides of the House).

5 **Presentation of Papers**
A formal process when ministers and chairmen of various committees present reports to the parliament. On some occasions such papers are the basis of statements and replies.

6 **Ministerial Statements**
The House gives leave for such statements which are normally the first public expression of a major matter of government policy, or some major development concerning the department for which the minister is responsible. Such statements are usually the genesis of a parliamentary debate.

7 **Matter of Public Importance**
Any member can propose a debate on any matter which is so defined and if eight other members support the motion, debate on the matter proceeds for a maximum period of two hours.

8 **Orders of the Day**
The Clerk prepares a notice paper for each day of sitting, setting out the precedence of items of business which are planned for the House, in collaboration with the government and the opposition. Such orders are almost inevitably government business—there are limited opportunities for the opposition or backbench members to have items on the notice paper, and if they do succeed, the items would have a low priority.

9 **The Adjournment**
At the close of a sitting day, a brief period of time (usually thirty minutes) is provided for members to bring before the House almost any matter they wish.

There are few times available to backbenchers as private members to raise issues of concern to them. Apart from the Address-in-Reply, the budget debate and the limited opportunities in question time, backbenchers have only the grievance debate and the adjournment debate for their own purposes. Under Standing Orders, certain periods during a session of parliament are put aside for any private member to address the House for a set period (ten minutes in the House of Representatives) on any topic. The allocation for the grievance debate is about two hours once every two weeks.

FROM A BILL TO AN ACT

Beyond these stipulated periods for wide discussion, the overwhelming time of a session of parliament is spent on government bills. There are normal procedures for the passage of a bill.

1 **Initiation**
The formal introduction of a bill by a minister, and the circulation of copies of the bill to the members.

2 **First Reading**
By practice this has become part of the initiation process, and consists of a reading of title of the bill by the Clerk. (At no time in the procedure of the passage of a bill is the full text read. The term 'reading' refers to a stage in the debate.) Only on very rare occasions is there any debate on a first reading.

3 **Second Reading**
Immediately following initiation of the bill, the minister usually proposes a motion for the second reading and gives the second-reading speech—usually a description and justification of the bill in general terms. The second-reading debate follows, with speakers able to range over the general field of interest of the bill. At the conclusion of the debate, the motion for the second reading is put and (in the modern Australian system of party government) automatically carried. The Clerk then again reads the long title of the bill.

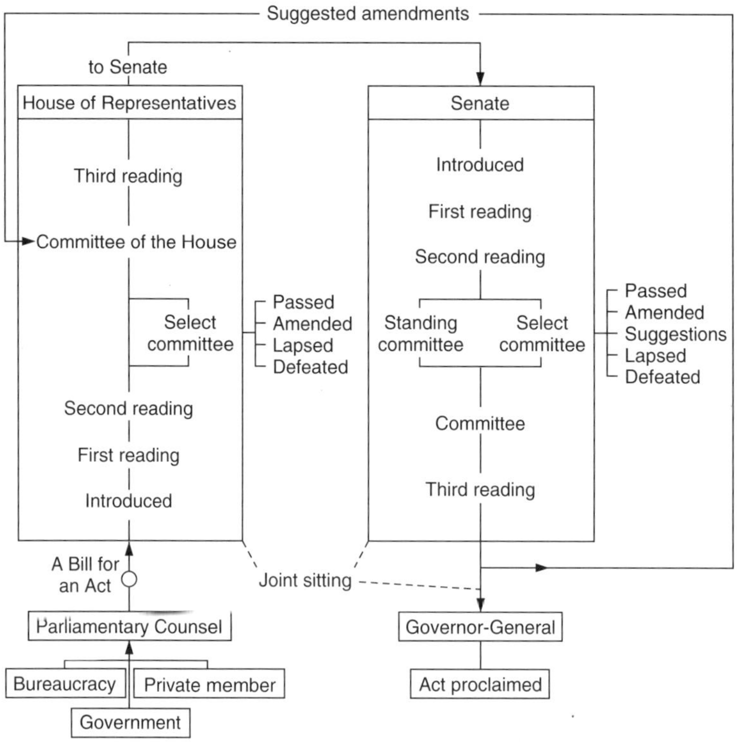

Figure 7.3 From a Bill to an Act

4 **Committee Stage**

Under normal circumstances, the House then becomes a committee of the whole House. This is achieved simply by the removal of the Mace from the table. In this stage, the House (as a committee) considers the bill in detail—sometimes clause-by-clause—and considers detailed proposals for amendment. The government itself may move amendments (which will be carried) and the opposition may propose amendments (which will be defeated), and the detailed progress continues, often over days of sitting, until the final form is accepted by the government. The chairman then reports to the Speaker who takes the chair and the House again becomes a House.

5 **Third Reading**

The final part of the debate in this first stage, usually carried without debate. The Clerk again reads the title of the bill.

6 **Transmission to the Other House**

Passage of any bill requires the acceptance by both houses of parliament. If the bill were initiated in the House of Representatives, the bill is transmitted to the Senate where a similar process is carried through: a) initiation; b) first reading; c) second reading; d) committee; e) third reading; after which the bill is returned to the House of Representatives. If the bill has been passed by the Senate in the form received, a message to that effect is the only document transmitted and the bill is then ready for the final stage. If the bill has been amended by the Senate, the House again forms itself into committee to debate the amendments and if they are accepted, the bill has been passed.

7 **Assent**

In practice, a formal process where the Governor-General signs with the words: 'In the name of Her Majesty I assent to the Act.'

8 **Proclamation**

The formal action putting the terms of the Act into effect. Some Acts, for example for emergencies or for penalties under industrial disputes, are carried but not proclaimed until required.

PRIVILEGES AND PERQUISITES

As the concept of representative and responsible government has been modified in Australian practice by the development from cabinet government into government by disciplined political parties, what effects have these changes had on the roles of the individual members of parliament? What freedom and protection do members have? What resources are available for members? The answers to such questions may help in assessing the role of parliamentarians in Australia.

PRIVILEGE

Parliaments are specially protected institutions, and members are especially privileged people. Parliamentary privilege refers to the special rights granted to parliament and its members designed to ensure the independence of both and to enable parliamentary business to be carried out without external pressure and fear of prosecution. The prime purpose of privilege is to enable members of parliament to have absolute freedom of speech; a member cannot be sued for slander or libel or defamation for any statements made under the protection of parliament. All papers and documents, including parliamentary debates (*Hansard*), published by parliament are equally under privilege.

In cases of an alleged breach of privilege by a member of the public against parliament, the parliament is prosecution, defence, judge, jury and 'executioner'. The offender is brought to the bar of the House, judged and sentenced, and has no right of appeal to any court. One of the most notable cases in Australia concerned the jailing of two journalists in 1955 for three months after they had been found guilty of publishing defamatory articles about a member. Given such an absolute privilege of freedom of speech, members of parliament have the duty to ensure that the right is not abused.

FACILITIES AND SALARIES

Any move by members of parliament to increase, or accept an increase in salary, allowances or benefits always brings in its wake a storm of protest in the correspondence columns of Australian newspapers. Yet how often does the public examine the facts of the life of a member of parliament, examine whether the facilities available to members are adequate or whether salary assistance and benefits are sufficient? The common public reaction to any suggestion of an increase in any such area is usually one of cynical pessimism.

The salaries of members of the national parliament are set by an independent remuneration tribunal. The members of the tribunal receive submissions from interested people, including members of the public, and determine salaries and allowances. All members of parliament receive a basic salary, equal for members of both the House of Representatives and the Senate. All members also receive an electoral allowance which is tax-free and is related to the area of the electorate the member represents. There are then additional salaries and allowances for ministers, and other office holders. The

1988 review by the Remuneration Tribunal proposed significant increases to basic salaries of members, from $49 180 in 1988, to a proposed $67 000 in 1991. This was rejected by the Hawke government. Current salaries (selected) and allowances are shown in Table 7.3. All members of parliament also receive electoral allowances, ranging from $21 005 for a senator, and a member whose electorate is less than 2000 square kilometres, to $30 458 for a member whose electorate is larger than 5000 square kilometres.

Members also have a wide range of other allowances and perquisites. All MPs and senators have a daily living allowance when in Canberra, or when away from home on some sort of official business. They have free first-class travel anywhere in Australia, and can use official government vehicles. All are provided with free telephones in their private homes and receive a stamp allowance as well as an entitlement to postage free envelopes when in Parliament House. Each member or senator is provided with an electorate office and two staff members.

Are these salaries and conditions justified? Certainly a conscientious member of parliament has much to do; speeches to prepare and give in the parliament, parliamentary committee work and party activities, and the most time-consuming occupation of parliamentarians—servicing the many demands of the residents of their electorates. Members have seemingly unending demands from their local parties and from their local electorates, and for most members, devotion to the party and the electorate will be the prime aim and occupy most of the time, especially if the electorate is marginal, or the member's name is last on the Senate ticket. There are constant calls on the time and finances of a member; local party meetings, dinners, speeches, opening shows and laying foundation stones, appeals for support—moral and monetary—from every local organisation, and a constant stream of electors at the local office seeking some kind of help or support. For almost all members of the national parliament

Table 7.3: *Parliamentary salaries and expense allowances, 1990*

	Salary	Further salary	Allowance	Total
Member/Senator	55 000	–	–	55 000
Prime Minister	55 000	56 931	29 255	141 186
Deputy Prime Minister	55 000	38 806	17 253	111 059
Minister	55 000	25 747	12 002	92 949
Leader of Opposition	55 000	29 809	14 268	99 077
National Party Leader	55 000	11 369	12 002	78 371
Chairman of Committees	55 000	9 064	2 474	66 538
Opposition Whip	55 000	7 519	2 474	64 993

and country members of state parliaments, the sitting days mean constant absences from home. Overall, any judgement about the monetary worth of a member of parliament needs to be made only after a full consideration of all such aspects.

DOCUMENTS

7.1 THE FUNCTIONS OF PARLIAMENT

Source: An official publication of the House of Representatives.

The principal features of the role of the House may be summarised as follows:

1 The power to make government.
2 The power to break governments if they do not retain the confidence and support of a majority of the Members of the House.
3 The initiation of the major part of legislation introduced into the Parliament.
4 Consideration of the nature and merits of legislation put before it and the proposal of such amendments as it thinks necessary.
5 Control of expenditure by scrutiny of financial proposals and their purpose. The principle of the financial initiative of the government vests in the government the right to initiate or move to increase appropriations and taxes, but this does not deprive the House of its right to make amendments which will reduce a proposed appropriation or tax to reject the proposal.
6 Examination of public accounts to ensure that public money is spent in accordance with parliamentary approval and in the best interests of the tax payer.
7 Critical discussion of government policy, both external and internal, and its implementation.
8 The maintenance of a watching brief over government administration.
9 The safeguarding and promotion of the best interests of the nation and its people by raising particular matters in the course of business before the House or through means otherwise available in the procedures of the House. The redressing of grievances is within this category.
10 The surveillance of delegated legislation, usually in the form of an ordinance or regulation, approved by the government pursuant to a general authority contained in an Act of Parliament.
11 The development and use of procedures which will enable the House to discharge its functions in the most effective form.

12 The establishment and use of adequate research and information facilities necessary for the conduct of informed inquiries and debate.

7.2 GIVING PARLIAMENT A JOB

Source: 'What's gone wrong with politics?', *Bulletin*, 20 May 1972.

Australians are beginning to wonder if it is right to saddle New Guinea with the 'Westminster' form of government. It would be a good idea if they now also began to ask whether it was right to saddle Australia with it. One of the greatest contributions a political scientist could make to Australian politics would be to come up with some new doctrine of representative government.

Australians just took parliaments over from London. But have they ever really learned to work them?

For instance, in Westminster, the tradition of picking ministers from among parliamentarians seems to work yet is this necessarily the best method for Australia? Shouldn't we experiment a bit more with picking some ministers from outside parliament altogether?

The immediate criticism of this is that it would be even harder to attract good men into politics if there were even less possibility for them to become ministers. But the answer is that as parliamentarians they can be given more sensible and useful jobs.

This could come from an expansion of the committee system from the Senate—now, unexpectedly, the real action-chamber in Canberra—to the House of Representatives and to the state parliaments.

Apart from being electoral colleges which decide who should be the government, parliaments should be the place where committees provide some of the nation's most important sounding boards—by calling witnesses and getting evidence about what is going on in the administration and what kinds of new policies might be possible.

Instead of being largely given over to be phoniness of 'debate' on matters that have already been decided in the party rooms, parliaments could be watch-dogs of the people by prying into administration—and they could be instruments of change, by canvassing new policies up to the point of political practicality.

7.3 A VIEW FROM THE BACKBENCH

Source: St John, E. 1969, *A Time to Speak*, Sun Books, Melbourne, pp. 22–3.

Normally the only time they spend in Canberra is when Parliament is sitting for its sixty-six days or so of the year. Their time is so fully occupied that they have little or no time to join in the life of the capital city or to become acquainted with its denizens. Their contact with public service and service officers is limited for the most part to an occasional meeting where a senior public servant or service officer may attend a Parliamentary or Government or Opposition Members' Committee. Except for Ministers from their home State or particular Ministers with whom they may have some personal relationship, perhaps stemming from the days when they were backbenchers together, there is a great gulf even between the Government backbencher and the members of the Ministry. Nor do the backbenchers have much contact with other classes of people with whom one might have hoped they would have had contact by virtue of their position and their role as members of Parliament—not only public servants and service officers, but the officers of national organisations, university people, foreign diplomatic representatives and visitors from overseas or interstate. Parliamentarians are in Canberra but not really of it. The knowledge of what is going on which they do manage to glean is derived partly from contact with a few Ministers and other Members, but mainly form the Press and pressmen. Because of the absence of other contacts, only the Press, and pressmen in private conversation, or perhaps a friendly Minister, can fill the void for them and provide the essential link, not only as to what is happening in the rest of Australia but even as to what is happening in Canberra. This would include, for example, information as to what is occurring in the Ministry or in relation to the conflicts which may be raging within the bureaucracy, or in exchanges between the Government and the particular outside interests who may desire to promote or oppose some change in legislation or policy, or even as to what is going on under the roof of Parliament House itself.

The senior political journalist, with his well-established links with the leaders of all parties and times to pursue information in numerous conversations, his contact with senior public servants and service officers, his knowledge of the history and personalities of Parliament and Canberra gained over a period of year, not to mention the interchange between the members of the Press Gallery themselves, is in a much better position to know what is going on than even the most experienced backbencher.

7.4 THE WESTMINSTER SYSTEM

Source: Carey, B. 1980, 'Executive control in the 1970s', in Mayer, H. & Nelson, H. (eds), *Australian Politics: A Fifth Reader*, Longman Cheshire, Melbourne, p. 227.

It is often asserted that Australia has a 'Westminster model' type of government but it is not always clear what this means. It is certainly true to the extent that as a description of Australia's institutional approach to government, Canberra is more akin to Britain's Westminster than to Washington, Paris, Bonn, Moscow or Peking.

In common with Westminster, Australia has two Houses of Parliament; legislative power is vested in parliament (section 1 of the Constitution); the members of the Lower House are 'directly chosen by the people' (section 24); executive power is vested in the Crown (section 61), with an Executive Council actually conducting government (section 62); ministers of state are chosen from among sitting parliamentarians (section 64); there is a Speaker (section 35); and money bills cannot originate in the Upper House (section 53).

7.5 THE SENATE: AN OFFICIAL VIEW

Source: An Introduction to the Australian Federal Parliament, 1959, Angus and Robertson, Sydney, pp. 26–7. Prepared under instructions from the President of the Senate.

Both Houses of the Federal Parliament are elected by the same body of electors. In choosing a bicameral legislative system, the founders of the Constitution had in mind, however, that the Senate should give expression to the interests of the States as partners in the federation; that is to say, that the Senate should be a States House...

The Senate was also designed to function as a House of Review—a function universally accepted as the role of a second chamber. With this in mind, the founders provided that senators should be elected for six-year terms and that one-half of their number should retire every three years instead of all senators retiring at the same time. This rotation principle ensures an element of continuity in the constitution of the Senate, and the six-year terms were designed to give senators greater independence and better opportunities for deliberation in dealing with proposed legislation.

7.6 PARLIAMENT AS A PARTY PLAYGROUND

Source: Davis, S.R. (ed.) 1960, *The Government of the Australian States,* Longman Cheshire, Melbourne, p. 667.

The second striking feature of parliamentary government...is the obsessive regard for party. No doubt, there can be dispute about what too much party is, but the extreme is always recognisable; it expresses itself in any number of ways. First in the absence of any obvious sense of the 'House' as a whole, or any transcendent interest which links one side in any way with the other unless it is in the provision of amenities or in an external attack on its privileges. Stripped of all its constitutional theory the parliamentary play in each House on almost every issue, large or small, is simply this—to stand behind the party at all times and 'knock' the other side whenever it raises its head. The idea of a free vote is almost unknown. To speak of Parliament versus the Crown or talk of Parliament as some collective entity whose business it is to scrutinise each item of the Government's work, is virtually meaningless where Parliament is really 'them' and 'us'.

ISSUES FOR DISCUSSION

1 When voting on legislation, should a member of parliament follow the directions of his or her political party ? Should a member of parliament decide what legislation is best for his or her constituents or should he or she follow their wishes? Give reasons for your opinions.
2 If the Senate is no longer an independent house of review or a house of and for the states, can its existence be justified?
3 Is a backbench member just a rubber stamp? What could be done to improve the effectiveness of the members of the backbench?
4 Is Australia over-governed? In what sense?
5 'Parliament discusses, debates, criticises, publicises and ratifies. It no longer legislates.' How true is this statement?
6 Is there an *effective* opposition in your state parliament? Why or why not?
7 Would a higher salary encourage better politicians?
8 How well does parliament carry out its functions? (See Document 7.1.) Is it more than a party playground? (See Document 7.6.)
9 Is the *Bulletin* (Document 7.2) correct to ask 'What's gone wrong with politics?'
10 If St John (Document 7.3) is correct, what power and role is left for the ordinary backbencher?
11 Does a formal, constitutional statement of the Westminster System (Document 7.4) mean that the system is working in practice?
12 Is the Senate acting as it was designed to? (See Document 7.5.)
13 Find out how many a) women b) people born overseas are in your state parliament. Why are the numbers so low?
14 Interview five civic leaders in your community regarding needed reforms in your state government. Phrase your questions to discover differing viewpoints. Report findings to the class and discuss the merit of suggestions offered for needed reforms. After class discussion, write brief individual reports giving your conclusions regarding the problems which would be involved in carrying out these reforms. Discuss these reports.

Chapter eight

RESPONSIBLE GOVERNMENT: CABINET AND PARLIAMENT

Political representation implies political responsibility. Those who are represented have every right to expect that the representatives they choose will be responsible to them. The previous chapter outlined the problems of practising the model known as parliamentary democracy in the Australian context. This chapter explores the meaning of the term 'responsible government', outlines the theory of the role of parliament in the processes of responsibility and analyses whether the Australian parliament is, or is even capable of, making government responsible.

CLARIFYING TERMS

General political discussions often use a number of political terms almost as synonyms. Words such as 'government', 'executive', 'cabinet', 'administration' are often used interchangeably, but there are important distinctions.

The word 'government', in its broadest sense, has been used to distinguish the public from the private sector. In another sense it refers to prime minister, the cabinet, the other ministers and the public service. The public service was established to execute the decisions of government, especially by applying the details of any Act of parliament, and by writing and administering the multitude of regulations which grow up around any Act. The combination of government, ministers and the public service is sometimes described as the executive branch. A government decision could therefore mean a cabinet policy statement, or minister's decision, a regulation established by the public service, a policy statement, or the official passage of an Act by the Governor-General and the Executive Council.

The formal authority of executive government in Australia is vested in the Governor-General and his Executive Council. In formal terms, the Governor-General appoints members of the Executive Council to be his principal advisers and they hold this office at his discretion. The Executive Council is defined as of the Governor-General and the ministers. A meeting of the Executive Council requires the presence of the Governor-General and a quorum of at least two ministers.

The Executive Council in modern Australian politics is a formal, official body which gives legal form when necessary to decisions made by, or under the authority of, cabinet. But cabinet, the body of people which dominates political decision-making in Australia, is not mentioned in the constitution. It has no constitutional existence. But it is the keystone of what has happened to responsible government. Cabinet is formed from, and remains part of, the parliament. It comprises the prime ministers and the ministers, all of whom have been elected as members of parliament.

THE GOVERNOR-GENERAL AND THE 1975 CRISIS

A brief comment is necessary in regard to the powers, responsibilities, and the authority of the Governor-General within this structure and process. Under the constitution, the Governor-General has wide reserve powers. He has the authority to dismiss a prime minister, a minister, a government, even a parliament. The *legal* power of the office is therefore not under question. But the events of 1975, the so-called 'constitutional crisis', raises questions about the role of the Governor-General in regard to the theories and practices of responsible government. His dismissal of the Whitlam government was legal, but was it legitimate? Did Sir John Kerr have a mandate? To whom was he responsible?

To attempt to answer these questions, a very brief summary of what happened in 1974–1975 is necessary.

December 1972	The ALP won government with 67 seats in the House of Representatives to 58 seats held by the Liberal–Country Party coalition. The new government, however, did not control the Senate where the party numbers were ALP 26 seats, L–CP 26, DLP 5 and Independent 3.
April 1974	Liberal leader Billy Snedden announced that the opposition would oppose the supply bills, and the opposition in the Senate voted to defer the supply bills.* The Governor-General accepted the advice of his ministers and called a double-dissolution of parliament.
May 1974	The Labor government was re-elected with a reduced majority in the House of Representatives (ALP 66 seats, L–CP 61). In the Senate the party numbers were in favour of the opposition (ALP 29 seats, L–CP 29, Liberal Movement 1, Independent 1).
July 1974	Sir John Kerr appointed as Governor-General.
February 1975	Senator Murphy appointed to be a Justice of the High Court. NSW Liberal Premier Lewis announced that the vacant seat would be filled by a non-Labor senator.* The Senate voted to affirm the convention of replacement of casual vacancies by a person from the same party. The NSW parliament still appointed a non-Labor senator to fill the formerly Labor seat.*
March 1975	Malcolm Fraser displaced Billy Snedden as leader of the opposition.
September 1975	The Queensland government also refused to follow the convention to fill the casual vacancy caused by death of a Labor senator* (ALP 27, L–CP 29, LM 1, Independent 3).
October 1975	Opposition leader Fraser announced that appropriation bills would be blocked in the Senate until the Whitlam government agreed to an election. The Senate deferred the bills* but Prime Minister

	Whitlam stated that the government would not resign.
11 November 1975	Whitlam and Fraser met and failed to reach agreement; Whitlam visited the Governor-General to advise a half-Senate election, and was dismissed from office.* The Governor-General appointed Fraser 'caretaker' prime minister. The Senate passed the appropriation bills. A double dissolution was proclaimed by the Governor-General.
13 December 1975	Liberal–Country Party government elected (L–CP 91 seats, ALP 36) in the House of Representatives and with the majority in the Senate (L–CP 36, ALP 26, Independent 1).

The events marked * raise the question of constitution versus convention. Each decision was within the terms of the constitution, but denied the convention. Most debate, however, has been focussed on the actions of the Governor-General.

In the first place, Sir John Kerr did not follow the advice of his ministers. He took the advice of the opposition that the Governor-General, who is responsible to no one, should dismiss a majority-elected government. To some, the defence is that the legal terms in the constitution must be followed. There are two responses to this. First, there are many instances in our constitutional history where the High Court has had to interpret the wording of the constitution. The

In the 1975 constitutional crisis, it was clear that the Governor-General held reserve powers.

document's meaning is not watertight. Second, and more important, if the crisis is to be judged only on the written constitution, then what is the status of all the other conventions essential to the workings of parliament and government in Australia? If some conventions can be declared as not relevant in 1975, then which conventions are next in line? If one set of conventions is ignored for partisan advantage, then the whole edifice of the Australian practice of responsible government is under question. Reid's conclusions are therefore important:

> Questions about the powers of the Senate, conventions of the Constitution, the role of the Chief Justice and the reserve powers of the Crown are important in themselves but, in retrospect, each is secondary to the significance of the Governor-General's initiative. The most important question is whether the Australian political system should accommodate an executive resolution of parliamentary conflict; and if so, when? (1980:10)

The point is that we need to go beyond the specific action of the Governor-General, and ask who put him into the position of having to decide whether to intervene.

The Governor-General was forced to intervene by the actions of the Liberal and National parties. It was their decision to break the convention and refuse to fill Senate vacancies with senators of the same party. It was their decision to break the convention and use their numbers in the Senate to refuse to pass the Supply Bill. It was their decision to put potential party advantage above the conventions of a responsible parliamentary system of government. The actions of the Governor-General can be criticised, but it should not be forgotten that it was only through the machiavellian behaviour of the anti-Labor parties that he was forced to decide.

THE WESTMINSTER MODEL

In its most simple terms, the model establishes a chain of accountability: public servants are responsible to a minister, the minister is responsible to cabinet, the cabinet is responsible to parliament and the parliament is responsible to the people. Does this apply to Australia in the 1990s? To answer this, we need to delineate the model further and then examine whether Australian practice accords with it.

The first, and fundamental, point is that as the constitution does not set out how responsible government should work, then the practices of responsible government are carried out through conventions, rather than by formal rules. Conventions are accepted methods of action, tacit agreements that certain things will be done. They are best described as the unwritten rules of the game which work effectively only if everyone follows them. But, if they are only informal agreements, then there is a potential problem: what happens if other considerations become important enough for the rules of the game to be ignored? The 1975 constitutional crisis was an obvious example of the role of conventions, but there are many other conventions of responsible government.

WESTMINSTER CONVENTIONS

The conventions of the Westminster model of responsible cabinet government emerged over a period of more than a century in the developing British system of parliament and were naturally accepted at the formation of the first Australian colonial parliaments in the 1850s and as a basis of the national parliament in 1901. In summary, the major conventions of responsible government are as follows.

1. The government is formed from the party or coalition of parties commanding a majority in the House of Representatives.
2. The government remains in office as long as it has the support of a majority in the House of Representatives. It resigns if it ceases to carry that majority in the House of Representatives.
3. The government meets in secret, and its deliberations are secret. In the parliament and in the public arena, the government presents a united voice.
4. Each minister is responsible to parliament individually for his or her conduct and the conduct of the department(s) over which he or she has control.
5. The government as a whole is collectively responsible to parliament for its policies and performance.
6. The Governor-General as the head of the executive acts on the advice of his ministers.

None of these conventions is legally binding. None can be enforced. All are totally dependent on the willingness of those participating to follow the rules of the game.

WESTMINSTER CONVENTIONS AND AUSTRALIAN PRACTICE

FORMING A GOVERNMENT

The first convention can be assumed to be automatically followed in Australia. In fact, in all but a handful of cases in this century, the government has been decided by the election result. Given that the parties are cohesive, then there is no doubt that the party (or coalition) that wins the majority of seats in an election will be the party which produces the prime minister and the government.

But there is a fundamental difference between the two major parties in the way they select members of a cabinet or shadow cabinet, a difference which reflects the formation, history and ideology of the Labor and Liberal parties. The Labor Party was born out of the concept of collective action in the trade union movement, and from the beginning emphasised and asserted control by the mass membership over the leaders of the party. The predecessors of the Liberal Party were formed in the parliaments of the colonies; they emphasised the necessity for strong leadership, and rejected the concept of control by the membership. Cabinet selection and authority reflect these divergent attitudes.

Any cabinet or shadow cabinet formed by the ALP in national or state politics is formed by election. The caucus of the party—the total membership of the parliamentary Labor Party, including members from both houses—elects the parliamentary leader (who becomes prime minister if in government; opposition leader if in minority in the lower house) and the deputy leader, and elects all members of the ministry. The leader then has the right to allocate to the elected ministers the portfolios which he or she thinks that each would best serve.

The national Liberal parliamentary party gives the elected leader sole right to select ministers and allocate portfolios. To some degree, the strength of this commitment within the Liberal caucus varies with the leader; during the terms of leadership by Gorton, McMahon and Snedden, the question of election of ministers was publicly canvassed on more than one occasion. From 1972 to 1974, the party elected the shadow cabinet under Snedden, but this has since been abandoned and is unlikely to be re-introduced.

There are arguments for and against both systems of cabinet formation. Selection by leader gives the leader tremendous potential power; it allows the quick disposal of a minister who is considered not to be up to standard (provided that the minister has not too strong a power base within the party), it allows the leader to choose a team which contains those considered the best and who will work best together, and it allows for quick promotion and demotion. At the same time, the system of selection by the leader offers no protection against favouritism and nepotism, and no protection to those members of the party who are of ministerial timbre but who are out of favour with the leader. It also has the potential to alienate some individuals or factions to the extent that they may cause problems within the party.

Election by the caucus is more democratic in that it ensures that the ministry is more directly responsible to caucus. Moreover, it allows for the representation of the broad elements within the parliamentary Labor Party in the ministry. But the system has shortcomings. The procedure is cumbersome, and caucus control also makes it difficult for the leader to demote or even to guarantee that an elected cabinet will contain only ministers with whom the leader can work—and relations within cabinet are important.

The prime minister will be a member of the House of Representatives. There was no constitutional bar to John Gorton in the late 1960s becoming prime minister in the Senate when he was heir apparent following the death of Harold Holt, and following the refusal of the Country Party to work under William McMahon. But the convention was followed; Gorton resigned from the Senate and was elected to the House.

The Australian convention is that there should be some ministers in the Senate. This, in fact, may be seen to conflict with an equally important convention of a federal parliament, namely that the Senate should be an independent house of review and a house of and for the states. But it has been an almost inevitable consequence of the party domination of the Senate. It has been justified on the grounds that there needs to be a core of senior government members in the Senate able to introduce and to defend government legislation. And, of course, some of the more senior members of a party are senators who would be less than pleased to be omitted from the ministry simply because of their house. In recent years, there has been a slowly growing number of members of parliament who have indicated a desire to remove ministers from the Senate, and thus return the upper house to its original function.

DEFEATING A GOVERNMENT

A government defeated on a major issue of confidence in the House of Representatives must either resign or request that the Governor-General allows a dissolution of the House. In colonial politics, before the growth of a disciplined party system, the parliaments controlled the government. Within a decade after federation, the situation in the

Australian parliament was completely reversed. Hence, the likelihood of events occurring to bring this convention into operation is indeed rare (except in the case of by-election results turning a narrow majority into a minority government, or where a governing majority collapses internally, as was the case of the UAP federal government in 1941). Such a case did occur in South Australia in 1970. The party complexion in the House of Assembly was Liberal (government) nineteen seats, Labor (opposition) nineteen seats and one independent (the Speaker) who had the casting vote. In a division the Speaker voted with the Labor opposition, defeated the government and forced a dissolution.

Factors which help to maintain this stability of government are various. Members, particularly those in marginal seats, would not be keen to face an election before they had to, and defection from their party on a crucial vote could bring about this result. Moreover, defection from the Labor Party means automatic expulsion from the party; in the Liberal Party it would be likely to bring future pre-selection into question. Loyalty in the Labor Party is enforced and hence this convention would not be brought into application under a Labor government. In non-Labor coalition governments, loyalty is not enforced with such formal, mechanical rigidity, but recent parliaments have shown that the party line is strongest when a narrow majority is held, and tends to be weaker when there is a large majority.

CABINET SECRECY AND SOLIDARITY

A minister is constrained by the convention that a decision of cabinet is binding on all members of the cabinet. A minister may argue in the secrecy of the cabinet room, but once a decision is made, his or her public position must be that of the majority of the cabinet. In a sense, this is similar to the enforced discipline within the political parties, and the convention of cabinet solidarity is one of the key components of a Westminster model.

Only rarely does this convention have to be 'enforced' following public dissent by a Labor minister. In 1983, S. J. West was required to resign from the Hawke Labor cabinet when he was unable to agree publicly with the government's position in favour of uranium mining. But the convention is frequently tested during a Liberal–National coalition government. There have been more than a few occasions when National Party ministers publicly expressed views which are not in full accord with the formal announcements of the government of which they are part. Why they have been able to do so, in the face of the convention, is explained by the politics of the coalition—the Liberal party needs the Nationals' numbers and it has been willing to ignore the breaking of the convention for the sake of the stability of the coalition.

INDIVIDUAL MINISTERIAL RESPONSIBILITY

In its simplest terms, this convention holds that an individual minister is individually responsible to the parliament for his or her actions, for the actions of the department, and for the actions of the members of the department. Obviously this is a simplistic summary of what has developed into one of the most complex of the conventions. Rather than a clear and unequivocal statement of theory and practice, this convention has become surrounded by a constellation of questions and issues.

What level of individual ministerial blunder can be forgiven by parliament, and above what level is resignation required? Obviously some actions (and some inactions) are clearly cases for resignation. If a minister is revealed to have misled parliament deliberately, then resignation would be expected immediately. But what if a minister has inadvertently given wrong information to parliament through no personal fault? Would the convention demand resignation?

In 1967, the Labor opposition raised a question of the use of the government's VIP airline fleet. The Liberal Minister, Peter Howson, after increasing opposition pressure, admitted to

> mistakes; not large in my view, and not harmful to any measure, but they have been made and I am the responsible Minister.

He offered his resignation, but the Liberal cabinet refused to accept on the grounds that

> we do not believe that these mistakes are of such magnitude that they would warrant us taking the step (Commonwealth Parliamentary Debates, House of Representatives 1967:2777, 2779).

This case appears to be a watershed in the interpretation of individual ministerial responsibility. It established an interpretation of the convention that if a minister makes a blunder, or a mistake occurs in the department, then all the minister has to do is explain it to parliament, apologise for it, promise that everything will be done to ensure that it will not happen again, and state that the damage caused by the mistake has been cleaned up.

We may even be able to accept this as a welcome interpretation—if we could be assured that when errors and mistakes occur, they will be fully reported to the parliament! Given one of the other conventions—that of the secrecy of the meetings of the cabinet—can we be sure that all mistakes are reported? Further, who decides what is a 'major' error and what is 'minor'? It may be enough for responsibility to be fulfilled in the case of a minor error if the error is simply rectified and reported, if someone admits fault and promises to do better. But if a substantive aspect of responsibility has been breached, who should judge that it is a major misdemeanour, and what should the penalty be? Take one of the most important conventions of ministerial responsibility—that a minister must not mislead the parliament. The penalty automatically applied by the conventions is that the minister should resign. But what is 'mislead'? Who should define it and apply it?

During one debate on a matter of individual responsibility, the then Liberal Attorney-General, Billy Snedden, set out a case for an interpretation of the convention:

> He may have to answer and explain to the Parliament, but not be absolutely responsible in the sense that he has to explain for (is liable to censure for) everything done under his administration... There is no absolute vicarious liability on the part of the Minister for the 'sins' of his subordinate. If the Minister is free from personal fault, and could not by reasonable diligence have prevented the mistake, there is no compulsion to resign (1966).

This does seem to be a reasonable interpretation. No one can expect ministers to be aware of everything that goes on in their departments. But it is not the Westminster convention!

COLLECTIVE MINISTERIAL RESPONSIBILITY

The convention of collective responsibility was an integral part of the Westminster tradition during the earlier, colonial cabinets and has been accepted by Australian cabinets from the beginning. Quick and Garran in their commentary on the constitution put the convention clearly:

> The principle of the corporate unity and solidarity of the Cabinet requires that the Cabinet should have one harmonious policy, both in administration and in legislation, and that the advice tendered by the Cabinet to the Crown should be unanimous and consistent; that the Cabinet should stand or fall together. The Cabinet as a whole is responsible for the advice and conduct of each of its members. If any member of the Cabinet seriously dissents from the opinion and policy approved by the majority of his colleagues it is his duty as a man of honour to resign (1901:706).

According to the official handbook of the House of Representatives 'Cabinet is collectively responsible to the people, through the parliament, for determining and implementing policies for national government.' The key phrase is 'through the parliament', and this raises the question: by what means can parliament call government to be responsible to parliament and how well does the Australian parliament achieve this?

This means by which cabinets can be forced to be responsible are few indeed. Effective means are almost non-existent. Scrutiny and control—essential aspects of responsibility—are presumed to be able to be implemented by a range of procedures: questions to ministers, urgency motions, debate on matters of public importance, grievance debates, adjournment debates, and reports from standing and select committees. But these are dominated by party discipline which always becomes absolute when the reputation of the cabinet comes into question.

Reports from select or standing committees, whether joint, house or Senate, are a potentially potent means of inquiring into a government's action or inaction. But these committees are more often than not made up of a majority of government members, hence any real critique is usually in the form of minority dissenting opinions from opposition members. And the committees' reports can simply be shelved and forgotten if the government so desires, simply by the use of the party numbers.

The ultimate formal test of the collective (and individual) responsibility of a government lies in the authority of the parliament under the standing orders to move a censure motion or no-confidence motion against a minister or the government. These are usually taken very seriously in the parliament and much energy and emotion is expended in the debates on both sides. But, again, the result is inevitable. The party lines will close, the debate will probably be gagged or guillotined and the vote will go the way of the government. The protagonists, as party members, will meet in solemn conclave and count up the score of points won and points lost. The participants are engaged, in fact, in what is essentially a theatrical performance—in which the actors believe that the Australian electorate is listening and watching and is not only interested, but will be affected by the performance.

Labor has had some problems with internal dissent in recent cabinets. But it is in coalition governments that the conventions of cabinet secrecy and collective responsibility are continually brought into question. When perceived special interests of the National Party have not been protected by cabinet decisions as the party and its ministers would desire, they have shown little hesitation in breaking the convention of collective responsibility. The coalition agreement has recognised the right of the National Party to make separate policy statements and election speeches, and there has been more than one occasion when the National Party has taken advantage of this to the point of breaking collective responsibility. Nothing has been done by the Liberal Party to 'discipline' the offenders. The reason, as in so many things in Australian politics, is that self-interest overrides the convention if there is a conflict between the two.

The Royal Commission on Australian Government Administration, the most detailed examination of how government works, cast doubt on the effectiveness of the various procedures of making government responsible, and described them as:

hampered by lack of information, or by not being pursued in the systematic form necessary for an adequate probing of executive and administrative action (1976:109).

These criticisms are valid, but they do not go far enough to identify the problem which is at the root of the issue; as Parker puts it, responsible government works 'essentially on the honour principle' (1976:179). The problem is that there is little in the way of honour exhibited, except, that is, the 'honour' of the parties.

There is a delicate balance necessary for the actual operation of the theory of responsible government. The cabinet must be unified, and collectively responsible, but not so disciplined, protective of party interest, and unwilling to report to and justify to parliament that its responsibility is to party and not to parliament. The parliament must also carry out its functions—to examine, debate, if necessary oppose and, in the case of ministerial irresponsibility, to be willing and able to take the cabinet to the people by forcing a dissolution.

RESPONSIBLE POLITICAL PARTIES?

Many observes agree that the balance between parliament and cabinet was upset as early as the first decade of national politics. There is little doubt that the development of disciplined parties has swung the balance almost exclusively to the cabinet, the prime minister and the executive, and that parliament has little real power remaining. The collective and individual responsibility are key aspects of the cabinet systems, but they tend to be observed in Australia on a contingent basis, depending on the political and party climate whether the convention is followed or not. Party numbers decide the collective responsibility, and the effects—especially the potential electoral effects—decide how much individual responsibility will be applied in each case.

The problem is that party politics do not function by what is reasonable, but through party confrontation. Hence, no opportunity is lost to try to embarrass the other side and to score points. Any question of 'error', no matter if it was impossible for the minister to be aware of it or to be able to prevent it, is taken as the next stage in the party warfare. The government seeks above all to cover up the event or to cover up any tracks. The opposition seeks above all to attack and to make public points at the expense of the government.

In practice, the government—the majority party—decides when a minister is responsible. There is little left of the Westminster convention in the practice of the Australian model today. A minister resigns only on a matter where the convention has been revealed as seriously breached. In almost all cases, the government opts to tough it out and, given that it has the numbers, it can usually do so. The risk of course, is the impact on the electorate. A governing party and cabinet will have to balance, on each individual case, the potential negative impact on the electorate if it opts to tough it out and the internal party damage if a minister is forced to resign.

Until the 1984 Federal ALP Conference, this decision, for a Labor government, rested in the hands of the caucus rather than the government. The caucus elected the ministers and the caucus removed them. Given the factional nature of the party, such events were inevitably traumatic within the party and inevitably received media headlines. In 1984, the Labor Conference inaugurated a procedure whereby a committee of cabinet—the two leaders and two deputy leaders from the two houses—would have the authority to demand a resignation; but they, too, will consider the party implications.

The Westminster conventions have been rewritten by Australian practice; a minister is responsible to prime minister, cabinet, and party, but is not responsible to parliament. If the government decides that there is less likelihood of public damage to the party and to the hopes of re-election by forcing the minister to resign, then resignation will follow. If the government decides that the resignation would cause more problems—within the party as well as among the public—then he or she will stay. The parliament has no say in the matter, except for the traditional time spent on ringing speeches of denunciation or defence, because the government has the numbers to back up its decision. Party discipline will be applied.

BICAMERALISM AND RESPONSIBILITY

By translating a bicameral system from the US federal presidential system and embedding it in a parliamentary system, the original constitution contained the framework for inter-house conflict, a dilemma about who was responsible to whom and the seeds for the constitutional crisis of 1975. The principle that a government must be responsible to the House of Representatives is a core aspect of parliamentary responsibility. By incorporating the US principle of a federal Senate with equal powers, the designers made the government also responsible to the Senate.

Party domination of the parliamentary processes has changed the Senate for both of the original intentions for it, a house of review and a house of the states. The Senate was granted equal powers with the House of Representatives, excepting the power to initiate money bills, or to amend such legislation. The Senate can, however, request amendments and has the power to defeat a whole bill—including the budget bill—if such requests are rejected. Constitutionally then, the Senate, for all practical purposes, is an equal partner with the House in the Australian parliament. But this conflicts with the basic convention that the government is formed in, and continues in office so long as it has a majority in, the House of Representatives. The 1975 crisis saw the Liberal–National majority in the Senate deny the latter convention.

Further, in the sense of responsible government, the Senate has always had the power to refuse a budget, and to force a majority elected government in the Representatives to an early election. This power, at the time of the writing of the constitution, was recognised as containing the potential for problems. But the majority of the constitution planners felt that reason would triumph. What they could not foresee was the development which put reason and principles and conventions of parliamentary democracy lower down the scale than the party self-interest.

THE DOMINANT CABINET

It is a common charge in modern parliamentary systems that cabinets have become too dominant, that cabinet government has replaced parliamentary democracy. In Australia, this is a result of the development of disciplined political parties.

There is no doubt that parliament can no longer carry out many of its core functions. The function of forming a ministry has passed to the majority party or parties, that of judging a government has passed to the electorate. But parliament has remained as a significant institution, at least on the media level. It certainly is one of the most newsworthy institutions in Australian politics. Most of the news items on political activities which are released (deliberately or leaked) for public consumption originate in parliament or relate to parliament. During its sessions, parliament carries out, with full traditional ceremony, those formal functions it has held since federation; cabinets are formed and reshuffled, the government is sustained, obstructed and opposed, laws are debated, amended, assessed or defeated and the many aspects of administration are reviewed, criticised and amended.

But how much of this behaviour within the walls of parliament is merely a formality? To what extent can parliament today carry out its theoretical functions within representative and responsible parliamentary democracy as we know it? Is it correct to describe parliament, as many observers do, as an impotent and irrelevant body of persons confronting a dominant body—the cabinet?

There is no doubt that the development of cohesive and disciplined political parties has had a marked effect on the relationship between cabinet and parliament. Parliament has increasingly become a matter of numbers. The party (or coalition) with the majority not only forms the government, but it controls all of the activities of parliament. There is no doubt that criticisms of the growth of cabinet 'dictatorship' and of the loss of independence, initiative and authority of the ordinary backbench member, do have some substance. The House of Representatives has undoubtedly become a house of party, for and against government. The cabinet controls all aspects of the business of parliament; government business dominates the legislative activity of parliament; the government can, and often does, limit the possibilities for the opposition as a body, and for individual backbench members, to probe, comment, criticise and seek to change government proposals. This is achieved by use of such parliamentary mechanisms as the gag and the guillotine; the procedures of parliament offer little opportunity to private members for business other than that of the government; above all, the party line, except on very rare occasions, hold firm at every vote or division.

The critics of this development use, as a comparative model, a vision of a parliament 'as it ought to be'—a deliberative assembly of independent individuals who discuss, debate and vote on matters of public concern, in context of a notion of the public interest and who control the government, vet its actions and, if necessary, change the government, again in the public interest. It is arguable whether such a model parliament ever existed in Westminster practice, let alone in Australia. Even in the colonial parliaments prior to the formation of political parties, cabinets and parliaments were based on factions, pressure groups, and private as well as public interests.

Cabinet, then, is an executive body which derives its authority from the parliament. In Australia, however, instead of the cabinet being controlled by the parliament, specifically by the House of Representatives, the cabinet controls the parliament.

However, despite its power, a cabinet is not a totally unchecked institution. Although neither the opposition nor individual backbencher members have much, if any, control over government in and through parliament, there are other checks. The party room offers an opportunity for individual members of the government party to debate, criticise and seek changes in policy. This is of more consequence in a Labor government, where the concept of caucus control is entrenched—there was more than one occasion during the time of the Whitlam government when caucus did modify the plans of cabinet. The party-room role of government backbenchers in the Liberal Party varies with the current play of personalities—especially the personality of the prime minister. Other checks of varying importance include pressure groups, the mass media, the limited opportunities at the disposal of the opposition (question time, grievance debates, adjournment debates), advice and pressure from the upper echelons of the public service and, ultimately, the decisive power of the electorate as a whole.

The growth of the power of cabinet has meant that not only does it occupy a pre-eminent position in the institutions of Australian politics (despite the fact that it is constitutionally non-existent), but it has an almost unlimited potential to decide the future direction of political, social and economic life. As government involvement in the Australian economy has grown—under both Liberal and Labor governments—so has the potential influence of cabinet over all aspects of Australian development.

Under Menzies, cabinet was a reactive institution, reacting to the ideology of its leader, containing social, economic and political pressures with the assistance of an apparently healthy economy which generated little demand from society, parliament or party for innovative national policy. Under the Whitlam government, the cabinet was like a particularly powerful generating station, and produced more activity than most governments. Between 1975 and 1983, the Fraser government was like a dam, attempting to limit and contain pressures for government action. After 1983, the Hawke cabinet was very slow and cautious, emphasising consensus before action. Following the amazing election victory in 1993, the Keating cabinet has been driven by Keating, but its activities have been directed more toward attempting to heal the recession and the economy than to formulating new initiatives.

CABINET IN OPERATION

Cabinet has many functions. It is the supreme, decision-making authority in the whole system of national government. Cabinet makes the major decisions of government; minor decisions are made by individual ministers, and still lesser decisions are made by departments (and can be checked by parliament). The line between major and minor decisions is not a fixed one, depending as it does on a number of factors, including the willingness of the prime minister to delegate authority to his ministers, and the willingness of ministers to delegate to departments. Cabinet is also concerned to co-ordinate all the decisions, tasks and activities of the various departments of government in order to produce a consistent and coherent policy. Once the policy is decided, then a collective and an individual responsibility applies. Cabinet as a whole accepts collective responsibility for its decisions and, as a collective will be required to explain and defend policies and decisions to the party in the party room, to the parliament and to the electorate. Equally, the individual ministers are individually responsible for supervising the implementation of cabinet decisions, whether such implementation involves parliamentary legislation, delegated legislation or administrative action.

In general terms, then, cabinet considers, discusses, co-ordinates, administers and supervises government activity, and explains and defends decisions, policies and activities to the parliament and the people. To achieve this, there have been other developments within Australian cabinet—conventions which include the formation of cabinet committees and of a secretariat for cabinet. Ministers whose responsibilities are relatively light (or whose responsibilities are judged as minor by the government—a quite different matter) assist ministers whose tasks are major (or considered so). Hence, the Minister for Housing assists the Minister for Industry and Commerce, the Minister for State assists the Minister for Defence and so on.

As the tasks of government have widened, so the size of the ministry has increased, until in 1956 Menzies instituted an inner cabinet of

The size of ministries has increased remarkably since federation. Above: The first government, 1901. Below: The Keating ministry, 1993.

twelve senior ministers; the remaining ten ministers remained out of the cabinet. Since then, all Liberal–National Party governments have utilised this two-tier system; under Fraser the fourteen ministers who constituted the cabinet administered their own departments and had the task of formulating government policy; the thirteen ministers not in cabinet administered their departments, but played a role in cabinet deliberations only when summoned to do so by the cabinet.

The Whitlam Labor government rejected this two-tier ministry, and included all twenty-seven ministers in the cabinet with all, excepting the four leaders, on the same rate of salary. At the same time, in an attempt to make effective what would otherwise have been an unwieldy committee of twenty-seven, the new government established five cabinet committees. Even then, the plenary sessions of these committees suggested that a cabinet of twenty-seven was simply too large for efficient operation. The Labor government in 1983, for the first time for a Labor party, followed the Liberal concept of a two-tier ministry, and established a 'senior' cabinet of thirteen members.

A cabinet secretariat is a recent innovation. From 1901 until 1940, the secretarial servicing of cabinet and the recording of cabinet decisions was *ad hoc*, and a far from formal process. Records of cabinet meetings in the early decades were often little more than scribbled notes; decisions were more often than not never formally recorded. In 1940, Menzies brought into cabinet the first official secretary who developed a small secretariat for full cabinet papers and discussions. The functions of this division of the Prime Minister's Department have broadened over time. It circulates documents to ministers, arranges meetings, plans an agenda, records decisions, carries out the correspondence for the cabinet and has many other functions besides. In fact, the Department of the Prime Minister and Cabinet has become the real driving force of executive government.

THE ROLE OF A PRIME MINISTER

The office of prime minister originated in Britain in the early part of the eighteenth century when the first Hanoverian king, a German, could not speak English and left the meetings of the cabinet to the senior minister. Since then, the authority and power of the office has grown to the extent that some analysts suggest that a further functional change has occurred; cabinet government and party government have been supplanted by prime ministerial government.

While a substantial growth in the status, power and prestige of a prime minister has occurred, there are implicit and explicit constraints on an Australian prime minister. A Labor prime minister is, by the rules of the party, specifically designated as no more than *primus inter pares* (first among equals) and his or her power and authority derive directly and constantly from cabinet and caucus. A non-Labor prime minister is not so constrained by party rules and hence has the potential to be a more dominating influence in his or her own right, but may well be constrained by such factors as having to lead a coalition government and hence recognise and acknowledge the authority of at least the leader of a coalition partner.

The role and authority of a prime minister, like so many other key aspects of the Australian political system, are based on convention and hence can be affected by intangible factors. The prime minister's power flows from his or her control over the majority party in the House of Representatives and, simply in becoming leader, is sufficient evidence of a tactician with support from at least the majority faction or factions in the party. But the prime ministerial style will depend on the individual. It will vary between attempts to involve cabinet as committee and encourage participation of the party in policy-making and an authoritarian approach to both cabinet and party. Where any one style falls between these extremes depends on personality, but also on the extent to which the party needs the incumbent leader. Hence, we can contrast the authority and style of such dominating leaders and prime ministers as Menzies and Fraser with that of McMahon as prime minister and Snedden as opposition leader, neither of whom could be said to have dominated the party.

A strong non-Labor prime minister is a powerful influence; he appoints, promotes, demotes and dismisses ministers; controls the time, agenda and conduct of cabinet meetings; decides what issues will even be put before cabinet and normally determines the decisions of cabinet by ruling as to the sense of the meeting, usually without a formal vote. Such a leader may also achieve a position where he or she personally symbolises the party and the government and is electorally indispensable to the party. Such a combination would provide great potential for prime ministerial rather than cabinet government.

The office of prime minister within the institutions of parliament and cabinet cannot be divorced from the influence of the political party. The natural forces of party organisation and loyalty naturally support the person identified with the success of the party. These factors are strongest when the party is in office and offer the greatest potential for power to a prime minister who has won a resounding majority in parliament for his party. Paul Keating is an obvious example. Since, in modern Australian elections, the voters see themselves as selecting a prime minister and government as well as a parliament, the electoral contests have increasingly developed into a battle between parties and essentially between party leaders. The leader will have toured the country, have been the prime focus of the mass media and the campaign and as a result becomes a symbol of the party. Any rival within the party or the cabinet starts at a disadvantage.

Both the power of the prime minister and the restraints on the exercise of power derive from convention. But the key to the understanding of the role of a prime minister in Australia is electoral success. The Liberal Party places more importance on electoral success than does Labor in judging its leaders. In both state and national politics, Liberal leaders, if they retain their positions after an electoral defeat, are definitely on probation, whereas Labor parties in government or opposition tend to demonstrate a longer-term loyalty.

For both parties, the authority of the prime minister and his or her power in cabinet (and hence in national politics) will depend to a large degree on the capacity, the wisdom and the personality of the individual. But there is no doubt that merely holding the office provides the person with tremendous authority in cabinet. The cabinet has become the key institution in Australian politics, dominating policy-making and the legislative process; it is the permanent executive authority. Parliament is in session normally for less than 100 days per year, but cabinet is constantly in session; as a leader of cabinet, the prime minister is the focus of political power.

REPRESENTATION, RESPONSIBILITY AND CABINET GOVERNMENT

Representation implies legitimate authority, which in turn implies responsibility. The basic tenet of a Westminster model of parliamentary democracy is that the ministers comprise a government which is collectively accountable to the elected legislature and that the individual ministers are individually accountable to the legislature for their own actions as ministers and for the work of their departments. Hence, the core principle of the Westminster system is that government should be responsible to the parliament.

The government is not directly responsible to the people, except in the sense that the people have the periodic right, at elections for the parliament, to judge what the government has or has not done. This, of course, is a very vague application of responsibility. The government is assumed to be indirectly responsible to the people through the parliament. Any assessment of responsible cabinet government in Australia, then, must focus on the interrelationships of cabinet, parliament and people, and especially on the role of parliament.

Part of the difficulty in analysing responsible government in Australia is that many observers make the assumption that the Westminster model was transmitted unchanged to Australia and put into practice. In fact, we developed a particular Australian model which seriously modified the Westminster original. Federalism divided responsibility, and resulted in the formation of the Senate. The written constitution, by omitting any principles, let alone practices, of responsible government, provided an environment where conventions became the norm and where sanctions become informal. Finally, the development of disciplined political parties weakened the potential for parliament to conduct its function of responsibility. To repeat, the system of responsible government depends 'essentially on the honour principle' (Parker 1976:179). Whether there is sufficient 'honour' in the Australian political system of representative and responsible government is a matter for argument.

DOCUMENTS

8.1 CABINET AND PARLIAMENT: A CRITICAL VIEW

Source: St John, E. 1969, *A Time To Speak,* Sun Books, Melbourne, pp. 6, 15. (St John was a Liberal M.H.R.)

It follows that in the Australian parliamentary democracy today most of the important decisions are not made by parliament as such, despite the fact that it is described in legal theory as the sovereign body. With rare exceptions the major decisions are made by Cabinet on the material and advice supplied by the public service. It is true that some regard is paid to the views of the members of the Government parties and to public opinion (chiefly as reflected or formulated in the Press and other news media), but the Government in power can rest secure in the knowledge that, due to the party system, a decision once made is almost certain to be endorsed and defended in the House of Representatives whether it is right or wrong. The decision will stand unless, in the case of legislation ... independently minded Senators choose to join forces with the ALP in opposing it in the Senate. If the Government backbenchers are able to make their voice heard in advance, they can have considerable influence: but when they are presented with a *fait accompli* ... the chances of their reversing the decision or of even trying to do so are in practical terms virtually nil ...

The malaise of the Australian people is reflected in our Parliament. It would be profitless to attempt to disentangle cause and effect. No doubt we have the Parliament we deserve; to a great extent Parliament reflects the values and the mores of the people whom it represents ...

The greatest of civil liberties is the right of the people to decide the major issues affecting their future through their own elected leaders in the Parliament. It is this liberty which is now in the greatest danger; unless this tendency is checked, all else will be gravely endangered also. If the Parliament fails to function effectively the rot spreads and must finally affect the freedom of expression, as it has already done in Australia, and even the working of our laws and the judicial system itself. The case of law reform will be a lost one. Repressive legislation already existing will be enforced and new repressive laws will be enacted without a free Parliament to serve as a bulwark against them ...

But if civil liberties—in which phrase I include all the traditional democratic freedoms and values—are to be effectively protected, we need not only an impartial administration of existing laws but a vigilant Parliament, watchful of new legislation, eager for law reform, ready and able to test the policies of government and to ensure that the great issues of the day are properly debated. Parliament must be in a position to prise the facts even from the tightest grip of official secrecy whenever this is necessary in the public interest so that Parliament, and not merely the bureaucracy or the executive, can be placed in a position to make the great decisions on behalf of the people it represents.

8.2 A NON-EXISTENT CABINET?

Source: Rodan, P.K. 1979, 'The prime minister and cabinet', in Lucy, R. (ed.), *Pieces of Politics*, Macmillan, Melbourne, p. 186.

Despite their important roles in the Australian political process, the prime minister and cabinet do not exist in strict constitutional terms. No mention is made of them in the Australian Constitution, and their existence is, instead, a matter of convention. The second chapter of the Constitution leaves all executive power with the monarch's representative, the Governor-General, 'advised' by a federal Executive Council. By convention, this Executive Council is the ministry, comprising certain members of the majority party (or parties) in the House of Representatives, whose parliamentary leader is the prime minister. The actual constitutional status of the ministry was highlighted by the novel events of 1975: its members are 'appointed' by the Governor-General and hold office during his 'pleasure'.

8.3 MINISTERIAL RESPONSIBILITY?

Source: Carey, B. 1980, 'Executive control in the 1970s', in Mayer, H. & Nelson, H. (eds), *Australian Politics: A Fifth Reader*, Longman Cheshire, Melbourne, pp. 234–5.

It may have made sense to speak of ministerial responsibility when government departments were so small that it was possible for the minister to know most of his departmental staff and to be on top of his job, given the relatively small number of matters demanding his close attention ... Now there is more for more government departments to do. Their work is more complex. It involves more money, legislation and programs. It is done by a greater number of officials. Ministers still have constituency and political party commitments which lessen considerably the time they can give to official ministerial (individual and collective) responsibilities. Ministerial control and accountability to parliament are not all they once may have been.

Parliament's role as watchdog over the executive has diminished. Parliament has been manipulated and bypassed ... Members of the judiciary are co-opted for the purposes of the executive. Freedom of information legislation, as proposed, represents a new political value distorted to fit with the old. Very little say can be had by the public even through the political parties. The media's effect is limited.

Responsible government in Australia has traditionally been viewed in Westminster terms. That view suited those satisfied with a representative parliamentary system of democratic government as well as those satisfied that strong executive government could be maintained. The democrats must be experiencing growing disappointment.

8.4 HOW IS CABINET RESPONSIBLE?

Source: Parker, R.S. 1976, 'The meaning of responsible government', *Politics*, vol. 11, no. 2, p. 179.

Essentially on the honour principle: ministers would see that parliament was adequately informed about government operations, would answer questions, would resign individually if found incompetent or worse, would resign in a body if the majority of the popular house of parliament voted censure on or no confidence in them, or defeated a measure the government held to be vital. And so that parliament would know where it stood, ministers would all belong to the same party, would stand or fall together on government policy, would not betray each other's confidences, would get rid of a minister who broke these rules.

8.5 MINISTERIAL RESPONSIBILITY IN AUSTRALIA

Source: Emy, H.V. 1976, 'The public service and political control: the problem of accountability in a Westminster system with special reference to the concept of ministerial responsibility' in *The Report of The Royal Commission into Australian Government Administration*, vol. 1, p. 35.

In Australia, the political reality of the concept has been undermined by factors similar to those in Britain. Therefore, it is difficult to argue that the concept is of such overriding significance in the political sphere ...

Unlike Britain, it is difficult to say whether ministerial responsibility is a significant influence upon the probity of ministers' personal behaviour. There have been several cases in recent political history where a ministerial resignation might reasonably have been expected, but none was forthcoming. This is indicative of a wider point: Australian parliamentary practice has been characterised by a reluctance to make rules or even to pass judgment upon the propriety of ministerial behaviour. The case of separate standards of public morality, or for an ethic of responsible government, has gone by default. Australian ministers have shown little inclination to accept the implications of a concept of absolute responsibility. Public criticism of their official advisers is not unknown: nor are attempts to shift the blame for political as well as administrative error on to public servants ... In Australia, the inadequacy of ministerial responsibility as a method of imposing a realistic degree of political responsibility upon ministers reflects the basic weakness of the House of Representatives as an institution ... The basic cause of this situation is the effect of party discipline upon a small legislature. But the House itself has taken too little interest in the procedures and devices it has at its disposal for securing information and accountability. It has failed to use the reports from either independent authorities such as the Public Service Board, or from its own committees such as Public Accounts, or from the public corporations as a basis for debate and inquiry. Parliament has failed to develop any systematic or constructive approach to the problem of scrutinising the actions of bureaucrats, the organisation and efficiency of the public service, or the personal behaviour and policy aspirations of ministers.

Consequently, even the concept of answerability is of little practical significance. It has even less significance if ministers themselves refuse to take this function seriously. There is widespread recognition that parliament does not possess the requisite influence seriously to embarrass ministers. Where ministers enjoy personal authority within the party, it is difficult to believe that the open or parliamentary processes provide any real threat to their reputation.

8.6 COLLECTIVE RESPONSIBILITY?

Source: Sydney Morning Herald, 5 March 1976, cited by C.A. Hughes in Mayer, H. & Nelson, H. (eds) 1980, *Australian Politics: A Fifth Reader*, Longman Cheshire, Melbourne, pp. 194–5.

A confidential document, the Cabinet handbook, issued by the Prime Minister's Department, lays down some of the rules for collective responsibility:

- Conventions relating to the collective responsibility of Cabinet are to be observed. Decisions in Cabinet and Cabinet committees are reached collectively and are to be supported collectively.
- Personal views on submissions should not be indicated publicly in advance of Cabinet discussions.
- Once a decision is taken, it is binding on all members of the ministry, and personal differences or reservations are not to be revealed.
- Ministers should deal with their own portfolios and not cut across the portfolios of their ministerial colleagues.

ISSUES FOR DISCUSSION

1. 'The conventions of collective responsibility and individual ministerial responsibility are obsolete.' Discuss. (See Documents 8.1, 8.3, 8.4, 8.5, 8.6.)
2. If it became the convention that no ministers would sit in the Senate, would this help to restore the Senate to what it was designed to be?
3. Is an Australian prime minister a potential dictator? What gives him or her this potential, and what limits it?
4. Is the office of Governor-General, as laid down in the constitution, too powerful?
5. Cabinet ministers are not chosen for expertise in certain fields: a Minister of Health is not always a medico, a Minister for Primary Production is not always a farmer. Should ministers be experts?
6. Does Australia have a working system of responsible government?
7. What qualities should a prime minister have?
8. How has a body of people which has no constitutional existence (see Document 8.2) become so powerful in the Australian political process?
9. Does the concept of collective responsibility (Document 8.6) mean too much secrecy of government?

10 Debate the question that 'Australia should introduce the US (republican) system of cabinet'.
11 Imagine you are the prime minister. If you could choose from any members of the national parliament over the last ten years, who would you select for your cabinet, and what portfolios would they have? Compare your list with others and justify your choices.
12 Prepare a list of subjects which you feel should not be made public by government. Give reasons for each subject.
13 Debate the topic that 'the Governor-General should be elected'.
14 Given the power of cabinet, is parliament still relevant?
15 Would a republican form of government be more democratic?

Chapter nine

THE PUBLIC SERVICE AND RESPONSIBLE GOVERNMENT

PUBLIC SECTOR/PUBLIC SERVICE

For many people, the terms 'public service' and 'public sector' are used as synonyms. The second term, however, is usually applied in the field of political economy, to distinguish between economic activity which is privately owned (private enterprise) and that which is organised, managed or controlled by one or other of the Australian governments or government authorities. In this sense, almost one-third of the total workforce of Australia is directly employed by government, by Australian and state government departments, by various authorities and semi-government bodies, by local governments and local government authorities.

There has been an explosion in the actual numbers of people employed in the public sector in the last fifty years, but, despite

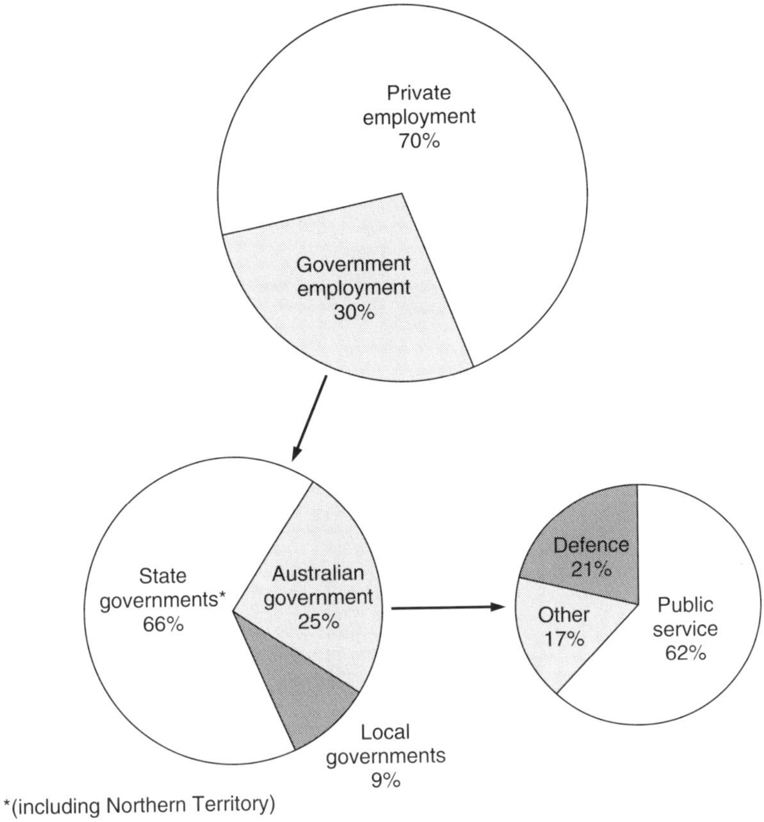

Figure 9.1 *Categories of employment, 1986*

popular opinion, employment in the public *service*, as a proportion of the total workforce, has increased at a slower rate.

Public sector employment over the years 1939–1990 increased by almost 600 per cent in the national government, by nearly 300 per cent in state governments and by over 200 per cent in local governments. It should be noted that the most rapid rate of expansion in the national sphere occurred during and immediately after the Second World War. It should also be noted that the state and local governments have consistently accounted for about 70 per cent of public sector employment, and that the explosion in these areas occurred in the 1960s and 1970s.

The public service is defined as a subset of the public sector, as those government employees who are covered by the Public Service Acts passed by national and state governments. Hence, while 402 000 civilians in the public sector were employed by the Australian government in 1983, only 159 190 (36 per cent) were in the Australian public service. The majority of government employees do not therefore come under those Acts which govern the nature and process of

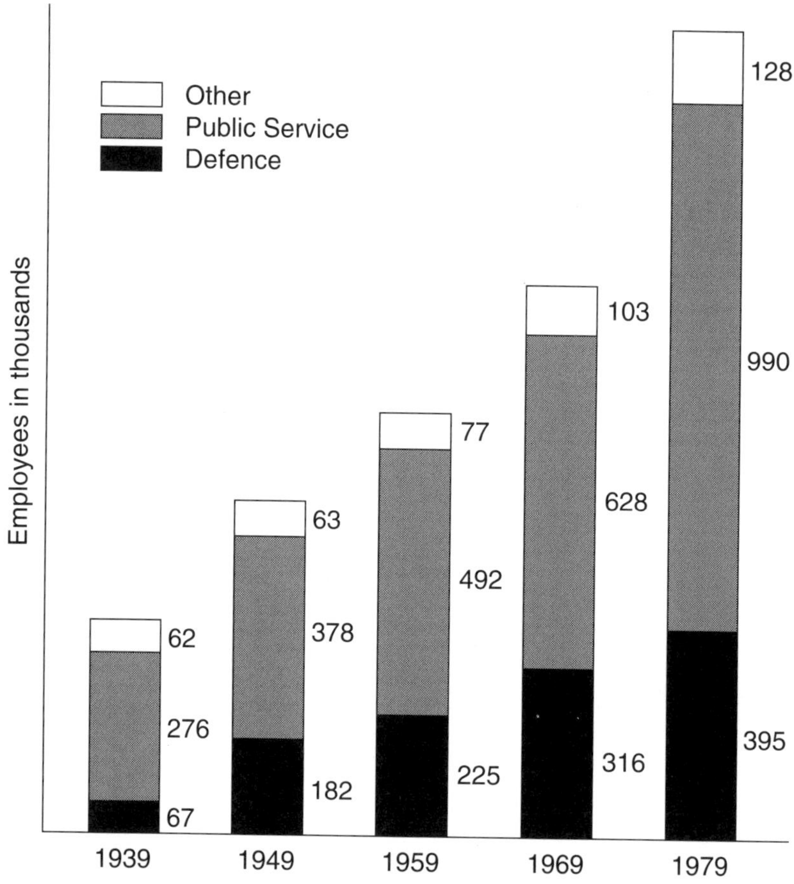

***Figure 9.2** Growth in public sector employment, 1939–1979*

employment recruitment, promotion, dismissal, and supervision by a Public Service Board or its equivalent. But groups of employees such as police, teachers and employees of most statutory authorities, as well as local government employees, will often be under the provision of separate Acts which establish their rights and duties as employees.

It has often been asserted, especially in the 1970s, that the growth of the public sector and public sector employment has been, first, a result of increasing intervention by the national government in areas which have traditionally been those of state and local authorities and second, the result of the policies of Labor governments which have given 'undue emphasis' to public sector involvement in the economy. But data of public sector and public service employment do not support these assertions. There has, in fact, been a greater increase in public sector employment, in both absolute and relative terms, in the state and local government areas than in the national government. During the 1970s, when accusations of a Canberra octopus were most strident, employment in the national public sector increased by just over 60 000 (by almost 18 per cent), while employment in the public sector in the states increased by over 230 000 (by almost 35 per cent). And comparison of the state public sectors in the 1970s shows clearly that the growth occurred under both Labor governments (South Australia, Tasmania and New South Wales) and Liberal–National Country Party governments (Victoria, Queensland and Western Australia).

PUBLIC SERVICE STRUCTURE

The organisation of the Australian public service rests on two bases: vertical by authority and, to some extent, by the nature of the duties of the public servant; and horizontal across departments and authorities.

Until 1985, when a major reconstruction of the Commonwealth public service was carried out, the vertical structure contained four divisions.

1 First Division: this top level of the public service consisted of the permanent heads of the departments of government (31 staff members in June 1983).
2 Second Division: this level included the top administrative and management staff, including the heads of some of the government authorities under the umbrella of departments (1354).
3 Third Division: this level included specialist, administrative and clerical staff, with entry to the division determined by formal results of examinations usually at the end of secondary school (71 753).
4 Fourth Division: the remainder of the public service, a level which did not require any standard qualifications, but may require some educational standards for specific tasks (86 052).

Most of the work force of the Australian public service was in the fourth division (54.0 per cent) and third division (45.0 per cent), and it needs emphasising that all of the first division were men, and only 34 of the 1354 in the second division were women.

Following a report of a Royal Commission in 1976, the Fraser government instigated reforms which were carried through in the early 1980s. As one observer put it (cited in Emy and Hughes 1988:350), these changes

> constitute a major administrative reform package. The individual components—ministerial consultants, the open Senior Executive Service, program budgeting, affirmative action and industrial democracy are each significant ... they are, as a group, the most wide-ranging reforms of the Australian Public Services since its creation at the time of Federation.

Table 9 1: Employment categories, 1985

	Male	Female	Total
Department Secretary	29	0	29
Senior Executive Service	1 473	67	1 540
Clerical Administration	42 386	19 285	61 671
Clerical Assistant	8 913	18 867	27 780
Keyboard	281	12 405	12 686
Other	32 861	5 304	38 165
Totals	85 943	55 928	141 871

The new structure is less hierarchical and offers much more opportunity to employees at the former third and fourth division levels for promotion and for job mobility. The 1985 structure established Departmental Secretaries at the apex of each Department and a Senior Executive Service (SES) replacing the former second division. The fourth division was abolished, and there is now a tripartite division in which much more potential for promotion and development is possible.

The overwhelming majority of public servants remain in the 'service' categories. The equal opportunity emphasis in the reforms has not yet had significant effects in the senior positions. But the reforms will in future produce a less hierarchical structure, and the possibility of more mobility within the service.

The remainder of this chapter will focus on questions of relations between the public service and government, cabinet, ministers and parliament. This involves a focus on the senior levels of the public service, the Departmental Secretaries and the Senior Executive Service which make up only 10 per cent of the total personnel. These are centrally involved in policy advice, responsible government and policy administration questions.

DEPARTMENTS

The horizontal division of the public service is based on the nature of the governmental authority. Most public servants are employed in departments of government, some are employed in statutory authorities and public business undertakings. Employees in the public sector who are not public servants (as defined above) are employed in all of the various authorities of government.

Of these authorities the *department* is that which is most directly connected with, and under the direction of, the government. Departments can be created, modified or abolished by a decision of government (given authority by the Governor-General in Executive Council). Departments are generally distinguished from other authorities of government both by structure, and by their relation to government. A department is a creation of government, not of parliament. Departments are responsible to a minister through a permanent head. Departments are also subject to control in regard to staffing (governments can, and do, set overall limits to the growth of the public service), buildings, accommodation, furniture and so on.

The growth of activity of government, especially in post-war years, is reflected by the growth of the numbers of departments and the breadth of their responsibilities. As government initiatives opened up new areas of activity, so new departments (and other authorities) were created. In 1904, there were only seven departments of the national government: Postal, Trade and Customs, Defence, External Affairs, Home Affairs, Attorney-General and Treasury. In 1939, there were eleven departments, only one of which resulted from new developments—that of Civil Aviation. In 1990, there were twenty-seven departments, the growth reflecting the broadening responsibilities of the national government; for example, Education, Primary Industry, Science, and Aboriginal Affairs.

The number of government departments and their nature, purpose and size, also varies from government to government depending on priorities set by each government. It is not unusual to have a reshuffle of ministerial portfolios, a change in the number of ministers and departments, or a change in the organisation and structure of departments, if not all three, in any one year. Hence, any statistics relating to departments can go rapidly out of date.

The five largest and five smallest departments as at June 1985 are shown in the table below; it should be noted that the five largest departments employed over half of the total departmental public service.

Table 9.2 *Public Service employment—largest and smallest departments, 1985*

Department	SES	Other	Total
Defence	152	23 720	23 874
Treasury	141	20 149	20 390
Social Security	37	16 702	16 739
Aviation	49	10 460	10 509
Veterans Affairs	47	8 667	8 714
Aboriginal Affairs	18	683	711
PM, Cabinet	47	608	655
Sport, Recreation	11	571	582
Arts, Environment	19	339	358
Minister of State	16	320	336

STATUTORY AUTHORITIES

A statutory authority, in broad terms, is an agency of government, an organisation established by a special Act of parliament, which has the legal status of a corporate body with an independent legal existence. Beyond these common criteria, the nature and responsibility of statutory authorities varies widely; the various authorities have no standard structure and their functions are very diverse. They differ significantly from a department of government. In the first place, such authorities are created by parliament, not by government and they cannot be modified at the desire of the government without approval by parliament. Second, statutory authorities are independent, to varying degrees, from control by government and ministers, whereas departments of government are not. Third, statutory authorities are required to submit regular reports to the parliament.

From the time of federation in 1901, the Australian government has formed more and more statutory authorities. Today, Australian governments have gone much further than British governments in allocating certain tasks and functions to such bodies; the tendency in Britain has been to keep most of the administration of government within formal government departments. Once again, then, we need to note a significant modification from the Westminster system. The use of departments for the great bulk of administration provides that the minister is directly responsible to parliament for the direction, planning and administration of a wide range of functions within the department. A statutory authority may also be directly responsible to parliament in that it may be required to submit an annual report to parliament, but it is not responsible in the sense that a minister cannot be called to justify its activities at any time in parliament.

An inquiry by the Senate Standing Committee on Finance and Government Operations reported in December 1978, with some surprise, that not only were there many and varied types of statutory authorities, but there was 'no fully comprehensive and updated list of authorities' available even from government! The report listed no less than 241 statutory authorities (and was by no means certain that it had managed to find them all), ranging from huge undertakings, such as Telecom and Australia Post, each of which employs over 100 000 people, to such authorities as the Custodian of Expropriated Property which employs only two or three part-time employees.

Statutory authorities undertake a wide range of functions and activities. These include (with examples):

- business undertakings (Australian Airlines, Australian National Railways)
- commodity bodies (Honey Board, Wheat Board)
- research (CSIRO)
- advisory (Commonwealth Grants Commission)

- tribunals (Industrial Relations Commission, Australian Broadcasting Tribunal)
- 'service' (Australian Electoral Commission).

There is a growing mood in both political parties, although stronger in the Liberal Party, that business undertakings, especially, should be 'privatised', and that governments should not be involved.

CAREERS AND CONTROLS

A CAREER SERVICE

In some countries, especially in the USA, the public service contains a high proportion of positions which are political appointments and which change with the government. The Australian public service, modelled on the British civil service, is based on the concept of a permanent career service. This concept includes the following general principles:

- Recruitment by merit, usually on the basis of results in public examinations, but increasingly on the basis of qualifications in a specialist field.
- Organisation and control of the public service, including recruitment and employment conditions, by an authority which is independent of direct government control and is not party political.
- Protection of public servants against arbitrary dismissal.
- A hierarchical structure of posts and positions with a graduated classification of salaries and benefits and promotion through this hierarchy by means of merit and seniority, protected by a right of appeal to a tribunal.
- A standard retirement and pension plan.

The public servant in Australia, whether employed by the national or state governments, has considerable rights and benefits, including lifetime tenure, an expectation of promotion through merit, a stable occupation and, when retired, an excellent (and often indexed) pension.

The process of reform in the 1980s decreased the emphasis on hierarchy, and gave more emphasis to merit as the basis for promotion. Further, the top levels of the service have been made more open to recruitment, whether for permanent or contract positions, from 'outside'. Thus specific expertise can be sought by the service to a greater extent than previously. At the same time, the public servant in Australia, in return for the obvious benefits of a career service, is under a number of constraints and controls and is expected to conform to what is, in effect, a code of conduct.

THE PUBLIC SERVICE BOARD

As with any employees, public or private, a public servant is expected to carry out his or her duties efficiently, effectively and within the terms set out by the employer. In the case of a public servant, the employer is a combination of minister, permanent head and senior officers of the public service. Common to Public Service Acts in Australia is the establishment of a form of centralised control of the internal structures, processes and functions of the public service through a Public Service Board (or Commission). Public Service Boards are wholly concerned with the efficiency and partially concerned with the effectiveness of the public service. As a monitor of efficiency, it has a number of tasks, the most important of which are the administration and enforcement of the Public Service Act and the recruitment, selection, placement and control of the public service itself. The Public Service Boards make an annual report to parliament and carry out functions of efficiency within the terms set by the government, especially in such areas as ceilings on staff numbers and on expenditure. As an internal co-ordinating and controlling body, Public Service Boards are only partially concerned with the effectiveness of the public service. The effectiveness and responsiveness of the public service is a matter for the government and the parliament, and, in terms of responsiveness, for an ombudsman.

In 1987, the Hawke government abolished the Public Service Board. The Board was replaced by a Public Service Commission, with authority to implement policies on recruitment, promotion and similar issues, and a Public Service Management Board. The stated purpose of the change was to develop more responsibility to the Departments and to increase cost-effectiveness. The roles of dealing with industrial relations within the public service, and the issues of employment classification were transferred to government departments themselves, under policies established by the Department of Finance and Industrial Relations. Hence, in fact, the public service moved to be more under the direct control of the government and cabinet.

RIGHTS AND OBLIGATIONS

From the inception of the public service, the key tenets of expected behaviour by public servants have been loyalty to the elected government, secrecy, and political neutrality. These tenets have not been fully codified in law and written regulation but there is little doubt about their importance if a career public service based on the requirements of a Westminster system is to function as it was designed. The demand for secrecy about the business of government in the Australian public service is enforceable. Under the Crimes Act,

> 70.-(1.) A person who, being a Commonwealth officer, publishes or communicates, except to some person to whom he is authorised to publish or communicate it, any fact or document which comes to his knowledge, or into his possession, by virtue of his office, and which it is his duty not to disclose, shall be guilty of an offence.
>
> (2) A person who, having been a Commonwealth officer, publishes or communicates, without lawful authority or excuse (proof whereof shall lie upon him), any fact or document which came to his knowledge, or into his possession, by virtue of his office, and which, at the time when he ceased to be a Commonwealth officer, it was his duty not to disclose, shall be guilty of an offence.
>
> Penalty: Imprisonment for two years.

The thrust of such constraints is essentially a censorship of public servants in regard to their work, and this has been a topic of political debate in recent years.

Such acts and regulations are attempts to enforce secrecy by law. But, increasingly in recent years, especially with the widespread use of the photocopier, there have been cases of documents and other secret material from the public service which have leaked to the parliamentary opposition and to the mass media. There are stringent penalties for such actions, but both governments and the public service have found the practice very difficult to police and virtually impossible to stop.

Recent Australian governments have been concerned with secrecy, almost to the point of obsession. Obviously some government decisions and related advice and administration, in and from the public service, need to be secret. Matters of national security are normally accepted as matters of total (and strictly enforced) secrecy, although questions are often raised about how much of which is declared 'national security' needs to be so described. Decisions to devalue the dollar, to impose different taxes or to modify tariffs obviously have to be kept secret until the formal announcement, because advance knowledge could lead to financial gains for a few. But the doctrine of secrecy, on occasion, has gone beyond such clear cases to include the protection of governments, ministers and political parties to an extent where the public's right to information has not been satisfactorily observed. The extent to which governments emphasise secrecy is shown by the frenetic activity and reaction when leaks are made to the mass media or to the opposition.

Overall, the issue of the degree and extent of secrecy will remain a contentious one, as it involves two contradictory values: the right of a government to keep its policies, activities and actions, and especially its reasons, a matter for itself, and the right of the public to be informed. The Freedom of Information Act was intended to set formal regulations for public access to public service (and hence government) material and documents. However, the Act includes clauses which can be used to limit public access rather than guarantee it. For example, a minister can rule that the material requested by a member of the public should not be provided on the grounds that it would not be in the national interest. It is the minister who decides.

NEUTRALITY

This tenet, like that of loyalty to the current government, is essentially a code of conduct and derives from one important aspect of the system of parliamentary government; while parliaments and governments change, and different political parties and party leaders win and lose office, the public service continues. A distinction needs to be made, then, with the political nature of much of the public service in the US presidential system where senior public servants are selected by the President and their appointments are partisan. On the other hand, appointments to the most senior levels of the Australian public service are increasingly on the basis of contracts. Hence, governments are more able to make 'political' appointments. As such, the Australian public service is moving away from its Westminster traditions.

The doctrine of neutrality of the public service is not, nor can it be, defined in law or regulation, but flows from the necessary conventions of the parliamentary system. A government department is headed by a minister who is responsible for its operations to parliament. The members of the department, the public servants, are therefore the agents of the minister, are expected to carry out orders, and are expected to implement and administer the relevant Acts proposed by the government and passed by the parliament, as well as the policies and programmes decided for the department by the minister or the cabinet.

The obvious implication is that Australian public servants will find themselves having to execute widely divergent policies as governments change, and possibly having to carry into action policies with which they personally disagree. Further, the public service has increasingly been involved in advising ministers and the cabinet about options for policies, alternative programmes and the risks and benefits of various actions. The convention of the public service in a parliamentary system demands that such advice should be honest and courageous, even if the tenor of the advice is, on occasion, politically unacceptable to the government. Naturally, it is the responsibility of the government to accept or reject such advice and to justify such decisions to the parliament and the public. But the necessity for the public service to be non-partisan and neutral is one justification for the protection and security of tenure granted to public servants. If public servants could be dismissed at the will of the minister of the government, then it would be unlikely that advice and administration would be as honest and neutral.

Neutrality does not imply that a public servant must have no political views or belong to no political associations. Many members of the public service in Australia are members of political parties and play an active role in them. Many public servants are members of trade unions—Public Service Associations, and the Council of Australian Government Employees Organisations (CAGEO), for example. On the other hand, public servants are specifically prohibited from formal, public involvement in partisan activities, such as standing as a candidate for a political party, without first resigning from the public service.

Nor does the doctrine of neutrality mean impartiality. In fact, neutrality means total and loyal support for the elected government, regardless of party, and has a positive expectation that the public servant will not only offer objective advice and impartially carry out executive directions, but will seek to apply the policy directions of minister and government.

CONTROL BY THE PUBLIC?

As governments, public service and the public became more intermeshed, so the public service came into more direct contact with the public. Most activities of a member of the public today will involve some contact with the public service—health, welfare, building regulations, property transactions, all areas of taxation, road laws, licensing laws—all manners of the activity of private citizens. As government and the public service have grown and become more pervasive, so pressures have increased for the provision of some means by which the ordinary citizen can be assured that he or she is obtaining fair, just and efficient service from the public service.

The oft-repeated charge that, while the public service may be constantly seeking more efficiency in its relationships with the public, it has become too impersonal and arbitrary, has prompted the appointment of an Ombudsman by Australian governments. The office of Ombudsman is a concept which developed first in Sweden but which has spread to a number of Western systems of government. In the broadest sense, an Ombudsman is an official watchdog on behalf of citizens, a person appointed by the parliament, but independent of government, to investigate complaints by the public against decisions of government authorities or officials, on the grounds that such decisions or actions were allegedly unjust, wrong, or even illegal. However, an Australian Ombudsman has no authority to make decisions and no authority to carry out or enforce action—the post is usually empowered to merely inquire into actions which bring complaints and to report and recommend action. If a case of maladministration is proved, then the Ombudsman usually reports to parliament with a recommendation for action. In some countries, but not Australia, the Ombudsman has the authority to initiate prosecutions in the courts.

In most cases and for most of the time, the process of responsibility in Australian government is based on the concept of an indirect control of the public service by the public. The Ombudsman provides a means for a member of the public to take issue with the public service over a specific matter. But the continuing task of ensuring that the public service and the public sector are efficient, effective and responsible is essentially that of the government and of individual ministers, of the parliament and of individual members of parliament.

How effective ministers can be in ensuring that there is administrative responsibility in their departments depends on a number of factors. The personalities of the minister and the permanent head may lead to the department becoming dominant. The appointment of a minister to a portfolio where he or she has no previous expertise may cause the minister to be dominated by the department from the start. And some departments—Treasury is the prime example—need professional expertise which is difficult for any minister or government to counter.

The extent of responsibility also depends on the willingness of individual members of parliament to inquire into the activities of the public service, and the willingness of government to grant parliament the opportunity so to inquire. Questions to ministers, the scrutiny of delegated legislation and the raising of grievances provide some potential for such responsibility to be enforced. Whether this potential is exercised or allowed is a matter for debate.

DELEGATED LEGISLATION

Concern is often expressed about the increasing power of the public service—the bureaucracy—and this has, as one of its bases, the growth of the involvement of the public service in law-making.

From the beginning of responsible government in Australia, parliament and parliamentarians have delegated certain responsibilities to the public service. In the second half of this century, this process has increased to the extent that the public service has taken on a new and important function. As noted above, the original functions of the public service were to administer and execute the laws made by parliament and the programmes laid down by cabinet or a minister and to advise the government about policy alternatives. To this, in modern times, has been added an important legislative function—the public service is increasingly involved with the making of laws, as distinct from the administration of laws.

This development has occurred as a result of a number of factors. The parliaments of Australia face an ever-increasing amount of legislation, of increasing complexity, on intricate social and economic matters. As well, the nature of the new legislation and the complexity of the subjects has meant that simple, straightforward laws are no longer sufficient. Members of parliament are ill-equipped to deal with the increasingly technical nature of legislation. As a result, parliament has come to depend more and more on the experts in the public service and on delegated legislation. Public service regulations, orders, warrants, rules and ordinances are, in fact, laws which flesh out the broad terms of an Act passed by parliament.

In principle, such powers of delegated legislation run counter to an important tenet of responsible government—that those who legislate should be directly responsible to the public for whom the laws are made. Its defenders point to the necessity for such delegation to aid in the efficiency of government and emphasise that all such delegated legislation must be tabled in parliament and can be disallowed by parliament. However, given the pressures of time in the parliament, its domination by government business and by political parties, it is not uncommon for the tabling of such legislation to be a mere formality.

BUREAUCRACY AND REPRESENTATIVE DEMOCRACY

In the 1970s and 1980s, the Australian public service became the focus of much interest and debate. The basic aspects of its structure, role and processes came under review; it has been forced to accept change and both internal and external pressures have brought a state of flux in, and about, the public service.

The public service has always been important in Australian politics and society, an early development which derived from at least two factors. The involvement of colonial, state and national governments in the social and economic life of the country was a central factor from the beginning, and such involvement brought a natural development of an administrative wing. This was assisted by a pervasive attitude of the Australian public which is summed up by Hancock's statement (1945:61) over forty years ago, that 'Australian democracy has come to look upon the State as a vast public utility, whose duty it is to provide the greatest happiness for the greatest number.'

The public service is often referred to as a bureaucracy. This term has two senses—positive and pejorative. In the former sense, it refers to a professional, efficient and effective organisation, which provides objective and sound advice to government, and which provides service to the public on the basis of fairness and objectivity. The tenets of the Westminster model of the public service, then, are professional and impartial service, neutral and courageous advice based on devotion to the public interest, and obedience to the will of the minister and the cabinet.

But this is not the stereotype of the bureaucracy which is often expressed by the Australian public. The Commission of Inquiry into the South Australian Public Service summarised this negative stereotype:

> It is often argued that the good qualities of this system bring with them inevitable defects. Public servants, immune from political dismissal, not required to explain publicly the reasons for what they do, and exercising considerable power, could become arbitrary, lazy, insensitive to criticism, flint-hearted and narrow-minded. Delay, passing the buck, caring more for technicalities than for the substance of just and fair treatment—these are the hallmarks of bureaucracy, and these are the defects to be feared in a system of government such as the Westminster model.

All government departments and most, if not all, large non-government organisations such as large businesses, have bureaucratic characteristics. That is, they contain an organisation based on specialisation of function, a hierarchical structure with defined rules and regulations which govern the organisation and its members, a career service based on promotion by merit and seniority, pervaded by a sense of neutrality and objectivity and a commitment to the purpose of the organisation. The danger of any bureaucracy is that it may tend to the stereotype summarised above.

The public service has come under criticism both from outside, on the grounds that government generally, has become too big, too involved, too dominant and too secretive about its actions and activities, and that the public service itself has become too rigid and too bureaucratic; and from inside, on the grounds of its over-emphasis on hierarchy, seniority, rigidity and conformity.

The development of a complex industrial society has produced a political paradox. As the economy and the society have become more complex, so parliament and government alike have had to depend more and more on decisions and advice from the public service. But this has meant that the bureaucracy has inevitably become more important in the whole political process. Has this development reached a stage where the bureaucracy, not the government, nor parliament, runs Australia? Are the usual formal and informal means of control of the bureaucracy—the ministers and the cabinet, the Ombudsman, the opposition, the press, and the Public Service Board—still able to carry out effective and democratic controls? Such questions may well be crucial to Australian democracy in the 1990s.

In the most simplified terms of the model, the public service has two functions. The first (and theoretically most important) follows the passage of an Act by parliament and assent by the Governor-General. The public service has the task of administering that Act, applying its various terms and interrelating with the public in regard to the legislation. An Act of parliament may be drawn up in general terms. It is up to the public service to then formulate details of its application, to designate the various procedures for the administration of its terms, to devise the many regulations which may be necessary and to apply these regulations in relation to the target of the Act, whether business, trade unions, the economy, the legal system, or the public at large.

This was the original and primary function of the public service but, increasingly over time, the public service has been granted (or has acquired through practice) a second, important function; that of providing expert advice to the government or to an individual minister. The public service was, originally, a simple extension of government and parliament, the administrative wing of government which managed the details of programmes set for it.

But one of the most striking facts about modern government in Australia, especially the national government, is the breadth of its activities. The tasks of government range from the eradication of weeds to negotiating international treaties, from the construction of the Snowy Mountains Scheme to the collection of fares on public transport, from provision of social services to the protection of native fauna, from protecting Australia's industry to caring for orphans, from the control and maintenance of a national (or state) economy to the registration of motor vehicles. Citizens have equally demanded more and more from government. They have sought government intervention in society to help them in distress, to promote and assist their interests, to protect them and to guarantee their rights, and to provide for many of their needs and desires. All citizens, groups and individuals seem to make constant calls on government—for more schools, better public transport, the control of crimes; the demands and requests seem unending.

The response from governments have been varied, from 'do it yourself', 'it's not our problem', 'it is the state government's responsibility', to an agreement that the government should be involved. As government has moved more and more into the society and the economy it has needed not only to expand its role in policy-making, but also in the administration of policies. From these developments has come the seemingly inexorable growth of the public service.

At the same time, as governments (and parliaments) have been involved in an ever-increasing range of activities, so the need for expert advice has grown. Governments have traditionally depended on their public services for such advice and this has resulted in the fact that, today, the public service occupies a central and powerful place in the system and is a key part of a complex interrelationship of government and parliament, policy-making and administration, decision and application.

DOCUMENTS

9.1 ON SECRECY

Source: Quoted in Spigelman, J.J. 1972, 'Secrecy and democracy' in AIPS, *Parliament, Bureaucracy, Citizens: Who Runs Australia?*, Angus and Robertson, Sydney.

A research worker at a US museum once wrote to the space agency NASA requesting a satellite photograph of his State for a museum exhibit. He was told that such photographs were classified. He received similar replies from the Weather Bureau and the US Air Force. As a last resort he wrote to the Soviet embassy in Washington—and got one.

9.2 THE DANGER OF BUREAUCRACY

Source: Report of the Committee of Inquiry into the Public Service of South Australia 1975, p. 11.

The Public Servant is protected, and has security of tenure in order to insure that his advice is honest and courageous, even if it sometimes has to be politically unpalatable to his Minister. This advice is confidential; the Public Servant is not permitted to say in public what he has advised his Minister to do, nor should the Minister disclose the views of his advisers, or attribute opinions to individuals within his Department. Public Servants are not supposed to make public comments on policy questions for which their Minister is responsible, nor are they free to disclose information acquired in the course of their work.

It is often argued that the good qualities of this system bring with them inevitable defects. Public Servants, immune from political dismissal, not required to explain publicly the reasons for what they do, and exercising considerable power, could become arbitrary, lazy, insensitive to criticism, faint-hearted and narrow-minded. Delay, passing the buck, caring more for technicalities than for the substance of just and fair treatment—these are the hallmarks of bureaucracy, and these are the defects to be feared in a system of government such as the Westminster model. The Ministers are supposed to prevent them, but when Ministers are unable to examine departmental matters in detail, and have to rely on what their officials tell them, then there is every danger of bureaucracy in the worst sense. Besides, there is always the danger that the permanent officials in a department will develop a strong departmental line of policy, which they then try to foist on Ministers of whatever political persuasion, sticking to it through thick and thin by every means short of open defiance of the Ministers' explicit orders.

9.3 CONTROL OF THE BUREAUCRACY

Source: Spann, R.N. 1980, 'Bureaucracy and the public service', in Mayer, H. & Nelson, H. (eds), *Australian Politics: A Fifth Reader*, Longman Cheshire, Melbourne, p. 254.

Formal and Informal Controls. Giving someone the legal authority to issue orders would be a case of a formal control. The bureaucracy of a department is formally responsible or accountable to some minister. The Public Service Board and the Department of Finance also have certain formal powers over the rest of the bureaucracy.

But there is also the question of informal controls. For example, we must also ask: to whose influences are public servants responsive? They are responsive to many other influences besides that of the minister, including their own internalised standards of behaviour, their colleagues, outside pressure groups, and so on.

Again, a minister may formally control his department, but he himself is also responsive to his public servants. He may depend on them for much information and advice; he wants to keep their loyalty and goodwill. So up to a point they control him; control is reciprocal. Ministers often protect their departments and are in league with their officials, rather than control them.

9.4 POLITICIANS AND THE PUBLIC SERVICE

Source: McClelland, Senator J.R. 1972, *Who Runs Australia?*, AIPS, Canberra, pp. 133, 139.

The first discovery that a politician makes after a brief stint as a legislator is that he is even more ignorant about public affairs than he had been prepared to admit to himself or to those who elected him. The second discovery that he makes is that there is a vast conspiracy to keep him in that state. Let me give you an example; an earlier speaker referred to the annual Estimates debate in the Senate and to the fact that senators are confronted with the impossible task of investigating the whole range of $3000 million of estimated expenditure. The speaker was over-polite in describing his task as humanly impossible. It is in fact a hollow farce ... My brief, disenchanting experience of the bureaucracy's ascendancy over parliament inclines me against any pussy-footing with this problem. This ascendancy is compounded by the conspiracy, and I use the word advisedly, between the Executive and the bureaucracy to keep the ordinary parliamentarians in the dark. I reject any reliance on the bureaucracy's alleged readiness to accept parliament's right to act as a watchdog. Parliament should put this right beyond doubt by enacting a statute giving its members the power that I have suggested.

ISSUES FOR DISCUSSION

1 In what ways can the public be protected from the worst features of bureaucracy? (See Document 9.2.)
2 'Except for matters of national security, all detailed reports and submissions prepared in government departments should be made public. The resulting public debate could be more useful to governments than their present secrecy. No other single measure could better inform public opinion.' (*Bulletin*, 20 May 1972.) Do you agree with this proposal? Discuss a) what benefits it would have, and b) what problems it would cause. (See also Document 9.1.)
3 Who controls whom in the Australian system of executive government? Who should control whom? How can this be achieved? (See Document 9.4.)
4 'Australia needs experts on tap, but not on top.' Discuss.
5 How should public servants be promoted—by seniority, or by merit, or by a combination of both? Is there any danger to democracy in a meritocracy?

6 Why do more and more pressure groups ignore parliament and cabinet and seek to apply their pressure to the public service?
7 Would the Australian public service be more responsible and effective if there were more cross-fertilisation with the private sector?

Chapter ten

FEDERALISM—AUSTRALIAN STYLE

CONSTITUTIONAL GOVERNMENT

A constitution is a means of arranging a system of government. Its function, in essence, is to provide a fundamental statement of laws concerning the organisational framework of government, the division of responsibilities between political institutions, the interrelationships, functions and activities of the various units within the polity and a systematic statement of the basic values of the political society. In sum, then, a constitution is concerned with values, structures, functions and procedures within a polity. It establishes the formal relationships between the government and the governed.

Constitutionalism is a commitment to the formation and presentation of a constitution as a fundamental statement of the protection of citizens from arbitrary government. This commitment is therefore a basic requirement in a democracy. Constitutionalism arose as a reaction against royal absolutism, as a demand for freedom for those who were defined as citizens and as a demand for life, liberty, and property. In short, it is embodied in the rule of law, in a principle of limited government. Its roots go back at least to Aristotle who defined a constitution as an

> organisation of offices in a state, by which the method of their distribution is fixed, the Sovereign authority is determined, and the nature of the end to be pursued by the association and all its members is prescribed.

Modern constitutionalists emphasise three core components:

> it should set out the 'ways' of how the various components of the State are organised; it should clearly establish the authority which each component has; and it should provide a clear description of how such authority should be used.

The Australian constitution has something to say about the first and second, but very little about the third component.

The British 'constitution' is taken as a model of democratic constitutionalism. It has unique characteristics. It evolved over a period of a thousand years, but it has never been systematically codified into a single document. It is an unwritten constitution, and constitutional law in Britain is indistinguishable from all public law. The British 'constitution', then, possesses no formal superior authority and it can be amended by the normal parliamentary processes. Constitutionalists in Britain have therefore been able to adjust the constitution to changing conditions in the polity, although not always easily, peacefully, or amicably. The structures, functions and procedures of politics, then, are dispersed among the various laws, and especially the conventions, of political life.

The more recent democratic States accepted the core theme of British constitutional democracy that government should be representative, responsible and accountable to the people and that government is authority granted by the people, held on trust which can ultimately be taken back by the people. The French Revolution and the American Declaration of Independence made that very clear (although what constituted 'the people' showed significant variations). Most democratic states formed a constitutional system based on the essential premise that the scope and range of the power of government should be defined, that power should be exercised within strict limits, and that such power should be controlled by law and, ultimately, by the people.

Most modern nations have codified the ideas of their constitutionalists into a single law—a constitution. That is, there is a supreme written document which can be amended only by special processes. The Australian colonies, embedded in the Westminster system, designed, and were granted by Britain, their own written constitutions. But the moves towards the formation of an Australian State brought the need for a different constitution.

FEDERATION

As the various communities in Britain were slowly brought together within a system of constitutional government, the paramount ideal was the formation of a nation. Over time, Britain developed a national government, a unitary system where authority was vested in a single parliament elected to govern the nation. In the USA, the context at the time of a formation of a nation in 1776 was fundamentally different. There were already in existence thirteen independent nation-states, each of which was jealous of its society, authority, and rights. The formation of a nation-state, the United States of America, was therefore a compromise of national and state powers.

The formation of the Australian nation-state was based on a similar federal compromise. At the time of the first moves towards a nation in the 1890s, there were in existence six independent nation-states in the colonies. Each was self-governing and had its own constitution, system of laws, practices and procedures of government and, most important, its own economic interest; it was not surprising that each treated with considerable caution any suggestion that it should submerge itself within a national, unitary government.

There were, in fact, two pressures. On the one hand, the colonies could understand and support the need for a new national authority to provide for common needs and common protection. In economic terms, it made sense to have free trade between the colonies and a national policy on duties and tariffs for overseas trade. A common defence, the need for a national transport and communications system, coupled with a growing sense of nationalism in at least some of the colonies, were some of the forces towards unity. On the other hand, the colonies, especially the smaller ones such as South Australia, Tasmania, and Western Australia (which had only received its self-government in 1890), feared that they would lose all of their independence in a unitary system and feared that they would be dominated by the larger populations and stronger economics in New South Wales and Victoria. Above all, the constitutionalists in the colonial parliaments were determined to protect their own, and their colonies', economic interests. A compromise was necessary—federation as in the USA, provided a possible answer.

In 1890, the formal processes began at a conference of Australasian governments—six colonies and New Zealand—where the delegates resolved unanimously for the union of the colonies, under one legislative and executive government, on principles just to the several colonies. The first National Australasian Convention, (excluding New Zealand), met in 1891 and reached a general consensus about applying US federalism to Australia and approved a draft Federal

Constitution Bill. That was the end of unanimity. In the following six years there were government and public discussions, and a second Convention, without New Zealand, met in 1897.

A revised draft was considered and sent to colonial parliaments. The Convention re-assembled in January 1898, completed the revisions and forwarded the draft bill to the colonies for a decision. But the opponents of federation, the first 'states rights' movements, had become vocal and influential. Referendums were held in four colonies in June 1898 and were carried in Victoria, South Australia and Tasmania, but defeated in New South Wales. Lobbying continued until a second referendum in five colonies in 1899 was carried, and Western Australia finally accepted federation in July 1900.

FEDERALISM

Federation established federal government which involved both structure and process. Like that of the USA, the Australian federal structure was based on a concept of 'dual federalism' where the national government and the state governments would have distinct spheres of activity and authority. While acting within their specified

The opening of the Australian Parliament, 1901.

sphere, each government would be independent and no government could encroach on the activity of another. Both national and state governments accepted a division of powers which involved four crucial components: each was to be directly elected by and to act directly on the citizens; each would have a substantial area of responsibility; each would be autonomous within its sphere of responsibility—not subordinate nor dominant in authority; each would be protected from encroachment by others by a judicial authority.

But politics and societies are not static. As the demands of people changed, as the activities of governments broadened, as issues, events and developments unforeseen by the 1890s planners occurred, so the original concept of 'dual federalism', of independent spheres of action and authority, became complex, conflicting and confused. The *structure* of federalism did not keep pace with the *processes* of federalism.

THE CONSTITUTIONAL STRUCTURE

The Australian constitution is essentially a document about the mechanics of government, setting out the essential structures of government. It says little about the processes, let alone the values, of government—a point to which we will return. The document is divided into eight chapters, the first three of which Parliament, Executive, Judiciary establish the basic structures of federalism. Chapter 4 focusses on Finance and Trade, Chapter 5 on the States, and the last three chapters set out rules for New States, some miscellaneous provisions and, finally, the important processes for Alteration of the Constitution. The following paragraphs distil the document into the essential structures that it established.

THE FOUNDERS' DESIGN

The constitution established a 'dual federal' structure, a dual Westminster system of parliamentary governments, based on a national parliament, a national executive and a national judiciary, in parallel with the parliaments, executives and judiciaries in each of the states. In fact, Australia's federalism is built on three tiers of government, but the third tier, local government, was not incorporated into the constitution. It remains as it developed in the colonial period, subordinate to, and controlled by, State governments. In the constitutional sense, then, Australia has a 'dual' federalism.

The constitution divided powers between the national and state governments so that the former was given authority to make laws in specified areas (Section 51), and authority to legislate over all remaining areas was in the hands of state governments. This division was not absolute. The national parliament had authority to legislate 'for the peace, order, and good government of the Commonwealth' in regard to the forty topics outlined in Section 51. There were, however, *concurrent* powers on which both the national and state parliaments had authority to legislate, including most of the powers set out in Section 51; in the event of a conflict between national and state parliaments, the national legislation would prevail. Some powers within Section 51, however, were established as exclusive to the national parliament; these included customs and excise, defence, currency, external affairs, and territories. There were some potential areas of legislative activity which were *prohibited* for all parliaments. Trade and commerce (s. 92), for example, as 'shall be absolutely free' between the states.

PROTECTIVE INSTITUTIONS

The founders were faced with the necessity to incorporate two essential protective components in the constitution: one structural, and essential for the existence of a dual federalism; one more political, but equally essential if the proposed federal nation were to be accepted in the colonies.

The Senate was established as a protective mechanism for the states, and especially for the smaller states, by means of both representation and legislative authority. Each state, regardless of population, elected the same number of senators—originally six, increased to 10 in 1949 and to 12 in 1983. This equality of representation, in fact a structural malapportionment, was planned to provide a house of the states, for the states. The second protection, to reinforce the power 'for the states', was that the Senate was granted equality of power with the House of Representatives, with one minor restriction that the Senate could not initiate, nor amend, a money bill. But the Senate could suggest amendments, and had the authority to reject any bill, including a money bill. In practice, then, nothing could pass into law without the agreement of a majority in the Senate. The problem with this design was that the almost immediate development of cohesive political parties destroyed both the house of the states and the house for the states. The Senate's grand design was rapidly overtaken by party politics.

The second necessary protective institution was the High Court, created in 1900 by the Constitution Act. We will return to its structure and role later.

A NEAR-STATIC CONSTITUTION

Obviously, even the structure of such a plan could not be sustained in its entirety. In the first place, the division of powers was based on the assumption that two *separate and independent* levels of government could be maintained. Second, the planners did not foresee developments in the society, polity and economy which interposed the need for new powers, or which demanded co-operation, even co-ordination, rather than independence. The constitution was drafted and accepted before radio, television, aviation, mass transportation, a national industrial network, satellites, a universal system of social security, and a national economy to mention only some post-1901 developments. The division of powers in 1901 made an explicit assumption that there would be little change necessary in the structures and institutions of basic dual federalism. As a result, the constitution has become anachronistic in many areas.

The founding fathers were well-satisfied with the product of their deliberations, so much so that they designed the constitution as one of the most difficult to amend of any in the collection of modern federal systems. The Australian constitution was designed to be rigid, to be very difficult to change, to survive the ephemeral changes in the society and the polity, to be a real 'Supreme Law'. Certainly, any constitution is usually protected to the extent that special measures are required to amend it (excepting the unwritten British constitution), and a federal constitution is usually surrounded by stronger protective measures. But the Australian founding fathers chose means to change the constitution which, with the subsequent addition of the impact of confrontational and disciplined political parties, have resulted in the defeat of a long list of attempts to reform it.

The structure of the constitution can be formally changed in three ways.

1 Referral of Powers

A state can refer powers which it holds to the national parliament, and any such powers referred apply only to the state which agreed to such a transfer. In theory, then, the federal division of powers can vary from state to state. In practice, this means of changing the structure of federalism has been resisted rather than used. The most recent transfer of powers occurred in 1977 when the South Australian and Tasmanian governments passed over to the national government the ownership of the states' country railway systems. In 1984, the Hawke Labor government put a referendum to the people proposing that commonwealth and state governments should have the right to interchange powers. This failed to pass.

2 New States

The constitution explicitly provides for the establishment of new states and for consequent changes in boundaries of existing states. Attempts have been made, with the backing of the National Party, mainly in the New England and Riverina areas of New South Wales, but they have been notably unsuccessful. It is unlikely that such efforts will ever be successful, as the constitution demands that the parliament of the state or states concerned, and a majority of the voters in a referendum, must consent to any modifications to present boundaries. States' rights are guarded with such intensity that any changes are unlikely. On the other hand, the formation of a new state from at least one of the two internal territories—the Northern Territory and the Australian Capital Territory—is a possibility.

3 Referendum

While the planners set out to write a document which would last, they recognised that some procedure for change should be incorporated. The process for an amendment to the constitution is complex. A bill for an amendment must first be passed by an absolute majority of both houses of the national parliament (although if one house rejects the proposal, and the other passes the bill twice, the Governor-General has the authority to declare the bill 'available' for the next stage). The second stage involves a referendum of all electors in all states and, since 1977, in the Northern Territory and the Australian Capital Territory. The proposed amendment needs a double majority; an overall majority vote in favour (including the Territories), and a majority in favour in at least four of the six states (excluding the Territories). This was incorporated as a means to protect the less populated states against domination by the electors in New South Wales and Victoria.

THE HISTORY OF REFERENDUMS

Since 1901, of a total of forty-two questions that have been put to the voters only eight have achieved the necessary double majority. The proposals which have succeeded have generally been non-controversial in terms of the relations between the levels of government, and have been questions on which the major political parties have been in general agreement. For example, the 1906 referendum made minor alterations in the laws governing the election of senators, a 1967 referendum granted the Australian government power to legislate for all Aborigines, and a 1977 referendum set a retiring age for federal judges.

The proposals which have failed to pass were of three main types:

- to increase the powers of the national government
- to change the status quo as it affected certain economic or social groups
- those on which the major political parties, at the time of submission to a referendum, were in disagreement.

(Document 10.5 sets out the results of all forty-two referendum questions.)

An emphasis on the third point is necessary as parties have not been overly consistent in their approaches to referendums, even to the same question offered a second or even a third time. This party confrontation for confrontation's sake was not foreseen by the planners, understandably, as they produced the constitution and the amendment process before the modern confrontation party system had formed.

One example provides enough evidence to prove the point, and to show that the Liberal Party's approach has had little to do with principles of reform, but much to do with simple pragmatism. In 1974, the Whitlam Labor government put a referendum to the people that Senate elections should be held simultaneously with those for the House of Representatives. The Liberal–National coalition opposed this vehemently. The proposal therefore was voted on in an atmosphere of party confrontation in an environment where most electors tend to follow their party, regardless. It was defeated: 48 per cent overall support, and majority support only in New South Wales.

In 1977, the Fraser Liberal government put the *same* question to the people, the federal Liberal Party and federal National Party (the latter somewhat grudgingly) supported it and recommended it, and the Labor Party maintained its support. That is, the coalition parties, in three years, had reversed their stand. The referendum received 62 per cent support overall, but was defeated when it failed to win majority support in Queensland, Tasmania and Western Australia. It had run into another problem—the tendency for state non-Labor parties to be as pragmatic as the national bodies. Where the Fraser–Anthony Liberal–National Parties proposed and supported the simultaneous elections referendum, Liberal parties in Tasmania and Western Australia, and the National Party in Queensland, campaigned heavily against it.

In 1984, the federal Liberal and National parties continued their political somersault and strongly opposed the Hawke Labor government's referendum to introduce simultaneous elections. On this occasion, the proposal again received an overall majority in support, 50.6 per cent, but it was again lost in Queensland, Tasmania and Western Australia.

It can be argued that the main explanation for the defeat of so many referendums is the combination of the pragmatism of the non-Labor parties (and *within* their federal structures), and the tendency for a majority of Australian voters to 'follow the party line' on all political decisions. Many other reasons have been suggested for the low success record. The Australian electorate has been described as conservative and unwilling to support change; the voters have been said to be embedded in a 'states rights' culture, tending to reject any suggestion of any transfer of powers to Canberra. It has also been suggested that constitutional issues are complex and that the relatively apathetic Australian electorate may vote 'no' as the easy way out. These, and other factors, may play a role, but the impact of party, party voting and party pragmatism is probably by far the major explanation.

THE 1988 REFERENDUMS: A CASE STUDY

The parties opposing referendums, often on grounds which had little to do with principles, have not been the only reactionary elements in the history of constitutional reform. Governments, too, have 'played politics', have presented ill-thought-out questions and have been just as pragmatic as their oppositions. In 1944, for example, a single referendum question included a transfer of fourteen specific powers to Canberra *and* three issues concerning rights, yet demanded a simple yes/no answer to the whole package.

The 1988 referendums were a case study of a government playing politics, and an opposition playing even harder. The Hawke Labor government selected six recommendations from the long list emerging from the Constitutional Commission and prepared four questions for the electorate. But it imposed a party modification to one recommendation and made a tactical mistake with another. The Commission had recommended a compromise between a fixed term for parliament and the existing maximum term. It recommended a four-year term, the first three years of which would be fixed. The Hawke government proposed only the first part, a four-year maximum, and campaigned along the lines that this would mean fewer elections. Obviously, without the second part of the Commission's recommendation, it would not. The tactical error was to include three separate issues as one question in the referendum (see Document 10.6), and when a number of religious groups, the Call to Australia Party, and the Liberal and National parties, vehemently opposed the extension of freedom of religion, all three proposals were likely to be defeated.

But the Liberal and National parties also played a major part in the worst defeat for referendum proposals in the history of Australian federalism. The campaign by the opposition parties was a model of 'the end justifies the means'. The Liberal and National parties sought the defeat of the referendums simply because Labor had proposed and supported them, for partisan ends, and their campaign was filled with 'fear and loathing'. The editorial in the *Age* (5 November 1988) correctly assessed the role played.

> The no case was inflated by an emotion-charged farrago of fallacy, falsehood and fear-mongering that was breathless in its audacity. At least three of the questions were entirely in accord with Liberal principles and arguably all four were compatible with Liberal interests. The defeat of the second question runs directly counter to Liberal interests as well as electoral fairness in Queensland. Mr Howard has served neither the good of the nation nor the good of his party.

The point is, the approach worked to the extent that the opposition believed it had won some party political points.

CONSTITUTIONAL CONVENTION, 1973–1985

The Constitutional Convention was established by the Whitlam Labor government as part of its attempt to bring about real constitutional reform. It was the first Convention since 1897, the first real attempt to bring about reform. Some earlier attempts had been made. In 1927, a Royal Commission proposed major changes, but the report was shelved. In 1959, a joint parliamentary committee reported with major recommendations, but party ideology and party politics intervened and the report was shelved by the Menzies Liberal government.

The formation of a Constitutional Convention in 1973 was therefore overdue. The potential for reform was, in theory, considerable. Membership was drawn from all three levels of government, from national and state parliaments and from local government, and a secretariat, research and advisory structure was established. If all delegates had approached the Convention with a promise of open-minded discussion then much constructive reform could have been achieved. Unfortunately, as with almost every other attempt to reform the federal structure, the Convention became a venue for party conflict, an arena for determined ideologies and an outlet for supporters of states' rights.

The Bjelke-Petersen Queensland delegation objected to local government involvement and temporarily removed itself from the Convention. In 1974, an intra-party Liberal split in South Australia (see Jaensch & Bullock 1979) almost ended the Convention. In 1983, the Tasmanian Liberal, and Queensland National governments refused to follow the established practice of equality of government/opposition representation.

There were some minor successes. Apart from the studies emerging from the research section of the Convention, three recommendations of the Convention were carried by referendum in 1977. These were hardly major reforms, proposing that federal judges should retire at 70, that a casual vacancy on the Senate be filled by a person of the same party (the first mention of party in the constitution), and that electors in the Territories should have the right to vote in referendums. By 1985, however, it was clear that party-based obstruction, especially by Liberal and National parties, the unbending commitments to states' rights by some delegations and the narrow structure of the membership of the Convention—party politicians—meant that the enterprise had failed. The Convention was brought to an end following the 1985 Brisbane meeting.

CONSTITUTIONAL COMMISSION, 1985–1988

This body was established by the Hawke government as a 'people's commission' in the hope that, in the absence of party politics, not only would the Commission produce recommendations of substance, but that these recommendations would receive wide and, especially, cross-party support. The former was achieved; the latter was a vain hope, given the nature and style of Australian party politics. The membership of the Commission contained expertise and promise: Sir Maurice Byers (former Solicitor-General), Sir Rupert Hamer (former Liberal premier of Victoria), E. G. Whitlam (former Labor prime minister), and two professors of law, Enid Campbell and Leslie Zines. Five advisory committees were established and a large supporting research team provided an opportunity for real and substantive reforms.

The report of the Commission in 1988 was a full review, and contained a multitude of recommendations. The review had been achieved, in three years, but the implementation process immediately faced the problems that had beset the earlier attempts—party politics, ideology, states' rights, and pragmatic electoral politics. The first attempt to implement six recommendations in the 1988 referendums incorporated all of these factors, and there is little evidence that future attempts at implementation are unlikely to be any less difficult. A detailed rewrite of the constitution has now been prepared; whether governments, parties and people have the open-mindedness and the will to carry it into practice is in question.

At the 1990 Premiers' Conference, Prime Minister Hawke set an agenda for the decade—the reform and restructuring of federalism. He received strong support from an unexpected source—the Liberal premier of New South Wales. Nick Griener went on to criticise his own party for its obsession with states' rights, and argued that Australia should move to 'a single market, a single economy and, indeed, a single nation' (speech to Liberal Federal Council, October 1990). Certainly there are some in the Liberal party who see the need for reform, but they apparently remain in a minority.

Since 1990, the federal and state leaders and ministers have been involved in a series of meetings in an attempt to make federalism more efficient and more effective. Changes in federal–state relations, in obtaining uniform laws and regulations, and in dealing with duplication, have been carried, but there is still much to do. And any suggestion of a possible agreement on a 'new federalism' is still to be tested by referendum. As well, the republic debate has introduced a further component for argument.

THE CHANGING FEDERAL PROCESSES

Changes over time in the process, operation and balance of federalism have inevitably occurred, and the effect, by 1990, has been a shift in the original division of powers of 1901—the 'dual' federalism—significantly in favour of the national government. Why has the expansion of national functions and national power occurred? It has not come about, as some States'-righters constantly assert, because of the desire of centralists (which usually refers to the Labor Party) to deliberately set out to consolidate power in Canberra. Such assertions are for party or electoral effect rather than for explanation. In fact, the drift of functions and powers to the national government has occurred as much, if not more, under Liberal–Country Party governments as under Labor.

The trend has occurred because society, the social system and the economic system have changed. The sparsely populated, essentially agricultural society has changed to densely populated urban complexes and the development of an industrial and commercial nation. The 'tyranny of distance' has been partly overcome by a network of transport and communication, much of which was not even envisaged by the constitution makers. Small business has become large; craft unions have become national trade unions; new urban and rural issues and problems have emerged, many demanding the expenditure of vast amounts of money; and the fragmented society of the 1800s has become developed federalism, with interlocking national, state and local demands and problems concerning a range of political, social and economic issues.

The changes in the *process* of federalism have come about through four major means:

- judicial interpretation
- unchallenged legislation
- increasing economic and financial control in the hands of the national government
- informal 'structures' of federalism.

JUDICIAL INTERPRETATION

Disagreements within a federal system often concern the areas of activity of the various governments, especially when the constitution is vague in definition, or where developments in the society and the economy are not mentioned in the constitution. Hence, the need for an interpreter of the constitution, an arbiter on disagreements. The High Court in Australia fulfils these roles and also acts as the supreme court of appeal in Australia. Until 1975, the High Court could allow appeals to the Privy Council in Britain, but since 1975 the decision of the High Court on any matter of the constitution or of federalism is final. The Court consists of a Chief Justice and seven other Justices who are appointed by the government. As the interpreter of the constitution, the High Court can modify the process of federalism in Australia. For this reason, there has been considerable interest and occasional dissension concerning appointments of new Justices, especially in regard to their party backgrounds. Decisions of the Court will naturally be affected by the ideologies and attitudes of the individual Justices. It is not surprising, then, that when vacancies occur, governments, whether Liberal or Labor, may seek to appoint people whose attitudes to federalism are in relative agreement with theirs.

The rulings of the High Court have modified the process of federalism in significant ways, although not always in the same direction. From 1903 until the early 1920s, the Court generally

The High Court, Canberra.

decided disputes in favour of the states and states' rights. For the next thirty years, through the depression and Second World War, the Court showed in its decisions that it saw little wrong with increasing the power of the national government. From the early 1950s, for twenty years, the Court's decisions returned to an emphasis on states' rights. This was also the period of the Menzies Liberal government. During the 1970s, the High Court showed a less consistent line, although it should be emphasised that there was no lessening of the power of the national government during the Whitlam Labor government or the Fraser Liberal government.

One reason for the changing emphasis of the Court is that it is faced with the problem of interpreting the words of a constitution written in the late 1890s in the terms of modern politics and society, and it is limited to a *legal* interpretation of the constitution—that is, it can make a ruling only when a case has been brought before it. A test of any legislation therefore requires the costly and time-consuming process of a High Court action.

The Court's decision in 1983, in favour of the Commonwealth government over the Tasmanian Franklin Dam issue, was one of its most important in terms of federalism. The decision re-affirmed the right of a national government to apply international treaties it has ratified, if necessary by a ruling from the High Court, and that state governments are not sovereign where national interests are involved.

The High Court found in favour of the federal government in the Franklin Dam controversy of 1983, overruling the Tasmanian state government.

This 'treaty power' has long-term implications and has the potential to bring further significant changes to the relationships within Australian federalism.

UNCHALLENGED LEGISLATION

If the national parliament, or one or more state parliaments, legislates in a manner which is in breach of the constitution, the High Court cannot so rule until one of the governments brings a case before it. If no challenge is made, the legislation remains in force.

The Australian constitution has been extended in practice (not in wording) by such unchallenged legislation, especially in areas not envisaged by the constitution planners. Such instances include specific cases of national intrusion in state areas of authority where the states have agreed to such involvement; for example, the Snowy River Scheme, the CSIRO and the Commonwealth Employment Service. The other extension of national authority concerns legislation on such matters as air navigation and the two-airline policy and radio and television, where the states have not exercised their reserve powers but have recognised the value of uniform laws and regulations.

FINANCIAL RELATIONS

Australia's constitution planners were determined to ensure that the division of powers reserved considerable authority and power for the states, but they could not foresee the implications of changed social demands which led to an imbalance in the process of federalism and moved financial power to the national government. The original financial foundations of the national government were met mainly by income from customs and excise, but even before the financial demands of the First World War, the government had been forced to apply a land tax to obtain sufficient revenue. During the war, the government was forced to borrow heavily and to institute its own income tax for the first time.

The major development in the slow but steady transfer of economic power from the states to Canberra was the 1942 legislation on income tax. Again because of the economic demands of war, the national government introduced measures which fixed the rate of income tax, provided that the Commonwealth would have 'first bite' at the taxpayer (the legislation did not exclude the states from the authority to tax incomes but asserted that the Commonwealth tax would be due before any state's impost), and provided for Commonwealth grants to the states as a reimbursement of lost revenue. The states originally refused to accept this legislation even as a temporary measure, and challenged it in the High Court, which declared the legislation valid.

In 1946, the Chifley government passed legislation to make the 1942 scheme permanent which, in effect, forced the states to vacate this field of taxation. In 1952, Prime Minister Menzies announced his intention to return taxation powers to the states but, whether or not he intended to carry such legislation through, the less affluent states which had benefited from the new scheme were not in favour of a change. The larger, more affluent states, at least at the level of rhetoric, have sought the return of taxation powers, but it was not until the 'new federalism' of the Fraser government that the question of modification to the Commonwealth's virtual monopoly of income taxation was seriously considered. Fraser offered the States a financial carrot which, on the surface, was hard to resist. He proposed to the premiers that they have access to income tax powers which would not affect their grants from the Commonwealth. No state government took advantage of the offer for good political reasons: the electoral life of any government offering increased income tax would indeed be short.

INFORMAL STRUCTURES

As the dual federalism of 1901 developed and gradually turned into co-operative federalism, a plethora of inter-government structures was established. The first important point about these—whether they are at the level of ministerial committees or the Premiers' Conferences—is that they have no formal authority in federal politics as they are not mentioned in the constitution. Any decisions they may take require legislation by the relevant parliaments and, if not in accord with the constitution, those Acts also require an agreement about unchallenged legislation. They are part of the conventions of the constitution (see below). Some have become more important, and one has been constitutionally ratified.

For the first twenty or so years of federalism, meetings of state premiers and the prime ministers were held on an informal and irregular basis to discuss matters of mutual interest. Since the formation of the Loan Council (see below) in 1923, Premiers' Conferences have been regular and increasingly important. They took on a greater importance following the 1942 Taxation Act. Usually hosted in Canberra, they provide a forum for discussions of and around federalism and a potential for mutual agreements about federal processes. However, two trends emerged early. One was that the Premiers' Conference increasingly became a party political theatre, where governments, especially state governments of whichever party, carried out political rituals which they hoped the media would report in terms favourable to them in their home states. The second is that the Conference, as a mutual exchange of views, became overshadowed with economic and financial issues, which added to the political theatre.

One problem which emerged only after federation was the one caused by competition between state governments, and state and national governments, for loan funds. In 1923, the Premiers' Conference inaugurated an advisory body in an attempt to co-ordinate loans and in 1928, one of a few successful referendums carried in all states established the Australian Loan Council. The national government won a powerful role from the beginning. The voting was established with each state having one vote and the Commonwealth having two votes, together with a casting vote. That is, even if the Commonwealth government can obtain the support of only two states, it can still carry a majority on the Loan Council.

Since its inauguration, as the financial position of the national government became dominant, and especially after the national government took over the income tax power in 1942, the role of the Loan Council changed from that of co-ordinating within a consensus, to allocating at the behest of the central authority. As the role of the Loan Council is to decide how much should be borrowed in the coming financial year and how the borrowing rights will be allocated among the governments, its decisions are crucial. Further, Loan Council decisions are binding on all governments, with constitutional backing and cannot be modified except by the Loan Council at a future meeting.

In recent times the Loan Council has not been a happy, let alone a consensual, meeting. As the Australian economy, since the boom of the Menzies era, has come under strain, national governments have increasingly sought to use the Loan Council as yet another means of economic, fiscal and monetary management and have sought firm controls on borrowings. The state governments, on the other hand, continually claiming they are starved of funds, have approached the Loan Council as a milch cow. The result has inevitably been confrontation, and intra-party as well as inter-party conflict.

CONVENTIONS—THE UNWRITTEN CONSTITUTION

No constitution can be all-encompassing. No constitution can cover every component of federal political structures and processes, nor can it foresee future developments in the polity and cover them. As a result, all democratic societies have had to learn to live with conventions of the constitution.

In a formal sense, conventions state the norms, procedures, and rules of political relationships. However, if they are ignored, or broken, there is no legal sanction which can be applied. They exist, then, to provide guidance for action where the formal laws or constitutional statements are ambiguous or are simply not present. As such, in more informal language, they are accepted practices, agreements, the 'unwritten rules of the game' or, in an older language, 'gentlemen's agreements'. Obviously, they depend on the players in the game all being 'gentlemen' who will accord the conventions the respect they deserve, and will not follow a machiavellian path. In Britain, almost the whole of the structure of the Westminster model of parliamentary democracy is built on conventions. These were imported into the Australian colonies and were assumed equally to apply to the national parliamentary system from 1901.

Australian federalism has had to *develop* a range of conventions, especially as the formal constitution has hardly been changed since 1901. The term 'develop' is important; conventions become necessary when a written constitution is not clear, not explicit, or even silent on an issue. At this point, a precedent is established and, if accepted as a sensible and logical solution, the precedent becomes accepted as an 'unwritten rule'. Conventions may change as circumstances change but a breach of a convention is a serious matter, which usually arises from a conflict of values and which may lead to an attempt to codify the convention formally into a written law to produce a barrier against further breaches. But the very unwritten nature of conventions may produce a situation in which a conflict can arise about precision of interpretation or further conflict situation, where there is a real dispute between the written constitution and the unwritten convention. At this point, the literalists and the conventionalists may have no common ground, and a crisis may result. The events of the 'constitutional crisis' of 1974 and 1975 were a prime example of such an impasse.

THE STATE OF THE CONSTITUTION

The concept of a constantly changing constitution is anathema to many people. There are many who argue that the document drawn up in the late 1890s should remain unchanged for all time. They argue that the constitution is fundamental to our federal, democratic system of government and that any change will weaken either federalism or democracy.

But simple logic shows that the constitution does and must change. Unless the 'written law' grows as the nation grows and changes as the social and political system changes, it will become outmoded and increasingly ignored. The powers of government, the division of powers, the various rights and constraints in the constitution may have been adequate in 1901. No one can sensibly argue that they are adequate for the 1990s. A constitution which was the result of a compromise between small, generally agricultural communities, between the political and economic interests of the turn of the century, is obviously not suitable for the mixed-economy, industrial nation of today.

More important, the basis of the federal process—co-operation—has been increasingly replaced, in the 1970s and 1980s, with confrontation, conflict and division, often with the aim of gaining partisan or electoral advantage by one party over another. When states' rights, regional jealousies and partisan advantage become the prime means of the political process, then the structure, nature and function of federalism comes seriously under strain. What, then, is the state of the constitution?

It will be clear from the discussion in this chapter that the Australian constitution is in need of rewriting. The 1901 document was written in a political climate permeated by the conservatism, parochialism and pettiness that characterised the Australian colonies at the end of the nineteenth century (Encel 1977:43). Federal politics in 1993 still shows these characteristics. After the failure of the proposed reforms at the 1988 referendum, reform of the document seems all but impossible while the party politicking which has characterised Australian federalism, certainly since 1972, continues.

The oft-claimed benefits of federalism, usually claimed by non-Labor parties, include prevention of authoritarianism, protection of diversity, protection of rights, a better reflection of localism and better representation. These 'benefits' are barely evident in modern Australian federalism, if they ever were present at all. And whatever benefits there are, are overwhelmed by a lack of uniformity of legislation and administration, complexity and duplication (even triplication) at all levels, over-government in every sense of the word, and division of what should be a nation into 'warring tribes' in the states and territories. These disadvantages have been exacerbated by the nature of party politics in Australia and there is no doubt that federalism has outlived whatever usefulness and value it may have had. The problem remains how to reform it, especially after the events, in regard to both structure and process, of the 1970s and 1980s. What has emerged in Australia is firm evidence to support the contention (Riker 1969) that federalism is nothing more than a legal fiction under which any system of political process is possible, and that it can be anything those with the power want it to be. Which, of course, may explain why it has survived for over ninety years.

DOCUMENTS

10.1 SOME DEFINITIONS OF FEDERALISM: CHANGING APPROACHES

a)
Source: Garran, R. 1929, *Report of The Royal Commission on the Australian Constitution*, Government Printer, Melbourne, p. 230.

A form of government in which sovereignty or political power is divided between the central and local governments, so that each of them within its own sphere is independent of the other.

b)
Source: Wheare, K.C. 1946, *Federal Government*, Oxford University Press, Melbourne, pp. 11, 15.

What is necessary for the federal principle is not merely that the general government, like the regional government, should operate directly upon the people, but, further, that each government should be limited to its own sphere, and, within that sphere, should be independent of the other.

c)
Source: Birch, A.H. 1955, *Federalism, Finance and Social Legislation*, Clarendon Press, Oxford, p. 306.

A federal system of government is one in which there is a division of powers between one general and several regional authorities, each of which, in its own sphere, is co-ordinate with the others.

d)
Source: Vile, M.J.C. 1973, *Federalism in the United States, Canada and Australia,* HMSO, London, pp. 2–3.

... the following characteristics when using the word federalism:

i) A constitution which guarantees to each of two levels of government an independence of each other sufficient to enable them to engage the continuing support of significant elements of the political system;
ii) A constitutional and political system which links the two levels with a significant degree of interdependence, such that neither level can subordinate the other to it, nor act wholly independently of the other across the whole range of government functions.

e)
Source: Livingstone, W.S. 1956, *Federalism and Constitution Change,* Clarendon Press, Oxford, p. 4.

Federalism is not thus an absolute but a relative term; there is no identifiable point at which a society ceases to be unified and becomes diversified... All communities fall somewhere in a spectrum which runs from what we may call a theoretically wholly integrated society at one extreme to a theoretically wholly diversified society at the other.

f)
Source: Riker, W.H. 1969, 'Does federalism exist and does it matter?', *Comparative Politics,* vol. 2, no. 1, October, p. 145.

Does federalism make any difference in the way people are governed?... Hardly any at all... federalism is no more than a constitutional legal fiction which can be given whatever content seems appropriate at the moment.

10.2 THREE AUSTRALIAN ATTITUDES TO FEDERALISM

a) J. Bjelke-Petersen (Country Party Premier of Queensland)
Source: Australian, 12 May 1973.

Every parent in this country will need to consider very carefully whether any extension of federal power, any denigration of the Crown's role and functions in our particular form of Federal democracy will not within our children's lifetime lead to a system of government involving fear and the midnight doorknock.

b) T.L. Lewis (Liberal Premier of New South Wales)
Source: Mathews, R. (ed.) 1976, *Making Federalism Work,* Australian National University Press, Canberra, pp. 212–13.

My theme has been federalism, genuine federalism, that is, a division of government functions, responsibilities and power in Australia between the Commonwealth and the States... We need to return to the basic issues. We do have a federal system. It reflected the wisdom of quite great men who put it together. The Australian people... do not want it changed... We must make federalism work... But we will only achieve this by returning from the new centralism to the original concept of federalism.

c) E.G. Whitlam (Labor Prime Minister)
Source: 'A new federalism', *Australian Quarterly,* 1971, vol. 43, no. 3, p. 11.

Ideally, our continent should have neither so few State Governments nor so many local government units. We should have a federal system of overlapping parliaments and a delegated but supervised system of local government. We should have a House of Representatives for international matters and nationwide matters, an assembly for the affairs of each of our dozen largest cities and regional assemblies for the few scarce areas of rural production and resource development outside those cities. Vested interests and legal complexities should not discourage or deter us from attempts to modernise and nationalise our inherited structure.

10.3 A NEED FOR CHANGE?

Source: Maddox, G. 1973, 'Federalism: or government frustrated', *Australian Quarterly,* vol. 45, no. 3, pp. 98–9.

There is still much that we can learn from the British constitution, which 'states' righters' praise and condemn in the one breath. Despite its size, Australia could move much closer to democracy by creating a unitary system with a single national government delegating authority to a vigorous network of small local government units. Local governments, laid out more rationally than at present, could be given real responsibility and real teeth. They could be designed to include effective popular participation in local affairs. Education and health services (over and above garbage collection) could actually be run by local people... It may be objected that such proposals would merely substitute one two-tier system of government for another. But there is a very important qualitative difference. Under the unitary system of central government with delegated authority to local governments, there is no cant about local 'sovereignty' by reason of which ancient mythology present state leaders stand on their own inflated dignity. There is no buck passing of responsibility, no doubts as to where jurisdiction lies. For the central parliament is ultimately responsible to the people for democratic government, for the protection of minorities, for the curbing of exploitation, for the balancing of interests. Where local affairs can be settled locally to the satisfaction of affected parties the national government need not be directly involved.

But an unfettered Commonwealth government, without the hindrance of state middlemen, can see that local authorities are adequately supplied and financed.

There is little likelihood that the inherent conservatism in human nature and the overpowering inertia of our present political superstructure could ever allow an easy transition to a unitary system of democratic government in Australia. At least we can learn to listen with greater sympathy to those who attempt to use national power to run our country efficiently and responsibly. And we can learn to view with deep suspicion the rantings of state politicians about the lurking threat of totalitarianism to their 'sovereign rights'.

10.4 PROPOSALS FOR CHANGES TO THE AUSTRALIAN CONSTITUTION

Source: Horne, D. 1977, *Power from the People: A New Australian Constitution?*, Victorian Fabian Society Pamphlet No. 32.

1 De-emphasise the monarchic basis of the present Constitution by a declaration that 'all public power comes from the people'.
2 Require equality of votes, and disclosure of party funds, and, perhaps, government funding of parties to ensure fairer elections.
3 Abolish the upper houses—State as well as federal.
4 Ensure that a majority of votes is reflected in a majority of seats either by a system of proportional representation or by 'topping up' the single-member constituency results with members-at-large to establish proportionality.
5 Provide that the prime minister is elected by and removed by the legislature, not the Governor-General.
6 Allow non-elected ministers on the European model.
7 Introduce 'open government'.
8 Entrench in the Constitution offices like the Ombudsman's which are intended to protect the public from abuses of power.
9 Provide an elected head of state for symbolic purposes, but stripped of real constitutional power.

10.5 HISTORY OF REFERENDUM RESULTS

Subjects	Year	Overall	States with majority 'yes'					
		% 'yes'	NSW	Vic	Qld	SA	WA	Tas
Senate Elections	1906	83	#	#	#	#	#	#
Finance	1910	49			#		#	#
State Debts	1910	55		#	#	#	#	#
Legislative Powers	1911	39					#	
Monopolies	1911	39					#	
Trade and Commerce	1913	49			#	#	#	
Corporations	1913	49			#	#	#	
Industrial Matters	1913	49			#	#	#	
Railway Disputes	1913	49			#	#	#	
Trusts	1913	49			#	#	#	
Nationalisation	1913	49			#	#	#	
Legislative Powers	1919	49		#	#		#	
Nationalisation	1919	48		#	#		#	
Industry and Commerce	1926	43	#		#			
Essential Services	1926	42	#		#			
State Debts	1928	74	#	#	#	#	#	#
Aviation	1937	53		#	#			
Marketing	1937	36			nil			
Reconstruction; Rights	1944	46				#	#	
Social Services	1946	54	#	#	#	#	#	#
Organised Marketing	1946	50	#	#			#	
Industrial Employment	1946	50	#	#			#	
Rents, Prices	1948	41			nil			
Communism	1951	49			#		#	#
Nexus	1967	40	#					
Aborigines	1967	91	#	#	#	#	#	#
Price Control	1973	44			nil			
Income Control	1973	34			nil			
Simultaneous Elections	1974	48	#					
Democratic Elections	1974	47	#					
Local Government	1974	47	#					
Simultaneous Elections	1977	62	#	#		#		
Senate Casual Vacancies	1977	73	#	#	#	#	#	#
Referendums	1977	78	#	#	#	#	#	#
Retirement of Judges	1977	80	#	#	#	#	#	#
Simultaneous Elections	1984	51	#	#				
Transfer of Powers	1984	47			nil			
Parliamentary Terms	1988	33			nil			
Fair Elections	1988	38			nil			
Local Government	1988	34			nil			
Rights and Freedoms	1988	31			nil			

Summary

42 questions—13 received overall majority
— 8 received majority of states as well

10.6 REFERENDUM RESULTS, 1988

Proposals

1 To provide for four-year maximum terms for members of both Houses of the Commonwealth Parliament.
2 To provide for fair and democratic parliamentary elections throughout Australia.
3 To recognise local government.
4 To extend the right to trial by jury, to extend freedom of religion, and to ensure fair terms for persons whose property is acquired by any government.

Results

	% voting 'yes' on each question			
State/Territory	1.	2.	3.	4.
NSW	37.1	35.6	31.7	29.7
Vic	36.2	40.1	36.1	33.4
Qld	35.2	44.8	38.3	32.9
WA	30.7	32.0	29.8	28.2
SA	26.8	30.6	29.9	26.0
Tas	25.4	28.9	27.5	25.5
ACT	43.6	52.0	39.8	40.7
NT	38.1	43.0	38.8	37.1
Aust	32.9	37.6	33.6	30.8

(All proposals were defeated)

10.7 A PREDICTION WHICH PROVED TO BE WRONG

Source: Davis, S.R. (ed.) 1960, *The Government of the Australian States*, Longman Cheshire, Melbourne, p. 711.

Is there reason then to expect the present relations of the Commonwealth and the States to undergo further fundamental changes? One may safely hazard the guess that at no other time in the past have their relations appeared so permanently settled as they do now, and at no time has there been a more mature understanding of each other's needs. Except for the annual feuding and fussing over the division of the tax spoils, the Commonwealth and the States have bedded down with sympathy and resignation, if without great love. For the past decade there has been less talk about constitutional revision than ever before and less enthusiasm for change. The States are neither as unhappy as they say, nor the Commonwealth as imperialistic as some believe. If there are many oddities still in the system what is important is that most of those who work it have come to understand the complexities and learnt to live with them without great discomfort.

ISSUES FOR DISCUSSION

1 From your current magazine and newspaper reading and from current radio and TV programmes, give illustrations of present-day conflict of opinion regarding the rights of the states in relation to the rights of the central government. Carefully check the results of public opinion polls which are published in daily newspapers. Is there any evidence of conflict over states' rights? (See Document 10.2.)

2 Give reasons why efficient and effective local government is of importance to the entire nation as well as to the immediate local community. How effective is local government in your area? How could it be improved?

3 In Australia, what duties and obligations do the states and the nation owe each other?

4 Some students of government have suggested that regional governments which would serve larger areas than local government should be established. Do you favour this proposal? Why, or why not?

5 One writer has likened our three levels of government—federal, state and local—to a 'marble cake' rather than a 'three-layer cake'. Discuss the idea in this simile.

6 Why has it been so difficult to change the Australian constitution? (See Documents 10.5 and 10.6.)

7 'All of the problems of Australian federalism arise from the near impossibility of changing the constitution.' Do you agree?

8 How federal is Australia? (See Document 10.1.)

9 Given the history of lack of success of referendums in Australia why were three out of four successful in 1977? (See Document 10.5.)

10 Why did the prediction by Davis (Document 10.7) not come true?

11 Discuss a referendum question which should be put to the Australian people.

12 Identify a local issue on which the three levels of government are all involved, and the manner in which they work together.
13 Carry out a survey in your local area asking 'why do Australians need a federal system of government?' Analyse the answers you receive and compare them with surveys by others.
14 Hold a debate on the theme that 'Australia no longer needs state governments'.
15 Prepare a list of activities which were originally granted to state governments but in which the national government is now playing a major role.
16 Prepare an argument to support a referendum that the Northern Territory should be the seventh state.

REFERENCES

The following works have been cited in the text:

Aitkin, D. 1973, 'Electoral behaviour', in Henry Mayer (ed.), *Australia's Political Pattern,* Longman Cheshire, Melbourne, p. 28.

Aitkin, D. 1976, 'Electoral behaviour', in H. Mayer & H. Nelson (eds), *Australian Politics: A Fourth Reader,* Longman Cheshire, Melbourne.

Aitkin, D. 1982, *Stability and Change in Australian Politics,* 2nd edn, Australian National University Press, Canberra.

Aitkin, D.A. 1977, *Stability and Change in Australian Politics,* Australian National University Press, Canberra.

Aitkin, D. & Kahan, M. 1974, 'Australia: class politics in the New World' in R. Rose (ed.), *Electoral Behaviour: A Comparative Handbook,* Free Press, New York.

An Introduction to the Australian Federal Parliament, 1959, Angus and Robertson, Sydney, pp. 26–7.

Australian Labor Party 1979, *National Committee of Inquiry,* APSA Monograph 23, 224 Bedford Park.

Beer, S.H. 1965, *Modern British Politics,* Faber, London.

Birch, A.H. 1955, *Federalism, Finance and Social Legislation,* Clarendon Press, Oxford, p. 306.

Bjelke-Petersen, J., The *Australian,* 12 May 1973.

Boyden, S. 1974, 'Australia and the environmental crisis', in Rob Dempsey (ed.), *The Politics of Finding Out,* Longman Cheshire, pp. 15–16.

Caldwell, A., *Advertiser*, 22 March 1967.
Carey, B. 1980, 'Executive control in the 1970s', in Mayer, H. & Nelson, H. (eds), *Australian Politics: A Fifth Reader*, Longman Cheshire, Melbourne, p. 227.
Clark, C. 1974, 'Parliamentarians by lot', *Quadrant*, 18(3).
Commonwealth Parliamentary Debates, House of Representatives, 1967, pp. 2777, 2779.
Connell, R.W. 1977, *Ruling Class, Ruling Culture*, Cambridge University Press, Melbourne, pp. vii, 58.
Connell, R.W. & Irving, T.H. 1973, 'Yes Virginia, there is a ruling class', in Mayer, H. & Nelson, H. (eds), *Australian Politics: A Third Reader*, Longman Cheshire, Melbourne, p. 33.
Dahl, R.A. 1976, *Modern Political Analysis*, Prentice-Hall, New York, pp. 103–7.
Davis, S.R. (ed.) 1960, *The Government of the Australian States*, Longman Cheshire, Melbourne, p. 667.
Dwyer, P. 1978, *How Lucky Are We?*, Longman Cheshire, Melbourne, p. 59.
Elcock, H. 1976, *Political Behaviour*, Methuen, London.
Emy, H.V. & Hughes, O.E. 1988, *Australian Politics: Realities in Conflict*, Macmillan, Melbourne.
Emy, H.V. 1974, *The Politics of Australian Democracy*, Macmillan, Melbourne, p. 355.
Emy, H.V. 1976, 'The public service and political control: the problem of accountability in a Westminster system with special reference to the concept of ministerial responsibility', in *The Report of The Royal Commission into Australian Government Administration*, vol. 1, p. 35.
Encel, S. 1977, 'The constitution as a social document', in Encel, S., Horne, D. & Thompson, E. (eds), *Change the Rules!: Towards a Democratic Constitution*, Penguin, Ringwood.
Epstein, L.D. 1980, 'A comparative study of Australian parties', *British Journal of Political Science*, vol. 7, no. 1.
Garran, R. 1929, *Report of the Royal Commission on the Australian Constitution*, Government Printer, Melbourne, p. 230.
Graetz, B. & McAllister, I. 1988, *Dimensions of Australian Society*, Macmillan, Melbourne.
Hagopian, M.N. 1984, *Regimes, Movements, Ideologies*, Longman, New York.
Hancock, W.K. 1930, *Australia*, Ernest Benn, London.
Home, D. 1977, *Power from the People: A New Australian Constitution?*, Victorian Fabian Society Pamphlet No. 32.
Hughes, C.A. 1977, *A Handbook of Australian Government and Politics*, Australian National University Press, Canberra.
Hughes, C.A. 1988, *A Handbook of Australian Government and Politics 1975–1984*, Australian National University Press, Canberra.

Jaensch, D. & Bullock, J. 1979, *Liberals in Limbo*, Drummond, Melbourne.

Jupp, J. 1966, *Arrivals and Departures*, Cheshire-Lansdowne, Melbourne, pp. 84–5.

Kemp, D. 1980, 'Political parties and Australian culture', in Mayer, H. & Nelson, H. (eds), *Australian Politics: A Fifth Reader*, Longman Cheshire, Melbourne, pp. 302–4.

Lasswell, H. 1936, *Politics: Who Gets What, When, How?*, McGraw-Hill, New York.

Livingstone, W.S. 1956, *Federalism and Constitution Change*, Clarendon Press, Oxford, p. 4.

Maddox, G. 1973, 'Federalism: or government frustrated', *Australian Quarterly*, vol. 45, no. 3, pp. 98–9.

Mannheim, J.B. 1975, *The Politics Within*, Prentice-Hall, New York.

Mathews, R. (ed.) 1976, *Making Federalism Work*, Australian National University Press, Canberra, pp. 212–13.

Mayer, H. & Nelson, H. (eds) 1973, *Australian Politics: A Third Reader*, Longman Cheshire, Melbourne.

Mayer, H. & Nelson, H. (eds) 1980, *Australian Politics: A Fourth Reader*, Longman Cheshire, Melbourne, p. 561.

McAllister, I. 1992, *Political Behaviour: Citizens, Parties and Elites in Australia*, Longman Cheshire, Melbourne.

McClelland, Senator J.R. 1972, *Who Runs Australia?*, AIPS, Canberra, pp. 133, 139.

McKinlay, B. 1977, *A Documentary History of the Australian Labor Party*, Drummond, Melbourne.

McQueen, H. 1972, 'Glory without power', in Playford, J. & Kirsner, J. (eds), *Australian Capitalism*, Penguin, Ringwood.

Parker, R.S. 1976, 'The meaning of responsible government', *Politics*, vol. 11, no. 2, p. 179.

Parker, R.S. 1978, 'Public service inquiries and responsible government', in Smith, R.F.I. & Weller, P. (eds), *Public Service Inquiries in Australia*, University of Queensland Press, St Lucia.

Parliament of Australia, 1977, *Australian Government Administration: Report of Royal Commission*, Commonwealth Government Printer, Canberra.

Parliament of Australia, Library 1991, Parliamentary Handbook of the Commonwealth of Australia, 25th edn, AGPS, Canberra.

Pitkin, H. 1967, *The Concept of Representation*, University of California Press, Berkeley.

Punch, L., Leader of the New South Wales Country Party, in the *Australian*, 14 April 1980.

Quick, J. & Garran, R.R. 1901, *The Annotated Constitution of the Commonwealth of Australia*, Legal Books, Sydney.

Reid, A. 1976, *The Whitlam Venture*, Hill of Content, Melbourne.

Reid, G.S. 1980, 'The changing political framework', *Quadrant*, no. 24.

Report of the Committee of Inquiry into the Public Service of South Australia, 1976, p. 11.
Riker, W.H. 1969, 'Does federalism exist and does it matter?', *Comparative Politics*, vol. 2, no. 1.
Roberts, G.K. 1971, *A Dictionary of Political Analysis*, Longman, London.
Rodan, P.K. 1979, 'The prime minister and cabinet', in Lucy, R. (ed.), *Pieces of Politics*, Macmillan, Melbourne, p. 186.
Rydon, J. 1965, 'The electorate', in John Wilkes (ed.), *Forces in Australian Politics*, Angus and Robertson, Sydney, pp. 177–84.
Snedden, B. 1966, 'Ministerial responsibility in modern parliamentary government', Third Commonwealth and Empire Conference.
Solomon, D. 1986, *The People's Palace: Parliament in Modern Australia*, Melbourne University Press, Melbourne.
Spann, R.N. 1980, 'Bureaucracy and the public service', in Mayer, H. & Nelson, H. (eds), *Australian Politics: A Fifth Reader*, Longman Cheshire, Melbourne, p. 254.
Spigelman, J.J. 1972, 'Secrecy and democracy', in AIPS, *Parliament, Bureaucracy, Citizens: Who Runs Australia?*, Angus and Robertson, Sydney.
St John, E. 1969, *A Time to Speak*, Sun Books, Melbourne, pp. 22–3.
Stevens, B. 1984, *Elections: How? Why? When?*, Rigby, Adelaide.
Stewart, R.G. & Ward, I. 1992, *Politics One*, Macmillan, Melbourne.
Sun, Sydney, 10 October 1969. Quoted in Mayer, H. & Nelson, H. (eds) 1973, *Australian Politics: A Third Reader*, Longman Cheshire, Melbourne, p. 336.
Sydney Morning Herald, 5 March 1976, cited by C.A. Hughes in Mayer, H. & Nelson, H. (eds) 1980, *Australian Politics: A Fifth Reader*, Longman Cheshire, Melbourne, pp. 194–5.
The *Age*, Editorial, 5 November 1988.
The *Australian*, Editorial, 'Our multi-racial society', 18 April 1980.
Thompson, E. 1980, 'The Washminster mutation', in Weller, P. & Jaensch, D. (eds), *Responsible Government in Australia*, Drummond, Melbourne.
Turner, K. 1973, 'The Liberal "Iceberg"', in Mayer, H. & Nelson, H. (eds), *Australian Politics: A Third Reader*, Longman Cheshire, Melbourne.
Turner, K. 1976, 'The Party contest in the 1970s', in Mayer, H. & Nelson, H. (eds), *Australian Politics: A Fourth Reader*, Longman Cheshire, Melbourne, p. 463.
Vile, M.J.C. 1973, *Federalism in the United States, Canada and Australia*, HMSO, London, pp. 2–3.
Westerway, P.B. 1965, 'Pressure groups', in *Forces in Australian Politics*, Angus and Robertson, Sydney, p. 120.
'What's gone wrong with politics?', *Bulletin*, 20 May 1972.

Wheare, K.C. 1946, *Federal Government*, Oxford University Press, Melbourne, pp. 11, 15.
Whitlam, E.G. 1971, 'A new federalism', *Australian Quarterly*, vol. 43, no. 3, p. 11.
Wright Mills, C. 1956, *The Power Elite*, Oxford University Press, Melbourne.

INDEX

ACKNOWLEDGEMENTS

Key to abbreviations: t = top, b= bottom, r= right, l = left

Photography

Andrew Chapman, 304; Australian Democrats, Western Australia, 131; Australian Information Service, 123 (br), 125 (tl, tr, bl, br), 128 (tl, tr), 217; Australian Labor Party, 12, 71; Commonwealth of Australia, 70; Sygma, 11 (r); Government Photographic Service, 260 (b); John Fairfax & Sons Ltd, 4 (Barry Chapman), 183; John Thwaites, MLA, 91; National Library of Australia, 120, 123 (tl), 212, 260 (t), 293, 303 (Henle Brusse); Australian News and Information Bureau, 123 (tr, bl); New South Wales Tourism Commission, 2; News Limited, 246; Photograph courtesy of Old Parliament House, Adelaide, 41; The *Age*, 26; The Australian Democrats, 74; The *Canberra Times*, 190, 230; The Herald and Weekly Times, 11 (l), 107, 194 (tl, tr); The Liberal Party, 72; The National Party, 73, 128 (bl, br); The Photo Library, 89.

Illustration

Randy Glusac, 9, 99, 144, 187.